WITH NIXON

WITH

RAYMOND PRICE

NIXON

THE VIKING PRESS
NEW YORK

Library of Congress Cataloging in Publication Data
Price, Raymond, 1930-
With Nixon.
Includes index.
1. Nixon, Richard Milhous, 1913-
2. Price, Raymond, 1930-
3. United States—Politics and government—1969-1974.
4. Presidents—United States—Biography.
5. Presidents—United States—Staff—Biography. I. Title.
E856.P74   973.924′092′4   77-13248
ISBN 0-670-77672-6

Printed in the United States of America
Set in Linotype Primer

ACKNOWLEDGMENTS

Dr. David Galin: From "Implications for Psychiatry of Left and Right Cerebral Specialization," which originally appeared in *The Archives of General Psychiatry*, October 1974

Harper & Row, Publishers, Inc.: *Nixon: A Political Portrait*, by Earl Mazo and Stephen Hess. Copyright © 1968 by Earl Mazo and Stephen Hess. Reprinted by permission of Harper & Row, Publishers, Inc.

Los Angeles Times: From a column by Nick Thimmesch. Copyright © 1970 *Los Angeles Times*. Reprinted by permission.

New York magazine: From a column by Richard Reeves, November 15, 1976

The New York Times: From an article by James Reston, March 11, 1977. © 1977 by The New York Times Company. Reprinted by permission

Dedication

To you, the reader, for whom this book was written.

I enjoyed writing it (most of the time). I hope you enjoy reading it (at least some of the time). And if we differ in our points of view, I hope that through these pages we at least can reach some better measure of understanding—so that if some day we should meet, we can "talk about our differences rather than fighting about them."

Author's Note

David Eisenhower, while working on a book about his grandfather, mentioned to me a bit of counsel he had gotten from a wise editor: "You've got to remember that you're not writing *the* book. You're writing *a* book." That is what this is: not *the* book about Richard Nixon and his presidency, but *a* book.

Some readers may wonder why this or that was not included —or why it was. The reason is: this is not the book, but a book.

Readers may also wonder about the sources of direct quotations from the President that appear in these pages Some are taken from the published transcripts of presidential tapes. Where this is the case, I think either the text or the context will make it clear. Some are from speeches or other public statements—quite obviously from the official public record. Many—including those from cabinet meetings—are from my own notes. These are substantially verbatim, but not always complete. I take notes quickly, in a sort of rapid, abbreviated scrawl that allows me to get almost everything but not quite everything. In conversations with the President, sometimes I took notes and sometimes I did not. Where I have not had verbatim notes, I have paraphrased, without using quotation marks.

In the writing of this book, many people provided help and encouragement that greatly eased its way. My special thanks go to Margaret Foote, my phenomenally gracious secretary throughout the White House years. She first came to the White House in 1953, tactfully instructed me in its workings when I arrived, and delayed her own retirement until after I left the staff in 1974—and then she lived through those years again, working with me as I wrote this book. Her kindness, her support, her unfailing helpfulness and skill contributed immeasurably to the writing of it.

My thanks go also to Ted Blanton, Harry Clark, and Steve Mathias, all of whom gave immensely valuable help with research; to my publishers, for their patience; to my editor, Alan Williams, for both gently and wisely showing me the occasional error of my literary ways; to the many former colleagues who generously shared ideas and information with me; and, not least, to the 37th President of the United States, for his inspiration, thoughtfulness, and consideration over the years—and for giving me so much to write about.

R.P.

Washington, D.C.
May 1977

Contents

WITH NIXON

WILD MIKE

I

HERE ENDETH . . .

10:00 A.M., August 9, 1974: The gleaming white-topped helicopter, so familiar, stood precisely positioned on the South Lawn of the White House, its rotor blades rigidly still against a leaden sky. Only moments before, the White House staff had gathered in the gold-and-white splendor of the East Room for the President's wandering, discursive, emotional farewell. When he had finished, we crowded along the stairways and balconies outside as Richard Nixon made his way for the last time down the long red carpet that led to the helicopter steps. The strain of the moment showed on his face, but his bearing was erect. He was still President. The authority of office would remain his until his letter of resignation was delivered to the secretary of state at 11:35 A.M.

He paused for a final handshake with his Vice-President, Gerald Ford; for a few brief words with soon-to-be First Lady Betty Ford; and, finally, for a quick embrace of his daughter Julie, who was staying behind to supervise the packing. Then, with his wife, Pat, his daughter Tricia, son-in-law Edward Cox, and a handful of staff already inside the helicopter, he mounted the steps. As he had done so often before, he turned for a final wave. The hundreds of people who were gathered waved back with hands and handkerchiefs, many sobbing openly, reaching out to one another, as the door swung shut, the rotors spun, and the chopper rose, turned, and gathering speed as it went, swung across the South Lawn, over the Ellipse, past the graceful spire of the Washington Monument, and into history.

Suddenly, in that brief moment, it was over. The finality of it numbed the senses. Every eye stayed fixed on the swiftly vanishing craft until it was out of sight.

Over. Done. Finished. But what was over?

Was it, as we had had drummed into us day after day and night after night, the end of the most corrupt administration in history, the republic saved in the nick of time from the subversion of its institutions and the rape of its liberties? Or was that vanishing speck in the sky carrying with it, as most of us gathered there had believed, America's brightest hopes since World War II for a new era of peace abroad and progress at home, sacrificed in a spasm of hysteria on an altar of hypocrisy? Or were both true, or neither, or did the truth lie somewhere in between?

Like most things in life, the Nixon administration was a mixed bag. It ended in scandal and disgrace. There were abuses of power, obstruction of justice, lies, and deceits. There were also high purpose and, in most things that mattered, high performance.

The contradictions and complexities of the administration mirrored the contradictions and complexities of Richard Nixon himself. Historians will be a long time sorting out the truth of the Nixon administration, and longer still evaluating and re-evaluating it.

I was a part of that administration from before it began until after it ended. As a speechwriter, I was the President's collaborator on his inaugural and resignation addresses. I liked and admired him. I still do. I believed in what he was trying to achieve. I still do. I was one of the relatively few people on the White House staff whose relationship was personal as well as official—I was a friend as well as an aide.

Obviously, all of this colors my judgments. It makes my perspective both better and worse than that of the observers-from-afar. I think I understand Richard Nixon pretty well. I doubt that anyone understands him totally.

The mystery, the contradictions are all a part of the enduring interest that surrounds Richard Nixon the man—and are among the reasons even those who revile him are fascinated by him. After the 1976 election, *The New Republic*'s "TRB"[1] column noted: "In 1962, when Nixon lost the California governorship and thought that his political career was over, he taunted reporters with the famous line, 'You won't have old [sic] Nixon to kick around anymore.' He

1. *The New Republic*, 20 November 1976. That week's "TRB" column was written by Richard Dudman of *The St. Louis Post-Dispatch*.

was premature but correct for the long run. We kicked him around for a long time. Now we don't have him anymore. And, at least subconsciously, we miss him."

The contradictions also are a reason why so many people see him so differently—why, for example, columnist Anthony Lewis could dismiss him as "a man without shame," and Mao Tse-tung could send him a message after his resignation calling him the greatest President in American history.

Nixon and Mao both spoke the language of power: the power to move nations, the power of war and peace.

Two and a half years earlier, the mood on the South Lawn was far different as Nixon boarded his helicopter for the start of another journey: to Hawaii, then Guam, and then, on Monday, February 21, 1972, to Peking. The world watched on satellite-transmitted television as *Air Force One* touched down at Peking's Capital Airport and rolled to a halt in front of the assembled honor guard. The door opened. The President stepped out into the winter sun, strode down the ramp, stepped on the soil of China, and grasped the hand of Premier Chou En-lai. The ice of a quarter of a century was broken. That same afternoon, the President was taken to the home of Mao Tse-tung. The two men, the two old antagonists, the two leaders, respectively, of what Nixon often referred to as "the world's most powerful nation and the world's most populous nation," talked for an hour. The next day, photographs of the two on the front pages of China's rigidly government-controlled newspapers were a clear signal to China's 800 million people: a new era is beginning, and the Chairman's blessing is on it.

For the rest of that week, Americans watched transfixed as cameras followed the President's party to the Great Wall of China, to the Forbidden City—the home of China's emperors for eight hundred years—to Hangchow and Shanghai, and as Chou and Nixon toasted one another at sumptuous banquets in the Great Hall of the People while a Chinese orchestra played "Home on the Range." For sheer historic drama, there had been little to rival it since Neil Armstrong set foot on the moon. But in their private sessions, Nixon and Mao, and Nixon and Chou, spoke the language of power.

Power, more than anything else, is what sets presidents apart. Others can advise, analyze, criticize, evaluate. But presidents decide, and because they decide, they live with the knowledge that they bear the ultimate responsibility not only for the rectitude of a decision but also for its consequences.

Nixon and Mao—and Chou—for all their differences, were

among that handful of men who shared the experience of exercising power on a global scale, and who were comfortable in its exercise. They were men who, as they met, were aware that what they said and did, what they agreed to, how they evaluated one another, would alter the shape of the world and shift the tides of history.

On February 29, the day after his return, on the stroke of noon, Nixon reported privately on those talks to his cabinet.

When the cabinet met, the members would gather in the Cabinet Room in the West Wing of the White House, mixing and mingling, then one by one take their seats around the long cabinet table as the scheduled time approached. Those members of the White House staff who were also attending would take seats in chairs placed against the walls. When all were seated, an aide would signal the President. When he entered, an aide would announce him. All then stood, until the President took his seat in the center of one of the table's long sides, his back to the tall windows opening onto the Rose Garden. The Vice-President sat across from him. The other cabinet officers sat from the center of the table outward, in order of official rank; the departmental secretaries sat in the order in which their departments had been created; and those named individually to the cabinet sat at the ends of the table. The secretary of state sat on the President's right, the secretary of defense on his left; the secretary of the treasury on the Vice-President's right, the attorney general on his left.

When the cabinet met on the day after a particularly crucial presidential speech or other event, members would sometimes break into applause as he entered. That day, February 29, the applause came loud and long.

The President himself was ebullient, despite his weariness from the long trip home. A wooden jewelry box with jade inset and a covered china teacup had been set out on the table in front of each member's place, brought back as gifts for those who stayed behind. He joked, bantered, and explained that the cups were replicas of those that he and Chou En-lai had used during their meetings. Then he went on to describe the meetings.

Characteristically, he opened with a dash of cold water aimed squarely at many of those who had waxed most euphoric over the visit, a euphoria he saw grounded in the wrong reasons:

"Some people have a naïve assumption that all problems will evaporate when we get to know each other. This is nonsense. But if we understand one another, we *may* find some common ground. If you don't talk, you don't find it. The idea that each is affected by knowing each other, by the nice gestures, is baloney. It helps. I don't believe in hot rhetoric when cool rhetoric will work. But let's be under no illusions that we will have instant peace. We have set it up so that we can explore common ground, and gradually expand it."

Then he talked about the Chinese leaders themselves:

"Mao and Chou are Chinese, and therefore extremely courteous. Mao is approaching eighty. In terms of his mental equipment, he is quick, earthy, one who does not get into tactics, though I am sure he is interested in them. But he sees strategic concepts with very, very great vision. Of course, he sees them through different lenses."

With Chou En-lai, he said, in addition to the dinners, the plenary sessions, the rides and other ceremonial occasions, he had held twenty hours of "head-to-head talks." Henry Kissinger and his Chinese counterpart were there, along with the interpreters, but the principals—Chou and Nixon—did the talking.

"Chou is seventy-three, but he has the vitality and mental vigor of forty. He works eighteen hours a day—far into the night—and he's as good at the end of the conversation as at the beginning. He never shows mental fatigue. His mind is quick; he has a fine sense of humor.

"I've known just about all the major world leaders since World War II—and except for Churchill, I've known them at their best. None that I have met exceeds Chou in terms of the ability to conduct conversations at the highest level in an effective way.

"He does as I do—we both sat across the table from each other, totally without notes, even on the most intricate problems. He didn't read any statements to me, nor I to him. This established a pattern of communication.

"He and Mao had done their homework about me. They knew my background. Also, Chou showed a remarkable knowledge of what is going on in the United States and the world. He has a great historical sense. His historical references were accurate even with regard to the United States—instead of seeing it through Marxist glasses, he saw it in terms of an objective historical perspective.

"My talks with him—in terms of their scope, and of the give and take—were an experience that perhaps will not be exceeded in my lifetime."

Then he described the nature and tone of the talks as the two men sought a new basis on which their nations could live together:

"You'd think there might have been a lot of nit-picking about the communiqué, about this problem and that problem, as would be the case with most Western leaders. We did discuss this and that issue, but he begins by looking at the whole world. He puts it first in a philosophical context, and then he goes on to reason from the general to the specific, as I also like to do.

"We talked about the forces in the world. Then we talked about the sub-Continent, India, Taiwan, and so forth. And that way we got a better concept of it.

"With regard to specifics, we engaged in tough, straight talk. We were tough in terms of substance, but we were totally elegant and courteous in terms of tone—both on my part and on his part.

"This is important: If in our private conversations we can discuss these profound differences in a *tone* that is civilized, the chances that we will not come to the brink of armed conflict and also the chances of finding that glimmer of common ground that can bridge our differences are greatly increased.

"We could have tried to gloss over our differences. Some do. That's a weakness. Or we could have gone to the other extreme— saying these people are enemies and we'll prove ourselves by taking them on. This too would have been bad.

"Chou is a total, dedicated Communist. He believes deeply, and he never let me forget it. I was a total advocate of our philosophy, and I never let him forget it. Not every hour on the hour—it was beneath the surface—we didn't let it color our conversation so as to become belligerent. There was firmness but never belligerence.

"Whenever he said something really tough, he became much cooler, and spoke more softly—which is exactly my approach. Therefore, when we talked about things that didn't matter, we were easygoing. But on extremely controversial things, we both spoke almost in a way that the interpreter couldn't quite hear. The more deeply you believe something, the more effective you think your point is, the more softly you can talk."

As for the substance of the communiqué, he told the cabinet that the most important things were "not the specifics about Taiwan, Vietnam, and so forth, though these were what the unsophisticated reports in the press emphasized." More significant were "those that concerned the profound new relationship. We both agreed we will not resort to the threat of force or the use of force in international relations and with each other. We agreed that no nation should dominate Asia. This is the heart of the communiqué. They understand that it's the heart of it."

The communiqué, he added, "avoids the temptation to gloss over differences. It states them. There will continue to be differences— the question is whether we're going to live with them or die for them."

Summing up, he put the changes in both personal and historic terms:

"The one thing that characterized my meetings was treating them with total dignity. I feel this toward all leaders—and also toward the Chinese as people, not as Communists. As we were riding to the Shanghai airport with the local Communist leader—a man of fifty-four, the most hard-line in the Politburo—we went by a beautiful children's park. He said, 'Twenty-five years ago—before the liberation—that was a golf course. There was a sign on it: 'No Chinese allowed.' Nothing more was said—or had to be.

"Far greater than the exploitation of China, or the military domination, was the affront to their dignity—treating them as inferior.

"As we look to the future—and I've seen this to varying degrees in every Communist society—as I see their regimentation, and compare this with what I see in free countries—and I say that what we have is good, we believe in ours—I *never* make the mistake of underestimating theirs. There are two reasons: first, the Chinese people. They are enormously capable. Second, whatever the failures of their system, in the leader class they're formidable, either as adversaries or, if not as friends, as people with whom we will have some form of understanding.

"Among the top leaders, and those young who have been exposed to the enormous discipline of their schools and so forth, there is a dedication, a belief in their system that is something to reckon with. It would be an error to say that because they are Communists, they are something we don't have to worry about. They believe in it, they know what they want, and they are determined to get it, and they are going all out for it.

"Our problem is that—not because of our wealth, or our power, but in terms of a sense of destiny, of dedication, and the rest, the leader class in the United States may in many cases lack the backbone—the strength—that they have. The history of nations tells us that as a nation becomes rich, and better educated, it becomes soft. This is still a great country. It is still the wonder of the world. If they could see it, they'd be popeyed. But as we look at the Soviets on one side and the Chinese on the other, with that iron control and discipline, even though their system is one we could never agree with, it's one certainly to be reckoned with. Therefore, it's necessary, if we are trying to build a peaceful world, to deal with it, to establish communications, and thus to reduce the dangers.

"I put it best in my return toast: 'What brought us together? Not common beliefs, but common interests.' They have an interest in not having a war that would destroy their growth, in maintaining their independence—and, therefore, we are finding those areas of common ground that will serve our interests.

"We are not going to make the mistake of supposing that we have had these years of hostility because we didn't know each other, and that therefore as we get to know each other the problems will evaporate.

"We have entered a new era. I'm confident that the chances for peace in the Pacific are better now than they were ten days ago. But this is a small plant, a delicate one, and it needs to be nurtured very carefully."

The President turned the meeting over to Secretary of State Rogers, and then to Henry Kissinger. They discussed the Chinese leadership, China as a nation, Chinese aims, and the terms of the agreements, and then Kissinger commented:

"This couldn't have been done at a lower level. The Chinese had to ask themselves: Do these people have a view of the world we can live with? Are they reliable enough as a people—and as leaders— to carry this out for a period of time? It is on this level that I believe the President scored his most notable successes.

"The approach was unusual. The President began by saying you have no reason to trust me because you don't know me. Then he talked extensively about why we are really trying to stay in the Pacific rather than getting out. The talk was on an extraordinarily philosophical level. I believe this is a better guarantee of the future than what we can deduce from the individual words of the communiqué.

"These are not trivial people. They have imposed on their society this tremendous wrench—the opening to the United States—because of profound requirements. What can make it worthwhile for them is that on those essentials that brought them there we can perform over a period of time.

"As these exchanges develop, and this may be faster than most people expect, I believe it is not going to be an easy challenge for us. They will challenge us in a moral way very profoundly. They have great discipline, not just through terror but by dedication.

"What the President has done is to set a major new direction. When the words of the communiqué are long forgotten, it may be considered a historical turning point, if—just as they looked at the President to see if he knew where he was going—they now look at our whole society, and see if there is enough there to be what they need. We are embarked on what will be a great adventure and a great challenge. The communiqué is a tremendous step forward, and beyond the communication that has been established, the trip has exceeded all of my expectations."

The President then turned to what would be important in the future:

"Their evaluation of us will be in two areas: Not wealth; *power* will impress them. More important will be purpose. I am speaking now of the leaders. Being as they are—dedicated, believing in the Revolution, believing they will prevail—they look at societies like ours and see the emphasis on material things as a weakness.

"They look for the strength of character of the people. This they have to an infinite degree. The willingness to sacrifice, and faith, belief—these factors are enormously important to them.

"In our talks, each of us made clear that they believe in what they are doing and we believe in what we are doing.

"The real question will be whether in their minds, in their relationship with the United States, they are dealing with a nation led by people who have the strength, the character, to be a *responsible* world power.

"That's why, despite the fact that they say get out of the Pacific, get out of Vietnam—and they must continue to say it—for the United States to fail to meet its responsibilities in the world, even though it would fit with their ideology, would lead inevitably to their figuring that we did not have that strength and that belief.

"We had good personal relations, but far more important than that is the question of the strength and character of our society. They speak glowingly of our early Revolution. But now, after two hundred years, are we too fat, too rich, too educated, too far from the soil to have the guts, the discipline, the steel to lead? If we're important, they will respect us and deal with us. But if not, we won't matter."

Commerce Secretary Peter Peterson then asked what was the most important thing to the Chinese? Why did they come?

"Cold-blooded interest," replied the President. "Not friendship. I don't believe what Malraux said about their wanting huge trade and aid. They see the Soviet Union, India, Japan—all of them, each in its way, encircling them—so they need *somebody* who is not antagonistic. They know the Soviets have more men on the Chinese frontier than against Western Europe. As for Japan, history has to give them some pause. With India, they've had a little squabble. As for the United States, first, we're a long way off; and second, while they would never state publicly that India, Russia, and Japan have designs on them, they know very well, I think, that we don't."

Between the anguished, cornered Richard Nixon of the Watergate transcripts and the confident, self-assured Richard Nixon speaking the language of power, the contrast is as stark as it was between his return in triumph from Peking and his departure in disgrace to San Clemente. But both were part of the man. Both are part of the record.

No presidency in the nation's history ever spanned such a range between its heights and its depths. None ended in such disgrace, damned even by its former supporters. Yet this end came less than two years after the second largest re-election margin in history, a sweep that carried the man once dismissed as a "loser" to one of the greatest political victories ever. It came less than two months after a triumphal Nixon reception in the Middle East, where, capping a phenomenal diplomatic tour de force, millions turned out in the streets to cheer the leader of a nation they had ranked as their second-bitterest enemy only a short while before.

If the lessons of both are to be understood, Nixon's triumphs and his downfall must be viewed together. They were the product of the same complex and contradictory personality, of the same staff system, of the same effort to deal with often hostile and intractable forces. Both also reflect a deep-rooted conflict of perspectives over where the nation's priorities should lie.

For me, the helicopter's departure on that final presidential journey was the end of an odyssey that began exactly seven years, five months, and twelve days earlier, on Washington's Birthday in 1967.

On that winter morning I woke late in my New York apartment, crushed under the weight of one of the worst hangovers of my life. The telephone rang. On the other end was the cheery voice of Walter Thayer. For nine years, until its collapse late in 1966, I had been on the staff of the New York *Herald Tribune*, the last two of those as editor of the editorial page. Walter had been president of the *Trib;* he was still president of the Whitney Communications Co., the umbrella organization formed by John Hay ("Jock") Whitney when he bought the *Trib* in 1958. Besides the money-losing *Trib*, it included the money-making broadcast and publishing concerns acquired by Whitney, enabling their profits to help offset the *Trib*'s losses—Corinthian Broadcasting, *Parade* magazine, *Interior Design,* and several others. Walter also had long been active at the higher levels of Republican politics and was very friendly with, among others, Dwight D. Eisenhower and Richard Nixon. We exchanged brief pleasantries, then he got to the point: Nixon had called him the day before, and asked him whether he thought I might be interested in joining his staff to help prepare for a possible run for the presidency in 1968.

"I told him I didn't know," Walter said, "but I'd try to find out. What shall I tell him?"

Silently, I cursed my hangover. I told him I really didn't know; that I still had not focused on who my candidate for 1968 would be, much less whether I would want to get involved in the campaign. Since the *Trib*'s collapse I had been writing a novel. I wanted to finish it. On the political side, as I explained to Walter, my starting premise was that after the 1964 debacle the Republican party probably needed someone fresh. On the other hand, I had never shared the anti-Nixon animus of so many "Eastern Establishment" Republicans. When Nelson Rockefeller challenged Nixon for the nomination in 1960, I favored Nixon for nomination as well as for election. But there was another consideration. We all assumed that Lyndon Johnson would run for re-election. I voted for Johnson in 1964, and in fact wrote the staunchly Republican *Herald Tribune*'s endorsement of Johnson. Though I had quite a few policy disagreements with Johnson, I still thought that he had generally done a creditable job. I supported him on the war in Vietnam. I would probably support the Republican nominee, but not automatically. In any case, I still saw all of these as future considerations; they simply were choices that I had not yet addressed. I spun all of this out to Walter, then summed it up by saying I thought there was less than a fifty-fifty chance that I would want to do it, but that if, understanding this, Nixon wanted to talk, I'd be delighted to meet with him.

Walter said he would pass it along. I sat back in the chair, sinking back into my hangover. The idea was intriguing, certainly. I had always been keenly interested not only in public policy but also in elective politics. I went to my first Republican National Convention in 1948, as a sophomore at Yale. (My candidate then was Michigan's Senator Arthur Vandenberg, the prewar isolationist turned postwar internationalist, who, as chairman of the Senate Foreign Relations Committee, was one of the principal architects of bipartisanship in foreign policy during the Truman era.) Two years later, as a Yale senior, I spent two or three days a week stumping Connecticut with the Republican candidate for the U.S. Senate, Prescott Bush. (In an agonizingly close finish—by 1000 votes out

of 1 million cast—Bush lost that campaign to the legendary advertising mogul and publisher of the *Encyclopaedia Britannica*, William Benton. Two years later Bush was appointed to a Senate
vacancy, and then won re-election in his own right. In 1968 his
son, then-Congressman George Bush,[2] topped my own list of
recommendations for Vice-President.) My first presidential ballot
was cast for the Eisenhower-Nixon ticket in 1952. During my nine
years of writing editorials for the *Trib,* I wrote a large share of
those on national affairs, some of those on foreign affairs, and
quite a few of those on politics. In 1964, together with Walter
Thayer and Jock Whitney, I was deeply involved in the Republican
party's prenomination maneuverings (our candidate for the presidency was Pennsylvania Governor William W. Scranton), and
served as General Eisenhower's collaborator on a major article
about the Republican choice that he did for the *Trib* just before
the crucial California primary, which the *Trib* released for use
nationwide. (The Eisenhower article prompted Arizona Senator
Barry Goldwater to pose in profile for photographers with an arrow
under his arm, so that it looked as if he had been shot in the back.)
Just the previous October—after the *Trib*'s collapse—I had spent
three weeks in Chicago, helping Charles H. Percy in the final stages
of the campaign that won him his Senate seat. Shortly before
Thayer's call, I had also turned down a bid by an ambitious young
congressman to join his staff in Washington. Neither the congressman nor I had the remotest idea that two years later we would
be serving together in the White House. His name was Donald H.
Rumsfeld.[3]

I had never met Richard Nixon, except once, briefly, in the
crush of the annual dinner of Washington's Gridiron Club, when
we merely shook hands and exchanged a few words. Yet I was very
much a part of what commentator Meg Greenfield later dubbed "the
Nixon Generation"—those whose whole adult lives had been lived
in the political presence of Richard Nixon. I was eighteen when he
shot to national fame with the Alger Hiss case, twenty when he won
his Senate seat from Helen Gahagan Douglas, twenty-two when

2. After his defeat in a race for the Senate in 1970, George Bush was
named by Nixon as ambassador to the United Nations. He later served as
chairman of the Republican National Committee, chief of the U.S. Mission
to China, and director of the CIA.

3. Rumsfeld was brought to the White House by Nixon in 1969 as an
assistant to the President and director of the Office of Economic Opportunity.
He served as director of the Cost of Living Council during the wage-price
freeze, then as U.S. ambassador to NATO. President Ford brought him back
to the White House as chief of staff, then named him secretary of defense.

Eisenhower chose him as his vice-presidential running mate. Whether people of our generation admired him or detested him, there was no way we could ignore him.

I was curious, fascinated, wondering what he was like close up; I wanted to meet him. But I doubted that I would, as I had stressed to Walter the less than fifty-fifty chance that I would be interested in working for Nixon in order to be sure that he was under no illusions that I was likely to sign on. I assumed this made it unlikely that I would hear from him, and wondered if perhaps I should have been a little less straightforward.

All this was running through my mind when, ten minutes after hanging up, the phone rang again. I answered. A deep voice on the other end said, cheerfully but a bit tentatively, "Hello—this is Dick Nixon."

We exchanged greetings. He told me Walter had called him, and then he asked if I were free that day for lunch. For a moment I thought of saying no, of trying to postpone it—of all times to be cursed with those dry eyeballs, the feathered tongue, the pounding head, the aching body, the angry furnace where a stomach should be!—but I said yes, I'd be delighted. He explained that he was at his office, but the office was closed because of the holiday. He said he would check on whether we should meet there or at his apartment uptown, and get back to me. A few minutes later he called again, saying he had arranged for us to have lunch at his apartment.

I showered and shaved, and dipped into my larder of hangover antidotes—milk, water, coffee, aspirin—all the time trying to think through what I should discuss. This was probably going to be the one time I would ever actually sit down and talk with this man who was already a legend, and who, but for a few thousand votes in 1960, would be President. Finally, summoning whatever powers of sheer will I could muster, I got the hangover halfway under control and set out across Central Park.

Already, Nixon had come a long way from Yorba Linda, California. His apartment—one full floor—at 810 Fifth Avenue was in one of those gracious older buildings facing Central Park that give Fifth Avenue its distinctive air as the Queen Mother of New York thoroughfares. At Sixty-second Street, it overlooked my favorite corner in all New York: Fifth Avenue and Fifty-ninth Street, where the Plaza Hotel holds court over the southeast corner of Central Park, while horse-drawn carriages wait for passengers in front of the graceful scoops of the Pulitzer Fountain. The apartment building was a co-op. Among the other owners were upstairs neighbors Nelson Rockefeller and William Randolph Hearst, Jr.

Arriving at the fifth floor, I rang. Nixon himself opened the door, greeted me, and showed me in. We went through the large foyer, through a sunny living room with a view of the park, and settled into the small room off the living room that he used as a study. It, too, had a view of the park—it was the southwest corner that faced both the park and Sixty-second Street. But the room's focus was inward, not outward, the furniture arranged with the backs to the windows. It had a comfortable, lived-in, worked-in look, with a small desk and desk-lamp, bookshelves behind the desk that looked as though they were for reading, not display, a brown velvet over-stuffed chair and matching ottoman, a couch, a coffee table, a few chairs.

The apartment had a formal dining room, but we had lunch on tray-tables in the study. The meal was served, not by a liveried butler or a maid in starched uniform but by a bouncy middle-aged man in shirtsleeves, tieless, with a quick grin and a twinkle in his eye and a heavy Spanish accent. When he appeared in the room, Nixon introduced us. The man's name was Manuel Sanchez, but Nixon used the familiar name I have known him by ever since, Manolo—and then engaged him in an exchange of quick, informal banter, playing straight man to Manolo's punch lines.

This was my first glimpse of the human side of Richard Nixon. It was only a glimpse, but I liked what I saw. The warmth was clearly genuine and infectious, the humor quick and spontaneous. Manolo and his wife, Fina, have been with the Nixons since January 1962, when Nixon was practicing law in California. (When they first went to work for the Nixons, Manolo and Fina spoke no English. I later learned that when Nixon lost the California governor's race in 1962, the Sanchezes, unfamiliar with the language, thought he had lost his job and would have no money to pay them. Tearfully, they offered not only to work free, but to take outside jobs to help support the family. In 1968 they worked desperately to complete their applications for citizenship in time to cast their first vote for Nixon for President. Their appearance in court to apply for final papers was scheduled for the same day Nixon was to fly to the Republican National Convention at Miami Beach from Long Island's Montauk Point, where he had secluded himself to work on his acceptance speech. At the appearance, they were required to have two sponsors. Mrs. Nixon was already in Miami Beach. Nixon detoured his plane by way of New York so that he and Bob Haldeman could stand up with them as their sponsors. They finally got their citizenship papers on November 6

—just one day too late to vote.) Like most friends of the Nixons, I soon came to regard Manolo and Fina as valued friends of mine.

As we talked, I also quickly developed a new appreciation of Nixon's intellectual range, the quickness and facility of his mind, his extraordinary capacity to leap continents and issues and subjects, and then tie them all together at the end. We ended up talking for three hours—about the nation and the world, politics and political philosophy, people and events, the strengths and weaknesses of other possible contenders as well as his own. In analyzing his chances, he spoke clinically, dispassionately, referring to himself in the third person as he dealt with Nixon, Romney, Rockefeller, Percy, Johnson, and the rest. He saw his own nomination and election as possible but not probable—enough to justify a try (though he was not yet committed to the idea), but still a long shot.

As he showed me to the door after we had finished, he asked me to think about it, and to give him an answer within a week. He was about to begin a series of foreign trips, and wanted to settle this staff arrangement before he left on the first of them.

Promising to get back to him, I set off toward home, walking through the park in the brisk February air, reflecting on what I had seen and heard. I had been vastly more impressed than I expected to be. Later I was to find that this was a common experience: that persons whose impressions were based on the public Nixon, and particularly those exposed to large doses of the public Nixon as presented through the media, were surprised or even startled when they met the man himself either one-on-one or in a small, informal group. Almost always their opinions of him rose, often dramatically so.

Having promised him an answer within a week, I set out to spend the next seven days intensively thinking it through. First was the question of whether he was my candidate. I tried to learn more about him. I read his own memoir, Six Crises; my Herald Tribune colleague Earl Mazo's 1959 biography of him, Nixon: A Political and Personal Portrait; Stewart Alsop's 1960 book, Nixon & Rockefeller: A Double Portrait; Arthur Schlesinger, Jr.'s Kennedy or Nixon: Does It Make Any Difference? (Schlesinger thought it did). They all had, until then, sat unread on my bookshelves. I dipped into a few other books, and pored through rather extensive clipping files I had that might have some bearing on the choice. All the while I was trying to check the preconceptions, the automatic assumptions, the prejudices that I had picked up during eleven years in journalism against what I could determine to be the facts. I was also trying to think through in my own mind how a person of his particular experience and characteristics, at his particular stage of life, would probably have developed during the six years he had then been out of office, and to measure him as nearly as I could against each of the other likely contenders. The more I learned of the facts, the more the old caricatures faded away. The more deeply I got into the comparisons, the more convinced I became that he would, after all, be my candidate.

Deciding whether to join the campaign was in many ways a harder choice. It would have to be pretty much a seven-day-a-week, twenty-four-hour-a-day commitment. It would mean abandoning the novel. It would cut deeply into my personal life. And I knew that Richard Nixon was anathema to many of those in the New York world I inhabited, and at least mildly disliked by most. Joining his staff would mean having to face down a lot of old friends. But as the deadline drew closer, I grew more nearly convinced that I should join. First I talked it over with Jock Whitney and Walter Thayer (even though the *Herald Tribune* was no longer publishing, its traditions were still alive, and therefore, I felt they were entitled to at least a say and, if they felt strongly, perhaps even an informal veto). Both gave the move their blessing. By the sixth day I was 90 percent decided, by the morning of the seventh day 95 percent. Finally, at midafternoon of the seventh day—Wednesday, March 1—I picked up the phone and called Nixon at his office.

"If you still want me to come aboard," I said, "I'd like to very much."

There. It was done; I couldn't take it back; it was irrevocable; I was committed.

He asked if I could come down to the office that afternoon. I said yes, and soon was entering the building at 20 Broad Street that housed the law firm of Nixon, Mudge, Rose, Guthrie & Alexander. Though twenty-seven stories high, it seemed squat sitting in the canyons of Lower Manhattan, crowded among the taller and older buildings that for decades had made the soaring skyline a New York landmark.

Nixon greeted me in his office. It was clearly the office of a public figure. Displayed on the walls and shelves were his collections of elephants and gavels, and on a large table behind his desk were inscribed portraits of presidents and prime ministers and kings and queens. But, for all the souvenirs, it still was basically a comfortable, traditional, unpretentious office, in its character very much like the one he later established in the Executive Office Building next door to the White House. It had a lived-in rather than a "decorated" look. In the cramped space outside it, Rose Mary Woods occupied one small desk, Pat Buchanan another, and sometimes Mrs. Nixon was there too, pitching in as a volunteer to help with the mail and the phones (when she did so, if she had to identify herself to telephone callers, she disguised her identity by saying she was "Miss Ryan"—her maiden name).

We talked for a while, then he called in some of the people I would be working with: Pat Buchanan, Len Garment, Tom Evans, John Sears. Buchanan, a feisty young former editorial writer for the St. Louis *Globe-Democrat,* had joined his staff full time the previous year, when Nixon was campaigning for Republican congressional candidates in the 1966 midterm election. Len Garment, the head of the firm's litigation department, a Democrat who put himself through Brooklyn College Law School playing jazz saxophone and clarinet, had become a Nixon enthusiast, and was spending part of his time informally on political planning (Garment later became my closest friend at the White House, and in the first unraveling of Watergate he succeeded John Dean as counsel to the President). Tom Evans, then one of the firm's more junior partners, was also spending part time on the fledgling political organization, handling, among other things, such housekeeping details as payrolls. Sears, a politically astute and politically ambitious young lawyer in the firm, became one of our chief delegate-hunters in the fight for the nomination; eight years later he came prominently into the national picture as manager of Ronald Reagan's 1976 campaign.

I was given a comfortable corner office on the twenty-seventh floor, with windows overlooking the spires of Lower Manhattan and, in the distance, the East River and New York Harbor. But I particularly liked one thing that seemed to me nicely symbolic: the windows also looked down on the corner of Broad and Wall streets, where the old Federal Sub-Treasury Building still stood, a tall bronze statue of George Washington, arm upraised, commanding its steps, marking the site of the first President's first inauguration.

It seemed a good place to begin the effort that might lead to another inauguration, one that I hoped and believed would make Washington proud of his successor.

I began work that evening.

GETTING ACQUAINTED

Ten years later, after a full decade of working with Nixon, traveling with him, sharing not only the tumult of the public stage but also many of the quiet moments with his friends and family, he remains—to paraphrase Churchill's description of Russia—a paradox wrapped in a contradiction inside an incongruity. Getting to know him, in fact, while lessening the air of mystery, heightens the sense of paradox.

Theodore H. White has written of "the essential duality of his nature, the evil and the good, the flights of panic and the resolution of spirit, the good mind and the mean trickery." White goes on to comment: "If one hates Richard Nixon enough, it is easy to describe the implacable vindictiveness and tenacity of the man as more important than the enormous courage; the recurrent gusts of panic or fury as more important than the long thoughtfulness; his coarseness of discourse and lying as more important than his exceptional sensitivity to others' emotional needs; the cheapness and nastiness of his tactics as more important than the long-range planning of his exceptional mind."[1]

In *Before the Fall,* his memoir of the White House years, William Safire has a remarkably perceptive section analyzing the multiple levels of the Nixon personality, in which he suggests thinking of Nixon as a layer cake.

The icing of the cake, he says, is the public face: "conservative,

---

1. *Breach of Faith* (New York, 1975), pp. 57, 62.

stern, dignified, proper." Underneath the icing he finds a whole series of separate layers: the progressive politician, capable of surprising grace; the pugnacious, self-made man, furious with loafers and leeches; the calculating, patient negotiator; the "hater, the impugner of motives"; the supreme realist, with an extraordinary understanding of what moves nations and power groups; the "observer-participant," assessing his actions even as he acts; the man of extraordinary courage, whose diplomatic triumphs resulted from a refusal to bend under pressure; the loner, mysterious, aloof, immersed in his briefing papers.[2] Safire's point: No one layer by itself, light or dark, gives the true flavor of the cake. The only way to slice it is vertically, not horizontally.

In probing for an understanding of the personality of anyone who holds high public office, there is a special hazard. The official both acts and reacts. Particularly in the case of a president, his choices are often circumscribed by an extremely complex set of conflicting pressures. As a result, the most carefully calculated move may appear the most irrational, or the most self-serving may appear the most generous.

He has to be "on stage" more than most people, his words and actions chosen for effect. Sometimes the public *persona* reflects the private personality; sometimes he drapes it over the private personality as a cloak, concealing rather than revealing. He feigns enthusiasm for people and policies he privately detests. He often acts from necessity rather than choice. Having to lead a disparate, shifting coalition of frequently conflicting forces, he bends one way and then another, buttering, cajoling, exhorting, juggling. This should be obvious, yet I constantly find myself amazed at the degree to which people who should know better seem oblivious to it.

After Nixon's resignation, I had lunch one day with a prominent New York psychiatrist, Dr. David Abrahamson, who was writing a book on the former President. He had done exhaustive research on Nixon's personal and family history. As we talked, it became apparent that he was planning to follow the currently fashionable trend of psychohistory, interpreting a public official's public acts by means of a sort of remote-control Freudian psychoanalysis. For anything Abrahamson considered "irrational," he found an explanation somewhere in the depths of Nixon's psyche; and he defined the Nixon psyche itself largely in terms of those supposed "irratio-

2. *Before the Fall: An Inside View of the Pre-Watergate White House* (New York, 1975), pp. 97–99.

nalities." It also quickly became evident that Abrahamson deemed "irrational" anything he happened to disagree with politically, that he was extremely naïve about the processes of both government and diplomacy, and that he was totally incapable of comprehending the role of external pressures in shaping a president's actions. It reminded me of a cocktail-party conversation I had had ten years earlier, shortly before the 1965 New York mayoral election, with three psychiatrists. Talk had turned to the campaign, in which columnist William F. Buckley, Jr., was running as a third-party candidate against Republican John V. Lindsay and Democrat Abraham Beame. Speaking of Buckley, one of the psychiatrists declared emphatically that he was a paranoid schizophrenic. I was quite taken aback. Buckley had been a close friend of mine for many years, and he certainly had never shown any signs of mental instability. I asked the doctor what he based his diagnosis on.

"He thinks differently," said the doctor. "He starts out from the same premises as other people, but he reaches different conclusions." (Relating the incident in a magazine essay shortly afterward, I commented: "Well, so much for the sanity of politics, and the politics of sanity.")

My first opportunity to get to know Nixon came in April 1967, just a month after joining his staff, when I went with him on a three-week round-the-world trip. In the spring of 1967, in preparation for his presidential race, he made four foreign-study trips. On the first, accompanied by Robert Ellsworth—a former congressman from Kansas, who was to become national political director of the campaign and later the U.S. ambassador to NATO—Nixon visited Europe and the Soviet Union. I went with him on the second, to Asia; we returned by way of Iran and Switzerland. The third trip, with Pat Buchanan along, covered Africa and the Middle East. The fourth, on which he took his long-time friend from Key Biscayne, Charles G. "Bebe" Rebozo—later much in the news—was to Latin America.

On April 2, I flew from New York to Los Angeles to meet Nixon. While he had dinner with some California friends, I got a briefing from John Davies, an official of Pacific Telephone, who had helped in several campaigns and had occasionally traveled with him. (Davies later was a member of the White House staff, in charge of handling visitors.) One thing Davies told me was that I would soon get a sense of when Nixon wanted to talk, and when he did not; that he liked to use flying time for work, and sometimes just for thinking; that when he wanted to talk, he would usually signal it by opening the conversation himself. Davies also told me that Nixon would usually want me to take the aisle seat, so that I could provide a sort of buffer between him and other passengers who might recognize him and would want to chat. For anyone as well known and readily recognizable as Richard Nixon, this could become a problem.

As Davies had said, I did soon learn to sense when Nixon wanted to talk and when he did not. On a plane, he usually traveled with his briefcase on his knees, dipping into it for things he wanted, using it as a writing desk when it was closed, scratching ideas on the yellow legal pads that were his trademark. Often he sat for long periods absorbed in thought, then suddenly launched into a conversation that might last moments, or might last hours.

On each leg of the trip I gave him whatever research materials I had brought along on the country we were about to visit—on its politics, its economy, its current problems—but there was little real need for these. He knew the countries, knew the problems, and in most cases he already knew the leaders he was going to meet. He was, however, always keenly interested in whatever scraps of information or impression I might have picked up in the countries we had already visited, fitting them into his own impressions.

Whenever possible at our various stops, I ducked out for an hour or so to walk around the city, through the back streets, studying the people, looking for the little things that give clues to the ways people of different cultures live and see themselves: the juxtaposition of old and new, the goods they display in shop windows; the inhabitants' bearing, their signs, the way they drive in traffic, how they look and sound when they congregate. The crowded capitals of Asia are rich in those little clues, and fascinating in the way they span centuries and cultures. In Bangkok, four young Buddhist monks wearing saffron robes, their heads shaved, stared eagerly at a store-window display of transistor radios. In the outskirts of New Delhi, an ancient Indian woman squatted in the dust, forming cowdung patties with her hands to be used for fuel, while a transistor radio in her lap played music from a Delhi station. In Rawalpindi, Pakistan, on the site where a modern house was being built, a two-man construction team worked with a single shovel, a string attached above the blade. One man pressed the shovel into the earth with his foot, then the other pulled the string, moving the dirt away. In Tokyo, where people had still been uncertain, subservient, self-effacing when I last was there thirteen years earlier, they now strode confidently, brimming with pride and self-assurance. Manila presented an overriding impression of a nation in search of an identity, the people racially mixed, the culture a conglomerate of Spanish,

American, and native influences. There was no dominant architectural style, no uniquely Philippine element. Street signs were randomly English or Tagalog, with no apparent rule or pattern. (I was also fascinated by the contrast between the presidential palace, a magnificent, imposing example of Spanish colonial opulence, meticulously maintained, and Vice-President Fernando Lopez' office—a tacky warren of plain, heavy wooden tables and Woolworth-modern furnishings, with a gaggle of secretaries peering in the door, giggling, kibitzing, and carrying on noisy telephone conversations from Lopez' desk while he and Nixon talked. Lopez himself, though a wealthy member of the Philippine "establishment," displayed the wheedling histrionics of a fugitive from *The Threepenny Opera*.) At 7:00 A.M., scores of people were already gathered by the busy waterfront outside the hotel where we stayed, doing calisthenics, reading, eating. In the huge public square in front of the hotel, a lone worker trimmed the grass with a pair of library scissors.

But the kaleidoscope of cultural impressions was incidental to the main thrust of the trip itself.

Each stop was heavily scheduled, with arrangements made in advance through the local U.S. embassy and the host country's embassy in Washington. There were extensive briefings by the U.S. ambassador, and sometimes by the embassy staff; calls on the presidents, prime ministers, foreign ministers, and frequently on other officials: for example, Nixon's old friend Carlos Romulo, then president of the University of the Philippines; Kozo Sasaki, the chairman of Japan's opposition Socialist Party; Morarji Desai, India's deputy prime minister and minister of finance (now prime minister). Frequently there were meetings with old friends, official or unofficial. Usually there were lunches or dinners, hosted by national officials: by India's Prime Minister Indira Gandhi, Pakistan's President Mohammad Ayub Khan, Nationalist China's President Chiang Kai-shek, Thailand's Prime Minister Thanom Kittikachorn, and others. Sometimes Nixon met with a group of Americans. Occasionally he met informally with members of the U.S. press stationed in the various capitals, although he tried to keep a "low profile" on all four of his trips that year.

In each capital, after his meetings with the national leaders, he made a point of giving the U.S. ambassador a full debriefing on what had been talked about, what he had learned, what attitudes the leaders had expressed. And each night, on the IBM portable dictating machine that he carried, he dictated extensive notes on what he had learned. Leaving Los Angeles on Monday, April 3, we then stopped at Honolulu, Tokyo, Hong Kong, Taipei, Manila, Bangkok, Saigon, Djakarta, Singapore, New Delhi, Lahore, Rawalpindi, Teheran, and Geneva before arriving back in New York on Monday, April 24.

Throughout the trip, the embassy staffs were exceptionally helpful. Nixon traveled on a lifetime diplomatic passport, issued when he left the vice-presidency. At each stop, a "control officer"—usually a second or third secretary at the embassy—was assigned to meet us at the airport. His task was to facilitate communications, help coordinate schedules, speed clearances, and generally assist with logistics and answer whatever questions he could. Though out of office, and though a part of the "loyal opposition" to the party then in power, Nixon was given the courtesies that would normally be extended a ranking official—one of those comities that transcend party lines and political contests, and that help to preserve a thread of continuity in America's relations with the world. In later years Nixon often expressed his respect for Kennedy's and Johnson's secretary of state, Dean Rusk. On that trip, we both had reason to be grateful for the cooperation we received from Rusk's State Department.

I sat in on most of the meetings, and was included in most of the official lunches and dinners, but not in all. Whenever the host indicated a preference for meeting privately, Nixon respected the preference. Thus I found other things to do when he lunched with Chiang Kai-shek, with President Ayub Khan, with the King of Thailand, and the Shah of Iran. But I did tag along when he visited with Japan's Prime Minister Eisaku Sato, Philippine President Ferdinand Marcos, India's Prime Minister Gandhi, Thailand's Prime Minister Kittikachorn, and others.

It was interesting to watch as Nixon dealt with the various leaders. This was my first experience with meetings at this level. There was always mutual deference, and great courtesy, but except in the setting of a lunch or a dinner there was very little small talk. He always showed a keen interest (genuine, not feigned) in the progress of Asia generally and of the host country specifically. He also would lead the conversation to the larger world picture, to the possible future roles of China, the Soviet Union, and the United States, and to the impact of those roles on Asia generally. Sometimes directly, sometimes by diplomatic indirection, he tried to size up the reactions of the various leaders to the Chinese and Soviet threats. He also encouraged each to evaluate the situations in neighboring countries—in Indonesia, for example, which recently had been narrowly saved by a coup from falling into the Chinese orbit, but which had also experienced a grisly internal bloodletting and which still faced a highly uncertain political and economic future.

Often, what the leaders told him in private was very different from what they were saying in public. One of the sharpest contrasts was provided by Indira Gandhi, who was then giving the United States vituperative public tongue-lashings for its role in Vietnam. Privately, she stressed that it was vital for the United States to hang tough. Her public posture was partly for domestic political consumption, and partly because she was walking a diplomatic tightrope in her relations with the Soviet Union. Privately, she was deeply worried about China's ambitions, and she saw U.S. perseverance in Vietnam as essential to checking those ambitions and thereby protecting India itself. (This attitude toward the U.S. presence in Vietnam was, in fact, almost universal among the Asian leaders we talked with. However much American opinion leaders might scoff at the "domino theory," the dominoes themselves did not. They believed in it, and they desperately wanted not to be toppled.)

Often the U.S. ambassador wanted to round up leaders of the American community for a social occasion with the former Vice-President. In most cases, we successfully resisted this. Nixon was trying to keep it a strictly working trip, and he had little enthusiasm in any case for cocktail-party-type gatherings. The lunches and dinners put on for him by the host governments, however, were another thing. These, in effect, were part of the job. The guests, for the most part, were officials of the host government. Treated as diplomatic occasions, they provided him an opportunity to talk informally with people whose interests paralleled his own. They always were lavishly prepared and presented, featuring an array of native delicacies. And always, at the end, there was an exchange of toasts.

This was my first introduction to Nixon as the formal diplomatist, the toastmaker, a highly specialized art form which requires an exceptional grace to do well, and at which—with a measure of surprise —I soon recognized him as a master. The toasts at a diplomatic dinner are never a simple "Here's to good old Joe, the greatest guy ever." Rather, they are speeches—sometimes lengthy speeches— that combine substance with just the right touch of flattery, directed not only toward the person being toasted but also toward his country, and designed both to extend a courtesy and to make a point.

He always spoke extemporaneously, without notes, and invariably his toasts were gracious, knowledgeable, and minutely sensitive to the feelings of the host country. As a guest, he always made the return toast; the first was offered by the host. And he always managed skillfully to make his a response to the one that had just been given, incorporating references to it in a way that demonstrated not only his attention but also his respect.

In some places we stayed in hotels, in others we stayed at the U.S. ambassador's residence. At our first stop after Honolulu, in Tokyo, we were the guests of Ambassador U. Alexis Johnson (a career diplomat later named by Nixon as under-secretary of state). The embassy residence in Tokyo is a palatial home that was used by General Douglas MacArthur during the postwar years, when MacArthur was the autocratic overlord of Japan. We were there for three days. As we prepared to leave, Nixon asked to meet with the household help—the maids, the cooks, the butler, the laundress. He thanked them, collectively and then individually, with a kind word and a warm handshake for each. Later he explained to me that he made a point of doing this whenever possible, especially abroad, both to show his respect and to express his appreciation: "They don't vote, but it means a lot to them." (When guests at an embassy residence, we also tried to handle the question of tips for the household help delicately. It was my job to find out from the ambassador whether they were welcomed or not, and, if so, to provide them discreetly.)

In all his foreign travels while out of office, Nixon adhered rigorously to one cardinal rule that he laid down for himself: that even though he was a potential challenger to the President then in office, he would not do or say anything that might embarrass the U.S. government, or that might make its diplomacy more difficult. In this, he demonstrated a sense of responsibility sharply in contrast to the actions of some of the Democratic contenders who traveled to Russia and other countries in their quest for the 1972 nomination.

Not only did he carefully refrain from criticism, or from otherwise undercutting administration efforts, but he went out of his way to be helpful. He freely exchanged information and impressions with the U.S. ambassadors. When being briefed by the ambassador before his talks with the government leaders, he always made certain to find out whether there were sensitive areas that should be avoided, or that needed to be handled in a particular way. When there were particular questions the ambassador wanted him to raise with the government leaders, he volunteered to do so, and then reported back to the ambassador. Since his own personal relationship with the prime minister or the foreign minister was often better than that of the ambassador, this was frequently useful.

The U.S. ambassador to India when we were there was Chester

Bowles, the former Democratic governor of Connecticut and under-secretary of state in the Kennedy administration. Bowles was a genial host. Because the Indian government had asked us to be its guests in New Delhi, we were staying at the government's Ashoka Hotel. But on the night of our arrival, Bowles and his wife invited us to a relaxed, informal dinner in the back yard of their home. The two old campaigners, the Democrat and the Republican, Bowles and Nixon, got along well. But Bowles did have a special favor to ask.

We were there at a particularly tense time in the often vexed relations between India and the United States. India and Pakistan were still locked in their bitterly emotional dispute over Kashmir. The United States had been insisting that the arms it provided Pakistan would never be used against India; but they had been, which infuriated India; a recent cut-off of arms to both sides had infuriated both; now India was doubly outraged by a new exemption to that policy, permitting the supply of spare parts for arms delivered prior to 1965. India claimed this favored Pakistan, because the United States had then been Pakistan's principal supplier, while the Soviet Union was India's principal supplier. Tensions were high and tempers were short. Bowles's request: that Nixon hold a press conference at the embassy the following day, so that he could explain the U.S. position.

In line with his effort to keep the trip low-key, Nixon had generally avoided press conferences. At Bowles's urging, however, he agreed to make an exception. The embassy sent out word that he would meet reporters, and more than sixty—mostly Indian, but some from other nations—gathered the next afternoon in a large hall at the American embassy. For an hour, Nixon fielded their frequently hostile questions about U.S. policy. In his answers he never criticized, he always explained, always treading the fine line between Indian and Pakistani sensitivities, trying to help them understand *why* the United States was taking the actions it was. After the press conference was over, the reporters trooped out, and Nixon, Bowles, and I gathered in a small anteroom off the main chamber. Bowles thanked Nixon profusely, and told him that his handling of that meeting with the Indian press was the best thing that had been done for U.S.-Indian relations in years.

Throughout the trip, Nixon was probing for new ideas, and also sizing people up—American as well as foreign. In Indonesia, we stayed at the home of U.S. Ambassador Marshall Green. Green was exceptionally insightful not only about Indonesia but also about the area generally. (When he became President, Nixon brought Green back to Washington as assistant secretary of state for Asian affairs.) Nixon encouraged me to meet with American correspondents in the various capitals, not to be interviewed by them but to pick their brains on the problems of the region. He sought out those Asian leaders with records as effective innovators, such as Thailand's economic wizard Pote Sarasin. In Vietnam, we had a long working lunch at the home of the legendary—and controversial—counterinsurgency expert Major General Edward Lansdale, together with Lansdale's whole top team of U.S. and Vietnamese deputies. Yet one of the most astute observers we met on the whole trip was not "new breed" at all, but one of the last of a vanishing breed: the British colonial administrators. He was Sir David Trench, governor general of Hong Kong, and he gave us this sage bit of advice: "The trouble with Americans in dealing with this part of the world is that you in America seem to have a passion for tying up all the loose ends. Out here, it's often better to leave a few loose ends dangling."

The trip had its tense moments. Because of the two nations' enmity, there were no direct airline connections between India and Pakistan. To get from New Delhi to Rawalpindi, we had to go by private plane—the embassy arranged for a little Piper Apache—to Lahore, Pakistan, and there connect with an Air Pakistan flight to Rawalpindi. Crowded into the Apache, we flew at one thousand feet over the scorched plains of northern India, keeping tight to our schedule. The plane was cleared to cross the border after 4:00 P.M. but if it crossed after 5:00 it would be shot down. We made it across in time, but at the tiny Lahore airport we confronted a raging mob of Pakistani demonstrators, scaling the low wire fence, carrying signs—"Nixon Go Home"; "Down with the U.S." Nixon studiedly ignored them. The consular representative who met us quickly pressed Nixon and Bob Ellsworth, who was with us on that part of the trip, into two of the three waiting cars, and they sped off, the second car keeping the space between them closed. I had stayed behind for a moment to clear up arrangements with the pilot for our return the next day. By the time I got to the third car, the mob was in full swarm. As the driver gunned the motor, one demonstrator who looked no more than sixteen tried to fling himself in front of the car. We missed him by an inch. I was glad we missed, for my sake as well as the youth's. Later the consul general told us he had been warned about the demonstration, and had asked for police protection. It arrived—after we were already gone. Shades of Caracas, I thought—even though this was puny compared with the mobs that had ambushed the Nixons and nearly killed them in that capital in 1958.

We waited at the consul general's house until time for the flight to Rawalpindi. The consul general, shaken by the incident, was profusely apologetic. Appearing unfazed, Nixon tried to relieve his host's embarrassment, by assuring him that such things had to be expected.

Some ten months later, aboard another small plane, Nixon and I fell to talking about that Asian trip. We were en route to Key Biscayne during a break in the New Hampshire primary campaign.
The first two Republican primary contests of 1968, on March 12 and April 2, took place in the biting Northern cold of New Hampshire and Wisconsin, respectively. That early primary season established my firm devotion to Key Biscayne. We developed a fairly general pattern: two or three weeks of intense campaigning, then off for a weekend of rest, recuperation, thinking, and planning in the Florida sun. Nixon had not yet bought the house on Biscayne Bay that would later become the Florida White House. Rather, he headquartered at the Key Biscayne Hotel. Key Biscayne has since undergone massive development, with towering condominiums rising where only palm trees and Australian pine stood before; but in 1968, it was still quiet, relaxed, informal, an unpretentious barefoot haven a world away from the glitter and tinsel of nearby Miami Beach.
On the first of those 1968 visits to Key Biscayne, only four of us went: Nixon, Pat Buchanan, Dwight Chapin, and myself. The campaign schedule had been grueling. We all were exhausted. At around 9:00 on a Friday evening we climbed aboard a chartered Lear jet. Buchanan and Chapin played cards in the front. Nixon and I were crowded into the back, unwinding with a couple of martinis. We talked about the campaign, the issues, the future, and then he began reminiscing about our trip through Asia the year before, and about his other earlier trips to Asia. He talked about the Indians, the Filipinos, the Vietnamese, the Japanese, the Chinese; about their similarities and their differences; about leaders he admired, such as Singapore's Lee Kuan Yew; about their ancient heritage and their struggle to survive. And then, in a voice tinged with both sadness and exasperation, he reflected on the strange inability of so many Americans, and particularly of so many liberal intellectuals, to take Asians seriously as human beings. They empathize with Europeans, but their thinking has an Atlantic tilt; too often, they instinctively, sometimes unconsciously, dismiss Asians as "little brown people." Passion welled up in his voice: " 'Little brown people.' I *love* those people!"
In the years ahead, as the nation was wracked by the traumas of

the Vietnam war, I often thought back on that moment. He did care about the 18 million South Vietnamese; whether they had a chance to determine their own future was, to him, a matter of real moral and human concern. And I think one of the reasons was that, more than his critics, he did take those "little brown people" seriously, as human beings, with the same feelings, the same worth, as the taller white people most Americans were more comfortable with.

One part of Richard Nixon is exceptionally considerate, exceptionally caring, sentimental, generous of spirit, kind. Another part is coldly calculating, devious, craftily manipulative. A third part is angry, vindictive, ill-tempered, mean-spirited.

Those of us who have worked with Nixon over the years often refer to his "light side" and his "dark side." The calculating, devious, manipulative parts are ones that I consign to neither side: These are necessary tools of statecraft.

But the light side and the dark side are both there, and over the years these have been at constant war with one another. I have seen the light side far more in evidence than I have the dark, and everyone I know who has worked closely with him agrees: while both are part of the "real" Nixon, the light side is by far the larger part, more central, the one that he himself identifies with. A lot of us routinely conspired with the light side to keep the darker side in check—and he was a conscious participant in that conspiracy.

Because of this constant conflict, he has always needed people around him who would help the lighter side prevail: who, when he issued an outrageous order, would quietly let it sit for a while until he calmed down, and then either ignore it or ask him whether he really wanted it done. For years Rose Mary Woods routinely did this. I did it. Bob Haldeman did it far more than most people realize (and one mark of Haldeman's self-effacement was his willingness to play the heavy, to appear as the grim Teuton hurling thunderbolts, when in fact he was quietly deflecting many of those thunderbolts).

I think probably the most important and least understood aspect of this light side–dark side conflict is the extent to which the dark side grew not out of his nature, but out of his experiences in public life. Almost invariably, his rages were directed at one aspect or another of the "double standard"—the standard that judged him harshly and his opponents leniently for the same actions. He wanted to be trusting, but he had had his trust too often abused. He had been burned too often by the press, and he reacted humanly rather than superhumanly. He accumulated resentments. Most of the time he hid them. Sometimes he let them show. Reflecting much later on the 1960 presidential campaign, he once rather wistfully commented, "We were babes in the woods"—in the big world of hard-knuckle politics, he was getting his jungle baptism. And over the years he learned, perhaps not wisely but too well: sometimes the only way to survive in politics is to do unto others before they do unto you.

In the Nixon White House, the President's "dark side" came to be personified, to many of us, by Charles W. ("Chuck") Colson.

Late one evening, several of us were gathered over drinks, swapping complaints about Colson. I asked John Mitchell—who despised him—just what the hell Colson's constituency was, anyhow? Mitchell quickly growled back: "The President's worst instincts." Mitchell was right. There would not have been a Chuck Colson if there had not been a dark side of Richard Nixon.

The tragedy was that, until Colson, the conspiracy had held: With occasional lapses, the dark side had been kept effectively checked. The light side had prevailed. But with Colson, the dark side had the ally and the outlet that it needed. Instead of discreetly ignoring the outrageous orders, Colson rushed to carry them out. No longer did the dark side face the constant frustration of being told that what it wanted shouldn't be done or couldn't be done. It could sneak around the light side, thumb its nose, and say "I told you so!"

Colson was brilliant, tough, immensely able, a shrewd political operator, but one who displayed no real comprehension of the underlying purposes of the political process, or any appreciation of the delicate balances, the patterns of mutual self-restraints essential to a democratic system in a pluralistic society. Unfortunately, he was also a man quite ready to push his way to the top by encouraging the President's worst instincts, playing on them, magnifying them—and, by magnifying the President's resentment of those who thwarted those instincts, weakening the grip of the lighter side of the President on himself.

As 1971 edged into the election year of 1972, Colson was more and more at Nixon's side, talking with him, feeding the fires of resentment against the "enemies," against those within the administration who were "disloyal" (a term increasingly used during this period to characterize those who objected to the more bizarre of Colson's schemes), persuading him that those who tried to keep the dark side in check were either too timid or too naïve, magnifying the sense of injury over the past sins against Nixon himself, feeding the desire to get even, building his outrage against the pervasive double standard by which, for example, the disruptive tactics of a Dick Tuck carried out against Nixon campaigns were "pranks" to be giggled over for their cleverness, while those against Nixon opponents were "dirty tricks" and an affront to the democratic system. (Personally, I was appalled when I learned of the Segretti dirty tricks; I saw them as neither clever nor funny. But neither did I think the Dick Tuck "pranks" were either clever or funny. The double standard constantly reminded me of a wry comment I had heard several times from a gruff old-timer on the *Herald Tribune* staff, that at the *Trib* there were always Republican "leaders" and Democratic "bosses.")

In terms of personalities, the Nixon administration was as complex and contradictory as the many sides of Nixon himself. Seldom has a national administration offered such a ministry of talent. Yet it also had its sprinkling of mediocrities, and a disturbingly large number of bright but inexperienced young people with responsibilities beyond their grasp. Leonard Garment, Henry Kissinger, Daniel ("Pat") Moynihan, Elliot Richardson, James Schlesinger, George Shultz, Caspar Weinberger—these and others like them were seasoned professionals, brilliant intellects, men of principle and of high public purpose. Then there was Colson. There also were the John Deans and the Jeb Magruders—ambitious young men on the make, with little concept of what government was about, but with an overweening desire to use government for their own self-advancement. Interestingly, most of the old hands from past Nixon incarnations tended to be a leavening influence: people like Arthur Burns, Robert Finch, Bryce Harlow, Don Hughes, Herb Klein, William Rogers, Maurice Stans, Rose Mary Woods.

This fact, to me, says something important about Nixon, and particularly about the balance between the two sides. These old hands, his associates over the years, had seen him in all of his moods. They were not moths attracted to the flame of the presidency. They were mostly people of independent stature, and uniformly people of high public purpose. They saw their loyalty to Richard Nixon as an extension of their concern for the country's welfare. They were natural, instinctive allies of the light side rather than the dark side. And they believed in him because over the years they had seen that he, too, was an instinctive ally of the light side. They themselves had been among the sentinels he posted to be sure the lighter side prevailed.

In late January 1975 I arrived in San Clemente for my first visit as a private citizen. I had already been there twice since Nixon's resignation, for a week in August and from mid-September to mid-

October. But these had been as a member of the White House staff, helping as a part of his transition team. Now I was back for a stay that I thought would be a month, but that lasted until early April. I found an oceanfront house, a couple of miles away from the Nixons', and worked in these rented quarters. (There was space at the office compound. But a campaign was still being waged in the Congress and in the press against provision to Nixon of the routine support facilities and staff allowances made available to former presidents. I felt that if, as a private citizen, I made any use of the government facilities there, it might be blown into an appearance of abuse. So I meticulously stayed away, except when coming down to the compound to visit Nixon or meet with members of his staff.)

After taking a leisurely eight days to drive from Washington, I arrived in San Clemente late on a Sunday afternoon. The Nixons invited me to dinner the next evening.

Twice during the previous autumn, once in September and again in October, Nixon had been hospitalized for treatment of the phlebitis he had developed on his Middle Eastern trip the previous June —an inflammation of the deep veins of the lower left leg. The principal danger in phlebitis is that it can cause clotting, and these clots, if they move to the lungs or the heart, can quickly prove fatal. When he was hospitalized in September, tests showed that a small clot had reached the lungs—evidence of a dangerous condition, but not itself large enough to be fatal. He was given intensive treatment, and released after ten days. Further tests two weeks later showed new clotting near the vein leading to the heart. At 5:30 A.M. on October 29, an emergency operation was performed to close off the vein. Shortly after the operation was completed, he suffered massive internal bleeding and went into sudden postoperative shock. His blood pressure dropped to 60 over 0; four doctors, together with a team of critical-care nurses, fought desperately for three hours to keep him alive. Their emergency efforts saved him, but for several days thereafter his condition remained critical. Sixteen days after the surgery he was finally well enough to return to his home, where a special hospital bed had been installed. But his recovery was slow and difficult. His left lung was still partly compressed by an accumulation of fluid. An area in his right lung was still devoid of air. His badly swollen, phlebitis-damaged left leg had to be kept elevated. His blood pressure was subject to abnormal rises, a condition made particularly dangerous because of the anti-coagulants he had to use for his phlebitis.

When I arrived for dinner, it was the first time I had seen him since before that brush with death nearly three months earlier. He still was thin, gaunt, haggard, moving with evident difficulty. Mrs. Nixon took me aside, and told me enthusiastically that he had improved "a hundred percent" in just the past week. He himself was proud to be getting his weight back at last. I wondered what sort of ghost he must have been the week before, and the week before that.

In the living room of their San Clemente house, the Nixons have a huge Spanish-tile fireplace. Manolo had made a blazing fire with weathered eucalyptus logs. Instead of using the dining room, we ate on tray-tables set out in front of the fire. The tray-tables, a gift from Tricia, were unsteady on the deep-pile rug, and Nixon still had only limited control over his phlebitic left leg. At one point during dinner his leg bumped his tray-table, toppling onto the floor a half-full bottle of wine that stood precariously on a corner. The deep-red wine flowed out onto the pale-yellow rug. I quickly got up, knelt down, sprinkled salt on it, and tried to soak it up with a Kleenex. The President, embarrassed as much at his own awkwardness as at the mishap itself, got painfully down on his own knees to try to help. Mrs. Nixon, protesting that we should both leave it to her, rushed out to the kitchen and came back a moment later with a bottle of club soda and a cloth, shooed us out of the way, and, kneeling in front of the fireplace, poured the soda on the stain and blotted it up. Her homespun remedy worked. The spot disappeared, and when Ronald and Nancy Reagan arrived for dinner with the Nixons the next night there was no trace of it.

If he were still President, that might have been the January night on which he delivered his State of the Union address to a joint session of Congress, a motorcycle escort clearing the way as his limousine, trailed by a procession of Secret Service and White House cars, sped him through the Washington night to Capitol Hill, 60 million television viewers watching as he acknowledged a standing ovation from the House, the Senate, the Supreme Court, and the diplomatic corps, all crowded into the chamber of the House of Representatives. Instead, he was an exile in his own country, on his knees, blotting wine stains from the rug.

To those who see Richard Nixon as evil incarnate, there is no tragedy in his fall from grace and power. It looks different to those of us who saw him as a good man, with flaws; as a statesman struggling to reshape the world so that peace would be secure for the next generation, brought low when he provided the weapon to those who sought to destroy him.

A few days after that dinner, Ron Ziegler, Frank Gannon (a former White House aide helping him with his memoirs), and I held a long session with him in the study of his San Clemente home.

I knew that emotionally, in approaching the writing of his memoirs, he was still having difficulty coming squarely to grips with the Watergate aspects, and, more broadly, with the whole light side/dark side dichotomy of the phenomenon that is Richard Nixon. The pain was still too intense, the disgrace still too near.

As I thought about it, I guessed that there was also another reason: that he probably imagined that he had been more successful than he had been at hiding the dark side from those he associated with the light side. So I decided to use the occasion to launch into a long, Dutch-uncle lecture.

I told him that there were a lot of us whose opinions I knew he valued, including myself, who had seen more of the dark side than he thought we had, who were well aware of it, and who admired him just the same. And I went on to argue that instead of being embarrassed by it, he should acknowledge it—that it was as important to an understanding of the Nixon triumphs as it was of the Nixon failures. If the country were ever to be restored to its senses, the public would have to recognize that a measure of scheming and duplicity are necessary in the real world of power politics. If we wanted great strengths in our national leaders, we would have to learn once again to accept the basic fact of human nature that great strengths come in a single package with great failings, or great weaknesses—and I argued that his own best claim on the favorable judgment of history lay in being judged on the whole record, the good and the bad together. But most importantly, the point I tried to drive home was that he could acknowledge the dark side, deal with it, without losing the support or the faith of those who were still his friends. He would not be telling us anything that we had not already counted into the equation.

I could see some of the tension drain away, and at one point he looked out of the window, then turned back, grinned, and commented: "Of course, it's true. We never could have brought off the opening to China if we hadn't lied a little, could we?"

A NEW DIRECTION

By the closing days of the 1968 campaign, the wide lead Nixon had held in the polls at the beginning had narrowed to a cliffhanger finish. After an anxious, frenetic last weekend in Los Angeles, on election day we boarded the campaign plane—the *Tricia*[1]—for the flight back to New York, with hope, apprehension, and uncertainty mixed in a confused emotional jumble. The day was clear. As we crossed the nation from West to East I kept looking out the windows at the tiny settlements nestled in the desert, the green-and-brown checkerboards of farmland, the spreading cities, knowing that down there, thirty-five thousand feet below, people in every state and every community were going to the polls, voting, pulling the levers that together would determine whether the long campaign ended in victory or defeat—and there was nothing, nothing whatever, that we could do about it. The contest was finished. All that remained now was the voting, and the counting.

Returning to New York exhausted but excited, the staff piled aboard a waiting bus that took us to our election-night headquarters at the Waldorf Astoria. I could have voted by absentee ballot, but I wanted to vote in person that year. It was more satisfying. So,

---

1. During the primaries in 1968, planes were chartered or borrowed on a trip-by-trip basis, except for one period late in the primary season when we chartered a Lockheed Electra for the month. For the postnomination campaign, we chartered a pair of Boeing 727s from United Airlines. They were christened the *Tricia* and the *Julie.* Nixon and most of the staff rode the *Tricia,* named for his elder daughter. Press, press staff, and any overflow from the *Tricia* rode the *Julie,* named for his younger daughter.

when we arrived at the Waldorf, I sped across town to my own apartment (the local polling place was in the lobby) to vote and to clean up before rushing back to headquarters for the counting.

The main election-night headquarters, where thousands of supporters milled about, were in the ballroom and adjacent public rooms of the Waldorf proper. But the inner circle gathered on the thirty-fifth floor of the Waldorf Towers, where the Nixons had their own suite. Scattered through the other rooms on the floor were television sets and refreshments and, of course, telephones. We circulated from one room to another, keeping tabs on the results, the tension mounting as the count dragged on. Through most of the evening Nixon clung to a thin but precarious lead. Around midnight Humphrey appeared to be surging forward, and for the first time my own characteristic optimism turned to a queasy pessimism. By 2:00, as more returns trickled in, it looked again as though we were winning. Shortly after 3:00, the man we thought was the President-elect invited a dozen of us to wait out the results with him in his suite. The banter was light, the campaign reminiscences good-natured, but there was a heavy tension in the air. Every once in a while, in a flash of impatient irritation, Nixon sent Mitchell or Haldeman or another aide to the next room to call headquarters in one of the states that had still not reported, and to try to get some sort of reading that might cut through the clouds of uncertainty. But by then there was little to report. Most had shut down their counting operations until morning. Texas reported before midnight that "mechanical problems" would delay the totals until morning— a report which sounded ominous to those with memories of 1960.

Another of the hold-out states was Illinois. There, Mayor Richard J. Daley was up to his traditional trick of holding back the results from key Chicago areas until the count was in from downstate. That way, if the results were close and a few thousand extra votes were needed to tip the state into the Democratic column, the Daley machine could usually manage to find those "votes." But this time, the Nixon campaign organization was prepared. Instructions had gone out to several Republican-controlled jurisdictions not to release their totals until Daley had released his. Demands did no good; Daley stubbornly sat on his vote counts. Then, at about 8:00 A.M., as we sat together in front of the television set, campaign manager John Mitchell put in a call to Mike Wallace of CBS. We watched the screen as Wallace, who was on the air, took the call. Mitchell prodded Wallace to challenge Daley—on television. Wallace did, and shortly thereafter the Illinois totals were released. Illinois fell into the Nixon column.

Finally, shortly before noon, Humphrey conceded. At 12:30 Nixon went down to the grand ballroom and delivered his victory statement to a cheering crowd, most of whom had waited through the night—a healing pledge to "bring us together."

For those of us gathered on the thirty-fifth floor during the long night, one thing that heightened the drama was that as the contest finally got down to a waiting game, three of the states from which we were awaiting results were Illinois, Missouri, and Texas. In this, there were resounding echoes of 1960. And the eerie parallels between election nights 1960 and 1968 were much in my mind five years later, as the Nixon presidency once again hung in the balance.

In 1960 the presidential race had continued close down to the election-day wire, leaving Nixon and John F. Kennedy virtually even in the polls. Then, on election night, Kennedy surged to a swift, early lead, both in tabulated votes and in the network projections. At 9:00 P.M., Eastern time—still an hour before polls had closed in the West—CBS predicted that Kennedy would win with 52 percent of the popular vote. By 10:30, NBC reported that its computers made the odds on a Kennedy victory 250 to 1. The *Herald Tribune* went to press saying Kennedy appeared headed for "a landslide of Rooseveltian proportions." But as the night wore on, the Kennedy margin narrowed. In the popular vote, Kennedy's lead reached 2 million in the early counting. Then it dropped to 1.7 million by midnight, to 1.6 million at 12:45, to 1.1 million by 1:30. Nor was the outcome of the electoral vote yet clear. At 1:30, CBS and NBC were still giving California to Kennedy—though it eventually went to Nixon. Nixon was being pressed to concede, but the outcome was still not certain. Finally, at 12:15, Pacific time—3:15 in the East—he went down to the ballroom of the Ambassador Hotel in Los Angeles. By then the popular margin was down to 900,000. Nixon had twenty sure states, against nineteen for Kennedy. Kennedy's nineteen gave him the lead in electoral votes, but he still had only 265, four short of a majority. Nevertheless, Nixon faced the cameras, thanked his supporters, and said that while there were "still some results to come in, if the present trend continues, Senator Kennedy will be the next President of the United States. . . . I want Senator Kennedy to know, and I want all of you to know that . . . if he does become our next President, he will have my wholehearted support."

When the vote count was finally completed, Kennedy led by a hairsbreadth 113,000 out of 68,800,000 votes cast. Kennedy got 49.7 percent, Nixon 49.6 percent. The electoral count stood at 303 to 219. Among the states in the Kennedy column were Illinois, with 26 electoral votes, Missouri, with 12, and Texas, with 25. Kennedy won Illinois by 8858 out of nearly 5 million cast. He won Missouri by 9980 out of nearly 2 million. He won Texas by 46,233 out of more than 2 million. There were strong suspicions that the election in Missouri had been stolen. There was clear evidence of massive vote frauds in both Illinois and Texas—enough to have swung the margins in those two states, and thus the presidential election. (There was no indication that Kennedy himself was responsible for the frauds—they were the work of the local Democratic machines —but, because they were in behalf of the Democratic ticket, he was the beneficiary and Nixon was the victim.)

In Texas, the state's election machinery, from precinct tally clerks to the State Board of Canvassers, was totally controlled by the Democratic party organization. In 1960 Earl Mazo was still the New York *Herald Tribune*'s Washington-based national political correspondent. As a walking encyclopedia of politics, he was a legend among the Washington press corps. Immediately after the election, spurred by tips from his own sources in Texas, Mazo launched an extensive investigation of vote frauds there and elsewhere. As he has since reported, the state board, "which ran the whole election operation in Texas and was also court of last resort on the vote tallies, was made up of three stalwarts, two of whom happened to be managers of the Democratic campaign in Texas. Under that board's eagle eye, the election shenanigans ranged from ballot-box stuffing and jamming the Republican column on voting machines to misreading ballots cast for Republicans and double-counting those for Democrats. Typical was the result in Precinct Twenty-seven, Angelina County, where 86 individuals cast ballots and the officially reported vote was 148 for Kennedy-Johnson, 24 for Nixon-Lodge. That remarkable tally and thousands of others somewhat like it were approved without apparent question by the Democratic campaign managers sitting on the state's election Board of Canvassers." Another favorite Texas vote-fraud technique uncovered by Mazo was made possible by a peculiarity of the Texas ballot. About half the votes cast in Texas were on paper ballots. Rather than checking the candidates they did want, voters were required to strike out the ones they did not want. In 1960, in addition to the Democratic and Republican nominees, presidential candidates were listed for the Prohibition and Constitution parties. It was obvious from his own checking of the ballots, Mazo reported, that "ballots on which voters had failed to scratch out the minor party candidates were more likely to be thrown out in areas that went for Nixon than in Kennedy territory." Typical was Fort Bend County. There, in Precinct One, which showed 458 votes for Nixon-Lodge and 350 for Kennedy-Johnson, 182 votes were voided. None was voided in Precinct Two, which went 68 to 1 for Kennedy-Johnson. Mazo's conclusion, after his investigation: "An exercise in elementary arithmetic —adding and subtracting—indicated that a minimum of 100,000 votes officially tallied for the Kennedy-Johnson ticket simply were nonexistent."[2]

In Chicago, the Daley machine's sophisticated skills at manufacturing election results have long been legendary. In 1960, besides his traditional desire to give the top of the ticket a little extra boost, Daley also had important fish of his own to fry. He wanted to get rid of a local prosecuting attorney, a Republican, whose aggressive law enforcement was threatening Daley's machine. Huge piles of sworn affidavits filed after the election by poll watchers and disgruntled voters told how it was done. In one precinct, by 10:15 A.M. the voting machine indicator showed that 121 votes had been cast after only 43 persons had voted. (The final tally in that precinct: Kennedy 408, Nixon 79.) In another, one voter was seen putting six paper ballots in the box. In another, where there were 22 voters on the official list, 77 voted. And so on, ad infinitum.

Washington Post editor Ben Bradlee tells in his book about a dinner with Kennedy shortly after the election. Kennedy regaled his guests with a tale of a phone call he had made to Daley while the Illinois results were hanging in the balance. He asked Daley how it looked. Daley replied, said Kennedy, that "with a little bit of luck and the help of a few close friends, you're going to carry Illinois." Bradlee goes on to note: "Later, when Nixon was being urged to contest the 1960 election, I often wondered about that statement."[3]

(Even in 1976, when the political process had supposedly been washed all squishy-clean with soap and Watergate, columnists Rowland Evans and Robert Novak quite matter-of-factly reported that shortly before midnight on election night, "Daley told Carter operatives not to worry about Illinois; he was withholding Chicago precincts that would clinch victory in a re-enactment of John F. Kennedy's 1960 triumph." Daley's reassurance was passed on to Jimmy Carter by veteran Texas party stalwart Robert S. Strauss, chairman of the Democratic National Committee.)

Within days after the 1962 election, fraud charges came piling in. Nixon was under heavy pressure to challenge Kennedy's election.

2. Earl Mazo and Stephen Hess, *Nixon: A Political Portrait* (New York, 1968), pp. 245–48.
3. *Conversations with Kennedy* (New York, 1975), p. 33.

The question of whether to challenge involved more than fraud. Several states were so close that even honest errors, of the kind commonly found on a recount, might have shifted them from one column to the other. Even without Texas, a shift of four thousand votes each in Illinois and Missouri, plus a total of three thousand to five thousand in any two states such as New Mexico, Nevada, or Hawaii, would have made Nixon rather than Kennedy the next President.

Nixon weighed whether to demand a recount, but soon decided against it. For one thing, the two large states with blatant vote frauds made effective challenges there virtually impossible. In Illinois's Cook County (Chicago), the laws were so written that a recount would take at least a year and a half. In Texas, there was no procedure whatever for a losing candidate to get a recount.

There were other considerations, too: a recount would embarrass the United States abroad; there was no certainty that it would change anything; on recount, close states might shift both ways. Also, as he later explained: "If I were to demand a recount, the organization of the new administration and the orderly transfer of responsibility from the old to the new might be delayed for months. The situation within the entire federal government would be chaotic. Those in the old administration would not know how to act— or with what clear powers and responsibilities—and those being appointed by Kennedy to positions in the new administration would have the same difficulty making any plans."

So he sent word to his supporters: No recount. No challenge. But he also did more. Earl Mazo's digging into the frauds produced a series of articles in the *Herald Tribune,* planned by the editors to run for twelve installments. Early in December, after the first four had appeared, Nixon invited Mazo to come by for a visit. Immediately afterward, Mazo wrote a memo for his own files:

"Right off, as we shook hands, he said, 'Earl, those are interesting articles you are writing—but no one steals the presidency of the United States.'

"I thought he might be kidding. But never was a man more deadly serious. We chatted for an hour or two about the campaign, the odd vote patterns in various places, and this and that. Then, continent by continent, he enumerated potential international crises that could be dealt with only by the President of a united country, and not a nation torn by the kind of partisan bitterness and chaos that inevitably would result from an official challenge of the election result."

At one point, according to Mazo, "Nixon said, calmly as though talking to himself: 'Our country can't afford the agony of a constitutional crisis—and I damn well will not be a party to creating one just to become President or anything else.'" Pleading the need for national unity behind the new Kennedy administration, Nixon asked that the series be dropped. And it was.[4]

In 1968, by the time the long night of waiting was over and the votes were finally in, Nixon had won Illinois by 134,960 and Missouri by 20,488. Humphrey won Texas by 38,950. Overall, Nixon got 31,785,480 votes, to 31,275,166 for Humphrey and 9,906,473 for George Wallace. Nixon took 301 electoral votes to Humphrey's 191 and Wallace's 46.

But those two election nights, one losing, one winning, each by so agonizingly close a margin, each with the outcome hanging shrouded in doubt until the following morning, must have had an effect on Nixon himself. And that impact must have been compounded, waiting through the night in 1968 for the results from Illinois, Missouri, and Texas, by the vivid memory of what had happened in those states in 1960.

As we geared up for our intensive re-election effort in 1972, I kept arguing, with the repetitive monotony of a metronome, that if we lost that election it would be because we tried too hard to win. As it eventually turned out, I was a pretty good prophet, but my timing was off. Still, I can't help wondering. If I had been he, by then I might have felt the need for an extra margin of safety, too. And, later, I never ceased to be amazed at the monumental hypocrisy of those keepers of the double standard who professed outrage at the Watergate break-in, but shrugged off the probable theft of a presidential election itself—because the victim of that theft was Nixon, and because when Democratic machines steal votes it isn't news. It's expected.

By inauguration day, January 20, 1969, the anxious uncertainties of election night were long past. It was a time of beginning.

For its campaign headquarters, the Nixon organization had leased the five-story building at the corner of Park Avenue and Fifty-seventh Street that previously housed the American Bible Society. It was dilapidated inside but imposing outside, one of those disappearing relics of a time when cities were built to human scale. I worked in a battered cubicle on the fourth floor. (Around the walls on the first floor, a single large room, Biblical quotations were

4. Mazo and Hess, *Nixon: A Political Portrait*, pp. 248–49.

painted in Gothic script on the moldings. I especially liked the one that read, "Verily I Say Unto You—Heaven and Earth Shall Pass Away. But My Words Shall Not Pass Away." Later, when the building was being torn down to make way for a black-sheathed slab of a new office building, a friend salvaged this molding for me. She also salvaged one for the campaign's finance chairman, Maurice Stans. It read: "Feed My Sheep.")

During the transition period between election and inauguration, most of us who still were involved in the operation continued to work in the old Bible Society building. The President-elect himself set up transition headquarters at the Hotel Pierre, on Fifth Avenue, just a block south of his own apartment. While putting together his new administration, he was also giving a good deal of time and thought to his inaugural address. He sought out ideas from many sources, but it was understood from the beginning that I would be his basic collaborator on it, and would be the one who worked with him on pulling it together.

As usual, I churned around in several directions at once, experimenting with various themes, trying out ideas, looking for inspiration, trying to think through what would be most appropriate to the moment. More than almost any other public occasion, a presidential inauguration has an almost sacramental element. Symbolism is important. Substance is also important. The American people look to it for an indication of what to expect from a new president, and of what he expects from them. So does the rest of the world.

Nixon did the same. He read every previous inaugural address. He jotted down ideas, dictated notes, gathered suggestions, all the time reaching for the central theme that would tie it all together. He wanted to keep it short: "Only the short ones are remembered." As we talked one day in early January, in his office at the Pierre, he reflected on the earlier ones. "The most memorable have come at turning points," he commented. "Lincoln's second was a great one— Theodore Roosevelt's was damn good, even though it came in the middle of his presidency. Wilson's was very good, and FDR's first. Kennedy's basically stands up because it has some good phrases, and because it caught the mood and it caught himself." He said that some people, recalling Truman's announcement of Point Four in 1948, were urging that he put some such specific in this one—for example, inviting the Soviets to join us in sending a man to the moon. But he rejected that sort of thing as "gimmickry," and said "it would stand out too transparently as gimmickry." As a matter of basic courtesy, he wanted to be careful not to "kick the predecessor while he's sitting there on the platform, as Kennedy did in 1960—

saying 'the torch has been passed to a new generation,' and so forth —but still to get the idea of something new." We should make clear, he said, "that this administration is going to be progressive, that we're not just going to be caretakers, that this is not just going to be a period of 'normalcy.' It's a time when great decisions are going to be made, and when we can all be a part of history." He wanted to exhort the people themselves to play a greater role, "not by telling them to put their nose to the grindstone, but by appealing to their better natures."

Shortly after the election, Nixon tapped Henry Kissinger and Pat Moynihan, both Harvard professors, as his assistants for national-security affairs and for urban affairs, respectively. The appointments dramatically demonstrated not only that Nixon was looking for top-flight talent but also that he was willing to reach across old barriers to get it. Kissinger had been a close, long-time associate of Nixon's long-time rival Nelson Rockefeller. Moynihan, a Democrat, was a veteran of the Kennedy and Johnson administrations (and, in 1965, a losing candidate for the Democratic nomination for president of the New York City Council). Nixon asked both for their own recommendations for the inaugural address.

Kissinger responded with three pages of text. His covering memo read:

MEMORANDUM FOR THE PRESIDENT-ELECT

From: Henry A. Kissinger

Subject: Proposed Foreign-Policy Section of Your Inaugural Address

I am attaching the outline of the inaugural. Some version of the under-lined sentences on page three should be in for the reasons we have discussed. I shall be happy to explain the grounds for the other passages. In general, the attempt was to strike a note of sober, precise, methodical, undramatic progress.

The "underlined sentences on page three" were:

"To those who, for most of the postwar period, have opposed and, occasionally, threatened us, I repeat what I have already said: let the coming years be a time of negotiation rather than confrontation. During this administration the lines of communication will always be open."

In passing the Kissinger material along, Nixon explained to me that this had been worked out with Soviet representatives as a public signal to confirm the private indications he had given that he really did want an "era of negotiation." But this—or some version of it— was the only part of the Kissinger material that was sacrosanct.

Kissinger might label his draft "the outline of the inaugural," but Nixon had his own ideas.

(Actually the Kissinger draft struck me as mostly standard boiler-plate rhetoric. But the brief passage on Vietnam had substance. It read: "We shall make peace in Vietnam. This is our aim in negotia-tions in Paris and on the battlefield in Vietnam. We shall be patient and we shall persevere in both efforts. We seek no permanent pres-ence in South Vietnam. We ask no more than that the people of that nation be allowed to determine their own fate free of external force. We shall settle for nothing less." Before passing it along, Nixon crossed out the last sentence. The line reflected his policy. But if he stated it that belligerently and that categorically in his inaugural it might hinder negotiations.)

Moynihan's response, characteristically, was brisk, breezy and to the point:

"You asked for thoughts concerning your inaugural address," his memo began. "I have only a small number, and they will be thor-oughly familiar to you."

First, he said, was "the matter of commitments. There are three groups which, by and large, were not important to your candidacy, but which can prove immensely important to your presidency. These are the black poor, the white working class, and the educated youth."

Among the first of those groups, Nixon had long been the target of such a fear campaign that Moynihan felt a special reassurance was needed: "The black poor desperately need to be reassured that you have no intention of turning away from the great goals of the civil-rights acts of 1959, 1964, and 1965, the goals of a free and open society in which equality of opportunity for blacks increasingly has the outcome of equality of achievement as well. It would be difficult to overstate the present anxiety. . . . I repeat the statement of your urban-affairs task force: The rumor is widespread that the new government is planning to build concentration camps."

One of Nixon's central aims, which he repeatedly stressed during the campaign, was to reverse the flow of power to Washington, to decentralize, to strengthen the states and localities. On this, Moyni-han wrote:

"I would urge you to consider the possibility of a brief acknowl-edgment that in the past the cry of decentralization was typically that of persons who wanted government, that is to say organized society, to attempt less, not more. This is not your purpose at all, nor is this why the surge toward decentralization arose. To the contrary, it has sprung from the desire that organized society should in fact achieve its goals, and that big, centralized government simply cannot deliver on its promises."

In the margin beside this, Nixon scrawled: "Decentralization is not an excuse for inaction, but a key to action." It was a point he wanted to make.

Ideas and suggestions poured in. Billy Graham wrote, urging a "strong spiritual emphasis," and saying he was convinced that young people would respond "to a tough and hard challenge." One of Nixon's closest friends is Hollywood gagwriter Paul Keyes, who was the creator of the old Rowan and Martin "Laugh-In" show,[5] and at the time was still its chief writer. Keyes also has a serious side, and he sent along five pages of suggested language. One passage in the speech was drawn from the Keyes material: "Let us take as our goal: Where peace is unknown, make it welcome; where peace is fragile, make it strong; where peace is temporary, make it permanent."

Nixon continued honing his own ideas, and developing his own themes. As usual, it was in the final week or so—as he himself began his own intensive concentration on it—that it really began to take form.

Rose Mary Woods and I joined him in Key Biscayne, where we worked on it until it said basically what he wanted to say. "We should try not for a blockbuster," he told me, as we started that final phase, "but to say what's in our hearts; what we believe." And he wanted to do it in a way that would heal a divided country, not divide it further: "In reading the better inaugurals—Wilson's, FDR's, Teddy Roosevelt's, Kennedy's—one very subtle but important point comes through. Each had problems, and talked about them. Both Wilson and FDR talked about them and tried to analyze them—but the theme of each was to kick hell out of someone else and tell the American people they're great. We've got to write the section about the spirit of America, about confronting ourselves, in a way that we don't condemn everybody. We mustn't appear to be scolding the people."

In writing the speech, he was also defining the goals of his presidency.

One of those goals was summed up in a theme we developed

5. One of the trademarks of "Laugh-In" was the line "Sock it to me!" followed, usually, by the dousing of the person saying it with buckets of water. At one point during the campaign Nixon made a cameo appearance on the show, consisting solely of his appearing suddenly on the screen, asking, in a puzzled voice, "Sock it to *me?*"

during the campaign: to break the pattern of the century's middle third at the start of its final third. In a neat bit of historical symmetry, the administrations from Franklin Roosevelt's through Lyndon Johnson's precisely spanned the middle third of the twentieth century. FDR was inaugurated in March 1933. He was the architect of the modern presidency, and of the vast expansion of federal powers that continued from his administration onward, reaching its zenith under Johnson, who came to Washington in the 1930s as a Roosevelt protégé. Even during the Eisenhower years—in all but the first two of which Congress remained solidly Democratic—the trend toward an expanded federal role continued.

One result was a weakening of government at the state and local level. Washington commanded the resources and wrote the rules. Washington collected the taxes, and then, when it passed money back, the money came wrapped in a tangle of federal red tape and regulations and reporting requirements. Increasingly, people got into the habit of looking not to city hall or the statehouse when they had a problem, but to Washington. As long as Washington was where the power was, and where the glamour was, Washington also was where the talent went—however much that talent was needed at the state and local levels.

As a result decisions minutely affecting local communities came increasingly to be made by faceless officials far from the scene, who, however highly motivated, had no way of responding to the infinite variety of local conditions. People felt helpless, confronted with a decision-making process that had passed beyond their control or even their influence, a process they frequently could not even locate or identify. At the same time, the more people expected from Washington, the less they were inclined to do for themselves.

Nixon's goal was not to dismantle the New Deal but to shift the direction of change, to shift the flow of power away from Washington and back closer to the people themselves.

In his own mind, the need for this change was rooted in more than the mechanics of government: It was rooted in the human spirit, and it was vital to the restoration of the American spirit.

At one point, as we worked on the speech, he was dissatisfied with the section of the draft that dealt with this. He looked up from the draft and, as he so often did, began spinning out his thoughts aloud: "This misses it. What we've got to say is, the emphasis in the past has been on material things and on government action. We've come to the ultimate limit in that respect. We've never had more programs, spent more money, or passed more laws than in the past third of a century. Yet we have these terrible problems today, and the reason is that we've reached the ultimate in what government can do by itself. The missing thing is what's at the heart of the American experiment. While the United States is thought of as the wonder of the world, in terms of its material progress, its wealth, its productivity, what matters is the fact that the United States has provided a place for individual self-expression. We've got to provide that opportunity. We've got to ask millions of Americans to join in, not only to get the job done but also because only as an individual gets involved in a cause bigger than himself is he really fulfilled. Man needs food, clothing, medical care. But, above all else, for a man to be whole he needs self-expression, a chance to create, to build, to participate."

The inaugural address was not the place to speak of the mechanics of government; that would come later. Rather, it was a place to signal directions, to suggest priorities, to lay a healing hand on the nation's fevered brow, and, importantly, to seek to enlist the people themselves in the "high adventure" that he saw ahead. (One theme he had stressed throughout the campaign was the need to encourage a renaissance of "voluntary action"—private-citizen efforts to deal with the problems of people and communities on a volunteer level. One of the major disappointments of the first term was that our attempts to do this, including establishment of a national information exchange on techniques that proved successful in various communities, failed really to get off the ground.)

But it was, as he had stressed, essential to signal change without "kicking the predecessor." Thus, he spoke of the middle third of the century as "a time of proud achievement." But he warned that "we are approaching the limits of what government alone can do. . . . What has to be done, has to be done by government and people together or it will not be done at all."

He reached out to assuage the blacks' fears, of which Moynihan had warned, and to dampen whatever hopes there might be among bitter-enders that they could turn the march of racial progress:

"No man can be fully free while his neighbor is not. To go forward at all is to go forward together.

"This means black and white together, as one nation, not two. The laws have caught up with our conscience. What remains is to give life to what is in the law: to insure at last that as all are born equal in dignity before God, all are born equal in dignity before man."

Nixon carefully warned potential adversaries abroad that in its pursuit of peace, his administration would also keep its powder dry:

"With those who are willing to join, let us cooperate to reduce the burden of arms, to strengthen the structure of peace, to lift up the poor and the hungry.

"But to all those who would be tempted by weakness, let us leave no doubt that we will be as strong as we need to be for as long as we need to be."

He also set his own first priority:

"The greatest honor history can bestow is the title of peacemaker. This honor now beckons America—the chance to help lead the world at last out of the valley of turmoil and onto that high ground of peace that man has dreamed of since the dawn of civilization.

"If we succeed, generations to come will say of us now living that we mastered our moment, that we helped make the world safe for mankind.

"This is our summons to greatness."

And he added "this sacred commitment: I shall consecrate my office, my energies, and all the wisdom I can summon to the cause of peace among nations."

In one of my own early drafts, weeks before, I had included a passage urging that, as a nation, we "lower our voices." It came back from Nixon with a note to "keep this theme." We did, and it became the theme most widely bannered in headlines the next day and most remembered since:

"The simple things are the ones most needed today, if we are to surmount what divides us, and cement what unites us.

"To lower our voices would be a simple thing.

"In these difficult years, America has suffered from a fever of words: from inflated rhetoric that promises more than it can deliver; from angry rhetoric that fans discontents into hatreds; from bombastic rhetoric that postures instead of persuading.

"We cannot learn from one another until we stop shouting at one another—until we speak quietly enough so that our words can be heard as well as our voices."

By the time we flew back to New York from Key Biscayne, the themes had been honed, and the speech was basically in shape. On the way to the airport, Nixon, Bebe Rebozo, and I stopped off at Key Biscayne's Jamaica Inn for a quick dinner. For years, the Jamaica Inn had been one of Nixon's favorite restaurants. The main part, where he normally dined, is built around a soaring, glass-walled botanical garden, with lights playing on lush tropical foliage. The inn also has a more informal annex, the English Pub, a warren of booths with plain wooden benches and tables, where a mostly youthful crowd drink beer from glass mugs while eating hamburgers and french fries. That evening, Nixon's last in Key Biscayne before becoming President the next Monday, we slipped in through a back door, past the kitchen, and, unnoticed, took a booth in the Pub. Bebe had ordered ahead of time, a hamburger steak for each of us. As soon as we finished, Nixon thanked a slightly flustered young waitress, and we slipped back out again past the kitchen to the car, to the waiting Air Force Jetstar, and New York.

Back in New York, we continued to work on the speech through Saturday, refining it, until finally, at midnight, we both were satisfied that it was finished. We were scheduled to leave the next afternoon, Sunday, for Washington. Sunday night Nixon was to stay at Washington's Statler Hilton Hotel, and then at noon on Monday, on the steps of the Capitol, he was to be inaugurated as the 37th President of the United States.

In his office refrigerator at the Pierre that final Saturday, he found a single bottle of Heineken's. He got out two glasses, and we shared it, as he put his feet up on his desk for a final few moments of relaxation. Then he, Rose Mary Woods, and I left his transition office for the last time, and rode the elevator in silence to the street floor. Leaving the Pierre by a back entrance, Rose and I walked him the one block up Madison Avenue and another block across Sixty-second Street to his apartment, with the Secret Service agents following a few steps behind. It was his last night in New York, his last in the apartment that had been home for the past five years. There was a feeling of finality about it. The transition was ending. Now, at last, the presidency was about to begin.

The next morning, it turned out that we were not quite finished, after all. While I was hastily trying to pack, the phone rang. It was Nixon with a last-minute idea. He said it had occurred to him that it would add a gracious touch if he were to invite the people to share with him "the majesty of this moment." But it would be important, we both felt, that if he did so it not be in a way that would seem overly self-celebratory. So I sat at my typewriter again, and in the course of three more phone calls back and forth we worked out the opening that he used:

"Senator Dirksen, Mr. Chief Justice, Mr. Vice-President, President Johnson, Vice-President Humphrey, my fellow Americans—and my fellow citizens of the world community:

"I ask you to share with me today the majesty of this moment. In the orderly transfer of power, we celebrate the unity that keeps us free."

That seemed to me not only graceful but a historically apt concept. In the latter 1960s the nation had been wracked by the worst violence and torment in a century—and beneath the riots, the burnings, the armed rebellions on campus, had been a profound challenge to the orderly processes of the exercise and transfer of power. The question, in its simplest form, was whether rule by mob would supplant rule by the democratic system. The peaceful inauguration of a new president, sharing the platform with his outgoing predecessor, the oath administered by the chief justice, the ceremony itself taking place on the steps of the Capitol—this was, in a very real sense, the supreme sacrament of the democratic system, bringing the three branches of government together in a rite as old as the republic to ratify the choice of the people, freely expressed.

January 20 dawned cold, gray, raw. The inaugural stand was set up on the steps of the East Front of the Capitol, facing the thousands of invited guests who sat, bundled against the chill, on benches stretched across the Capitol grounds. Outgoing President Lyndon Johnson, who had helped carry John F. Kennedy to victory over Nixon in 1960, was there. Outgoing Vice-President Hubert Humphrey, defeated by Nixon in 1968, was there. Chief Justice Earl Warren, the sometimes bitter Nixon rival from their days together in California politics, was there. But old feuds were submerged now, old differences eclipsed, as Richard Nixon, his hand on his family Bible, repeated after Earl Warren the words from Article II, Section 7 of the Constitution:

"I do solemnly swear that I will faithfully execute the office of President of the United States, and will to the best of my ability, preserve, protect and defend the Constitution of the United States."

The power had passed. The man who sought it eight years earlier now held it, confident in its exercise, and eager to get on with the job.

GHOSTS OF PRESIDENTS PAST

When each new president moves into the White House, he finds that he shares it with the ghosts of his predecessors. They all live on, their legacies part of a newly inaugurated president's inheritance.

Of the thirty-five[1] men who had been president before Nixon, three were still living when he took office. Four years later there were none. Of all those thirty-five ghosts, three in particular roamed the White House with the 37th President: Dwight D. Eisenhower, who died less than ten weeks after Nixon took office; John F. Kennedy; and Franklin Delano Roosevelt.

With Eisenhower, the links were deeply personal, a combination of father/son, mentor/protégé, commander/subordinate, predecessor/successor, forged during an association that spanned seventeen years. Nixon's administration was sprinkled with old friends who had served with him in the Eisenhower administration—Arthur Burns, chairman of Eisenhower's Council of Economic Advisers, named by Nixon first as counselor to the President and then as chairman of the Federal Reserve Board; Maurice Stans, Eisenhower's budget director and Nixon's secretary of commerce; William Rogers, Eisenhower's attorney general and Nixon's secretary of state; Bryce Harlow, Eisenhower White House aide and, in

---

1. Nixon is counted as the 37th President, but only thirty-five persons preceded him. Grover Cleveland—elected in 1884, defeated for re-election in 1888, and elected again in 1892—is counted as having been both the 22nd and the 24th.

the general's retirement years, counselor and confidant,[2] chief of congressional liaison in Nixon's White House.

Nixon was already a national figure when Eisenhower chose him as his vice-presidential running mate in 1952. But Eisenhower, a generation older, was a world figure. While Nixon was an obscure navy lieutenant[3] in the Pacific, Eisenhower was a five-star general of the army, supreme commander of the allied forces that defeated Nazi Germany, the man whose decision to go ahead launched the largest amphibious force ever assembled across the English Channel on D-Day, 1944, the war hero whose name, as both soldier and diplomat, was already engraved in history with those of Roosevelt and Churchill.

Nixon first saw Eisenhower shortly after V-E Day in 1945, when Nixon, thirty-two, on naval duty in New York, watched from his twentieth-story office window as a triumphant Eisenhower rode through the streets of Lower Manhattan in what was then the greatest ticker-tape parade in New York's history. Seven years later, when the young California senator was picked to run with the general, the two had met only twice, and really talked only once— for forty-five minutes in December 1951, when Nixon called on Eisenhower, then NATO commander, at his headquarters outside Paris.

Ironically, considering Nixon's chronic difficulties with the Eastern Establishment, one of the key roles in bringing together the Eisenhower-Nixon team was played by former New York governor Thomas E. Dewey. Dewey himself had been the Republican presidential nominee in the two previous elections, in 1944 and 1948. In 1952 Dewey worked vigorously behind the scenes to win the nomination for Eisenhower. Herbert Brownell, the manager of both Dewey campaigns, was one of the principal coordinators of the Eisenhower effort. Together, Dewey and Brownell also concluded that if Eisenhower got the nomination, his best running mate would be the junior senator from California.

---

2. I first met Harlow in Gettysburg in 1964, when I went there to work with Eisenhower on an article he was writing for the *Herald Tribune* on the Republican presidential choice. Eisenhower had asked Harlow to come up from Washington, where he represented Procter & Gamble, to advise him on it and to work with us. At the White House Harlow had, among other things, been Eisenhower's favorite speechwriter. Over lunch at a little coffee shop across the street from Eisenhower's office, Harlow gave me my first briefing on the subtleties of how to function as a president's—or, in that case, an ex-president's—"ghost."

3. He was promoted to lieutenant commander in October 1945.

"I had heard a lot of very fine things about him," Dewey said later. "I checked with a lot of people who worked with him in both the House and the Senate. Everybody whose opinion I respected said he was an absolute star, a man of enormous capacity. They liked and admired him. So I pretty much made up my mind that this was the fellow." But first, Dewey wanted to see Nixon in action. So he arranged for Nixon to be invited as speaker at the $100-a-plate New York State Republican dinner on May 8, just two months before the convention. Dewey was very favorably impressed with Nixon's off-the-cuff performance, and, after the dinner, invited Nixon up to his twenty-fourth-floor suite at the Roosevelt Hotel. They talked for an hour. It was then that Dewey broached the possibility of the vice-presidency.

"I couldn't believe he was serious," Nixon said later.

But he was.

In Chicago, on July 11, the Republican National Convention nominated Eisenhower, and then recessed. Immediately, Brownell offered Nixon's name to the general. Eisenhower, while favorably disposed, asked Brownell to get "the collective judgment of the leaders of the party." Brownell called together some two dozen leaders.

Dewey recalled:

"There were a lot of people with a lot of views. I waited until they had gotten down through the list. I didn't say much about it, until finally they had gotten from the East all the way across to the West. Then I named Nixon as the logical nominee."

The committee then voted unanimously for Nixon.

The pattern of political collaboration between Eisenhower and Nixon was set from the beginning: Eisenhower the world statesman, the politician-above-politics; Nixon the political gut-fighter, carrying the battle hard against the Democratic ticket.

If Nixon gained experience from the Eisenhower years, those years also gave rise to many of the enmities that pursued him and the myths that haunted him throughout his own presidency. Of the myths, perhaps the most galling—and one of the most damaging—was that inspired by the "Nixon fund." The fund crisis contributed in large measure to Nixon's bitterness toward the press, and very nearly sundered his relationship with Eisenhower at its beginning.

Barely two months after his nomination as Eisenhower's running mate, on September 14, 1952, Nixon appeared on "Meet the Press."

One of the reporters interviewing him was Washington columnist Peter Edson. After the show, Edson took him aside and asked,

"What's this 'fund' we hear about?" Edson said there was a rumor to the effect that Nixon had a supplementary salary of $20,000 a year, contributed by a hundred California businessmen.

Nixon assumed the rumors must relate to the political-expense fund set up after his 1950 Senate election. He explained the fund, and suggested that if Edson wanted details, he contact its trustee, Dana Smith, and Nixon gave him Smith's telephone number in Pasadena. Edson called Smith, who was delighted to talk about it. In establishing the fund, Smith and Nixon regarded it as a campaign reform. There was no way a senator from a state so distant from Washington as California could meet his political obligations between campaigns without some sort of funding apart from his salary (then $12,500). The fund was created to meet necessary political expenses. It was publicly solicited, meticulously accounted, regularly audited, kept in a separate Pasadena bank account, all disbursements made by check, and contributions limited to a maximum of $500. Over the two-year period, seventy-six contributors had given a total of $18,235. The fund had paid for Christmas cards sent to campaign workers, for recordings of speeches, for political travel, for postage on political mailings (rather than using the Senate frank); and for a few smaller items, leaving a total balance of $66.13.

By coincidence, on the same day Edson called, three other reporters also approached Smith about the fund. Again, he discussed it freely. He and Nixon were proud of it, believing it should serve as a model for other senators. One of the three was Leo Katcher, a Hollywood reporter for the rabidly anti-Nixon *New York Post.*

Shortly afterward rumors reached the Nixon campaign train that newspaper stories were about to break on a Nixon "fund." Nixon dismissed the rumors, assuming they referred to the Edson story, and that the story would be accurate.

But then, at 10:00 on Thursday morning, September 18, the early edition of the evening tabloid *New York Post* hit the streets with a screaming page-1 headline: SECRET NIXON FUND. On page 2, the story itself appeared under another banner headline: SECRET RICH MEN'S TRUST FUND KEEPS NIXON IN STYLE BEYOND HIS SALARY. Underneath, Katcher's story began: "The existence of a 'millionaire's club' devoted exclusively to the financial comfort of Senator Nixon, GOP vice-presidential candidate, was revealed today."

Together, the story and the headlines were a fraud, a lie, the grossest of political libels. Katcher's story nowhere claimed that the fund was "secret." That was an invention of the headline writers—

and, thanks to those *New York Post* headline writers, the notion of a "secret Nixon fund" has remained in the popular political mythology ever since. But the story itself was a malicious distortion-by-innuendo, in calling the contributors a "millionaire's club" (a charge made in the lead but not supported in the body of the story, which pretty much reported the facts as Smith had given them) and, by saying it was "devoted exclusively to the financial comfort of Senator Nixon," in managing to imply without actually saying so that it was for his personal rather than political use.

Yet lies travel as quickly as truth—and even more so when the lies are sensational in content and bannered on page 1. The report sent panic waves through the Republican high command, and through the Eisenhower campaign train. Soon, leading Republicans were joining the Democratic national chairman in calling on Nixon to resign from the ticket—without regard for whether the charges were true or false. Even the New York *Herald Tribune* (this was five years before I joined it) declared editorially: "The proper course of Senator Nixon in the circumstances is to make a formal offer of withdrawal from the ticket. How this offer is acted on will be determined by an appraisal of all the facts in the light of General Eisenhower's unsurpassed fairness of mind."

The *Trib* editorial was a special blow, because Nixon was sure it would not have been written without at least a tacit signal from the Eisenhower high command.

Nixon pressed his staff for reports on the attitudes aboard the Eisenhower train, but insisted that he himself would speak only with the general, not with his aides. The reports that came back were gloomy: more than 90 percent of the press on the Eisenhower train now saw Nixon as a liability on the ticket, and they were predicting that he would be forced off. Most of Eisenhower's staff and advisers were also saying privately that he should resign or be forced from the ticket. On Sunday afternoon Dewey called, telling Nixon he should go on television—and then let the American people, rather than Eisenhower, make the decision. That way, "if you stay on, it isn't blamed on Ike, and if you get off it isn't blamed on Ike."

That evening, Eisenhower finally called. He said it was a difficult thing for him to decide, and he thought that Nixon himself should decide—but that first he should go on a nationwide television broadcast, and tell the people "everything there is to tell." Nixon, increasingly annoyed and impatient, asked whether, if he did so, an announcement could then be made one way or the other. Eisenhower replied that he hoped no announcement would be necessary, but that "maybe after the program we could tell what ought to be done." Nixon then told the former supreme commander that in matters like this, "there comes a time to —— or get off the pot."

Recalling the incident, Nixon wrote later that "one of Eisenhower's most notable characteristics is that he is not a man to be rushed on important decisions."

They chatted some more; Eisenhower told him to go on television, wished him luck, and told him to keep his chin up.

With the necessary $75,000 pledged by the Republican National Committee and the Senatorial Congressional Campaign Committee, the Nixon staff arranged to buy a half-hour of network television time just forty-eight hours later, on Tuesday, September 23. Nixon broke off his campaign tour, and returned Monday afternoon to Los Angeles. All day Monday and Tuesday, working on his yellow legal pads, he outlined his speech. His staff scrambled to assemble every detail of his financial history. Thinking it would "irritate my opponents and delight my friends," he decided to work a variation on Franklin D. Roosevelt's invocation of his dog Fala during the 1944 campaign—"and now they attack my little dog Fala." Nixon's "Fala" was a cocker spaniel puppy named Checkers, a gift to the Nixon daughters from a Republican supporter in Texas just after his nomination.[4]

The broadcast was scheduled for 6:30 P.M. California time (9:30 Eastern time). At 4:30, just two hours before Nixon was to go on, live, with no script—only an outline—Dewey telephoned. He said he was calling on behalf of some of Eisenhower's closest aides, and implied that he was doing so with the concurrence of Eisenhower himself. His message: that Nixon should explain the fund, but then say that even though he believed he had done nothing wrong he did not want his presence on the ticket to be a liability for Eisenhower;

---

4. After laying out his financial history in the minutest detail ever given by a candidate, Nixon added:

"One other thing I probably should tell you, because if I don't they will probably be saying this about me, too. We did get something, a gift, after the nomination. A man down in Texas heard Pat on the radio mention the fact that our two youngsters would like to have a dog and, believe it or not, the day before we left on this campaign trip we got a message from Union Station in Baltimore, saying they had a package for us. We went down to get it. You know what it was?

"It was a little cocker spaniel dog, in a crate that he had sent all the way from Texas—black and white, spotted, and our little girl Tricia, the six-year-old, named it Checkers. And you know, the kids, like all kids, loved the dog, and I just want to say this, right now, that regardless of what they say about it, we are going to keep it."

that therefore he was submitting his resignation to Eisenhower and insisting that he accept it.

Dewey asked how he was to report back Nixon's intentions.

Angry, shaken, rattled, Nixon barked: "Just tell them that I haven't the slightest idea as to what I am going to do; and if they want to find out, they'd better listen to the broadcast. And tell them I know something about politics too!"

He slammed down the receiver, and, in a daze, shaved, showered, and dressed for the broadcast, trying to get the outline of the speech back into focus in his mind—a focus badly jarred by Dewey's last-minute call. Then he made a decision he had been debating all afternoon. He would ask viewers to write or wire, not to him, not to Eisenhower, but rather to the Republican National Committee.

He rode to the studio, scanning his five pages of notes, and at 6:30 he began, still extemporizing. Sixty million people watched or listened.

Eisenhower was scheduled to address a rally that evening in the Cleveland Public Auditorium. With a group of aides, he watched the Nixon telecast in the auditorium manager's office. Then Eisenhower strode down to the rally, discarded his speech on inflation, and told the cheering crowd: "I happen to be one of those people who, when I get into a fight, would rather have a courageous and honest man by my side than a whole boxcar of pussyfooters. I have seen brave men in tough situations. I have never seen anyone come through in better fashion than Senator Nixon did tonight."

But the Nixon party was unaware of that Eisenhower reaction. The general also sent Nixon a wire, which began, "Your presentation was magnificent," and went on to say he felt a need to meet with Nixon personally, saying that he would be in Wheeling, West Virginia, the next day. The wire itself got lost in the torrent of telegrams flooding Nixon's hotel. The Nixon staff got a partial text of it from a wire-service reporter—but the partial text omitted the opening line, and appeared to be simply a declaration that he could not decide until they met. Nixon was furious. He declared to his aides that if the broadcast had not satisfied the general, there was nothing more that he could or would do. He dictated a telegram of resignation. Campaign aide Murray Chotiner quietly took the telegram from Rose Mary Woods, and tore it up.

Finally, the two did meet in Wheeling. Eisenhower bounded up the steps of Nixon's plane, held out his hand, and said, "You're my boy!" Together they rode to an exuberant rally in Wheeling Stadium. Eisenhower read to the crowd a telegram from Arthur Summerfield, chairman of the Republican National Committee, saying that the members of the committee unanimously wanted Nixon kept on the ticket. Eisenhower himself declared that Nixon had "completely vindicated himself."

No total count was ever made of the letters and telegrams that poured in in response to the "Checkers" speech. They deluged not only Republican National Committee headquarters but Eisenhower's office, Nixon's office, and almost anything with the name "Republican." But the Republican headquarters in Washington alone got three hundred thousand signed by a million people.

In office, Eisenhower gave Nixon more responsibilities than any vice-president before him. But it was only gradually that their relationship ripened and mellowed into a warmly personal one. As President, Eisenhower had his cronies, and Nixon had his, and Nixon was not one of Eisenhower's. In 1956, as several of Nixon's Republican rivals were trying to engineer a "dump-Nixon" movement, Eisenhower declared both privately and publicly that Nixon should "chart out his own course"—a statement interpreted by many as an invitation to withdraw as a candidate for renomination.

For two months, after Eisenhower's announcement on February 29, 1956, of his own candidacy for renomination, the question of Nixon's future was left dangling. Pointing out that no one had been elected president directly from the vice-presidency in more than a century, Eisenhower suggested that a cabinet post in the second term might serve Nixon's own interests better, and offered to let him choose almost any except state (firmly in John Foster Dulles's hands). Nixon did not want a cabinet post; it had to be the vice-presidency or nothing. Characteristically, Eisenhower kept telling friends of his reluctance to "dictate" to the Republican National Convention. Nixon considered this an abdication of responsibility. The choice belonged to the President. Nixon was confident that he had served well, particularly during the difficult time of Eisenhower's 1955 heart attack. As Vice-President, he had then had to walk an extremely delicate line between being too assertive, on one hand, and, on the other, holding the government together and assuring both the nation and the world that it was functioning smoothly during the President's extended incapacity. But he did not want to petition the President for renomination. He would not crawl. And he did not want to be renominated unless the President wanted him.

Finally, with party chairman Leonard Hall running interference, Nixon was persuaded that Eisenhower really did want him to "chart out his own course," and that he, Nixon, would have to take the initiative. On April 26 he met with the President, and told him he would like to run again. Eisenhower broke into a wide grin, called in Press Secretary James Hagerty, and instructed Hagerty to set up an immediate White House press conference at which Nixon could announce his decision—"and after he finishes his announcement, you say I was delighted to hear this news from the Vice-President."[5]

By 1960 Eisenhower was firmly committed to the idea that his successor in the White House should be Richard Nixon. When Nixon was defeated, Eisenhower said he felt as though he "had been hit in the solar plexus with a ball bat," and later called it his "greatest political disappointment." But it was in the years afterward—as both grew older, as, out of office, they were no longer senior and subordinate, as the friendship between Nixon's daughter Julie and Eisenhower's grandson David deepened into engagement and then marriage—that the ties grew closest.

Eisenhower spent the last ten months of his life in a three-room suite on the top floor of Washington's Walter Reed Army Medical Center, where he was taken after suffering a heart attack while on a California golfing vacation in April 1968. Gaunt by now, his age and infirmities telling, he waged a dogged struggle against recurring heart problems. He told friends that he was determined to live long enough to celebrate two events: the wedding of his grandson David to Julie Nixon in December, and the inauguration of Richard Nixon in January. From his hospital suite, he issued a preconvention endorsement of Nixon for the Republican presidential nomination—a sharp break with his firmly established rule, since leaving the White House, of not endorsing candidates for nomination. He also addressed the Republican National Convention, by television, from Walter Reed. And he lived long enough to achieve his two ambitions. On December 22 Julie Nixon came down the aisle of New York's Marble Collegiate Church on her father's arm, and, while David waited and the five hundred guests watched, turned impulsively to plant a kiss on her father's cheek before repeating the vows after the Reverend Norman Vincent Peale. In January, on the day before inauguration, Eisenhower placed a call

---

5. Later, Harold Stassen, acting on his own, but trying to create the impression that he had Eisenhower's blessing, tried at the last minute to engineer Nixon's replacement on the ticket by Christian Herter. With Eisenhower's behind-the-scenes help, the move was squelched; at the convention, Eisenhower pressured Stassen into seconding Nixon's nomination.

to Nixon. The general said he wanted to use that last opportunity to say, "Hi, Dick!"—because from then on he was going to call him "Mr. President."

On February 23, just a month after Nixon's inauguration, Eisenhower underwent abdominal surgery. A few days later he contracted the flu, and then, on March 15, he developed congestive heart failure.

More than twelve years earlier, on October 8, 1956, in an eighth-floor suite at Denver's Fitzsimmons Hospital, Nixon had paid his first hospital visit to Dwight Eisenhower. That was two weeks to the day after Eisenhower had been stricken with a massive heart attack, and it was the first time a vice-president had ever been at the bedside of a seriously ailing president. Now, on March 26, 1969, at Walter Reed, Nixon paid his last visit to Eisenhower. Eisenhower grinned, held out his hand, and said a cheery "Hi, Mr. President!" Nixon had just returned from a trip to Europe. He discussed the trip, and passed along greetings from a number of the leaders he had met with.

Two days later, shortly after noon, Eisenhower died.

With him when he died were his wife, Mamie, his son, John, and David and Julie. Julie telephoned her father at the White House. Nixon had already been notified moments earlier by his physician, General Walter R. Tkach, who had been flashed word by the hospital's executive officer. A few minutes later, with Mrs. Nixon and Tricia, Nixon went to the hospital, where they were greeted by Mrs. Eisenhower, and, together, talked quietly for twenty-five minutes. Then he returned to the White House and left by helicopter for Camp David, sending word for me to join him there the following day.

The elaborate funeral plans called for Eisenhower's body to lie in state in the Capitol Rotunda, and for the traditional eulogy to be delivered there. Eisenhower had specified that he wanted it delivered by his friend and protégé, Nixon. For Nixon, it was an intensely personal moment. By now the bonds of official and then personal friendship had been cemented by bonds of family. His affection for Eisenhower was deep, and real. (Years later, on the eve of his resignation, when he broke into tears saying farewell to a group of old congressional friends, he commented that "the last time I cried was when Eisenhower died.") He wanted the eulogy to be right, and he knew that to be right it had to be both personal and official—from the heart of a friend and from the heart of the nation, to Dwight Eisenhower the man, and yet also to Dwight Eisenhower the commander of the mightiest expeditionary force ever assembled, receiver of the surrender of the German armies in World War II, president of Columbia University, supreme commander of NATO, and 34th President of the United States.

It would have been difficult in any case. It was made more so because Nixon was laid low that weekend with a severe bronchial infection, his strength drained, working much of the time in bed with an old-fashioned croup kettle at his side.

On the day Eisenhower died, I happened to get a call from an old friend, Dick Wald—now the president of NBC News—who had been executive editor of the *Trib* when I was editorial-page editor. While he was on the phone, I asked whether he had any suggestions for the eulogy. He thought for a moment, and then said that one thing that particularly set Eisenhower apart was that he was truly loved throughout the world: that often great heroes are loved in their own countries, or admired by the people of other countries, but almost never are they really loved by the people of other countries. Ike was, and Wald thought this said something important about him.

It was a good insight. I used it in some of the material I was putting together, and mentioned it to Nixon the next day at Camp David. It set him to ruminating about why Eisenhower was so widely loved—why he occupied that unique place in the hearts of the world.

"Everybody loved Ike," he mused, sitting by the fire in the mountain retreat Eisenhower had renamed for his grandson. "But the reverse of that was that Ike loved everybody. In politics, the normal reactions are to have strong hatreds one way or the other. But Ike didn't fit that format. There were many who disagreed with him, but nobody hated him. And the reason was that Ike didn't hate anybody. He was *puzzled* by that sort of thing. He was puzzled by the kids in these recent years. He was puzzled by Joe McCarthy. He would disagree with people and he'd take a strong stand for principle—but, on the other hand, he never allowed those arguments to get him *emotionally* involved, as a *personal* antagonist. He didn't think of people who disagreed with him as being the 'enemy.' He just thought: 'They don't agree with me.'

"I remember talking with Foster Dulles," he went on, "about how he even loved Khrushchev and the Russians. It was naïve, but he did. When Khrushchev was here at Camp David Ike got the message, and he toughened up. But still, in a personal sense, he had no hate, no personal dislike. He always had a great feeling of affection toward people as people.

"He never hated his critics, not even the press," Nixon added. "He'd just say, 'I'm a little puzzled by those fellows.'" Then, pausing a moment, he added a qualifier: "Well, maybe he did, but he never *said* that he did."

I could picture Nixon's mind working, catching himself: Ike might never have *expressed* hatred of his critics, "even" those of the press, but it was just too much to believe, and certainly for Nixon to believe, that he had never *felt* it.

In framing the eulogy, Nixon decided to focus on the qualities of character that set Eisenhower apart, and which had made him "truly, first citizen of the world": the love of country, the ideals of freedom and democracy that to him were not clichés, but "living truths," the capacity to bring out the best in people, the "unique moral force that transcended national boundaries, even as his own deep concern for humanity transcended national boundaries." But also, as Nixon pointed out, he was strong. He was shrewd. He was decisive.

Sunday afternoon was cold and gray as Nixon returned to Washington. In the Rotunda of the Capitol, as the Eisenhower and Nixon families stood in silence, together with the Congress, the Supreme Court, the diplomatic corps, and other dignitaries, and as millions watched on television, the 37th President spoke his own and the nation's farewell to the 34th: "We gather today in mourning, but also in gratitude. We mourn Dwight Eisenhower's death, but we are grateful for his life. We gather, also, conscious of the fact that in paying tribute to Dwight Eisenhower, we celebrate greatness. . . ."

His mentor was gone. The torch had been passed.

The Kennedy ghost haunting the Nixon White House was partly that of a person, a political contemporary, sometime Nixon friend, sometime rival, whose own path and Nixon's kept crossing and recrossing as each made his way to the top. More broadly, it was also the ghost of Camelot, that mystic, mythic time graced, as Ben Bradlee effused more than a decade later, by "this remarkable man who lit the skies of this land bright with hope and promise as no other political man has done in this century."[6]

Wherever Nixon turned he confronted Kennedy memories, old Kennedy loyalties hardened now into bitter anti-Nixon antagonisms, old dreams conjured by courtiers and embellished by time, held up as standards against which presidents should be measured. Johnson,

6. *Conversations with Kennedy*, p. 10.

too, was haunted throughout his presidency by the ghost of Camelot.

Nixon and Kennedy both served in the navy in the Pacific in World War II. Both came to Washington in 1947, as newly elected members of the 80th Congress. As freshmen, both were assigned to the Education and Labor Committee, Nixon as the most junior Republican member, Kennedy as the most junior Democrat. Though on opposite sides of the issue, both served on the small subcommittee that drafted the Taft-Hartley Act. In 1950, at age thirty-seven, Nixon was elected to the Senate. In 1952, at age thirty-five, Kennedy was elected to the Senate—winning his seat by defeating Henry Cabot Lodge, Nixon's running mate eight years later against Kennedy and Lyndon Johnson. The presiding officer of the Senate during Kennedy's entire eight years as a senator was Vice-President Richard Nixon. Nixon was the nation's second youngest Vice-President, and the first one born in the twentieth century. Kennedy was the nation's second youngest President, and the first one born in the twentieth century.

But if their careers ran along parallel and often intersecting lines, their personal backgrounds were strikingly different: Kennedy the patrician, Harvard-educated son of Roosevelt's immensely wealthy ambassador to the Court of St. James's; Nixon the child of near poverty who grew up in the little Quaker community of Whittier, California, who worked his way through Duke University Law School in the depths of the Depression, struggling, striving, determined to have the education his father had not had so that he could make his own way in the world.

Nixon felt no personal animus toward Kennedy, and Kennedy, in the early years, at least, seemed to bear none toward Nixon. In 1950, when Nixon was locked in his bitter struggle against Helen Gahagan Douglas for a Senate seat, Kennedy personally delivered to Nixon a $1000 campaign contribution from Kennedy's father—and he told Nixon privately that he himself thought Nixon would be a better senator than Mrs. Douglas.

While Nixon liked Kennedy, even admired much about him, he also envied him: envied his easy grace, and above all the *acceptance* he was accorded because of his wealth and his style. Nixon and Kennedy were both tough, shrewd, often conniving politicians. But Kennedy, quoting Yeats and Aristotle, had his sins applauded as virtues; Nixon, lacking that "special grace," had even his virtues condemned as sins. The double standard stung.

The ghost that dogged Nixon's footsteps, that disturbed his nights and plagued his days was less that of Kennedy himself than it was of Camelot—and not so much that of the Camelot that was, but rather of Camelot as remembered by the tastemakers generally, and those of the media in particular. The brief Kennedy years gave the media what they wanted: glamour, style, excitement, drama, flattery.

In the first months of the Nixon administration, Meg Greenfield, deputy editorial-page editor of *The Washington Post*, wrote: "There has been no more traumatic clash of cultures than that which marked the confrontation between the arriving Nixon administration and the awaiting resident press since Pizarro first dropped in on the Incas."

In that "traumatic clash of cultures," the clash was partly of interests. The Washington press corps tends to identify with the old elite that the Nixon administration sought to displace, if not totally from its power, at least from its primacy. It was also a clash of styles—in that swirl of power where style becomes substance, style becomes interest, and style becomes power. John Kennedy's was, in the modern idiom, the quintessence of the politics of style.

Kennedy had wit, charm, intelligence, money, the unstudied presence of the rich and well-born. But more important, he was celebrated by the tastemakers because he celebrated the tastemakers. They held up his portrait and saw their own idealized image of themselves reflected. In celebrating him they celebrated themselves. They confirmed that they were, indeed, "the best and the brightest," the natural elite, that glorious few graced by divine right to prescribe for the grateful many.

In Camelot, the lords temporal of government had the exquisite grace to pay lavish homage to the lords spiritual of the media, which, by the canons of those particular lords spiritual, is the first duty of lords temporal. And thus, the lords temporal were abundantly blessed by the lords spiritual.

It was a tough act to follow, especially for Lyndon Johnson and Richard Nixon.

Although the political ghost that constantly dogged Nixon's footsteps was that of John F. Kennedy, the ghost that did most to shape his presidency was that of Franklin Delano Roosevelt.

It was FDR who inaugurated the modern presidency—what Arthur M. Schlesinger, Jr., would later, when Nixon occupied it, dub "the Imperial Presidency"—and it was under FDR that those practices began which later cost Nixon his presidency. It was the Roosevelt pattern in domestic policy that Nixon sought to reverse, the Roosevelt coalition he sought to replace, the Roosevelt legacy he sought to supplant.

Franklin Roosevelt and Richard Nixon were the only presidents who ran five times for either the presidency or the vice-presidency. Each won four of those races, and lost one. Each was a dominant figure in American politics for a generation. Neither completed his final term—Roosevelt's ended by death, Nixon's by resignation.

Each was a world statesman, with a global view, and with a compelling sense of America's role in the world. Each sought to lift America's eyes to see its destiny and to meet its responsibility. Each was a consummate politician, fascinated by the trivia of politics as well as by its exercise on a grand national scale. Each was exhilarated by a campaign. Each was devious, plotting, conniving—but each plotted with a purpose. Each could, on occasion, be cavalier about the restraints of law or constitution that stood in his way.

FDR's presidency began in an inherited Depression and ended in war. Nixon's began in an inherited war and ended in a recession.

Each strove to put together a new coalition that would insure that the stamp of his approach to government would last for a generation. FDR succeeded, and the entire middle third of the twentieth century bore his imprint. Nixon, too, seemed for a time to have succeeded, but then the reins of leadership were wrenched from his grasp by those whose power he sought to curb.

For one like myself, who first came to political awareness during the Roosevelt years, the words "President" and "Roosevelt" were synonymous. This was as true for those of us who opposed FDR as it was for those who worshiped FDR. He held the office so long, he so dominated the political process and shaped the presidential office that he was not only *a* president, he was *the* President. One of the most wrenching adjustments of our lives was the adjustment, after his death, to the notion that this was, in fact, an office and not an individual; that it was one filled not by divine right, but by democratic election; that the office continued while its occupants came and went.

The New Deal began in an orgy of improvisations. Only later would these improvisations begin to jell into a pattern that, for better or worse, would set the path of government for decades to come.

Nixon, by contrast, entered office with a very clear set of ideas on what he wanted to do with the federal government, and, more importantly in his own eyes, on what he believed the role of the United States must be in the world. Many of his ideas went sharply against the grain of then-fashionable thought. Many also required battle with the ghosts.

Shortly after Nixon's second inauguration, Walter Lippmann told an interviewer that "His role . . . has been that of a man who had to liquidate, defuse, deflate the exaggerations of the romantic period of American imperialism and American inflation. Inflation of promises, inflation of hopes, the Great Society, American supremacy—all that had to be deflated because it was all beyond our power. . . . His role has been to do that. I think on the whole he's done pretty well at it."

In doing battle with the ghosts, however, the legions he confronted were not spectral. They were very much alive, and determined to preserve their power.

TAKING HOLD

On taking office, Richard Nixon inherited a bitter legacy—that of the 1960s. In the sense that it came with the job, he asked for it. But that in no way lessens the ironies. Most of his presidency was spent trying to clean up the mess he inherited—from the war in Vietnam to the shrill discords and brutal patterns of violence at home. And those who most vociferously attacked him for his efforts to deal with the mess were, to a large extent, those who had done the most to create it.

For Nixon, the middle years of the 1960s were a time out of office, surveying events from a distance. Taking office, he felt confident that of all those who might have been president, he was the one best equipped to deal with those events. For me, the campaign, and then the move to the White House, marked a shift from the role of commentator to that of participant. As an editorial writer during most of the decade ("lecturing the world on how to run itself," I sometimes wryly called it) I had watched the gathering forces of that strange decade with fascination and sometimes with horror. Now I shared in the responsibility for actually dealing with them— and I read the press commentaries with fascination and sometimes with horror.

Twice during the transition period, while on visits to Washington, I drove by the White House and the Executive Office Building, gazing at them with a new kind of awe. I had visited the EOB only once before, and the White House only twice. During the Kennedy administration, I had called on my friend Jim Symington (later a congressman, but then deputy administrator of the Food for Peace program) at his majestic EOB office, and had visited Kennedy aide Ralph Dungan in the White House office I would later know as Bob Haldeman's. Later, as editorial-page editor of the *Trib,* I had attended a one-day conference at the White House hosted by President Johnson, from which my most vivid memory was of an awkward presidential gaffe. With the two hundred guests seated in the East Room, the center doors swung open. An aide announced the President. Johnson strode down the aisle, flanked by Secretary of State Dean Rusk and Secretary of Defense Robert McNamara. Standing at the podium, he made some brief remarks, and then said he wanted to introduce two of the finest public servants it had ever been his privilege to know: the secretary of defense, the honorable Robert McNamara, and "the secretary of state, the honorable Dean Acheson—er, Dean Rusk."

On one of those transition-era visits, the outgoing White House staff very graciously hosted a private cocktail reception in the White House staff mess for some of us on the incoming staff. We met and mingled not as political antagonists but as people sharing a common interest. They were generous in offering pointers, and we were grateful to get them. In fact, all my subsequent encounters with members of the Johnson staff were invariably cordial. In part, this was a matter of simple courtesy. In part, it reflected the common experience of working at the White House, which does transcend partisan and political differences. In part, too, I suspect, it reflected a certain unstated bond, forged by the experience of having been targets of the same sort of vitriolic attacks, from many of the same quarters. (Later, one White House staffer who served under five presidents, from Kennedy to Carter, commented to me that Nixon and Johnson had suffered a common fate: "Both were clawed to shreds by lesser men.") When Washington gets a good hate going, life becomes very difficult for those associated with the objects of that hate. We and the Johnson staff bore a lot of the same scars.

On our writing staff, when we came to the White House we filled two key roles with Johnson holdovers: Ceil Bellinger as chief of research, and Eliska Hasek in charge of special presidential messages for organizations, anniversaries, conventions, and the like. Both jobs were politically sensitive, but both Ceil and Eliska were highly professional—and the continuity was helpful. That first year, when Washington burst into the full bloom of springtime—a spectacular season in Washington—I sent a warm note of appreciation to Mrs. Johnson for her beautification efforts, which had done so much to enhance our own enjoyment of the city. At Christmas

1972, Johnson sent me an autographed copy of his memoir, *The Vantage Point*. He died a month later. I was with Nixon in his EOB office, working on his speech for the following day announcing the Vietnam peace agreement, when we got word via the Secret Service first that Johnson was stricken, and then that he had died. It was a sad moment for both of us—and, for Nixon, it was particularly poignant that Johnson had not lived to see the announcement that Johnson himself had so hoped to be able to make. Even now, I never look at my copy of *The Vantage Point* without recalling that moment —and without regretting that I never got around to thanking him for it.

The writing staff was housed in the Executive Office Building (later renamed the Old Executive Office Building), a vast granite pile of a structure that took seventeen years to build, from 1872 to 1889. Originally built for the State, War, and Navy departments, it later became the State Department. Then, in the late 1940s, State moved to its new quarters in the section of Washington known as "Foggy Bottom" (it was known as that even before State moved there) and the structure, next door to the White House, became the EOB. During the Eisenhower administration, a move was launched to tear it down, but preservationists countered with a successful drive to save it. They were aided by the fact that, with its four-feet-thick granite exterior walls and its two-feet-thick interior walls, it would have cost more to demolish than it originally cost to build. With its design inspired by French Renaissance châteaux, it was a center of architectural controversy from its first days. But whether the beholder's eye sees it as ugly or beautiful, tackily ostentatious or graciously imposing, it does stand as a powerful presence. I grew to love the old place, with its high ceilings, marble fireplaces, meticulous detailing, wrought-iron spiral staircases, its balconies and columns, its sense of timeless solidity, and the echoes of the past in its long, marble-tiled corridors. Separated from the White House by a private street, West Executive Avenue, closed off by gates at each end, the EOB forms part of the White House compound. Nixon was the first President to establish an office of his own in the EOB. When he first told me, during the transition period, that he was going to do so, I thought it was probably as a sop to those of the staff who were going to be quartered there—in prior administrations, the place had been regarded as a place of exile and this may have been one of his reasons. In status-conscious Washington, proximity to the President is a sensitive matter, and this gradually elevated the EOB, or at least its first floor, to rough parity with the West Wing of the White House. But Nixon was serious about using it. It became his principal working office, where he could escape the rigid, ceremonial formality of the Oval Office.

In the Oval Office, Nixon worked at the "Wilson desk"—a huge, meticulously preserved desk which for many years had been in the Vice-President's formal office in the Capitol. Nixon had used it as Vice-President. According to Capitol lore—which Nixon proudly believed to have been true—it had been used by Woodrow Wilson. On becoming President, Nixon had Haldeman ask the Architect of the Capitol whether, as a courtesy, it could be moved to the White House. Somewhat embarrassed, the Architect of the Capitol explained that Lyndon Johnson had already taken it to Texas. But Johnson agreed to have it returned, and it was duly installed in the Oval Office.

For his EOB office, Nixon requested and got the desk that Eisenhower had used as President. But this desk was seldom used. Instead, he worked more comfortably in an overstuffed club chair with an ottoman for his feet, and a telephone and dictating machine at his side. But from either office, the view in January 1969 was grim.

In Vietnam, more than five hundred thousand U.S. troops were sustaining losses as high as three hundred a week. Short of continuing to send more men and supplies, the previous administration had left him no coherent plan either for winning the war or for ending it. Public revulsion was intensified by the fact that this was the first American war ever to have been brought into the nation's living rooms night after night, in living color.

Nixon knew the war had to be ended, but he also believed that *how* it was ended was vital—and there was no way of predicting how soon it could be ended in a way that preserved the integrity of America's commitments and that would contribute to a larger peace, rather than leading to another war. He needed time. He needed some relief from the relentless pressures to "get out now," without regard for the consequences of *how* we got out.

Beyond Vietnam, the Soviet Union posed an increasingly powerful threat. NATO was in disarray, SEATO an empty shell, the nations of Latin America restless and dissatisfied. In the wake of the Six Day War of 1967, the Middle East was a cockpit of potentially catastrophic conflict. Mainland China glowered outward in seething hostility.

Though Vietnam presented the most acute strain on America's patience in the short run, what mattered most in the long run was the pattern of relationships among the superpowers. This would determine whether we had "a generation of peace," or whether we drifted or blundered into World War III.

At home, the costs of the Vietnam war—together with the Johnson insistence on "guns-and-butter" budgets that financed its costs by borrowing—had fueled a gathering inflation that threatened the dollar and frightened the housewife. When Nixon took office, prices already were rising more rapidly than they had since the Truman administration; and, to complicate matters further, the international monetary system was being shaken by two and three crises a year—so that the prospect of its collapse was the subject of nervous speculation in the capitals of Europe. Interest rates were the highest they had been since the Civil War. The average factory worker's "real" income—after allowing for taxes and inflation—had been stagnant for the past three years.

Since 1960, crime had increased 89 percent—seven times the growth in population. Farm prices, as a percent of parity, had dropped to their lowest level since the Depression, and one farm in four had closed down. Two and a half million people had been added to the relief rolls. Labor unrest was at a peak, with more man-hours lost through strikes in 1968 than in any previous year in the decade. The "public strike" had made its appearance on the American scene —walkouts by police, firemen, teachers, garbage collectors, and other public employees endangering the public's health and safety.

More broadly, the 1960s were a time of escalating rhetoric, escalating expectations, escalating frustration, escalating violence —as well as of escalation in Vietnam. The nation's people were divided more bitterly than they had been in at least a generation— young against old, North against South, black against white, urban against suburban, civilian against soldier, student against nonstudent. Since 1964, every summer had seen cities erupt in flame and riot. In 1968, following the assassination of Martin Luther King, Jr., parts of Washington were burned, and smoke from that orgy of destruction drifted over the White House and the Capitol.

By the time Nixon took office, the campus rebellion that began at Berkeley in 1964 as the Free Speech Movement had already brought great universities across the nation to their knees.

Fear and violence spread to the nation's high schools as well. In January 1969 New York City's High School Principals Association, appealing to the city for help, warned that "disorders and fears of new and frightening dimensions stalk the corridors of our schools. ... The hour is late, our schools are in peril." In Chicago, Philadelphia, Kansas City, Harrisburg, and other cities, police and armed guards were stationed in the schools in order to discourage student violence. Based on a monitoring of 1800 daily newspapers, the Center for Research and Education at Columbia University reported a tripling of disturbances over the four-month period from November 1968 to February 1969, with 348 schools in 38 states experiencing disruptions, 239 of them "serious episodes" such as strikes, sit-ins, or riots. By May of 1969 the director of the survey, Dr. Alan F. Westin, estimated that at least 2000 high schools had suffered disruptions. The U.S. Office of Education put the damage from school vandalism at $100 million a year.

In 1967 Paris reported only 20 armed robberies, London 205, Washington, D.C., 2429. Toward the end of the 1968 campaign, Gallup polls showed that "the most emotionally charged issue" was crime and disorder in the cities and on the campus.

Protest, often violent, reached epidemic proportions. And this violent protest was romanticized by those who saw themselves marching in the cultural vanguard. Surveying the wreckage, sociologist Robert A. Nisbet gloomily concluded: "I think it would be difficult to find a single decade in the history of Western culture when as much barbarism, as much calculated onslaught against culture and convention in any form, as much sheer degradation of both culture and the individual passed into print, into music, into art, and onto the American stage as the decade of the 1960s. . . ."

The 1960s were also a time when illusions about what government could do reached their most inflated level—and this, in turn, exacerbated the disillusion when the promised miracles failed to take place. It poisoned the political atmosphere, contributing to the widespread belief—particularly among the young—that the ills plaguing mankind resulted from a "conspiracy" of the "special interests."

As Peter F. Drucker observed:

"For seventy years or so—from the 1890s to the 1960s—mankind, especially in the developed countries, was hypnotized by government. We were in love with it and saw no limits to its abilities, or to its good intentions. Rarely has there been a more torrid political love affair than that between government and the generations that reached manhood between 1918 and 1960. Anything that anyone felt needed doing during this period was turned over to government—and this, everyone seemed to believe, made sure that the job was already done."[1]

In the 1960s politics became the new religion, the new romantic vision. Politicians responded by competing to see which one could

1. *The Age of Discontinuity: Guidelines to Our Changing Society* (New York, 1969), p. 213.

evoke the most extravagant dreams, paying for votes with promissory notes drawn on those dreams themselves. The "fiscal dividend" of an expanding economy, the basic belief in human progress, the promises of automation and cybernation, all were drawn upon to support the illusion that a beneficent government could provide more for everyone at no additional cost to anyone.

To many, and especially to the naïve and the romantic, this was exhilarating. It offered the spiritual uplift of appealing to the noblest in man's instincts, while also offering the ultimate luxury of doing well by doing good.

Many were conditioned to believe that government had only to decree a public good, and it would come to pass. Those who raised warning flags about the limits of what should be expected of government were dismissed as mossbacks at best, venal conspirators against the public interest at worst. The "public interest" was portrayed as something apart from—and superior to—the totality of private interests. Too little heed was paid to the warning of the late Justice Louis Brandeis: that we should "be most on our guard to protect liberty when the government's purposes are beneficent. The greatest dangers to liberty lurk in insidious encroachment by men of zeal, well-meaning but without understanding."

In politics, every force generates its counterforce. By the late 1960s a whole cluster of these were building into what came to be called "the social issue." This encompassed sharply contrasting attitudes on crime, race, life-styles, sex, drugs, clothes, work, aesthetics, authority, patterns of expression, and sensibility. It found expression in racial conflict, generational conflict, cultural conflict, and political conflict. Because they were so personal and so emotional, these cultural issues put the final edge on the shrillness of the political debate.

At the heart of the social issue was fear. White feared black, and black feared white, though each often wrapped his fear in belligerent bravado. The older generation feared the counterculture as an assault on the citadel of family and community. The alienated of the counterculture feared the police power of the state, sometimes with reason.

In 1933 Franklin Roosevelt rallied a distraught nation with his ringing declaration that "the only thing we have to fear is fear itself —nameless, unreasoning, unjustified terror which paralyzes needed efforts to convert retreat into advance." The fears of the 1960s were fully as real as those Roosevelt addressed. But they were less powerfully articulated and less sharply portrayed, partly because many were fears felt *by* the less articulate *about* what the more articulate were doing to them.

These fears of the less articulate found their sharpest focus among the followers of George C. Wallace. At the heart of Wallace's appeal was the fear felt by those who had little for the little they had.

To the Wallace voter, the impersonal "they" who enforced rules and promulgated decrees were a real and crushingly omnipresent force. "They" squeezed limited incomes with burdensome taxes, "they" ordered the busing of helpless children, "they" coddled criminals and opened the floodgates of permissiveness, "they" manipulated the news, "they" conspired to raise prices and increase profits. "They" were pointy-headed bureaucrats, far-out professors, greedy tycoons, lying politicians, radic-lib newscasters. "They" were the power elite, unreachable, unresponsive, uncaring, contemptuous of the ordinary fears of the ordinary American.

Essentially, to the extent that it embodied such fears, the social issue divided the manipulators from the manipulated. It set those who viewed themselves as movers of the human pieces on the chessboard against those who saw themselves as the pieces being moved. (The principal exception, of course, could always be found among the members of whatever might be the currently fashionable segment of the underprivileged, to whom the process of manipulation would appear as the most promising avenue of their own advance.) Just as war tends to be more fun in the planning rooms of the general staff than it is in the trenches, social planning tends to be more appealing to the planner than it is to the people whose lives are being planned.

This division reached its emotional zenith in the controversy over school busing, which became the human equivalent of the urban-renewal bulldozer. The strong arm of government was used to press small children into a mold crafted in the image of the planners' ideals, while the wishes of the people concerned were dismissed as irrelevant, unworthy, or immoral.

Largely because of this, the fears of the 1960s had another important element: for the first time, the courts themselves became one of the leading sources of fear. As the courts took themselves more and more deeply into the political thicket, ordering children taken from their home environment and thrust into one that was alien or even threatening, while parents and public officials stood helpless to prevent it, even those symbols of the rule of law came to be seen by many as threats to their freedom. If the aggrieved could not go to the courts for remedy—if the courts themselves had become the source of the threat—then where could they go? Many took to the streets or flocked to the banners of a George Wallace or a Louise Day Hicks, applauding defiance of the law as vociferously as a younger generation applauded defiance of the draft.

For Nixon, the passions aroused by the social issue were both an opportunity and a constraint. Pursuing his own middle course, he used it against his opponents on the left. Surveys showed that most Wallace voters in 1968 would have been Nixon voters in a two-man race between Nixon and Humphrey. Nixon reached out to this group for support in checking what he considered liberal excesses, and particularly for support on matters involving the war and national defense. At the same time, he himself was frequently a target of their wrath and resentment, and the forces generated by the "social-issue conservatives" were a powerful factor in Congress, contributing heavily to the trouble some of his more liberal initiatives, such as welfare reform, encountered.

But of the 1960s-era hatreds, those that plagued his presidency most were those nurtured on the left. It began within moments of his swearing in. As he took the oath of office, his left hand rested on a family Bible opened to Isaiah 2:4, a passage expressing the hope that nations "shall beat their swords into plowshares. . . ." Then, as the inaugural parade made its ceremonial way down Pennsylvania Avenue from the Capitol to the White House, some three hundred young antiwar demonstrators, part of a larger "counterinaugural" group, hurled rocks, bottles, and obscenities at his car.

On that cold January day we were a vast nation, torn and uncertain—in the words of his inaugural address, "rich in goods, but ragged in spirit"—bearing on its shoulders the responsibility for war or peace in the world, yet frightened of that responsibility, and many of its people unwilling to bear it; a nation weary of its burdens, tempted by visions spun from the rhetoric of the 1960s— the rhetoric of Camelot, of Utopia, of "wars" that would banish disease and poverty and unhappiness from the human condition—a rhetoric that conditioned millions to expect nirvana as their due, and to see any failure to receive it as the fault of someone else, not of themselves.

Now that he had the power, many of Nixon's first moves were structural: to get the decision-making machinery in shape, so that the decisions themselves could be approached in a more orderly and rational way.

He revived the National Security Council, which had played a major role in the Eisenhower administration but had since been allowed to lapse. With the hard-driving Henry Kissinger as its executive director, the NSC—and particularly the NSC staff—soon became the administration's foreign-policy center.

Nixon created an Urban Affairs Council, with his assistant for urban affairs, Pat Moynihan, as director of its staff; the cabinet secretaries with domestic-policy responsibilities were members. (Later, in the same reorganization that turned the old Budget Bureau into the present Office of Management and Budget, the Urban Affairs Council was metamorphosed into the Domestic Council; by then the council's staff functions had been gathered under John Ehrlichman's jurisdiction.) "The remarkable thing about the council," I wrote shortly afterward, "is not that it has now been created but that it had not been created before. In a simpler past, problems each cabinet department dealt with were largely contained within that department. But that simpler past is now a distant past. The most fundamental fact about our complex of urban problems today is that they are interdisciplinary and interdepartmental in nature. Patterns of transportation, for example, determine the accessibility of jobs within an urban complex. How well crime is controlled in the core city determines what kind of education is possible. . . . Only if the departments work together—and only if each secretary can learn to see his own area of responsibility from the perspectives of the others—can the cooperative attacks which are so essential be effective."

To improve cooperation with states and localities, Nixon established a new Office of Intergovernmental Relations under the Vice-President. He established a new Cabinet Committee on Economic Policy, to provide better coordination in that area. He restructured the field organizations of the principal departments providing social services, to decentralize their operations. (Each department's field operations had developed independently of the others'; until the Nixon reorganization, the various departments' regional headquarters were scattered in separate cities. As a result, mayors dealing with the various departments had to flit from city to city, and interdepartmental coordination was virtually impossible except in Washington. This field reorganization was an early effort to move power out of Washington, to get decision-making closer to the local community, and to make it more responsive to local needs.)

One of the Republican party's leading intellectual lights, Stephen Hess (who at the time was Pat Moynihan's White House deputy), commented during those early days that Democrats tended to be fascinated by programs, and Republicans by structure, and that perhaps the most notable legacies of the Nixon administration would be structural. If Watergate had not happened, and if Nixon had been able to get his later, more ambitious reorganization plans through the Congress, that forecast might have been very substantially borne out. Nixon's later reorganization proposals would radically have reshaped the executive branch. In a broader sense, many of his policy initiatives were also "structural"—aimed, like revenue-sharing, at moving decision-making power out of Washington, or at creating essentially self-regulating mechanisms that would lessen the need for "programs" of federal intervention.

In the beginning, however, the structural focus was on getting a firm grip on the government, and on putting the decision-making process in shape.

To many commentators at the time, this was all empty nonsense, undramatic and unnecessary. They wanted action—legislative proposals—and they wanted them now, and hang the content. Nixon himself, conscious as always of the demands of public relations, eager to assert command, concerned lest he lose the initiative, was torn and tempted. He was like a bull at the rodeo gate, wanting to charge out. Yet he knew, however he might *want* to send a sudden torrent of proposals to Congress, that he had to take his time about it.

In an internal memo at the time, I argued that we should not yield to temptation; that rather than play by the old rules, we should insist on having our performance scored by a set of new rules.

For a third of a century, the fashionable critics have been measuring progress according to the standards established by Roosevelt in his first 100 days. If we're going to change the pattern of government, we've got to change the standards of measurement. This is central. . . .

The fact of the matter is that the nation still is suffering from the first 100 days of Johnson, from the first 100 days of Kennedy, and even, lingeringly, from the first 100 days of Roosevelt. It should be neither our plan nor our style to repeat those 100 day stunts—and we should present this not defensively, but as a positive virtue.

Certainly if there is one premise on which we all can agree, it is that the critics' scoring rules are wrong—and if we share one common conviction, it is that the nation has suffered grievously from past Democratic administrations' grandstanding, their fascination with quantitative measurements, their frenzies of activity for activity's sake, their extravagant rhetoric, their "wars" on every real or imagined social ill, their piling of promise on over-promise, their rush of half-baked legislative proposals, their substitution of emotion for reason, their basic premise that to pass a law means to solve a problem.

These absurdities have gotten us into the mess we are in. We know we are not going to get out of it with more of the same. . . .

Declaring that "Our aim is to insure that what we do is done responsibly," I went on to urge that "scrapping bad proposals is fully as important a part of the decision-making process as advancing good ones—and a part that has been too often slighted in recent years by the sillier commentators who measure progress in numbers of laws passed, billions spent, and slogans coined. . . . In short, we ought to be as proud of what we've *not* done as we are of what we *have* done. And if we're ever to break the destructive cycle of silly laws in response to silly demands, we've got to change the scoring rules: we've got to get across the idea that to do less is often to achieve more."

The pressures on Nixon to move precipitately with his own legislative agenda were internal as well as external. There were many in the administration who were afraid he would risk his opportunity to lead if he did not get there "fustest with the mostest." Characteristically, his own response was to strike a balance, moving quickly with a few highly visible—and symbolic—actions, while taking time on others. Also characteristically, these first highly visible actions had something to calm the apprehensions of both liberals and conservatives: politically, he was strengthening his base; substantively, he was uniting the country.

He began this balancing process just eleven days after his inauguration, when he set forth a broad new program for the District of Columbia, which he had branded during the campaign as the "crime capital" of the nation. On one hand, it included tough new measures to strengthen the District's police and to reform its courts; on the other, it cut through red tape to begin a quick rebuilding of riot-devastated areas. He also named Walter E. Washington, a black originally chosen as mayor (then still an appointive position) by President Johnson, to a second term, and pledged his close cooperation.

He thus reassured conservatives and others concerned about crime that he was serious about "doing something" about it, while also seeking to reassure blacks and liberals that in his case "law and order" was not a code for racism.

Keeping a campaign pledge, he moved within days of taking office to get politics out of the post office, a reform presidents had shrunk from since the days of Benjamin Franklin. Postmasters would no longer be patronage appointees named by the President. Instead, they would be picked on merit in the competitive civil service.

One of the most controversial organs of government was the Office of Economic Opportunity, created by Johnson as a catch-all instrument for his War on Poverty. The OEO was viewed as a crucial symbol both by the right, who wanted it abolished outright, and by the left, who wanted it strengthened. Nixon's second legislative message to Congress dealt with the OEO. Again, he struck a balance: keeping the agency, but moving to shift some of its operations to the cabinet departments, and to return the OEO itself to its function as an "incubator" for experimental programs.

Fulfilling another campaign pledge, he created a new Office of Minority Business Enterprise in the Commerce Department, to assist blacks and other minority members in developing their own businesses.

He launched a well-publicized campaign to cut back spending, and to get the federal budget under control.

In his approach to social programs, in sharp contrast to Johnson, he continually emphasized how much was unknown: "In the maze of antipoverty efforts, precedents are weak and knowledge uncertain. These past years of increasing federal involvement have begun to make clear how vast is the range of what we do not yet know, and how fragile are projections based on partial understanding. But we have learned some lessons about what works and what does not. . . ."

He debated whether to make his own State of the Union address, a prerogative open to incoming presidents, but not required of them. The outgoing President normally delivers one in January, and Johnson had done so. Again, Nixon struck a balance (or, some might say, a compromise). On April 14 he sent a written message, announcing that he had decided against an address, but setting forth a list of areas on which he was going to follow with legislative recommendations. These ranged from an increase in Social Security benefits to reform of the tax structure, and from a start on revenue-sharing to a comprehensive labor and manpower program. Thus he staked out his territory, while still keeping his options—and buying time to fashion the specific proposals in an orderly way.

At the same time, he was moving swiftly to re-establish U.S. leadership in world affairs.

Within days of taking office, he secretly set in motion studies of how an opening to China could be advanced.

Less than five weeks after taking office he embarked on a tour of allied capitals in Western Europe. While determined to open a new dialogue with the Soviet Union, he considered it vital to move first to rebuild the Western Alliance. Speaking to NATO's North Atlantic Council in Brussels, he set the theme of the trip, noting that "there have been rumblings of discontent in Europe—a feeling that too often the United States talked at its partners instead of talking with them, or merely informed them of decisions after they were made instead of consulting with them before deciding."

Henceforth, he said, the United States would "listen with a new attentiveness to its NATO partners—not only because they have a right to be heard but because we want their ideas." Then he got to the heart of his new approach to the foreign-policy process: "In creating new policy-making machinery in Washington, one of my principal aims has been to shift the focus of American policy from crisis management to crisis prevention."

Henry Fairlie—a British journalist working in Washington—argues in his book[2] that from the beginning to the end of the Kennedy administration the American people "lived in an atmosphere of perpetual crisis and of recurring crises." Noting that Kennedy wrote, in *Profiles in Courage*, that "Great crises produce great men," Fairlie observes sardonically: "It is not a thought which should enter the mind of a statesman, but it appeared to enter his own without resistance. If he did not actually enjoy leading his country to the edge of danger, one could not tell so from his words or from his actions. The remark which he made on 20 October 1962—'Well, we earned our pay this month'—is rightly famous, if not for the reason given by his admirers. It was characteristic of him that he considered that he had done his job only if he had confronted peril, and let the nation confront it, whether in the Cuban missile crisis or in the violence at the University of Mississippi, the incidents to which he was referring on this occasion."

The pattern of the Kennedy years, says Fairlie, was that "policy was subjected to crisis, and the crisis was used in turn to stimulate the response of the people. . . . So they lived for a thousand days in expectation of danger, and of rescue from it."

The legacy of recurrent crises, of the exaltation of crisis as the epiphany of international relations and the focus of domestic politics, was what Nixon sought to reverse on taking office: to move, as he put it, from crisis management to crisis prevention.

2. *The Kennedy Promise: The Politics of Expectation* (New York, 1973).

DIFFERENCE AND DEFERENCE

In the fall of 1973, shortly after the "Saturday-Night Massacre," I got a note from an old college friend. It was written in longhand, on "TWA—In Flight" stationery, datelined "30 October—en route New York–Geneva."

He wrote:

I know that it is your integrity and loyalty that keeps you from defecting from hopeless—and in this case unworthy—causes. I respect that. . . . But, as I wrote last spring, I think this case is different from any other in which you have been involved. I know that historical credit is not what you are after, but I do not believe that you will even derive personal satisfaction from loyalty to a man who is at least venal, selfish, and the worst traitor to our country in its history—at worst, a felon. I am convinced that out of this crisis will emerge some genuine American heroes, and they will take their places with the founding fathers at our bicentennial. I urge you to consider joining them by resigning with an eloquent statement. It would not be deserting a sinking ship. The ship deserted you in one of the ports early in the voyage.

Other letters came in a similar vein. My friends, for the most part, were variously amazed, appalled, or dismayed that I continued to defend Nixon and to work on his staff. It was partly that they and I interpreted events differently, from our different perspectives. During that period, I commented to one of them that "if I had to depend for my information on *The Washington Post, The New York Times,* and CBS, I'd hate the son-of-a-bitch too." Many, of course, were appalled when I first joined him, and Watergate only deepened their dismay.

Quite apart from Watergate, many had difficulty understanding the submerging of differences which is necessary on a political team. Knowing I disagreed with him on some issues, they felt that this made it wrong for me to work with him, despite my agreement on the larger issues. Or, alternatively, they interpreted my working with him as sort of presumptive evidence that I did agree on all things, and they found this puzzling and unsettling.

To me, give-and-take is an essential part of the political process, compromise and accommodation the cornerstones of a working democracy. Thus it seemed perfectly logical to me to subordinate my differences on smaller things, as long as I felt that Nixon's leadership on the larger issues was what the nation needed. Even during the worst of Watergate, I continued to see its events—whatever they might turn out to have been—as of far less real consequence than the efforts Nixon was engaged in to cement a new structure of peace abroad, and to set domestic policies on a new and, I thought, more rational course. To cast it in rather extreme terms, I saw getting on with the prevention of World War III as more important than the bugging of Larry O'Brien's telephone. Many of my friends, particularly in the press, were outraged when I suggested this order of priorities. I thought that in reversing this order of priorities, they were standing reason on its head.

But we did have our differences—differences of style, of approach, of priorities, of policy.

To begin with the trivial: Nixon prefers the more formal; I prefer the more informal. He has a penchant for coats and ties, even in the seclusion of San Clemente; I wear them when I have to, and when I do I wear conservative suits and button-down shirts. But the rest of the time I'm more likely to be found in a pair of old Levis. (He has a rather stuffy tendency to equate dignity with formality, and, on taking office, he was determined to restore dignity to the presidency—he thought it had slipped under Johnson. During the transition period, word came down via Bob Haldeman that henceforth staff members would always wear coats and ties in the presence of the President-elect. I still remember sitting on the lawn of his newly bought Key Biscayne home by the edge of Biscayne Bay, working on the inaugural address, and sweating in my coat and tie in the hot Florida sun while Nixon uncharacteristically lounged in a sport shirt. I thought it was silly, but he saw these little things as important.)

On New Year's Eve, 1958, novelist Jack Kerouac—then newly

famous as the creator and chronicler of the "Beat Generation"—brought a half dozen of his friends to my New York apartment at the start of the evening, and then, to usher in the New Year, we all went uptown to the home of a young stockbroker whom Kerouac knew. Kerouac was wearing a dirty orange sweatshirt, while his date wore a loose sheath with—apparently—nothing underneath. The rest of us were all casual, and two or three were a bit on the rowdy side. Arriving uptown, we burst in on a party at which six couples, dressed in black tie and evening gowns, were sitting in a circle eating TV dinners in their foil freezer containers from tray-tables. It was a classic collision of cultures. Nixon, had he been there, would have been appalled at us, and would more nearly have identified with those who put on black tie to eat a TV dinner in its foil container.

On social questions—especially those often equated with "morality"—Nixon tends to be a traditional conservative; I tend to be more of a libertarian conservative, believing that essentially private matters are none of the government's business. In 1972, when his own Presidential Commission on Marijuana and Drug Abuse came out with a report favoring the decriminalization of marijuana, Nixon treated the report as if it were a spider that had just landed on his brow. He was afraid of it politically, as well as disagreeing with it substantively. The issue was a red flag to most of his conservative supporters. He himself believed not only that marijuana use had to be curbed as part of the drive on harder drugs but also that its use was an important contributing factor to the malaise, the anomie that he saw sapping the self-discipline of the young and threatening the nation's will. I welcomed the report; I favor not only decriminalization, but legalization. I don't use pot—as of this writing, I have tried it only once—but I class it with alcohol as something people have a right to decide about for themselves, and to me the real tragedy is represented by those thousands of young people whose lives have been ruined not by pot, but by arrest and imprisonment for its use. I see it as disastrously wrong to place practically a whole generation outside the law, and hypocritical for my contemporaries to do this while sipping their third martini.

In general, Nixon tended to be more sensitive than I to the concerns of the "social issue" conservatives; I tended to be more sensitive than he to the concerns of minorities, the young, the alienated. But this was often a matter more of nuance than it was of substance.

As a former newspaperman myself, I thought he often misread the nature of the press antagonism toward him, and often needlessly exacerbated it by his own overreaction. I shared his belief that he was unfairly treated. But where he ascribed this primarily to ideological bias, I ascribed it primarily to the internal dynamics of the news business itself. When he let his anger boil over, as he frequently did, he had a habit of issuing petulant orders that only made the situation worse: pronouncing anathemas on *The New York Times,* for example, and forbidding any member of the White House staff to speak with anyone from the *Times.* You can't run the government that way.

The atmosphere in the White House was much too political for my taste. In the presidency, I tend to believe—within limits, and with exceptions (I sometimes cite as a rule: Moderation in all things, including moderation)—that the best politics is the least politics. When Nixon actually got his teeth into a major problem he could often be remarkably forbearing about the politics of it, making decisions that he thought might cost him millions of votes because he believed they were right. But in the interstices between these decisions, politics had a way of suffusing everything. There was nothing especially novel about this. People get to be president by being master politicians, and certainly Johnson, Kennedy, and FDR, among modern presidents, were every bit as compulsively political as Nixon. But I wished our administration could have been different.

Recently I ran across some notes dated April 18, 1973, which I apparently had written as part of an unfinished memo to the President. It was at a time when Watergate pressures were building, only twelve days before Haldeman's and Ehrlichman's resignations, only nine days before I got swept into the Watergate battle, writing the speech in which the President would announce those resignations. But it was not Watergate I was addressing in these notes; it was a continuing concern I had had with the pattern of some of our actions. I wrote:

There has been a curious dichotomy in our approaches to public policy. On the one hand, we have led a crusade against the accumulation of massive federal power to intervene in state, local, and individual decisions, quite properly asserting that America was built by individual initiative and that it stands for individual liberty. On the other hand, in a number of our separate actions we have embarked on a course of quite unprecedented repression—of attempting to use the criminal law to impose our own personal standards on individuals who may not share those standards; of a cavalier and sometimes vigilante-ish use of the instruments of criminal justice; of heavy-handed and sometimes quite crude efforts to intimidate the media.

We've got to face up squarely to the fact that our basic belief in restraining the arbitrary and untoward use of federal power means, in the present instance, restraining ourselves. Pogo's famous "We have met the enemy and they is us" sums it up pretty aptly.

Part of the trouble, I think, stems from our habit of regarding everything in competitive terms of winning and losing, of friends and enemies, of with-us-or-against-us, of all's fair in love, war, and politics. Yet our great successes in foreign policy have stemmed precisely from rejection of this approach—from following, instead, a highly sophisticated and carefully, dispassionately rationalized approach, which recognizes the overriding importance of establishing an accepted set of procedural restraints—a "structure of peace"—that we as well as the other side will follow.

Virtually every one of our domestic or political disasters has represented either an emotional spasm or else a short-term political grab, which has had results that would have been quite predictable if we had applied to the situation the long-headedness that has characterized our foreign-policy approaches—and that has also characterized our *major* domestic-policy initiatives.

Looking back at those notes now, they seem a bit hyperthyroid, as if I had been reading *The Washington Post* too much. Had I completed the memo, I might have edited it down somewhat; I have no idea what got me steamed up to write of "quite unprecedented repression." We were guilty of repressive measures, but of very few that were unprecedented. But the notes, in this raw form, do give a flavor of the concerns I often felt. In particular, the contrast between Nixon's careful farsightedness in foreign policy and his sometimes belligerent shortsightedness in domestic political matters was one that troubled me often. Too frequently, by treating various groups as adversaries we made them enemies. When we should have rolled with a punch, we counterpunched instead. Abuse—even unfair and unjustified abuse—is part of a president's lot.

Another difference is one of roots. My own roots are planted deep in that same Northeast that looked so skeptically on the works and ways of Richard Nixon—in the harsh puritan soil of the Massachusetts Bay Colony, where two of my ancestors were among the early governors, and where another, the poet Anne Bradstreet, was among the first to establish a literary tradition in the colonies; among the glacial rocks and salt spray and potato fields of eastern Long Island, where other branches of my family settled in the 1640s, and stayed, and where I grew up, graduating from the local public high school in a senior class of twelve; at Yale, where I absorbed the lore and ways of old and new New England; in the raucous, competitive bustle of New York City, where I settled to live and work, and ultimately to direct the editorial page of the solidly Eastern Establishment New York *Herald Tribune*.

One result is that I think I know the East, not as a sociologist from another planet or from west of the Hudson might know it, but as the East knows itself, with its prides and its prejudices, its strengths and its insecurities, its high nobilities and its sometimes heartlessness.

It followed that in our various battles with the Eastern Establishment, I tended to react differently than Nixon did. When he moved to New York from California, even though he had been Vice-President (selected for that nomination by Dewey himself) and the party's most recent presidential nominee, he was elaborately snubbed by Nelson Rockefeller's New York Republican organization. Nixon was, somehow, always the outsider in New York. His responses were the visceral ones of a man too often burned. I, too, could get furious at the cavalier behavior of the Eastern Establishment, at its obsessive insularity, its self-righteous arrogance, its supercilious air of moral authority, its intellectual snobbery. But I tended to personalize this somewhat less, and to weigh it in the balance as the dark side of the Eastern Establishment, just as I weighed the dark side of Richard Nixon in the balance along with his better side. Also, I found myself often more bemused than offended by the trendy, turn-the-other-chic vacuities of the intellectually fashion-conscious, as they pirouetted from one cause to the next. Having lived as part of their world, it was easy to take them less seriously.

Growing up where one's own family through the generations have raised their young and buried their dead, where they have tamed the land and built their churches and forged communities out of the wilderness does have a subtle but powerful impact. It instills a sense of history, and also of the continuity between past and future. Like most whose roots in America go back to the first colonial days, ours were not the rich or aristocratic families, but rather those who lived out their ordinary lives in ordinary ways, not in the high drama of the history books but in the everyday drama of everyday life. Yet, because they had been *there,* they had a cumulative presence. When I visited my maternal grandparents in Southampton, it would be at the house on Bowden Square that my great-great-grandfather had built for his bride, and the talk would often be of distant cousins who were only names to me, but who, because my mother's family had *been* in Southampton for three hundred years, made the town seem somehow a part of the fabric of their existence, and therefore of my own. (Not fashionable summer Southampton but quiet, year-round Southampton. It was fairly typical that my grandparents had divided the house in two and rented out half—the only way they could afford to keep it. It was also fairly typical that, although both my mother's and father's families had lived on Long Island since the first English settlements, my mother was born in Pennsylvania and my father in Colorado, before the parents of each returned to where their roots were. Work took my mother's father—an engineer and inventor—to Pennsylvania. Tuberculosis took my father's father to Colorado, where my father was born in Kit Carson's sister's adobe hut, and where, two years later, my grandfather died at age twenty-two. Colorado was still a frontier then, and it must have held scant promise for the young widow from the East who slept every night with a pistol under her pillow. Already pregnant with a second son, she packed up her few belongings and made her lonely way back home. She buried my grandfather not in Colorado, where he died, but on Long Island, where they had lived. In later years she often wished aloud that she might go back sometime to those Colorado mountains for a visit. But she never did.)

I grew up with a rather stern sense of duty, with a rather rigid code of ethics, in a staunchly Republican family and a heavily Republican area. (Back in those days, there still were heavily Republican areas. Suffolk County—the eastern, rural half of Long Island —regularly voted Republican during my growing-up days by margins of 3–1 or 4–1.) I tended to see ethical questions, however, not as simple choices between good and evil, but often as conundrums that required a rather complex weighing of the balances.

Even beyond the ambiguities, I seldom expect essentially political questions to be settled on purely ethical terms. These questions, by definition, involve principles in conflict, and interests in conflict. As social commentator Irving Kristol has put it:

There is no unequivocal "moral" answer to our social and economic problems. These problems are complex, and so the relation between reality and morality will also be complex. Doing the "right" thing cannot be divorced from doing the effective thing. And, to complicate matters even further, doing the "right" thing in one respect always means doing the "wrong" thing in other respects. . . . The reason the human race is a political species is because it generates moral principles which, when coping with reality, turn out to be inconsistent with one another. These principles then have to be adapted to one another, and to the concrete circumstances that provoked the inconsistency. This, in turn, involves the compromising—the "betrayal," if you wish—of every single principle regarded in isolation. And that is what politics is all about.[1]

This, perhaps, is where many of my friends and I most sharply diverged in our reactions to Watergate. As an editorial writer, I had the luxury of passing judgments in the abstract. Those judgments could therefore be as ethically pure as I chose, though I tried to temper ethical purity, at least to some extent, with practical realism. In the White House, I was always acutely conscious that a president bears responsibility not only for the purity of his choices but also for the consequences of those choices—and the choice which, on the surface, seems ethically unexceptionable may have quite dire consequences for millions of people. The other side of that coin is that he may have to cut legal corners in order to meet a national emergency or to serve the national interest.

In Watergate, I was less concerned with whether there had been an obstruction of justice than I was with whether Nixon would have a chance to complete what he had begun, domestically and internationally. This, it seemed to me, was where the real stakes lay for the nation and the world. I care less about whether a president breaks a law than I do about whether he keeps the peace.

Recently, a transcript was leaked to the press of President Georges Pompidou's conversation with Mao Tse-tung, when the French leader visited China in 1973.

"As for Nixon," Mao lamented, "his situation is difficult because of Watergate. We cannot understand why there is such a row over this affair."

"Neither can I," Pompidou replied. "There are too many technicians and journalists in the United States."

To Mao, of course, the issues involved in Watergate would have been foreign in any case; the niceties of due process are not exactly central to the Chinese Communist experience. But as Pompidou's reply suggests, a scale of priorities that puts the fate of nations first comes naturally to those responsible for the fate of nations.

Many readers probably accept John Dean's book as the final truth about Watergate, and about the Nixon administration. Yet even if every word of that book were true, in its totality it would be a gross distortion—not because of what he says but because of what he leaves unsaid. In his total absorption with self-promotion, self-aggrandizement, and self-protection, and with the trivia of personal contests for power and influence, he seems totally oblivious to the

1. *The Wall Street Journal,* 19 November 1976.

larger concerns that weighed on Nixon himself and on his administration—even, and in some respects especially, during Watergate.

Dean reports that of all the critical things written about him when he emerged as the President's accuser, the one that made him angriest was Joseph Alsop's characterization of him as a "bottomdwelling slug." Yet it seemed to many of us apt at the time, and even in retrospect it seems—as confirmed by Dean's own book—at least partly appropriate.

My own feelings about Dean are mixed and somewhat contradictory. I have not seen or spoken with him since he left the White House. When he was there, I thought I knew him fairly well. I liked him. Our offices were near one another, mine in the southwest corner of the Old Executive Office Building, his midway down the South corridor. My staff and his staff shared that South corridor. He and I were both part of a small group of department heads and aides to chief of staff Bob Haldeman who met regularly, two or three times a week, in Haldeman's office—the "ten o'clock group," which was our regular meeting hour—to thrash out problems, swap information, get quick decisions. (Other members included Chuck Colson, personnel chief Fred Malek, appointments secretary Dwight Chapin, Alexander Butterfield, Haldeman's assistant Lawrence M. Higby, and staff secretary Bruce Kehrli.) My relations with Dean were always cordial, and in fact I looked to him as an ally in shooting down some of the wilder schemes that came from Colson. He was always personable, ingratiating, and I thought that what he lacked in experience he made up in balance and common sense.

As I became caught up in mounting our Watergate defense, however, Dean appeared to me in a different light: as a totally selfconcerned opportunist who would do anything or say anything that might save his own skin, without regard for its cost to the President, to the country, or to the world. Once, in early August 1973, as Nixon and I rode back to the White House in his bullet-proof limousine from a dinner cruise on the presidential yacht Sequoia, he fell to musing aloud about Dean, speaking of him utterly without malice, and commenting that he could understand why Dean felt he had to do what he was doing. I was not nearly so forgiving. I replied that I thought Dean's conduct was outrageous, and that in a similar situation I would have shot myself before following such a course. I meant it. At the time, I still believed that most of Dean's story was a tissue of lies concocted—and dribbled to the press in deliberately tantalizing bits—for the sole purpose of buying immunity from prosecution for himself. Even now that much of his story has been confirmed as true, however, the scale of priorities that would set his own personal welfare above all, heedless of what he destroyed in his effort to protect himself, remains, to me, utterly incomprehensible—despite the fact that at that point he was the one following the dictates of law. When issues of war and peace are at stake, obedience to the law seems to me no excuse for conduct at once so self-serving and so consequential.

Almost from the beginning, the chief focus of my own intellectual interest was on politics and public policy. Yale, at the time I was there, provided a fertile field for the development of that interest. The postwar classes through that of 1950 were overwhelmingly dominated by World War II veterans. Mine—1951—was the first made up primarily of nonveterans. The veterans were not only older than the normal college undergraduate but also substantially more mature, more purposeful about education and at the same time more keenly involved in the world around them. Through my junior year, those World War II veterans set the tone of campus life —and one key element was a keen, serious, and widely shared interest in things political.

One of my strong influences at Yale was Bill Buckley, who was a year ahead of me and who was a dominant personality on campus from his freshman year on. We were close personal friends and, though I was not quite so conservative as he, we were regular political allies. Even as an undergraduate, he showed the wit, the finely honed debating skills, the analytical incisiveness that later became his trademark as a columnist and television host, and as chairman of the *Yale Daily News* he made the *News* not only a lively vehicle for his own particular views, but also a catalyst for an engaged discussion of public issues.

The largest extracurricular organization on campus, and one of the most active, was the Political Union, a parliamentary debating society modeled after the Oxford and Cambridge unions. I served two terms as chairman of its Conservative party, and at the end of my junior year lost a bitterly fought battle for the Union presidency by a seven-vote margin. (In that election, incidentally, I connived in a "dirty trick" that backfired, and which I thought of often, years later, when the Segretti shenanigans surfaced in the Watergate era. My opponent was the chairman of the Liberal party, but the editor of the Liberal party newspaper was supporting me. A couple of days before the election, the editor secretly prepared a special edition of the paper with an editorial repudiating the party's own candidate and endorsing me. I saw this as a major coup that could swing what was clearly going to be a close election, and collaborated with the editor both in planning the move and in distributing the paper to all of the Union's four hundred-odd members. When the issue appeared, there were immediate cries of double-cross and dirty tricks, and the net effect was—deservedly—to set my campaign back, and probably to cost me the election. I was not only ashamed of what I had done, but was also sobered by the result. It was a good lesson.)

In those days I used to assume that I would someday be a candidate for public office (I particularly had my eye on the Senate). Having been through a few campaigns, any such desire has, by now, been thoroughly washed out of my system. But at that time, I still liked the cut-and-thrust of elective politics. I cared about the issues, and tried to examine and debate them in depth. And even then I was fascinated by the central dilemma facing the conscientious political leader in a representative democracy: when his own personal convictions on a particular issue run contrary to the strongly held views of his constituency, to what extent should he follow his own lights and to what extent should he represent his constituents? It seemed to me then, and still does, that the answer has to lie, on a case-by-case basis, somewhere in the realm of a weighing of the respective importance of things. On matters that he sees as fundamental, the representative should hew rigorously to the dictates of his own conscience. If that displeases his constituents, he should invite them to replace him. But on less important matters, he may even have a duty to do the "political" thing in order to maintain his capacity to follow conscience on the larger matters.

This is, of course, one of those ethical gray areas in which no answer can be wholly satisfactory. It is one that I wrestled with often in later years, not only during the Watergate era but also as the Nixon administration strove to put together and hold together its "new majority," as we angled for support from various groups and played politics with controversial and emotionally charged issues. But because on balance I thought the administration was headed in the right direction, none of my particular disagreements ever led me to the brink of defection.

When President Ford's first press secretary, Jerry terHorst, resigned in a blaze of righteousness over the Nixon pardon, he was roundly applauded and given awards for conscience. My own conscience works differently. If a press secretary is going to quit in protest the first time he disagrees with his boss, he should never take the job in the first place.

Of course, just as there are "one-issue" voters, ready to vote a candidate up or down on the narrow question of his stand on one particular issue—such as gun control or abortion—so there occasionally are "one-issue" staff members whose interests center so narrowly on that one issue that their support depends on it.

The principal, however—especially if he happens to be President —has no such "one-issue" luxury. He has constantly to give a little here in order to get a little there, to juggle competing principles and accommodate competing interests. Statecraft is the engineering of consent, if not always of consensus, and the leader who refuses to bend is destined to fall. If he has large purposes that require large sacrifices—as Nixon's large purpose of establishing a new structure of peace in the world required, in his view, persisting in Vietnam until the war could be ended on a satisfactory basis—then the engineering of consent may require even greater compromises, even more "political" measures in areas not central to that purpose. In passing moral judgment on such compromises, no assessment that fails to take into account this need is worth the breath required to speak it.

Toward the end of 1973 I did try to resign from the White House staff—though not in protest, and not as an act of moral condemnation. I was tired. I was stale. And, as I wrote in a memo to the President:

"I no longer feel able personally to argue our Watergate case, and so I want to get myself into a position where that's argued by people who can, and I can duck the issue. Having been as deeply involved as I have been in our presentation of the case heretofore, I think the best way to resolve this is to get out—but to do so, of course, without acknowledging that this is a contributing reason."

My doubts about our Watergate case were not so much specific as they were a general concern, by then, that there was more than Nixon had admitted to, more than I had been told. This was personally troublesome because I had written—or, more precisely, been Nixon's collaborator on—his Watergate speeches and "White Papers." Even if he were guilty, I wanted him to win the fight, to complete his term of office, to finish the work that he had begun. But I knew that if my doubts were reinforced by the hard evidence that I suspected was there, it would be difficult for me to go on arguing his innocence, and I also knew he was already too far down that road to change course. If he were guilty, I wanted the ball carried for him by advocates who were more comfortable than I would be arguing a case they didn't believe in.

This was before I had seen any transcripts or heard any tapes. It was after the eighteen-and-a-half-minute gap had appeared in the tape of Nixon's June 20, 1972, conversation with Bob Haldeman, a gap which seemed to stretch belief in coincidence to the breaking point. It was after months of going up the hill and down again, as new evidence surfaced that seemed to point to the President's guilt; as we then found innocent explanations that were at least equally plausible, and often conclusively so; and as new bombshells then exploded.

Nixon continued to protest his own innocence, privately as well as publicly. My doubts were still only doubts, my guesses still only guesses. But my nerves were getting frayed, and I wanted to get out.

On November 26, 1973, I wrote my memo to the President, asking to be released from the staff. Despite the demurrer about feeling unable to continue arguing our Watergate case, it was warmly supportive. I said that "how the crisis comes out will of course depend as much on how the country views the rest of the Nixon record as it will on the Watergate questions themselves." I said I could argue "with great conviction" the way he had handled America's national and international challenges, that I wanted to do this, and that I wanted to do it "not as an agent of the President I'm praising, but as one who is clearly putting his own beliefs on the line." I sent it over to Al Haig, who then was chief of staff, with a brief covering note, saying: "The timing on this is a bit awkward, because I'm scheduled to leave tomorrow (Tuesday) night for USIA talks in Berlin, returning the following Tuesday. But I think it ought to go to the President sooner rather than later, despite this, since it affects planning for such projects as the State of the Union."

I had wrestled with the decision to leave for a long time before making it. To me, it was more self-indulgent than self-sacrificing. Trading in the chauffered cars, the helicopters, the White House telephones, the invitations, for a little freedom and privacy, was better than an even exchange. The perquisites of the White House could be pleasant. They were useful for getting the job done. I liked the people I worked with, and I felt privileged to have a hand in events that had changed the world. But I had come increasingly to feel like a prisoner in a gilded jail—weary, worried, angry, tense, wracked by the hatred and hysteria that suffused the capital, frustrated at watching as the hordes at the gates tried to batter into splinters all that we had worked to build. I didn't know how much more I could take, and I was sure that if I failed to get out then, I was going to be stuck for the duration.

I took off for Berlin feeling more relieved than I had for months—feeling guilty at dropping the task of writing the State of the Union in someone else's lap, but even that sense of guilt was tempered by the feeling that it might all be for the best. Stale and distracted as I was, I had failed miserably at my efforts to get its main lines pulled together early. Perhaps someone else, coming at it fresh, could do it better.

Returning to Washington a week later, I looked forward to clearing off my desk and preparing to say farewell. But I found that Haig had held my memo back. He wanted, first, to try to talk me out of leaving, or at least into postponing it. The President needed me, he insisted, and beyond this there was the "cosmetic" problem —how my departure would be interpreted. I was regarded as one of the White House "good guys," and if I resigned it would be made to appear as a renunciation of the embattled President. I had been aware that this was a danger and that was why I had first worked out how I could do it in a supportive way. Now I offered to buttress this by remaining as a part-time consultant—just as long as I could get off the staff. Al persisted. I insisted. Time passed. Nothing happened.

Finally, late in December, I raised the question one day while talking with Ron Ziegler. By then Ziegler was not only press secretary, but also a constant confidant of Nixon's. I gave him a copy of my memo, and said I had doubts that Haig had ever passed it along. I was getting anxious, because the time for the State of the Union was getting closer. Whoever was going to do it was going to have to get cracking.

A few hours later the phone in my office rang. The Nixons wondered if I could join them and a few friends that evening for a sort of family dinner, celebrating the Christmas season. I could, of course, and so one by one and two by two we arrived at the yellow oval sitting room in the second-floor family quarters of the White House: Bryce and Betty Harlow, Pat and Shelley Buchanan, Barry Goldwater, Mary Brooks (an old friend of the Nixons who was then director of the Mint), Rose Mary Woods, and myself, together with the President and Mrs. Nixon and David and Julie Eisenhower.

On the surface, it was a relaxed, convivial evening, pre-Christmas good cheer shared with family and friends. But Nixon was working, hard. Goldwater—who arrived in pain, on crutches; he had fallen down a flight of hospital stairs that day and injured his leg—was one of the keys to Nixon's support in Congress, and Goldwater had been publicly voicing irritation with the way the White House was handling Watergate. Harlow, who had served in the White House for Nixon's first two years, then returned to his old job with Procter & Gamble, had been prevailed on to come back to the White House in 1973, but he was again trying to leave; and, of course, I was trying to leave, as Nixon probably learned for the first time that afternoon from Ziegler. (In *The Final Days,* Bob Woodward and Carl Bernstein prominently feature this dinner, but in a grossly distorted account, picturing Nixon as drunk, rambling, incoherent, repeatedly telling Harlow, "Bryce, explain what I'm saying to Barry," then interrupting to talk about Watergate. Apart from the cast of characters I found their account virtually unrecognizable, including what they say "Price was thinking." Harlow, Buchanan, and I all told them their version was untrue, but they used it anyway. As with so much else in that book, the distorted version better supported their dramatic thesis.)

Over drinks in the oval sitting room the talk was largely light, but by the time we moved into the family dining room for dinner Nixon was busily spinning his webs. He talked on about problems in the Congress, on which Goldwater's leadership was going to be needed. He tossed out assignments for Harlow, saying "You'll do that, won't you?" And, through about half of the dinner, he discussed what he wanted in the State of the Union, telling me how he wanted it written, ticking off ideas he wanted me to pursue—then, in a quick, seemingly casual aside, setting timetables and asking me to agree to them. Of course, I had to. Around the dinner table, not only with staff but also with family and Goldwater there, there was no way to say, "Sorry, Mr. President. I won't be here." At the end of the evening, smiling, he bade us all farewell at the elevator. As we walked together through the ground-floor passage from the residence to the West Wing, I grinned wryly at Harlow, and said, "Well, Bryce, I guess we've both been had."

"I guess we have," Bryce replied.

There was no way out. I was aboard for the duration.

"NOT WITH WOOLLY-HEADED IDEALISM"

Barely two months after his second inauguration, Nixon himself was swept up in the Watergate tide. On March 23, 1973, Judge John J. Sirica read in open court a letter from Watergate burglar James W. McCord, Jr., charging that he and others had been under "political pressure" to plead guilty and remain silent, suggesting perjury had been committed in the original Watergate trial, and declaring that others were involved besides those convicted. Two days earlier, White House counsel John Dean had met with the President to tell him the Watergate cover-up was becoming "a cancer—within —close to the presidency, that's growing." Dean told Nixon that large sums of cash had already been secretly provided to the Watergate defendants, and that E. Howard Hunt was, in effect, trying to blackmail the White House for more, threatening otherwise to reveal some of the "seamier" things he had done as a member of the White House "plumbers" team—activities that included breaking into the office of Dr. Lewis Fielding, psychiatrist to Daniel Ellsberg, the former government official who had pirated and made public the top-secret Pentagon Papers. Less than three weeks after warning Nixon about the extent of the cover-up and its possible implications, Dean himself was in the federal prosecutors' offices, trying to bargain for immunity for himself by inculpating his former friends.

From the day of McCord's letter until Nixon's resignation sixteen and a half months later, Watergate almost totally dominated the news that was sent to the rest of the country from the national media centers in New York and Washington.

For the final ten days of March and through all of April, Nixon himself struggled desperately with Watergate, trying to learn what had happened, to assess its dimensions, to weigh its threat, to contain its damage.

Meanwhile, the pressures mounted. I sent Bob Haldeman an "eyes-only" memo, urging that he resign. It wrenched me to do it. Despite Haldeman's public reputation as a mean martinet, despite the fear and trembling he inspired in much of the White House staff, I liked and admired him, and I thought Nixon needed him. The Bob Haldeman I knew was brilliant, dedicated, principled— tough, yes, but also fair, honest, straight-shooting, and, contrary to public impressions, rigorous about insuring that dissenting views got in to the President rather than being kept out. I told Haldeman that whether he was involved or not, I felt the point had been reached at which it was necessary to "divide the presidency in order to save it." The way to do this, I urged, was for Haldeman—in the manner of a British cabinet member faced with a scandal in his department—to assume a ministerial responsibility for whatever had gone wrong, and to resign his post on that basis: the only sacrificial offering big enough to appease the gods of the media. He never responded, but soon the question was moot. (I was told later that he had discussed the memo with others, that he disagreed with it and was irritated by it. But we remained friends.)

On Friday, April 27, Ron Ziegler asked me to come by his office. It was early evening. Even in the darkest of times, Ron retains a capacity for quick humor. Often, in the midst of a crisis, we relieved the mood with the kind of banter surgeons exchange over the operating table. But that evening he was more serious than usual. The President, Ron said, wanted to go on television Monday night to discuss Watergate—and to announce the departures of Haldeman, Ehrlichman, and Dean. It would be his first Watergate speech. Nixon wanted me to write it.

At the start of the second term, I had asked for and been given a new role at the White House. I turned over the writing staff— which I had headed for the previous two years—to David Gergen, who had been my deputy, and along with it turned over all responsibility for involvement in day-to-day operations. I took along one secretary, Margaret Foote, and one assistant, Tex Lezar, and moved around the corner to a small suite a few doors down from the President's EOB office. In a sort of free-floating capacity, I prepared to launch what I called my "house philosopher" project. I planned to spend about a third of my time trying to bring in new ideas from around the country, and about two-thirds pulling the disparate elements of Nixon's own philosophy of government into a form in which its aims and interrelationships could better be expressed and understood within the administration as well as by the public. When Nixon agreed to this, a part of our informal understanding was that I would, of course, still be available for those speeches that he particularly wanted me to work on—beginning with the second inaugural. I thought I could complete the philosophy project in about a year, and then planned to return to private life. Already, I was getting a bit itchy to leave. Getting rid of operating responsibilities was a first step. But I thought the philosophy project was an important one to get done. As things worked out, the project itself went glimmering, a minor casualty of Watergate. First things would have to come first, and, though neither of us knew it, that session with Ziegler began a long series of "first things." As the world closed in on him, Nixon seemed to turn to me more rather than less as collaborator on his major speeches—including all those on Watergate, and finally his resignation.

Reading from his notes of his own conversation with the President, Ron spun out some of the things Nixon wanted to say: that in the wake of Watergate, he had repeatedly been given assurances that none beyond those subsequently indicted was involved; that since March, when he had learned that there was potential wrongdoing at a higher level, he had tried to get to the bottom of this "bizarre, senseless, wrong activity"; that the man at the top must assume responsibility for what happens in his organization, and "I assume that responsibility"; that he was "not going to pound the gavel of justice," that he would not prejudge matters that were properly going through the judicial system; that whatever had happened had to be looked at against the background of the violence, the disruptions, and the radical threats to the lives of public officials which had also marked the 1972 political season; that it was important to ensure that past violations were investigated and punished, and future ones prevented, but it was also important to get on with the nation's business.

Ron quoted Nixon as commenting, "Ray will want to do it differently, but I want to do it in narrative"—relating the number of times he had asked for assurance that no one in the White House was involved, saying that he had immediately asked for a full investigation, that he had then and since ordered full cooperation, that now his top staff members were being put on leave of absence. (During the weekend he continued to debate whether a leave of absence would be sufficient; he finally concluded, reluctantly, that they would have to resign.)

I said I hoped that in laying out the facts, Nixon would lay out the truth, whatever it was; that if we had lumps to take, this was the time to take them. If we were trying to hide anything, in the bitter adversary climate then existing it was going to come out sooner or later, and better that we put it out first rather than have the press dig it out later.

Ron indicated that Nixon had anticipated that I might have doubts, but that he had insisted that on this I *had* to believe him: "Those guys *must* know that I didn't know!"

Ron and I talked at length as he went through his extensive notes from Nixon, and as we kicked around our own ideas for the speech. But time was short. I went back to my own office to get started. The next morning Ziegler and I went to Camp David.

It was a strange, tortured weekend. In the past, whenever we went to Camp David, Haldeman was usually there too, sometimes with his wife, Jo, and often John Ehrlichman, sometimes with his wife, Jeanne. Now the sound of their absence was deafening. Zeigler and I shared a newly constructed cabin, New Maple, larger, more elaborate, and more modern than the older ones, with a vaulted ceiling, a large living room with a high glass wall opening onto a patio in the woods, two bedrooms, a huge fieldstone fireplace with a large supply of extra logs, neatly cut, arranged by the door. A table in the living room became the weekend's activity center; Ziegler now was the one person Nixon had left to turn to for the roles that he, Haldeman, and Ehrlichman had played as both sounding boards and channels of command. I had a typewriter set up in my bedroom, and retreated there to do my writing. On Sunday Len Garment came up for the day, to meet with Nixon and accept the post of counsel to the President, replacing John Dean, and to debate the crisis with Ziegler and me. On Sunday Bill Rogers also arrived—secretary of state, Eisenhower's attorney general, Nixon's long-time friend, whom Nixon wanted to be there for moral support when he had to fire Haldeman. (Nixon asked Rogers to do the firing for him; Rogers refused, but agreed to be at Camp David while it was done. He and Nixon then had dinner together that Sunday evening.)

Throughout the weekend, Ziegler and I repeatedly interrupted our work to review the arguments and worry through the question, over coffee during the day or over a double scotch in the evening:

Was this the right course? Did Bob and John have to go? In this, Ron was reflecting Nixon's own doubts, his own reluctance, his own pain. Intellectually, Nixon had concluded—with less than 100-percent certainty, but with more than 50-percent certainty—that it had to be done. Emotionally, he was wracked by the doing of it. Ron, in turn, was wracked by having to advise the President that it was necessary. Before joining the campaign in 1968 Ron had worked for Haldeman in the Los Angeles office of the J. Walter Thompson Advertising Agency—a job Haldeman gave him after Ron had worked under Haldeman in Nixon's 1962 gubernatorial campaign. Then Bob had brought Ron into the 1968 campaign. Each time we debated it, however, we came to the same reluctant conclusion: Yes, it had to be done.

On Sunday afternoon Haldeman and Ehrlichman also both came to Camp David, going to cabins at the far end of the compound. Each met individually with Nixon, to receive the word in person. Each then left. Looking out of a window, I saw Ehrlichman striding along the footpath as he left the President's lodge, arms swinging, his head facing grimly forward, looking neither to right nor to left.

Through the weekend I worked with Nixon indirectly, sending speech drafts over to his lodge, then getting them back with his changes marked in ink, conferring with him, when I did, by telephone rather than in person. Sometimes Nixon relayed his thoughts through Ziegler, as he so often had previously through Haldeman or Ehrlichman. Not until Monday afternoon did I sit down with him face to face.

As we usually did at Camp David, we met in the study of the presidential cabin, Aspen Lodge. The study is a small room, its windows overlooking a graceful stretch of lawn that slopes down to the forest beyond. A log fire crackled in the fireplace. I knocked, entered, and found Nixon sitting in his corner chair, his back to the windows, facing the fire. He was emotionally ravaged, his hands unsteady, anguish written in every one of the deepened lines of his face.

There were only a few hours left now before he had to face the cameras. The speech was basically done, but he had a few more changes he wanted to make. Neither before nor since, not even during the bitter ordeal of resignation week, did I ever see him so unraveled or so distraught as he was that afternoon. At one point he dropped the pages he was working on, and they simply lay on the floor beside him. He seemed not to notice. (I had seen this happen only once before, and that, too, was at Camp David, just after President Eisenhower's death, as we worked together on the eulogy he would deliver at the Capitol Rotunda. But that time he was not only emotionally torn but physically ill as well, summoning strength to work from a sickbed.)

Now, as he worked on the speech that he hated to give, his mind kept drifting away from it and back again, his gaze shifting away to the windows and back to the fire. Finally, his voice flat, distant, defeated, he turned to me and asked: "Maybe I should resign. Do you think so? You've always been the voice of my conscience. If you think I should resign, just write it into the next draft, and I'll do it."

Few questions that have ever been directed at me have hit with such force. Being asked, suddenly, by a beleaguered president to decide for him whether he should resign his office that evening is not only uncommon but also uncommonly sobering. I had, and have, no way of knowing how serious he was about it. He clearly was reaching out, looking for reassurance. But it also was obvious that he had been giving a great deal of thought to resignation; that he was deeply tormented, wracked by a sense of personal responsibility for what he had been forced to do to people close to him, his nerves frayed, his conscience torn—and, in retrospect, I would also guess that he was plagued by a heavy sense of foreboding. I have suspected ever since that at that emotional nadir of his presidency he could, in fact, very easily have been pushed over the brink into resignation.

I paused briefly before answering, trying to collect my thoughts, knowing my answer was important to him and thinking it might be important to the country.

I told him he had a duty to stay in office. In essence, I argued that there was a lot of unfinished business of the presidency—that he had made beginnings that had to be completed both at home and abroad, but most particularly that Vice-President Agnew—whatever his other qualities—simply was not up to carrying forward the delicate diplomatic maneuverings that the United States was engaged in, in its efforts to prevent war and preserve the peace. For this, I argued, it was essential both for the nation and for the world that he, Nixon, remain in office and finish what he had started.

Twice more that afternoon he pressed on me the question of resignation, each time saying that if I thought he should resign, he would, and each time, when I said he should not, pressing again for reasons why he should not.

Each time I came back to the same central point: That if the Nixon "structure of peace" were to be completed, Nixon would have to complete his term.

This argument finally snapped him out of the worst of his depression, and got him to talking instead, first about the dangers and opportunities in our relations with the Soviets and the Chinese, and finally about the Middle East—which he pinpointed once again, as he so often had before, as the most dangerous potential flash point for a U.S.-Soviet nuclear conflict, and at the same time as the most difficult, most delicate diplomatic challenge confronting the United States.

Late in the afternoon, as we talked, he decided to go for a swim. He got up heavily from his chair, and went down the corridor to his bedroom to change into trunks. The minutes were ticking rapidly by. The speech still had to be put through at least one more draft. Rose Woods was waiting in her cabin to type it, and it was still going to take time for me to work out the changes we had discussed and incorporate them. But Nixon was in such a state of depression and disorientation that I was reluctant to let him go out across the terrace and down the broad concrete steps to the deep pool alone—afraid he might stumble, slip, bang his head on the concrete, or whatever. So I waited, and walked down with him. On the way he kept stopping, on one step and then another, to talk more about the Soviet Union, about the great powers, about the Middle East. The more deeply he got involved in his discussion of the intricacies of diplomacy, of the Soviet challenge, and particularly of the Middle East, the more readily he agreed that it was going to take his skills, not Agnew's, to navigate those treacherous shoals, and the more his old animation began to return. He stopped talking about resignation.

As soon as he was safely in the pool I hurried back up to the house, alerted his valet, Manolo Sanchez, to keep an eye on him, and rushed off to race through putting the finishing touches on the speech.

Ziegler had already gone back to the White House. The resignations were announced in a statement issued from the White House press room during the day. Ziegler and I conferred several times during the afternoon by phone, both of us anxious about whether the President would be sufficiently "up," psychologically, by air time to deliver the speech successfully. Shortly before we left, I took a call from Ron, on the run, on the telephone at the Secret Service post outside the Aspen kitchen. He asked me to tell the President that he had watched the evening news, talked with members of the press, and gotten a report on congressional reaction—and that "everyone applauds the actions taken today." Further, indications were that the country was behind the President. All three networks had sent reporters out to do man-in-the-street interviews, in places like Chicago, Los Angeles, Kansas City. Support for him was solid —asked if they would vote again for Nixon, the people interviewed said, "Absolutely." Ron reported also that members of the press he had talked with had said the President very courageously did what he had to do. Ron asked me, in passing this along, to add that he thought the imperative thing now was for the President to be "up" for the speech; that in terms of delivery, what the public wanted now was to see a president who was "in control, in charge, stating a problem—if he pulls it off, he wins the battle."

We both understood that what we were doing was psychological conditioning, trying to bolster the President's mood, to help him live with what he was doing, so that by the time the cameras went on he could successfully mask his feelings and could speak to the nation as a calm president, rather than as a tortured man. But by then I was able to tell Ron that I thought the worst was past, and that Nixon was going to be all right. And that this report from Ron would be a further help. By the time we boarded the helicopter for the return to Washington, the President, though still somber, was in full control of himself.

Day or night, in any season of the year, the helicopter ride from Camp David to the White House is beautiful—flying low over Maryland and Virginia countryside, farms blanketing the land by day, the lights of towns and villages twinkling by night, then along the curve of the Potomac, past Georgetown, circling the monuments of Washington, and settling gently on the South Lawn of the White House itself. As the helicopter landed, Nixon asked me to walk with him past the press toward the entrance to his office. I continued on to my own office, and waited there for the speech to begin.

Watching the speech on the television set in my office, my principal reaction was relief—relief that he had gotten himself sufficiently psyched up to make it through, calmly and authoritatively. In the circumstances—the haste, the emotional trauma, the tension, the stakes—and believing its facts to be essentially true, I thought that it was a pretty good speech. It had a few corny touches, but not many. He said he would "not place the blame on subordinates" for what had gone wrong, but rather that the responsibility "belongs here, in this office. I accept it." He pledged to "do everything in my power to ensure that the guilty are brought to justice and that such abuses are purged from our political processes." He urged that there be no hasty prejudgment of those against whom charges were being leveled, but rather that "we let the judicial process go forward, respecting those safeguards that are established to protect the innocent as well as to convict the guilty. It is essential that in reacting to the excesses of others, we not fall into excesses ourselves."

But the press pounced ferociously on one line of the speech, and flayed him with it ever afterward. In stating that he had accepted the resignations of Haldeman and Ehrlichman, he called them "two of the finest public servants it has been my privilege to know." Perhaps I should have tried to talk him out of saying it. But he believed it. He was determined to say it. And I believed it, and I thought he had a right to say it. In the whole Watergate battle, there were few things I resented more deeply than the brutal press reaction to that one decent, generous, and totally honest comment.

For the next fifteen months the Watergate battle continued to rage, and Nixon continued to fight as hard as he could to defend his position and retain his office. The Watergate transcripts have shown some of the seamier aspects of that fight. But throughout, he kept in the forefront of his own mind the larger purposes he sought to serve with his presidency, and particularly his determination to do what he could toward building "a generation of peace."

Just eleven months earlier, on May 22, 1972, the wheels of *Air Force One* touched down at Moscow's Vnukuvo Airport. Richard Nixon, who as Vice-President had engaged Nikita Khrushchev in spontaneous debate in the kitchen of a "typical American house" at the American Exhibition in Moscow in 1959, was back in the Soviet capital as President. He sped by motorcade past empty fields and crowded housing developments and through the streets of downtown Moscow itself to the ancient, walled fortress of the Tsars, now the heart of the Soviet empire. There, for the first time ever, the Stars and Stripes were raised above the towers of the Kremlin.

Three months after his visit to Peking, Nixon was completing the third leg of his diplomatic triangle.

In May the weather in Moscow is warm, and the days are long —by 3:00 or 4:00 A.M. dawn has already come, and light floods in through the windows. The President, Dr. Kissinger, and a few members of their staffs were quartered within the Kremlin itself, in the Grand Palace of the Tsars—a palace meticulously maintained by its new Communist owners in all its imperial splendor. The rest of us—including Secretary of State Rogers—stayed across

Red Square in the huge Rossiya Hotel. Because I was helping Nixon with the televised address he was scheduled to broadcast from a room in the Kremlin palace to the Soviet people, I worked a good deal of the time in the rooms set aside for us in the Kremlin.

Sometimes, rather than taking the chauffeur-driven cars provided for us by the Soviets, I walked the short distance between the Kremlin and the hotel. The Kremlin grounds themselves were a pleasant place to stroll, and, particularly if I were leaving in the afternoon, there was a certain wry satisfaction at the idea of striding, briefcase in hand, through the Kremlin to the Spassky Gate, lost in the bustle of Soviet bureaucrats leaving their offices.

One thing I found particularly fascinating on that trip was the kind of national treasures the Soviets chose to show off to us: the magnificent Kremlin palace itself, where they hosted the arrival dinner in the fourteenth-century Granovit Hall; the Bolshoi, still resplendent with its imperial trappings; in Leningrad, the incomparable Hermitage, and the Pavlosk—once the summer palace of Tsar Paul, destroyed by the Nazis during World War II and now, in a triumph of the restorer's art, re-created in its original splendor; and not a tractor factory on the entire tour. Dedicated to their Communist cause, yes; but also an intense, nationalistic pride in their Russian heritage.

But for all the perhaps unconscious symbolism of their pride in tsarist traditions, there were sharp reminders of the nature of Soviet society. At the Rossiya, each time we left our rooms, even briefly, we had to pack up our briefcases, and take them to a special room with a twenty-four-hour U.S. Marine guard. In the President's own quarters in the Kremlin, as we sat one day discussing his speech to the Soviet people, I called his attention to one passage I had in the draft and asked, aloud, whether he wanted to make so pointed a critical reference to the Brezhnev Doctrine. He quickly aimed a finger at the ceiling, glanced sharply at me, and changed the subject. It was a lapse of caution on my part; thereafter, whenever I had anything at all sensitive to raise, even in the President's suite itself, I remembered to write a cryptic note that he could reply to with a silent nod or gesture. Whenever I had anything sensitive to discuss with another staff member, I got into the habit of going for a walk with him around Red Square, where, lost in the crowd, we presumably could talk beyond reach of the listening devices.

One basic problem at international gatherings is that of language. It can make state dinners, for example, difficult occasions for the guests. Like most of our party, I spoke no Russian. Most of the Russians who attended the various official lunches and dinners that were put on for us spoke no English. Doing our best to keep up a conversation, we often relayed questions and answers through the occasional bilingual guest we found seated nearby, while also expansively using gestures—and smiling a lot. Fortunately, the Russians like to do a lot of toasting, and the vodka, wine, and brandy glasses were kept filled. Toasts could often be substituted for talk, using a phrase or two of the other's language, and producing at least as much international conviviality—and by sipping the drink rather than downing it, it was possible to share quite a few toasts during the course of a meal.

(English has become enough of a lingua franca so that in most parts of the world at least some rudimentary dinner-table conversation is possible for English-speaking guests. But I do remember particularly difficult times at state dinners in Indonesia, Poland, and Rumania. The Rumanians are basically Latin rather than Slavic, they have a Mediterranean flair, and French is widely spoken. There, between my own rudimentary French and his rudimentary English, I was able to manage a semblance of conversation with one guest, an ebullient cabinet minister seated across the table from me—though even so, it was a constant matter of groping for some word that could convey some comprehensible meaning. In Indonesia, where few spoke any English, I chiefly remember long, awkward silences. In Poland, the Polish guests were so warmly outgoing, so eager to be friendly, that the language barrier was doubly frustrating.)

A State Department interpreter traveled with us to Moscow, and his nose was put badly out of joint when the President made clear that he intended to use Brezhnev's interpreter, Viktor Sukhodrev, both for his talks with the Soviet leaders and to give the simultaneous translation of his televised talk to the Soviet people. As the speech approached, the State Department man agitatedly warned me of the dangers: it would be easy to skew meanings in subtle ways, so that Nixon could be made to appear to be saying things that the Soviets might want said, rather than as he wanted to say them. I was uncertain to what extent this was a matter of wounded vanity, and to what extent it was a real problem; I thought perhaps the President was making a mistake. I passed along the translator's concern, but Nixon still wanted to use Sukhodrev, whom he had known before. (Sukhodrev became a familiar figure to American television-watchers when he served as Khrushchev's interpreter on Khrushchev's visit to the United States.) As a precaution, when we gave Sukhodrev the text of the speech early in the day it was to be broadcast, we asked him to do a written translation that the State Department man could then check. He did, and our own interpreter pronounced it fair.

As soon as I got to know Sukhodrev—or Viktor, as we all soon called him—I could readily see why Nixon chose him. Polished, urbane, genial, witty, he turned out to be not only a master linguist but also a pleasant companion—and, more important from the standpoint of the speech, he used his exceptionally expressive voice almost as a musical instrument, catching all the nuances of tone and inflection. At the President's return dinner for the Soviet leaders in the U.S. embassy, Viktor and I shared the same table. The son of a foreign-service officer, he had lived a number of years in England—and as we talked, he demonstrated his technique, slipping easily back and forth between a faultless British accent and a perfect idiomatic American. Having gotten acquainted with Viktor, and having heard the broadcast (which I watched on Russian television in my own suite at the Rossiya), I was glad the President had been bold enough to use the Soviet translator rather than his own. While the speech was Nixon's, the fact that the voice the Russian audience followed was Viktor's probably added substantially to its effectiveness.

Being directed at the Soviet people, in making its points the speech drew heavily on the sort of homespun analogies and simple folk tales so popular in Russian tradition. It also played to the strong emotional feelings the Russians still have about World War II, and particularly to the intense concern for children which is characteristically Russian.

In his speeches, Nixon always gave special attention to the close —the peroration. The day before his speech on Soviet television, we made a one-day trip to Leningrad. There, we split into two groups. While some of us, including Secretary Rogers, were being whisked through a forty-five-minute tour of the Hermitage (a frustrating experience; two weeks would have been too short a time to appreciate it), the President was taken to a memorial to those who died in the nine-hundred-day siege of Leningrad in World War II. That siege was burned into the city's soul, and was one of the epic sagas of the Soviet Union. Nearly three-quarters of the city's people lost their lives. From a population of some 2 million before the war, only an estimated 560,000 were left by 1944. All of the city's dogs and cats were eaten. Thousands of people died in the streets of starvation. At the memorial, Nixon was shown the diary of a twelve-year-old girl, Tanya Savicheva, telling of the deaths, one by one, of all the members of her family, until, finally, "All are dead. Only Tanya is left."

In his toast at an official luncheon that day in Leningrad's Mariinsky Palace, extemporizing, Nixon spoke movingly of the diary itself, and of the picture of Tanya displayed alongside it, and then expressed the hope that the summit talks would advance the prospects that "the little Tanyas and their brothers and sisters will be able to grow up in a world of peace and friendship among people—all people in the world." Tanya was a natural for the television speech, too, and so he used the story of that twelve-year-old girl and her diary as his peroration the next evening as well. There were snickers from the American press—which became guffaws when he used the story again three months later in his speech at the Miami convention accepting renomination. But the Russians, to whom it was addressed, did not snicker. At the close of the speech, when I stepped out into the hotel corridor, the maid on duty—who had been watching the speech on a set in a room behind her desk—rushed to embrace me, tears streaming down her cheeks.

Essentially, what Nixon sought as President was to seize the opportunity presented by a particular confluence of forces in the world that might not be repeated, and to use this opportunity to create a new structure that could maintain peace among the major powers for the balance of the twentieth century and beyond. The keys to this were provided by the tensions between Moscow and Peking. But if the triangular great-power diplomacy these keys could unlock were to succeed, then several other conditions would also have to be met. First, continued U.S. military strength. Second, a stance toward the war in Vietnam that would command the respect of the major Communist powers. Third, a refurbishing of the Western alliances. Fourth, a restoration of the American spirit, and a strengthening of the American will to bear the burdens of world leadership. And fifth, an entirely new approach to the conduct of diplomacy between the United States and the major Communist powers.

As for the other corners of the triangle, the new relationship with China might well prove more important in the long run. But in terms of immediate significance, the main action lay with the Soviet Union. With the Soviets, it was essential to narrow differences, to develop areas of common interest, and, above all, to build a mutuality of interest—perceived as well as actual—both in limiting arms and in maintaining the peace. This meant weaving a fabric of interdependencies that would raise the prospective cost to the Soviets of incurring American displeasure. It meant remaining strong enough so that the Soviets would be dissuaded from the ultimate gamble. It also meant recognizing the virtues of a balance of power. As Nixon put it in a copyrighted article in *U.S. News and World Report* shortly after his return from Moscow:

"Those who scoff at 'balance-of-power diplomacy' on the world scene should recognize that the only alternative to a balance of power is an imbalance of power—and history shows us that nothing so drastically escalates the danger of war as such an imbalance. It is precisely the fact that the elements of balance now exist that gives us a rare opportunity to create a system of stability that can maintain the peace not just for a decade, but for a generation—and we hope beyond."

The capstone of the first Moscow summit was the first SALT agreement—the first treaty of the nuclear age in which two superpowers agreed to a limitation of their strategic nuclear arsenals. There were other agreements: to cooperate in reducing pollution and improving environmental quality, in medicine and public health, in science and technology, in space exploration, in expanding U.S.-Soviet trade, in lessening the chances of dangerous incidents at sea between U.S. and Soviet ships and planes. But the big prize was SALT, not only as an agreement of historic importance in itself but also as the foundation for a series of future treaties to limit and eventually reduce the burden of arms, while assuring security for both sides.

Beyond the specific agreements, that first Moscow summit gave the leaders on both sides a chance to take the measure of one another, and to establish a level of personal confidence that made it possible to narrow differences to the essentials of their competing national interests.

When Nixon met with his cabinet on June 16, a few weeks later, the purpose was not to discuss the summit. The main purpose of that day's meeting was political. The Republican National Convention was coming up soon, and so Republican National Chairman Bob Dole and Platform Committee Chairman John Rhodes were invited to meet with the President and the cabinet for a discussion of the platform committee hearings and of the platform presentation. But as the discussion wound on, Nixon commented at one point that probably the area in which the sharpest distinctions would be drawn between himself and Senator George McGovern

—the odds-on choice at that point to be the Democratic nominee —would be in defense and foreign policy. He then mused aloud that "maybe it would be useful to have a brief reflection by me on what our policy is at the present time." He warmed to the subject as he went on, the platform forgotten as he shifted into the role of professor-President.

"Too many people in the media," he began, "columnists and editorial writers, were for both the Russian and Chinese trips for the wrong reason. They say look at China—it was never a threat to the United States, it was a great mistake for us ever to have a policy of antagonism. They say now finally Nixon saw this, which means that we will get along with them.

"People want to believe the best about the world, and about other people. They don't want to believe the truth that nations are motivated by self-interest, and not by love and understanding. This does not mean that understanding is not good—but this won't change the Mexican position on salinity of the Colorado River, and it changes the Communists even less.

"As we look at what happened with the Chinese and Soviets, the reason China and the United States finally got together is not because we or they finally reached the conclusion that we had been mistaken. It was because at this juncture in history there were very fundamental shifts in the world balance of power that made it imperative that they look elsewhere, and useful to us to have better relations with them.

"The leaders of the Chinese government are more dedicated to communism as an ideology than the Soviets, because they are in an earlier stage. Also, they are more dedicated to supporting the 'third world.' They consider themselves weak. When it comes to Africa, to Southeast Asia, to the Middle East, the Chinese speak out strongly to those nations. Also, they do it for another reason —not because they love all those people, but also because the overriding Chinese and Russian concern is the fact that both are in competition for the leadership of the Communist world. When the Russians are trying to make an accommodation with the major powers, the Chinese see this as an opportunity to make gains with minor powers around the world. This hasn't worked very well.

"The fundamental point, however, is why the Chinese felt it was in their interest. Put yourself in the position of the Chinese leaders—with eight hundred million people, on one border they see the Russians, with more men there than against Western Europe. To the south, there is India. The Chinese have contempt for the Indians, after the 1962 war. But it gives them pause to see what

India could do with the support of the Soviets against China's friend Pakistan. To the northeast, they see Japan. They have no reason to fear Japan, because Japan has no nuclear weapons. But they have enormous respect for Japan, which has invaded and occupied China. Also, Japan is now the third and will soon be the second economic power in the world, and they could well develop nuclear weapons soon on the industrial base that they have.

"Then there's the United States. As far as our system is concerned, we are much more antagonistic toward them than anyone else. But Mao and Chou make no decisions on a personal basis. They do it only on cold calculation, which is true of most world leaders.

"So, if you were the Chinese, you would welcome better relations with the United States—giving you on one flank not an enemy at the very least, and also a nation that because of its interests might restrain some of China's neighbors.

"One of the major Chinese doctrines is that Japan must never rearm. Also, they say that the United States and Japan should dissolve our defense arrangement. But they don't *want* this. Japan, if it were unprotected, facing Russia and China, with its enormous economic capacity, would not be neutral—it would either go with one of the others or rearm. The Chinese know that.

"These clowns who write for the media don't understand this. They see it all in terms of their own prejudices from the past."

Then he turned to the Soviets: their motives, their goals, their interests, and what these meant to the United States.

"Now look at the Soviet Union. Why is the Soviet Union interested in talking to the United States in a number of fields? While they of course jump through the ceiling if you talk about linkage, they link everything.

"What are the Soviet Union's problems? They look at China—they know they have nothing to fear now from China, but they also know what they themselves have done economically in fifty years in a relatively backward country. They respect the Chinese people. They know that a billion Chinese in twenty-five years could be an enormous threat in the future.

"The Soviets' major purpose with the United States is to weaken the European alliance, and to erase the idea that the Soviets pose any threat to NATO.

"As they look to the future, they realize their interests at this time would not be served by allowing the U.S.-Chinese opening to ripen into, not friendship, but a possible accommodation which down the road might threaten them.

"So—did we go to China to play against the Soviets, and vice versa? We have to say no. If we ever said yes, they'd have to react the other way. But put yourself in their position.

"On arms control, there would have been no agreement whatever if we hadn't had the ABM. And we won that by only one vote in the Senate.

"The Soviets are no more interested in peace as an end in itself than the Fascists were. They prefer it. Their people don't want war. But as for the leaders—their goals, while not as violently expressed as the Chinese, have not changed. They still want communism to spread to other countries, by subversion perhaps. They play it down. No Soviet soldier has been lost since World War II. But, because they have avoided a military confrontation with the United States, this does not mean that the Soviet leaders have abandoned their ultimate goal—the victory of communism in other areas of the world.

"Every one of the East European countries is a potential problem for the Soviets, except perhaps for Bulgaria.

"These countries are pulled toward Western Europe. They have differences with the Russians. Communism hadn't sunk in there. So the Russians have Eastern Europe on one side, China on the other—and also internal problems.

"Anyone who went to the Soviet Union twelve years ago, and has gone again now, has to be impressed by the changes. But theirs is still a very primitive society by our standards. They want more consumer goods. So: Where's the logical place to turn? France and England don't matter anymore. The Soviet and Chinese leaders are total pragmatists. They know where the power is.

"Unless the United States has not only military strength but also leadership that makes us respected and credible, they wouldn't be interested in talking to us.

"That's why I took the action I did in mining Haiphong. If we were to lose in Vietnam, it would have pleased the Soviets and the Chinese, but there would have been no respect for the American President, no matter who he was—because we had the power and didn't use it. When the United States does become involved, we must be credible. We must stand by our commitments, our allies, our friends.

"So the Soviets look at the situation—the arms race—in major categories, they have caught up to us. But they do respect our enormous economic power, and they believe that if they get into a race with us on the military side they cannot hope to gain an advantage and win it.

"Therefore, we have reached these agreements.

"The ABM agreement is final, but it can be abrogated if violated. The offensive agreement is temporary, and limited to a few categories. We *are* entering a new period in our relations with the Soviets. We want to go forward. Pete Peterson is going to Moscow in July for some very tough negotiations on trade. A deal will be worked out. But the fundamental point is that the Soviet leaders' goals have not changed. They are dealing with us in nonmilitary areas because they think it will help them with their economy, and so forth. They are dealing with us on the military side because the choice is not very attractive—either go ahead with a race which neither side would be allowed to win, or make some attempt to limit or control it, by hard bargaining.

"We'll have the second round in October, assuming the Congress agrees to the first agreements. There will be a tendency for the Congress to go through some nonsense as it did with ABM—to put things in escrow. I went through forty-three hours of conversations. Bill [Rogers] did a lot. If you have something in escrow, forget it—don't take the trip.

"In the Soviet leaders we have people who will make a deal and keep it—because they are pretty sure if they cheat we will know it.

"We confront a situation—in order to capitalize on the most significant arms control agreement in history—one in which two superpowers, two nuclear powers, each with the capacity to destroy the other, agreed to restrain themselves. This affects the vital security of each, and each had to have basic incentives.

"We know that public opinion in the United States, as reflected in the present Congress, makes it terribly difficult to get what we need. People will grasp at almost any straw.

"In terms of capitalizing on it—the offensive agreement covers only a few categories, and unless followed with a permanent freeze neither agreement is going to amount to anything. We will get the permanent freeze only if we have a credible defense posture. We have to be able to deal from strength.

"At this point, in Vietnam the military situation is better and North Vietnam is hurting. For the United States to throw in the towel would seriously erode the chance that the Soviets would deal with us as a respected power.

"In terms of defense, it is essential we have a credible position. I hope we don't have to build the B-1s. But unless we are moving forward in these fields—" He paused, then added ominously: "Brezhnev made it clear that *they* are going forward."

He continued:

"This may be the last time in history when the United States could negotiate such an agreement. If we didn't negotiate it, they'd be ahead.

"We have the legacy of the McNamara era. The United States is in an inferior position in terms of land-based missiles, and we face potential inferiority even with submarines. If we didn't have this agreement, the Soviets could look down our throats five years from now.

"Why, then, were they interested?

"First, because of the Chinese. Second, because of their need for consumer goods. Third, because of their fear—maybe somewhat groundless—that the United States might go off on another arms kick, and get the edge on them. They fear our superiority, though we can't say that.

"If we don't do it now, I'm convinced we can't do it three or four years from now.

"For the United States unilaterally to cut back on defense spending would torpedo the agreement. For us not to go forward with our defense program would torpedo it. For the Soviets to get the idea that the United States may have power but not the will to use it would seriously endanger it.

"That's why this is so delicate—a walking-on-eggs process."

Then he turned to a discussion of the leaders with whom he had dealt in Moscow:

"We tend in the West always to underestimate the leaders of societies that are different from ours, because of their manners.

"I'll never forget when Khrushchev came on the scene—he was treated as a clown, but he was only a clown when he wanted to be. Robert Conquest classified the present Soviet leadership as third-rate intellectually. The leadership has major problems. The bureaucracy practically suffocates ideas. In negotiations, I had more freedom. I could make the critical decisions, while Brezhnev had to check with his other people.

"But simply because the guy on the other side of the table is a Communist, or because his manners are not up to Western standards, don't underestimate him.

"Kosygin can handle himself with anyone on the economy. He could handle any job in our cabinet.

"Brezhnev is different. He prides himself on not being an intellectual. What they do have is stamina, and a steel-like determination which can compensate for the lack of college degrees and things of that sort.

"I'm simply suggesting—not that we should feel an inferiority in this new world we are developing, and which is developing not because communism has changed, or because we have. The Communist world is now split. It's having problems. This offers an opportunity for us to accommodate to, and even to affect, this change. But to do so we have got to maintain our strength and credibility in the world.

"If you stand by your allies, you're worth talking to. If you let them down, you are not worth talking to.

"Most of the media approved the China initiatives, and were even quite glowing about the Russian ones. I'm convinced that as a result of what we have done, the chances of having a more peaceful world fifty years from now are substantially increased. But this would not have been done with woolly-headed idealism. If we've come this far, it's because we have not been belligerent; we have avoided exacerbating the problem by engaging in a shouting match. Our personal relationship is as good as it can be. I never believe in letting personal relationships make difficult decisions more difficult. But—you've got to put yourself in their position— how are they going to evaluate us? If they think we are weak, they are going to pounce on us. If they think we are strong, they are going to deal with us. . . .

"We're not in Vietnam because we want to bomb little children. We're not buying defense because we want to strut around the world. When we deal with budget problems, we see how much we need the money in the domestic field.

"But it isn't being for peace that matters. It's finding an effective method of doing something about it that matters.

"When I had my last long talk with de Gaulle, and I imagine that he was thinking what he'd do if he had our power, his major criticism of U.S. policy was that we are good at fighting wars, but not good at negotiating peace. We didn't succeed after World War I. After World War II it was a disaster. Now we are trying to *prevent* war—to *learn* from the past.

"We have one of those opportunities that may never come again. Meanwhile, you'll all have to take a lot of heat.

"Wouldn't it be nice if Bill, Mel,[1] and I could go to college campuses and say, 'I'm for peace,' 'I'm trying to cut the defense budget by thirty billion dollars,' 'I'm going to go to Hanoi and bring the Americans back'?

"Put someone with those views in this chair, and you'd better head for the hills."

1. He was referring to Secretary of State William Rogers and Secretary of Defense Melvin Laird.

VIII

THE NIXON REVOLUTION

In the immediate aftermath of Richard Nixon's fall from grace and power, his administration was remembered chiefly for its end. But to see it only in these terms is to miss the central significance of one of the most momentous six-year periods in the nation's history. To view it merely in terms of crime and punishment is not only to distort history but to deny history.

The battles over Watergate, impeachment, and resignation were the final battles of a presidency that, from its outset, was perhaps the second most fiercely embattled in our history. The most embattled President, of course, was Abraham Lincoln, whose election sparked the Southern secession, who was inaugurated against the backdrop of the gathering clouds of civil war, who was bitterly reviled by abolitionists as well as by Southern sympathizers and antiwar activists, and who was viciously caricatured throughout his presidency as an incompetent bumpkin and unprincipled knave, and as a subverter of the Constitution who ruled with a dictatorial hand.

The final battles of the Nixon presidency cannot be understood except in the context of those that went before; nor can those earlier ones be seen completely except in the context of the one that ended his presidency.

Those earlier battles were partly over policy—over fiercely competing views of the proper role of the United States in the world, and of the federal government here in the United States. They were also over power and primacy. In many key respects, they were confrontations between an old elite and new forces that marched under the banner of what could fairly be called a Nixon Revolution.

Nixon sought to define old concepts in new terms. He struggled to shift the direction of change. He fought to turn a nation still mired in the ways of mid-century around, and start it on a course charted for the final third of the century.

From the outset he was embattled over the conduct of the war in Vietnam, and, in an inextricably related sense, over what America's role in the world should be, and how that role should be pursued and supported. This was a battle for the highest stakes: basically, it was no less than a debate over how best to prevent World War III. It included fiercely fought questions of what price the nation should pay, both in lives and in money, for its defense, for its influence, for the military and economic underpinnings that might make its diplomacy succeed.

With violence in fashion, he was embattled over the basic question of where and how the nation's policies should be set: by the President and the Congress, operating through the processes of representative democracy, or by mobs in the streets and bombers on the campus.

At home, he was embattled over the tortured questions of race, of schools, of the extent and the limits of the proper federal role in enforcing the conscience of the community and the mandates of the Constitution—and over what that conscience commanded and what those mandates were. Beyond this, he faced a broad range of divisive issues of social policy: welfare, labor relations, taxation, crime and punishment, the rule of law, the balance that should be struck between the newly recognized claims of the environment and the continuing claims of economic progress.

He also was engaged in constant battles over the competing powers of the President and the Congress. Institutionally, tensions between the two branches are often acute. They were more so with the White House in the hands of one party, Congress in the hands of the other. Nixon was the first President since Zachary Taylor 120 years earlier who took office with both houses of the Congress in opposition control. And because he was Richard Nixon, the lingering bitterness from earlier partisan battles carried over into congressional attitudes toward his presidency.

More fundamentally, he was embattled over a set of basic philosophical divisions about the role of the central government in relation to those of the states, the communities, and the people themselves. This was a dispute over the extent and division of political power in a free society, and at the same time over the competing concepts of a pluralistic or a monolithic nation.

But one of the most basic battles of all was a war for supremacy between an old elite—which dominated the media, the academic world, the literary world, the tastemakers and trendsetters—and the new forces that sprang essentially from the nation's heartland, and that found their political focus in Nixon himself. This was a fight over values, and the way those values would be determined, and by whom. On both sides, it came to be seen as a struggle for survival. It was this battle, more than the others, that stoked the fires which eventually consumed the Nixon presidency.

What Nixon sought to bring about was indeed a revolution. This Nixon Revolution set out not only to reverse a forty-year trend in domestic social policy, but also to give primacy to a hierarchy of values that paid the same respect to Main Street that it did to the Main Line. If this revolution succeeded, it would shake the snobbish assumption of natural superiority that lay in the fashionable East.

For years the custodians of fashion—including most of the national media—had made fun of traditional middle-class values. In striking back in behalf of the equal right of those values to a decent respect, Nixon touched deep chords of response in millions of Americans. But he also won the contempt of the self-consciously fashionable.

One gauge of the style an administration sets for the nation is the selection of its White House entertainments. Those of the Nixon administration were deliberately eclectic. Beverly Sills performed at the White House, but so did Johnny Cash; the Johnny Mann Singers, but also Isaac Stern and Leonard Bernstein. For Duke Ellington's seventieth birthday, Nixon gave a full-fledged White House dinner in his honor, and the greats of the jazz world joined in an East Room jam session till well past the witching hour (with presidential assistant Leonard Garment sitting in with his clarinet), but not until after Nixon himself had sat down at the piano and banged out an unabashedly old-fashioned rendition of "Happy Birthday, Dear Duke."

By firmly rejecting the notion that all wisdom lay in Washington and pressing instead to get the power of decision-making out to the hinterlands, the administration quite consciously echoed Bill Buckley's classic observation that he would rather be governed by the first hundred names in the Boston telephone directory than by the faculty of Harvard University.

This was not an exclusionary policy: quite the contrary. Even before taking office, Nixon reached out to recruit Henry Kissinger from Harvard and from Nelson Rockefeller, and Pat Moynihan from Harvard and the intellectual round table of the Democratic party. As Theodore H. White (Harvard '38) has pointed out, "the cabinet and staff of [Nixon's] second administration were more heavily dominated by Harvard men than those of any of the six Harvard men who had been Presidents of the United States." But while welcoming—while seeking—individuals from the old elite, he was seeking to strip that elite of its corporate power to set the national agenda, to define the national values and to prescribe the national goals.

In speaking of the old elite, it is important to be clear about definitions. Time and again, when charges have been raised of Eastern domination of the media, for example, I have seen figures trotted out showing how many commentators and editors and network chiefs came originally from Iowa or Nebraska or Alabama— the intended point being that they therefore do represent the nation at its broadest, not the Eastern Establishment at its narrowest. But, like the Nixon administration, that Establishment is not exclusionary. It renews itself by absorption. It maintains itself by co-option. What it demands is not that a person be born to the right family, but that he celebrate the right values—its values. It demands the flattery of taking it seriously, the obeisance of following its fashions. To those who celebrate its style, and who have the importance that goes with power, it accords the grace of acceptance; to those who follow its fashions, it offers the currency of mutually reinforcing self-esteem, the white hat of the "good guy," the celebrity of inclusion. The process is subtle, seductive, and effective, and it is no coincidence that as the national press have acquired celebrity status they have also tended to acquire the elitist values—and that those who adopt the elitist values are most likely to acquire the celebrity status. It operates by osmosis, not consciously or deliberately, but as a natural function of their own self-esteem.

Against this, Nixon came on as almost aggressively square. But the collision of styles was also a collision of purposes. In fighting the cultural and intellectual fashion-setters, his real targets were the fashions they were setting.

In 1970 syndicated columnist Nick Thimmesch saw the contending forces in these terms:

> The Nixon Administration gets small affection or even tolerance in the very special world here of people who make a good living producing

and selling ideas. Massive "Middle America" might support President Nixon, but the tiny constituency of creative folk doesn't.

These are the imaginative, sometimes fantasizing souls who work in the confines of mid-Manhattan's entertainment and communications shops—the TV networks, magazines, publishing houses, Broadway, the music houses, art galleries, photographic and film firms, advertising agencies, and, of course, the power-house *New York Times*.

Though they number no more than a town, say, the size of Hannibal, Mo. (pop. 20,028), their influence is enormous because they pump ideas and attitudes into the minds of nearly everybody in the Republic.

From this boiling cauldron, the more extreme souls sputter that: American society is "repressive"; "genocide" is inflicted on the Black Panthers; and the United States is a brutal, imperialistic force in the world. They pant for the politician who proves to be King Dove on the war; indeed, there is something of the Spanish Inquisition here in the way candidates must attest to their "peace" positions. To show how wild it gets, consider the nationally televised "talk show" where Orson Welles and Norman Mailer gave currency to the nonsense that Mr. Nixon might call off the 1972 elections.

One day, toward the end of the 1972 campaign, Nixon, Haldeman, Ehrlichman, and I sat in the Oval Office discussing speeches Nixon might make during the final weeks. Presumably, a semi-audible version of that conversation exists on a tape somewhere. It was never published because it had nothing to do with scandal. But it was much more nearly typical of the vast majority of conversations that took place there than were the Watergate tapes. It was a relatively relaxed morning, and as we talked Nixon fell to ruminating on the differences between his "New American Majority" and FDR's coalition, and on the differences between his view of the essentials of national unity and the traditional liberal views of persisting antagonisms. He launched into it from a familiar corner: from his own deep resentment of the fashionable Northern attitude toward the South. He mentioned that he had been reading a biography of Sherman, "about the utter horror of the march to Atlanta and then to the sea—the devastation, the hatred, and then what happened in Reconstruction."

To understand the South, he said, "you have to remember that Southerners are terribly sensitive. They've got enormous pride, and a feeling of history. It's a great mistake to go into the South and talk of the South as a region apart. It's important to talk of it as a part of the country. People talk about a 'Southern strategy'—well, it's about time, after a hundred years, when a Southerner like Dick Russell *could* be elected President."

I knew he believed this. Richard Russell had been one of the giants of the Senate, a man Nixon admired enormously. I had often heard him, in private conversations, cite Russell as a man who could have been President if it had not been for Northern bigotry against the South. The day before Nixon was to deliver the 1971 State of the Union address, Russell died. As we went over a draft of the speech, Nixon said he thought he would do an ad-lib introduction, mentioning Russell, and asking for a moment of silent prayer in his memory. He then remarked to me that he considered Russell "perhaps the greatest senator of our time. The only other one in his league was Taft. He was an enormously capable man—though completely Southern on the race question."

Continuing the conversation with Haldeman, Ehrlichman, and me, he went on to comment:

"The South is finally teaching the Democrats a lesson—not because they think I'm a racist, they know I'm not, but because they're proud, because they care about a strong national defense, about patriotism, about life-styles, about morality. I don't satisfy 'em on race. But Southerners have basically the same sort of characteristics as a lot of union leaders—a belief in abiding by the law, and respect for the presidency. Like George Meany—he was talking awhile back to some British trade union leaders, and when they questioned one of his actions, he said simply, 'I'd given the President my word.' If he gives his word, he keeps it."

And he defined what he saw as his "New American Majority":

"When you talk about the heartland, the South, about ethnic groups, the McGovern people make a great mistake in developing this in terms of antagonistic groups.

"The Roosevelt coalition was just that—a coalition. He played one against another—big city bosses, intellectuals, South, North. By contrast, our New American Majority appeals across the board —to Italians, Poles, Southerners, to the Midwest and New York— for the *same reasons*, and because of the same basic values. These are people who care about a strong United States, about patriotism, about moral and spiritual values. They may differ about what those moral and spiritual values ought to be, but they agree that you ought to have some. They're turned off on welfare, not because they don't want to be generous, but because they don't think the country can be built that way. They think there *are* elitists who want to take their money, and give it to people who won't work. These are not just Southern or ethnic notions—they're American to the core. The South, of course, leans more heavily toward a strong defense. They're not poisoned so much down there by the loud voices of the media. But even so, support in the South is not significantly higher on the great defense issues than it is among Polish- or Italian-Americans, for example.

"Where support on those issues is weak is in suburbia, and the universities. It's here you've got the softness.

"When we think about the march of the hardhats, and so forth —about those times when we had support for the really tough presidential decisions, including the first support for the May 8 bombing and mining—where did it come from? From business? No. From educators? Not one college president called me, because they have no guts, no character. No—maybe one or two do. But, generally, the support came from those areas the elitists look down their noses at—from the farmers, the ethnics, from cattlemen, and so forth. But thank God for it! If it hadn't come—if they hadn't provided it—America's foreign policy would be down the tube.

"The new majority is not coming from those Americans the pollsters urged we appeal to. They said our strength is in places like Evanston and San Marino. But we're doing no better there than before. Where we turned it around was in areas that were very different. Nobody's written this. The media say we're getting support from Catholics because of abortion. That's not true. The main point is that they can't bear the thought that 'the movement' has had it. Square America is coming back—to their great discomfiture."

(Nixon did, of course, get some support from Catholics because of his opponents' identification with abortion, and some support in the South because of his opponents' identification with busing. And he sought this support. But his basic point was valid: essentially, his appeal was to the "square" values, while the media tended to see the contest through the prism of their own obsession with the fashionable.)

"The point I'm making," he went on, "is, if people interpret this election in terms of just getting together a bunch of haters, it's not true. The real issues of the election are the ones like patriotism, morality, religion—not the material issues. If the issues were prices and taxes, they'd be for McGovern. On the economy, the Democrats will always promise more. We've done things labor doesn't like. We've held wages down. But they're supporting us for these other reasons."

He went on to ruminate about the divisions in the world: "McGovern says, 'I don't have to worry because the Russians wouldn't jeopardize our friendship.' It has to do with *interests*, not friendship." And divisions at home: "The students stopped blowing up college libraries because they couldn't get jobs. We've helped—by saying let's have more civility—but the professors haven't helped. They whine, they whimper, they blame Washington."

Then he came back to this central point:

"When you proceed on a soft-headed philosophy that if only people know each other the problems among them are going to evaporate, and they're going to love each other, you're finished. Black, white, old, young, men, women—all are different. Nations are different. Individuals are different. The idea that everybody's the same is crap. The Chinese doctors were different from Walter Tkach. Chou and Nixon, Brezhnev and Nixon are very different. It would be a dull world and a dull country if all were the same. But the great secret of the American experiment was that people and regions, though they were different, finally learned that the things that united them were more important than the things that divided them."

The President paused for a moment, reflecting, and then added: "And when you get right down to it that's the real secret of the Nixon policies, both foreign and domestic."

In January 1973 Herman Kahn, the guru of the Hudson Institute, met with a group of us in the Roosevelt Room of the White House to spin out some of his ideas on the forces moving the nation. Describing an "intellectual" as "a man who deals with ideas and gets most of his information from secondhand sources," Kahn noted that "the strength *and* the weakness of the intellectual is that he deals in ideas. The strength and the weakness of the average guy is that he can tell black from white—but he gets confused in the gray areas." Roughly 20 percent of Americans, he added, "achieved the ability to confuse night and day during the early 1960s."

The fashionable liberal, the denizen of that small community of workers with words and ideas described by Nick Thimmesch, is essentially a romantic. Like Kahn's intellectual, he depends on secondhand sources. He likes to think of himself as an idealist. He wants always to be in the vanguard of the new, properly dressed in the latest slogans, pressing the latest causes, always on the "humanitarian" side, speaking to the noblest side of man's nature.

He has a fascination with "leadership," and particularly with "strong leadership"—as long as he sees himself on the inside rather than the outside, the leader rather than the led. For a third of a century, he had grown accustomed to being on the inside. As a romantic, he craves glamour, excitement, action. He particularly craves social action, and especially the improvement of man by the remaking of whole societies. As the sculptor creates in clay, the social activist yearns to create with communities and with nations. But to make this possible, the people, like the sculptor's clay, must be kept malleable. And he, like the sculptor, must have the power to mold.

For a time, during the post-World War II years, the social activists had the whole world for a studio. There were old nations to be rebuilt and new ones to be created, all in the image of the activists' own twentieth century, Judeo-Christian, parliamentary ideal. For a time this glorious ambition ran parallel with the aims of the Marshalls and Achesons and Dulleses—those who saw the postwar world as a place of serious confrontation and potential collision between superpowers, and who believed that the strengthening of alliances, the deployment of forces, the use, where directly challenged, of military might, all were essential if the outward thrust of a new totalitarianism were to be checked and freedom preserved where it existed.

As a result, foreign policy was a less divisive issue in that period than it later became. Both the high-minded and the hard-nosed then believed in an active U.S. role in the world. The dismantling of the old colonial empires, and the struggle of the newly independent nations to achieve their first footings in the wake of that dismantling, made both groups actively internationalist, though for different reasons.

The one was messianic in its outlook, the other essentially defensive (though the two were not mutually exclusive. Dulles certainly had a strong streak of the messianic). The one was primarily concerned with human uplift, with bringing civilization to the unwashed, with spreading the gospel of Western democracy and indoor plumbing. The other was primarily concerned with the balance and disposition of power in the face of the expansionist ambitions of the Communist nations.

Through the 1940s and 1950s, the interests of both groups coincided more often than not. Rebuilding Europe from the devastation of World War II was a grand humanitarian effort, and at the same time an essential counterthrust to the Soviet challenge. Washington, Moscow, and Peking were vying for influence in the newly emerging nations; to the extent that those emerging nations could be won to Western ways, Western ideals, and Western methods, and integrated into the interdependencies of the Western economic system, they could be made more resistant to Soviet or Chinese political and military penetration. By the same token, only if they could be made resistant to that military and political penetration by the expanding Communist powers could their people hope to enjoy freedom. In deploying its power to check the Communist advance, the United States was using that power in the service of both its ideals and its interests.

Eventually, however, the two groups parted company.

One of the fashionable liberal's defining characteristics is his fascination with words. In general, he can accept *acts* that contravene his ideals more readily than he can accept *words* that contravene his ideals. He can accept with equanimity the results of Stalin's casual assertion that you can't make an omelet without breaking eggs—the eggs, in this case, being the lives of some 20 million men, women, and children—because the *words* behind which the Soviet legions march are those of liberal idealism; the lip service is to truth and justice and human uplift—and, in his world of words, lip service is real service. The gods have been appeased. If the gods demand the sacrifice of virgins, well, that's the way the cookie crumbles.

Not that he approves of totalitarianism. He would prefer that the eggs not be broken, the virgins not sacrificed. He reacts in genuine horror when the stark realities of a Gulag Archipelago are presented with the literary mastery of a Solzhenitsyn. At the drop of a petition, he stands ready to organize for the defense of imprisoned writers, even in the Soviet Union. But these flaws are not fatal flaws. Common cause is still possible because the system celebrates the words of human concern and of remaking society for the benefit of the least among us. He likes omelets, and deep in his heart there is even a trace of envy, for his own Mitty-ish dream would be to be the grandest social omeletmaker of all (without breaking any eggs, of course).

But the right-wing authoritarian evokes a sharply different response. For the right-wing regime spurns the rhetoric of liberal idealism. It lacks the grace and the style to mask its deeds in contrary words. It forces us to confront them as they are. If hypocrisy is the tribute vice pays to virtue, then, in this case, hypocrisy is also the tribute virtue demands of vice. The left-wing regime pays its tribute, but the right-wing does not. As the custodian of the world's virtue, the liberal idealist, wearing his garlands of words, must have this tribute.

As an example of this curious double standard in action, I have long been fascinated by the contrasting patterns of liberal reaction toward U.S. dealings with two European military dictators, both of them resistant to Soviet power, though in different ways and different degrees. Traffic with Spain's Franco was condemned as traffic with the devil, while traffic with Yugoslavia's Tito was hailed as being what any enlightened government would seek. In neither country were the people spectacularly free, though freedom was probably somewhat greater in Spain. Neither government was, as a matter of principle, unfriendly to the United States, though that of Spain was somewhat friendlier.

Tito runs afoul of the American liberal when he imprisons a writer like Milovan Djilas—but his cardinal sin in doing so is not that he imprisons his political opponents, or that he commits the violations of human liberty that a Djilas complains of. Rather, his cardinal sin is that he imprisons a *writer*. Tito can imprison all the farmers or shopkeepers he wishes to, as long as he says it is in the cause of human uplift and the liberation of the masses—as long as he pays that tribute that virtue demands of vice.

It always strikes me as curious that left-wing prisons liberate while right-wing prisons repress. Maybe it shows that God must love the inhabitants of left-wing prisons, because he made so many of them.

In America's relations with other countries, Nixon's primary concern was not their internal policies, or, if they were authoritarian, whether it was an authoritarianism of the right or of the left. Though their internal policies might properly be a moral concern of individual Americans, there was a distinction to be kept between moral force and military force, between what an individual might properly say and what a nation should do.

His own overriding concern was with establishing a structure of peace: that is, with curbing aggression, and creating a lasting set of restraints that would deter potential aggressors in the future. In World War II, the Western democracies fought toe-to-toe against three expansionist powers commonly identified as right-wing regimes: Nazi Germany, Fascist Italy, and Imperial Japan. But in the three decades since World War II, the expansionist powers have been those of the left. Right-wing dictatorships have posed no threat to their neighbors. Left-wing dictatorships, however, have posed military threats to their neighbors, from China to the Soviet Union to Cuba to North Vietnam. Maintaining international peace means, quite specifically, restraining expansion by force of arms. And maintaining peace, not imposing our own system on other nations, is the central purpose of America's alliances as well as of its arms. In terms of its relationship to the structure of peace, what matters is not whether another nation is right wing or left wing, or whether its institutions are democratic or authoritarian, but whether its aims are expansionist or nonexpansionist. If peace is to be preserved, the first requirement is for the world's nonexpansionist nations to make common cause in restraining its expansionist nations.

This sharp difference in perception of America's role—and of the morality of America's role—was one of the principal points of dispute between Nixon and his liberal critics.

In terms of international relations, the Nixon Revolution was not a contest over ultimate goals. He and the old elite both wanted peace. They both cherished this country's free political system, and hoped it could serve as a model for other nations which had not yet achieved it, or which had enjoyed it but lost it. But it did represent a conflict over priorities, over how peace could best be achieved, over what price should be paid to achieve it, and over the criteria for intervention in disputes within or among other nations.

Domestically, Nixon meant what he said about returning power to the people—and by the people he did not mean the self-appointed spokesmen of the people. He meant the people themselves. And the people themselves protested increasingly that they did not want to be pushed around, they did not want to be experimented with, they did not want to be taxed, they did not want to be herded, they did not want to be driven, they did not want to be lectured at and patronized and catered to.

For years, it was intellectually fashionable to say that Nixon's support was a mile wide and an inch deep—but this was never really true. He had millions of passionate supporters, just as he had millions of passionate detractors. But his supporters were mostly found in those places where the arbiters of intellectual fashion seldom ventured: out west of the Hudson and south of the Potomac, in the towns and cities of Middle America, in the broad reaches of Ohio and Indiana and Nebraska, among the farmers and the steelworkers and those who flew the flag from their front porches, and who joined the American Legion because they were proud to have served their country. They found in Richard Nixon not only a kindred spirit but also one whom they respected because he respected them, and because he insisted on their right to a decent respect from others; because he shared their belief in the basic goodness of America, and defended that belief; because he shared their belief in the need for a strong America and fought for that belief. Just as he touched basic, primitive emotions in those who hated him, so too did he touch basic, primitive emotions in those who defended him.

The first Nixon term saw the battle-lines form and harden for the Nixon Revolution. But it was the election of 1972 that threatened to make the transfer of power permanent. For that election produced a landslide of phenomenal scope: the largest popular vote margin in history (18 million), and, even in percentage terms (60.7), only a hairsbreadth behind the Roosevelt sweep of 1936 (60.8), and Johnson's crushing of Goldwater in 1964 (61). In carrying every state except Massachusetts and the District of Columbia, Nixon equaled Franklin Roosevelt's feat of sweeping all but Maine and Vermont; his support came from the East and the West, the North and the South, from old, young, blue-collar and white-collar and professional.

Much has been written of the hubris that overtook the Nixon administration in the wake of that phenomenal victory, and of our tendency to misread the size of the mandate: to overestimate the degree to which it could be regarded as a Nixon win rather than a McGovern loss. To some extent we did. Self-puffery is one of the motor responses of politics, and, for a political organization, maintaining morale is one of the first rules of survival. The election results were an enormous morale booster, and every effort was made to milk them as much as possible, and to use them to counter the arguments of those Nixon critics who for the previous four years had proclaimed themselves the authentic voice of the American people.

But if we overplayed the self-serving interpretations, both internally and externally, the fact remains that it was a stupendous victory; and that however inept McGovern might have been, however his extremism alienated many who would have preferred another Nixon challenger and finally chose Nixon as the lesser of two evils, McGovern's campaign was the quintessence of that value system we had been struggling against for four years. McGovern himself was a Western populist, not an Eastern "elitist." Nevertheless, he represented contemporary "liberalism" carried to its logical —or illogical—extension. If we accept the premise that the government owes everyone a living, then why *not* a gift of $1000, for heaven's sake? If we are going to make the military the universal scapegoat, then why *not* trim the Pentagon's budget by $30 billion? If we are going to damn the war and America's participation in it, then why *not* openly welcome a victory by the Viet Cong?

McGovern's sin was not extremism, so much as it was the logic of suggesting concretely that the federal government deliver on what the fashionable elite for years had been promising. But that very concreteness, by bringing the pieties into focus, scared the pants off of most of the American people.

There clearly was a conservative tide running in the country. In part, this was a reaction against the orgies of mindless violence that punctuated the late 1960s. It was also an upwelling of resistance to the new, more permissive moralities, and to the social engineering epitomized by the wholesale busing of schoolchildren to achieve an arbitrary racial balance—to impose through the schools an ideal of a multiracial society that the adult world had failed to achieve for itself. It was an eruption of resentment by a hard-pressed middle class that saw its taxes taken, and then parceled out to what its members perceived as the lazy and unworthy. In part, too, it was a reaction against a pace of change that threatened to become overwhelming, to submerge the individual, to carry him on an ever-swifter course to an unknown and therefore frightening destination. There was a gathering determination to cry "Whoa! Enough!"

Running through the currents of this conservative tide was another current, strong and fierce: a gut-level love of country, a pride in what America was and what America meant, and, in those tortured days of the late sixties and early seventies, an injured pride, as people saw the leaders of intellectual fashion sneer at what they had striven to achieve, disparage their dreams, mock their flag, and attack the undergirdings of the economic and social system which had made America the richest and freest nation in the whole experience of mankind.

To the extent that the Nixon victory in 1972 was an anti-McGovern vote, it was a vote against the targets of these Middle American resentments, a crying out for some measure of respect for their own values, their own interests, their own right to belong. It was a vote of no confidence in the style-setters.

For forty years, power had been accumulating in Washington, there to be exercised by the inheritors of the New Deal–activist tradition. The liberal activist needs the psychic satisfaction of being hailed for his power and celebrated for his benevolence. With his dominance over the world of ideas, he had the power to bestow the blessings of acceptability on those he approved, and to condemn or consign to oblivion those he disapproved. Thus he still had the power of self-celebration. But he also needs an arena in which to act, players to move about, resources to reallocate, and the power to compel the moves and command the allocation. He needs political power. And now Nixon was determined to disperse the power away from Washington—and thus to leave the players of the power-game with no pawns to move. It was a specter to recall that plaintive exchange between Glendower and Hotspur:

Glendower: "I can call spirits from the vasty deep."

Hotspur: "Why, so can I, or so can any man; But will they come when you do call for them?"

On a more philosophical plane, of course, the debate was both profound and important, and by no means susceptible to the glib or black-and-white answer: To what extent and in what matters *should* the nation act as a nation in response to a single articulated national will, in behalf of a single, focused national goal? And to what extent should it preserve and enhance the diversities of a pluralistic society, with the right of each community, of each segment of the society to be different, and, by extension, to be wrong—to make its own mistakes rather than have the mistakes of others imposed upon it?

As with most questions so sweeping in scope, the answer would have to be found in a combination of approaches. The demands of national direction and local option would have to be fought out, accommodated, compromised, meshed, and the result would not be clean or clear. But the direction of change was clear: a shift from homogeneity and toward heterogeneity, from paternalism and toward individualism, from national direction and toward local option, from the bureaucratic process and toward the political process, in all its multiple forms, variations and responses. For the armies of those who had grown accustomed to commanding the Washington heights, and from those heights directing the battles across the grand sweep of the national plain, it would mean, if not technological unemployment, then at least a severe and wrenching deprivation. It would require a yielding of power by those grown accustomed to power.

OF TWO MINDS

On Tuesday, April 16, 1974, I was having lunch with Presidential Counselor Dean Burch in the White House's Conference Dining Room, when one of the red-coated Navy stewards brought a telephone to the table.[1] Al Haig was calling me from Florida. A major constitutional collision was building over the House Judiciary Committee's escalating demands for more and more tapes of presidential conversations. Now, Haig told me, the President planned a bold stroke: after nine months of fighting to maintain the privacy of those recorded conversations, he was going to go public with them himself. The latest committee subpoena demanded forty-two additional tapes. Nixon was going to turn over transcripts of all the relevant portions of those tapes—all having anything to do with presidential knowledge or presidential action with regard to Water-

---

1. The basement level of the West Wing—the "West Basement"—contains a dining room for the staff, called, in Navy terminology, the "Staff Mess." Early in the Nixon administration a second dining room was added, somewhat more plush—tablecloths instead of place mats, for example—less crowded and more exclusive, its membership limited to the Vice-President, the cabinet and about twenty of the top-ranked senior staff. Sometimes it was taken over for special luncheon meetings, but its name of "Conference Dining Room" was largely a euphemism. When I had guests, I normally took them to the Conference Dining Room. When I went over by myself, I usually joined the large round table in the regular Staff Mess. Once the Conference Dining Room was in operation, however, several of the senior staff shunned the regular Staff Mess entirely. Both were operated by the Navy, and staffed with Navy stewards, as had been the custom since Franklin Roosevelt's time. Camp David is also a naval facility, established by FDR during World War II.

gate—and at the same time release those transcripts to the public, while announcing firmly that that was it: this many and no more; the hemorrhage has to stop somewhere. He had decided that the only way to stop it was to go over the committee's heads to the public, even at the expense of publishing the transcripts, warts and all. These would answer the central questions: What did the President know, when did he know it, what did he do when he learned about it? He planned to announce the move in a speech to the nation from the Oval Office. Haig said that Ron Ziegler, who also was in Florida, had been briefing his assistant, Frank Gannon, on what Nixon wanted to say, and that Gannon—who was in Washington—could give me a fill-in that afternoon. Nixon, Haig, Ziegler, and the rest of the Florida party were to return to Washington that evening. Time was short. Nixon wanted to make the announcement the following Monday, April 22, the eve of the committee subpoena's due date.

For the next two weeks I was to live with the speech, with the transcripts, and with the continuing question of whether we should go ahead with their release. (It quickly became clear that there was no way they could be ready by the twenty-second. The target date was therefore moved to the following Monday, the twenty-ninth, with the committee meanwhile informed that the President would make a submission in response to its subpoena—though not what form his response would take.)

My own initial reactions to the idea of disclosure were mixed. I felt strongly, on both practical and constitutional grounds, that the principle of presidential confidentiality should be maintained. This would be a serious breach. By doing it on his own terms and at his own initiative, however, he at least would preserve the essential constitutional principle that none of the three branches of government can compel either of the others to disclose confidential communications against its will. To me, this was at the heart of the doctrine of separation of powers in a system of coequal branches. A congressional committee might *request* records of private conversations between the President and his principal aides. But to *demand* those records was, to me, as outrageous as it would have been for the President to demand the records of private conversations between the Speaker of the House and the rest of the Democratic leadership. If Nixon had ever had the effrontery to make such a demand—whatever the provocation—cries of "dictatorship" would have scorched the paint off the White House walls. The moment any branch can make and enforce such demands on either of the others, they cease to be coequal, and the balances that have sustained our system of government since the Constitution was ratified are destroyed.

On a practical level, presidents have to be able to talk freely with their aides and others in the firm expectation that the privacy of those talks will be maintained. There is no other way they can get the information they need, explore all alternatives, candidly discuss personalities, let off the steam that builds up under the pressures of the office, or plan the often devious maneuvers that are an essential part of the job. Presidents not only need this privacy for themselves; they also have to be able to guarantee it for those they talk with. If the price of such privacy is letting an occasional misdeed go unpunished—as had always happened quite routinely—this is a small price to pay for enabling the presidency to function.

At this point, I still had not seen the transcripts or heard the tapes, except for a brief excerpt from one of the tapes that lawyer J. Fred Buzhardt, Jr., had played for the cabinet to show what they sounded like. From what I knew of the events and had heard about the tapes, I doubted that they were going to be overwhelmingly conclusive one way or the other. For one thing, I was well familiar with Nixon's habit, in conversation, of pursuing one avenue and then another, exploring hypotheses, putting questions in the form of statements and statements in the form of questions, thinking aloud, giving vent to irritation one moment and then catching himself the next, playing to his various audiences—and I shuddered at the thought of what might be on the tapes of his conversations with Colson. I was also familiar with the way the major media operated. If there were anything that could be excerpted, lifted out of context, sensationalized, and used against him, it would be. Whatever else they might contain, the transcripts were certain to provide a rich cornucopia of precisely such excerptable gems. And those excerptable gems were bound to be damaging.

Thus, I began with the assumption that publishing the transcripts would be a high-risk venture, quite apart from the breach of confidentiality. But we were playing for high stakes, and we had reached a point at which such risks might be necessary. Further, on March 6 Nixon had ordered that all materials previously provided to the special prosecutor should be turned over to the Judiciary Committee. These included nineteen tapes—including the tape of the crucial "cancer on the Presidency" conversation between Nixon and Dean —as well as more than seven hundred documents from private White House files. The committee already was busily engaged in selectively leaking those materials. I was pretty sure the whole would be better than the selectively leaked parts.

In working on the speech, I began plowing through the transcripts. What came through to me from these, overall, was a picture of a beleaguered President confronted with a situation that could destroy his presidency, trying to find a way out of it, trying to do what he had to do, but to do it at the least possible cost to trusted aides and valued associates whose own involvement had come, often, either accidentally or incidentally as they too tried to contain the damage, and trying at the same time to minimize the political damage in a bitterly adversary climate in which his troubles were being exploited to the hilt by vengeful opportunists in the Congress and the media.

The situation he confronted was not one in which I expected him to be reciting from Blackstone, quoting Sophocles, or lecturing his aides on the finer points of public philosophy.

I also thought they showed very clearly that during this period he was groping for information, trying to find out what had happened, trying to assess liabilities, getting different stories from different people, all of whom had interests of their own to protect, and, quite properly, resisting pressures to prejudge cases that had yet to go through the criminal justice system. (Three years earlier, in a slip of the tongue, Nixon inadvertently referred to mass murderer Charles Manson as "guilty" before Manson's trial was completed. Despite a quick correction, his critics made it a cause célèbre, and continued ever after to harp on it as an example of Nixon's supposed disdain for due process. During Watergate, however, those same critics insistently demanded that he pronounce the guilt of his aides before that guilt had been tried.)

We continued going up the hill and down again on the basic question of whether to go ahead with the original plan to make the transcripts public. As he typically did with any major decision, Nixon kept weighing and reassessing it.

At noon on Friday the twenty-sixth, Haig and Ziegler stopped by my cabin at Camp David. They had just come from meeting with the President. His inclination now, they reported, was to go ahead with it—"This is it," Haig commented. "We've got to bring it to a head. This is as grave an issue as we've had."

We talked about the speech, Ziegler arguing that it should focus on four basic things: (1) The shifting charges, and how every time evidence was provided to disprove one charge, a new charge was substituted, together with a new and more sweeping demand for tapes and documents; (2) "An honest story of the tapes—how it's sort of a *Rashomon* theory, with different people talking from totally different perspectives. The President recognized the political and the human sides, and different people were telling him different things"; (3) The constitutional separation of powers; and (4) "Why he's making them public—and a ringing call for an end to it all."

In discussing the transcripts themselves, Ziegler suggested, we should not only state what they show, "but also use examples of how sections can be taken out of context to prove any theory—but they have to be taken in their entirety."

Later that day Ziegler stopped by again. The question of whether we were right to go ahead with releasing the transcripts to the public still nagged at all of us. He had been thinking about it some more.

We were all worried, not so much about the overall thrust of the transcripts, as about the tone of some, the "expletives deleted," those excerptable nuggets we knew would blossom into headlines. Now Ziegler suggested that the public perception of Nixon's involvement centered on John Dean's Senate testimony about two meetings, those of September 15, 1972—the first Nixon-Dean meeting, with Haldeman also present, on the day the original seven Watergate defendants were indicted—and March 21, 1973. One of Ziegler's assistants, Diane Sawyer, had put together a detailed analysis of the March 21 transcript, showing how much Dean concealed from Nixon at that meeting about Dean's own involvement in illegal cover-up activities. Now Ziegler argued that "from the transcripts we can see that the President's confusion post-March 21 was because Dean didn't level with him. The only way—it seems to me— that we're going to make the *emotional* case is to demonstrate *why* the President acted the way he did after March 21. And it seems to me the only way we can do this is to show what Diane showed— that Dean was as deceptive with the President on March 21 as he was with the American people and the Ervin committee about those conversations on September 15 and March 21." That, he said, "seems to me to argue irrefutably for putting out the transcripts of September 15 and March 21." But an alternative to publishing the entire batch of transcripts, he suggested, might be to get several key congressional leaders in, to show them how Dean had acted, and then make just those two transcripts public—so that the congressional leaders could help focus public attention on the fact that in his testimony Dean did systematically and consistently twist the facts to load them against Nixon.

Though we continued to explore alternatives, and though we continued to debate the wisdom of making public the full batch of transcripts, we kept moving forward on the assumption that we would. For me, the argument kept getting back to one basic fact:

that the Judiciary Committee already had those nineteen tapes, including the key ones that the special prosecutor had gone to court for. On the basis of the committee's behavior so far, it seemed to me as certain as sunrise that the worst parts would be systematically and selectively leaked, with the worst possible spin put on each—so that the question was not *whether* they were going to be made public, but how and by whom.

My own prediction of the transcripts' impact turned out to be disastrously wrong.

I expected a strong favorable reaction to Nixon's Monday-night speech, April 29, announcing his plan to release them, and spelling out his own account of what he had done and why in trying to come to grips with Watergate. On this I was right. The public response was strongly positive.

I then expected a strong second-wave negative reaction, as the media pored through for all the worst things and gloatingly bannered them, out of context. On this I was also right.

Where I went totally wrong was in forecasting a third-wave reaction, as the public began wading through the transcripts in their totality. This reaction never came. We had gambled on their eventually being taken as a totality, the good and the bad together, and read with some understanding of the pressures at work, the forces in contention, the stakes at issue. But this never happened. People were shocked, dismayed, appalled, overwhelmed, angry, disillusioned. Nixon's critics crowed and his supporters cringed.

Predictably, *The New York Times* saw in the transcripts "the ethical decay that pervaded the Oval Office." But papers which had been former Nixon supporters were, in this case, even harsher. To the *Chicago Tribune*, they showed him "immoral," "inhumane," "devious," "vacillating," "profane," and the "miscalculation" of releasing them "demonstrated an essential Nixon defect—an insensitivity to the standards of ethics and morality that Americans expect of their leaders." Calling on Nixon to resign, the *Tribune* declared that although the transcripts "may clear Mr. Nixon of direct complicity in the Watergate burglary and the early stages of the cover-up, nobody of sound mind can read them and continue to think that Mr. Nixon has upheld the standards and dignity of the Presidency which he proclaimed himself as a candidate in 1960. He hoped that, if elected, a mother or father would be able to 'look at the man in the White House . . . and say, "Well, there is a man who maintains the kind of standards personally that I would like my child to follow." ' " The *Norfolk Virginian-Pilot* declared that "no one can read the edited transcript of the White House tapes without being saddened and sickened by them. The documentation of the moral squalor within the White House is totally unrelieved. . . . The Oval Office was a moral pigsty."

Man-in-the-street reaction frequently followed similar lines, with those who had opposed Nixon all along feeling vindicated, and those who had supported him feeling betrayed. And what sparked the most violent reaction was not what the transcripts showed that Nixon did, but what, in those tortured private moments, he said. With the privacy of the Oval Office invaded, its dignity was stripped away.

(Interestingly, much of the most strident reaction was to the things that were *not* there: to the absence of that exhalted rhetoric people had come to associate with the presidency; to the lack of moralizing; and to those deleted expletives. People tended to let their imaginations run wild on the deletions, and soon were accusing him of profaning the Oval Office with language worse than a longshoreman's. It was a case of the mind filling in the blanks, and then seeing the picture with the blanks filled in.)

In *Breach of Faith*, Theodore H. White presents an impassioned thesis that Nixon's "true crime" was that "he destroyed the myth that binds America together."

In White's view, certain basic unifying myths are central to the American experience, and at the heart of these is the myth of the presidency: that the office exalts the man, that at that apex of power stands one person dedicated to the law, who will brook no breach of the law. This myth, this faith, transforms ordinary mortals into extraordinary leaders, and serves as symbol and inspiration for millions of Americans struggling with the meannesses and pettinesses of everyday life.

Americans do shroud their presidents in myth, and presidents wrap themselves in myth. To the extent that White's thesis is valid, publication of the transcripts might be said to have been Nixon's ultimate offense. Though what they laid bare was not particularly new to the presidency—as the post-Nixon revelations about prior presidencies have made amply evident to those willing to confront the evidence—it was new to public perceptions of the presidency. It was difficult for the old myths to coexist with the new realities as shown in the transcripts. The question of which is healthier—to preserve the myth, or to reduce the office to human terms—offers no easy answer. We do need unifying myths. We need ideals that enlist the spirit and summon forth the noblest side of human nature. But we also need to be able to synthesize the various parts of the human experience, and we need the kind of faith that can survive the buffetings of an imperfect world. Myth and illusion provide a shaky foundation for this kind of faith.

Publication of the transcripts was only one of many cases in which we badly misjudged what the public reaction would be to various Watergate events, underestimating the shock effect they were going to have. Reflecting on it now, I think our failure to gauge the reaction in advance was somewhat akin to my own puzzlement at the public reaction to President Kennedy's murder. I could understand the grief, the shock, but not the hysteria—certainly not the stunned, even panic-stricken sense that such an occurrence was simply *unthinkable,* and that it therefore must prove the nation was corrupt, evil, falling apart, in the grip of the damned.

Certainly, if anything about the presidency is utterly, totally thinkable, it is the prospect of assassination. Four presidents—more than one in ten—have actually been assassinated. Very nearly successful attempts have been made on the lives of several others. The fact that assassination is so very thinkable is precisely why presidents have Secret Service protection, and all the elaborate security that goes with it. Assassination is a danger presidents live with, the way pilots live with the danger of crashes and soldiers live with the danger of dying in battle. Statistically, the risk to presidents is greater than it is to pilots or soldiers—a higher percentage of presidents get killed.

But this is a logical answer; the national hysteria that followed the Kennedy assassination was an emotional spasm of the sort that sweeps all logic before it.

It was in September 1975 that a chance conversation one morning first introduced me to a phenomenon that I think goes a long way toward explaining these patterns of reaction. Usually, three or four mornings a week, I drop in at the Booeymonger, a small delicatessen across the street from my house, to pick up a copy of *The Washington Post* and browse through it over a cup of coffee. The Booey is a young, friendly, informal neighborhood place, in atmosphere sort of a Georgetown equivalent of the old-fashioned country store, where the regular customers and the staff all chat with one another on a first-name basis. Another Booey regular, a friend and neighbor of mine for several years, is Dr. Norman Tamarkin, a prominent young Washington psychiatrist. (Ironies abound. Not only is my morning reading at the Booey our old nemesis, *The Washington Post,* but Dustin Hoffman—who played the Carl Bernstein role in *All the President's Men*—stayed at Norman's house

during the movie's Washington filming, and had breakfast at the
Booey every morning. But that was before I had gotten into the
Booey habit.) Anyway, Norman and I were both in the Booey that
September morning, having coffee, when somehow or other he happened to mention to me the experimental work being done on lateral
specialization of the brain—that is, the separate and distinctly different functioning of the brain's left and right halves. It was new to
me. Intrigued, I kept pressing him for more details, and the more he
told me about it the more fascinated I became. It just might, I
thought, hold the key to a lot of the seemingly contradictory, and
often irrational, ways in which politicians and public react to one
another. More particularly, I thought it might help explain both
Nixon himself and the intensely emotional responses that both he
and Watergate triggered in so many of his critics.

Norman lent me a couple of books from his library, describing
and evaluating some of the research that has been done. Another
friend with whom I discussed it also alerted me to Maya Pines's
book,[2] which, in popular fashion, deals with the same research.
Going through them became an exciting voyage of discovery. While
the right-brain–left-brain phenomenon hardly explains everything,
I think it does throw an important new light both on the events we
have all lived through, and on the differing ways in which we perceive those events.

It turns out that the major, conscious portion of our brain—the
cerebrum—is divided by a solid membrane into two distinctly separate halves. Physiologically, the two halves function in different
ways. They are adapted for different modes of thought. In some
situations one side dominates, while in other situations the other
side dominates. Some people tend more to be guided by the left
brain, while others tend more to be guided by the right brain. But
we all are guided in various degrees—and in varying ways—by
both.

One of the unsolved mysteries is precisely how the two halves interact with one another. Apparently they sometimes act independently, sometimes act in conflict, and sometimes act in conjunction.
They are specialized not only in terms of function but also in terms
of what is called "cognitive mode." The left half of the brain (which
controls the right half of the body) is organized for a linear, logical,
analytical mode of thought. The right half (which controls the left
half of the body) is specialized for sensory, holistic, gestalt-type
perceptions and reactions.

2. *The Brain Changers: Scientists and the New Mind Control* (New York,
1973).

Though emotional responses are actually triggered from a separate, tiny part of the brain called the hypothalamus, in conscious terms—in terms of cerebral function—they tend to be associated primarily with the right half of the brain. The right half also is specialized for such functions as spatial relations, and music, while our analytical processes are carried out by the left brain.

The two halves are quite distinct. As one of the leading authorities, Dr. David Galin, has put it, "Not only are they separate minds, but because of their specialization they are different, not duplicate minds."[3] The relative dominance of one or the other half differs among individuals, and even in the same individual the relative dominance of the two differs from one situation to another. There seems to be a more or less constant tension between the two.

A great deal of our developing knowledge about the separate halves of the brain has come from experiments with patients in which one or the other side has been severely damaged, or in which the connection between the two—the *corpus callosum*—was severed through surgery, a technique sometimes resorted to as a treatment for extreme cases of epilepsy. That surgical separation requires the two halves to function independently. Therefore, their separate ways of functioning can be studied independently.

One thing researchers have found is that in a split-brain patient, one side will sometimes direct an action, and the other side will then stop it. For example, one case is frequently cited in which a person's left hand (controlled by the right brain) picked up a knife and started to attack someone else, and then his right hand (controlled by the left brain) grasped his left arm and forcibly restrained it.

The right brain is musical, the left brain verbal. A patient with left-brain damage may still be able to sing the lyrics of a remembered song, yet not be able to use the same words in a sentence.

The left brain analyzes, while the right brain synthesizes. The left brain processes information in a linear, sequential mode, while the right brain simultaneously assimilates large numbers of unarticulated impressions. When we have a "gut feeling" about something, what we are experiencing is a right-brain response. We cannot put it into words because it does not come from that part of the brain that uses words.

Specialization between the two halves develops during a child's early years, and as the two become increasingly specialized, excellence in one area of specialty—either the verbal, analytical, sequen-

3. *Archives of General Psychiatry*, October 1974.

tial logic of the left brain or the musical, spatial, intuitive perception of the right brain—often tends to inhibit excellence in the other.

Many people, early in life, develop into "left-brain" types, functioning primarily in a verbal-analytical mode, or "right-brain" types, functioning through primarily nonverbal modes of perception and expression. Dr. Galin sets up categories of "convergent" and "divergent" thinkers:

"Convergent types are those who excel at rational analysis but do relatively poorly in open-minded tests requiring mental fluency and imaginativeness. Convergers tend to specialize in the physical sciences and divergers tend toward the arts. These 'types' are consistent with the cognitive specializations of the left and right hemispheres."[4]

Apparently the two halves of the brain represent separate conscious systems, through which we see the world in different ways and respond in different manners.

One of the remaining mysteries is how the two sides interact, in normal people, in the course of normal activities. There are theories that they alternate, that they synthesize, that they compete—with the patterns perhaps depending both on the degree of one side's dominance in the particular individual and on the nature of the triggering activity. Galin hypothesizes:

If the usual condition then is either alternation between the two modes, or parallel but independent consciousness with one of them dominating overt behavior, what factors determine which hemisphere will be "on"? Which will gain control of the shared functions and dominate overt behavior? There are two factors suggested by experiments performed with split-brain monkeys and humans. One could be called "resolution by speed"; the hemisphere that solves the problem first gets to the output channel first. This seems the most likely explanation for the observations in the human patients that "when a hemisphere is intrinsically better equipped to handle some task, it is also easier for that hemisphere to dominate the motor pathways. . . ."

A second factor determining which hemisphere gets control could be called "resolution by motivation"; the one who cares more about the outcome pre-empts the output. . . .

Einstein once explained that his own creative ideas—his theoretical breakthroughs—came to him not in words, but in nonverbal images: "A thought comes and I may try to express it in words afterward." It would seem that in some manner, he had mastered

4. Galin, op. cit.

the synthesis of left- and right-brain functions—enlisting the creativity of the right brain, its holistic, conceptual, intuitive strength, and then translating what that produced into the verbal, analytical mode of the left brain in a way that changed the world.

Robert M. Pirsig's book[5] became something of a cult object in recent years, but I also found it quite a remarkable tour de force—at once an allegorical novel and an excursion through the history of philosophy. In effect, Pirsig's protagonist is seeking a synthesis of those values, those perceptions, that are represented by the two halves of the human brain. He describes them as the "romantic" and the "classic" sides of our nature. The romantic mode "is primarily inspirational, imaginative, creative, intuitive. Feelings rather than facts predominate." The classic style, on the other hand, "is straightforward, unadorned, unemotional, economical and carefully proportioned." Motorcycle riding is romantic; motorcycle maintenance is classic. To the romantic, mechanical drawings or electronic schematics are dull, uninteresting. To the classic, the romantic appears frivolous, irrational, shallow, primarily interested in pleasure-seeking. "And so in recent times," notes Pirsig, "we have seen a huge split develop between a classic culture and a romantic counter-culture—two worlds growingly alienated and hateful toward each other with everyone wondering if it will always be this way, a house divided against itself. No one wants it really —despite what his antagonists in the other dimension might think."

As we learn more about the interaction of the two halves of the brain, we almost certainly are going to come closer to a resolution of those dichotomies which have seemed so deeply rooted in the human experience, and which have fascinated philsophers through the ages: the classic and the romantic, the Yang and the Yin, the linear and the nonlinear, the intellectual and the "sensuous," the reasoned and the intuitive, objective reality and subjective reality. The key, of course, is that both are necessary, both are real, both are essential elements of the human experience. Each, in its own way, represents "truth"—though only part of the truth.

The same dichotomies also lie at the heart of our political processes, which are a combination of intellectual and emotional responses to the world, to the community, to particular leaders, to our own perceived needs and wishes, and to our concept of the possible and the desirable.

In contemporary political terms, the "romantic," right-brain

5. *Zen and the Art of Motorcycle Maintenance: An Inquiry into Values* (New York, 1974).

response tends more frequently to be found on the liberal side of the spectrum, and the "classic," left-brain response tends to be found more on the conservative side. Relatively more artists are liberal, and relatively more engineers are conservative. But the distinction also cuts sharply across ideological divisions. Abortion, pornography, and gun control, for example, are issues that arouse intense passions on both sides, with conservative opponents of all three tending to argue their case in highly emotional terms. These clearly arouse an instinctive, intuitive, right-brain reaction. (I happen to be pro-abortion, anti-censorship, and pro-gun control, and sometimes run into a buzzsaw when discussing these issues with conservative friends.)

Against this background, it becomes easier to see how one person's falsehood can be another's truth—how, in fact, a great deal of our public debate really represents a clash among competing truths: among realities differently perceived, because they are perceived in different modes.

Those of us conditioned to discipline our emotions are going to react differently than will those conditioned to "let it all hang out." Our response to political events, or to political personalities, is going to depend in large measure on whether we perceive "truth" to lie more nearly at the end of a progression of linear logic, or in intuitive, gestalt visions.

Between "intuitive reality" and "empirical reality" there *are* competing perceptions. The one who perceives a "truth" intuitively is fully as certain of its reality as is the one who observes it empirically, but the two will see it differently. Neither pattern is necessarily wholly "right" or wholly "wrong"; as the two sides of the brain are different, so the two patterns of response are different, reacting in differently programmed ways to different *kinds* of reality.

The 1960s were essentially a romantic decade, and a decade of expressionism—of emotional release—and the generation that came of age in the sixties came of age conditioned to see "truth" not in terms of observable, hard facts, or of laboratory experiments or linear logic, but rather in terms of emotional "truth"—what seemed right because it felt right, what felt right because it made them feel good, what pleased the senses, what excited the libido or gratified their hungers. Theirs was a right-brain age—aural, tactile, sensory, holistic. It collided explosively with the "classic" left-brain, linear-logical forces Nixon represented, which were trying to reimpose the basic disciplines of the fifties and before. We viewed their charges of "repression" as absurd cant. And yet, in a sense, from their perspective, we *did* represent "repression" in that we tried to discipline—to "repress"—the role of emotional responses, to subordinate these to the dominance of logic; and to those conditioned to regard emotional expressiveness as the highest good, this indeed *is* repression.

Viewed in this light, the 1960s admonition, "Never trust anyone over thirty," has a certain—if you will excuse the term—logic to it. The over-thirty people tended to see things differently, to perceive reality differently, because they were formed in an age when the old perceptions still were dominant. It was not that the person over thirty was inherently untrustworthy, but rather, from the standpoint of the under thirty, that he could not be trusted to see the world in the way that the 1960s generation saw it.

The 1960s were the time of Timothy Leary, of LSD, a time when life was something to be *felt* through the insistent pulse of a rhythmic beat, something to be *seen* through the phantasmagoric kaleidoscope of hallucinogens, something to be *experienced* in a spiritual way rather than lived in a material way.

By and large, those critics who viewed Nixon most harshly viewed the sixties generation most favorably (I hesitate to say sycophantically, not because it would be inaccurate, but because it would be pejorative). This was no coincidence. Nixon represented the antithesis of that experience. The Nixon Revolution was the opposite of the Youth Revolution.

Just as the human mind is not complete without both of its halves, the political experience is not complete without both its classic and its romantic components.

A society needs those values the romantic brings to it, just as a person needs those qualities governed by the brain's right side. These let us see the Mona Lisa as more than just another pretty face, and the majesty of the Alps as more than something Hannibal had to get his elephants across. This side gives our lives depth, humanity, meaning. But the other side puts food in our stomach and clothes on our backs. If we are to make sense out of our political process, we have to learn to accommodate both—to give the spirit its due, and also to render unto reason what is reason's.

The rationalist revolution that had its roots, intellectually, in eighteenth-century France and England, in a sense reached its full flower in twentieth-century-industrial America. A technocratic society is one that enshrines the rational process, the mathematical and physical realities, and that requires the submergence of emotional needs to the rigid forms of a structure of rewards and penalties devised to serve ends that celebrate the triumph of pure reason. Against this, the emotional side of our nature is likely to be in more or less constant rebellion. Thus, when the banners of anarchy are raised, or when the cry of revolt is sounded, those who feel themselves oppressed by this "antihuman" structure are going to flock to the cause—as happened in the 1960s. The soul is going to cry out for release from its bonds.

Like the more violent outbursts of the same era, the sensitivity explosion of the 1960s was a right-brain rebellion against left-brain dominance: it was an effort—probably both valid and valuable in individual, human terms—to let the whole person emerge, and to accommodate the sometimes suffocatingly structured complexities of modern society to man's essential humanity.

However, there is a danger inherent in any movement that draws its strength essentially from our emotional selves: the natural drive of emotion is to displace reason, to break down the barriers that reason necessarily places in the way of our own gratification.

Linear logic is a learned discipline. In our personal development, we respond to things emotionally before we learn to respond to them logically. Because the romantic is an instinctive response, the logical a learned response, the logical component of our minds, like Avis, has to work harder in order to prevail.

The concept of deferred gratification is a discipline we come to accept only as we mature, and this is central to the classic approach. Our romantic nature rebels against it: we want what we want, and we get mad at whatever stands in the way of having it now. But our logical side tells us that the candy now is going to spoil our dinner, that we have to put that dollar in the savings account rather than spend it at the circus, that the only way to get inflation under control is to cut the federal budget where it hurts. In each of these cases, the classic side is the cautionary voice telling us, not that what we want is bad, but that if we indulge that wish now we are going to be sorry for it later: that over the course of our whole lifetime we will be better off if we give more attention to the *processes* on which we depend for our ultimate well-being, and rein in our passions, our hungers, our demands for gratification now.

The classic is more disposed than the romantic to compromise, to seek a workable accommodation, rather than pursue an unachievable vision. The romantic sees this as a sell-out; logic tells us it is a means of achieving the greatest possible good. The notion that politics is the art of the possible is a classic concept. The True Believer is a romantic.

The "myths" Teddy White accuses Nixon of destroying belong

to the romantic vision. The Kennedy assassination had the disorienting impact it did because, for a terrible moment, it shattered the romantic vision. To the romantic, myths *are* realities, and often the most important realities. The myth can be life itself. Which brings us back to the transcripts.

In miscalculating the impact of many Watergate events—including release of the transcripts—we probably failed to give sufficient weight to the centrality of this romantic vision. And we certainly failed—or at least I did—to anticipate the extent to which these would send persons who cherished the myths into a sort of right-brain shock, producing the visceral, intensely emotional reactions they did. In the wake of that shock, efforts to discuss them rationally were in vain. It was as if the doors of the mind had been slammed shut. There was a *corpus callosum* between us and our audience.

The same differing perceptions carried over into the realm of social policy.

The romantic tends toward a politics of abstract idealism, preferably couched in utopian rhetoric—a "politics of compassion," as many would assert, or, as Hubert Humphrey rather unsuccessfully tried to make it, a "politics of joy." The classic's is more a politics of *process:* a primary attention to means, to the machinery of doing things, to the creation of a set of rules and procedures that can establish a self-regulating system. It reflects Stephen Hess's comment that Republicans tend to be fascinated with structure.

However, our romantic, right-brain side is not all soaring idealism. Emotional responses cut both ways. Like the split-brain patient whose right brain told him to pick up a knife before his left brain told him to restrain it, they also encompass resentment, rage, hatred. Just as the sixties were a romantic decade, the riots of the 1960s were the quintessence of the politics of emotion.

Essentially, the left brain is our disciplinarian. Its learned, linear logic serves as a check on those instinctive, sometimes infantile desires that the right brain presses upon us, and thereby makes a civil society possible. As with any imposed discipline, we sometimes rebel against it—in thought and word, even if not in action. When the tax bill comes, we curse the tax collector and kick the mailbox (right brain), but then we pay it (left brain). The greater the pressure of intense discipline in one area, the greater the pressure for emotional release in another: for example, the businessman who comes home from a particularly hard day at the office, explodes at his children, and sends them to bed crying. The children may have triggered his outburst, but the office pressure caused it

—and his real target was not the children but the pressure. While eighteenth-century France gave us the Age of Reason, it also gave us the bloody excesses of the French Revolution.

One of Nixon's most remarkable personal characteristics was the iron self-discipline that kept him welded so ferociously to his tasks. When he proclaimed that in a crisis he was the coolest one in the room, in effect he was saying that he had mastered the technique of separating emotion from reason, and laying emotion aside while dealing in a coldly rational way with a coldly rational problem.

In fact, this often was his way: and in the meticulous, far-sighted planning of maneuvers vis-à-vis the Soviet Union, for example, he did it brilliantly. But there often were times when he did yield to emotion, and here, frequently, was where he got into trouble.

When the dark side fought the light side, it was often that repressed, right-brain emotion fighting to be set free. And when the light side set up fail-safe mechanisms to keep the dark side in check, it was the stern left-brain taskmaster saying no.

However much we might try, we cannot be automatons on everything. In Nixon's case, he not only rigorously disciplined his thought and actions on major policy questions but he also felt the need constantly to be "on stage" in his public appearance—in the appearance, that is, of every aspect of person and presidency that was exposed to the public. He denied himself most of the little releases that other presidents found. Johnson railed at his staff, bellowing through the corridors of the West Wing, alternately damning and praising. Truman had his all-night poker parties. Eisenhower took his frustrations out on a golf ball, or in those explosions of temper that the public seldom saw but his staff often witnessed. Yet some form of release is necessary. Presidents deal with larger quanta of pressure than most humans ever experience, and with pressures that are constant and unrelenting. The pressures alternate not between high and low, but between high and higher. And there are outer limits to the amount of self-discipline that the human spirit can take. So Nixon sounded off, in the privacy of his office, to trusted members of his staff—and had the bad judgment to record it on tape.

Ironically, if Nixon had allowed himself a more open show of emotion—a greater spontaneity, including spontaneity of anger, unapologetically—it probably would have been accepted. What inspired distrust was the discontinuity between his professions of total control, total calm, total dispassion, and those rare public examples that belied the pretense.

Now that the tape transcripts have become part of the national folklore, a more important distorting factor has been introduced: popular impressions have become shaped more by what was *said* in those private discussions than by what was *done*—or, more significantly, not done. Often, these were his emotional safety valves—the occasions when he could let off steam, bring out his resentments, let loose locker-room bravado about how he was going to "get" his "enemies," safe in the knowledge that calmer heads (including his own the next morning) would prevail, and that the fail-safe mechanisms he himself had set up would work. ("Sure I have a temper," he once commented, much later. "Publicly, I control it pretty well. Privately, I sometimes blow off some steam.") The fact that these private comments often stood in stark contrast to his public actions should hardly be surprising. If public officials all were judged by what they said privately in anger rather than by what they did on reflection, every one of them would be impeached, unless he were tarred and feathered first.

But that, of course, is a left-brain argument.

THE OLD COLLEGE TRY

"It's disgusting to see the Vice-President unable to finish a speech, and to see the spectacle of crowds booing Teddy Kennedy.

"What's this system about? When dissent becomes destructive, it's totalitarianism in reverse."

That was not President Nixon complaining about the heckling of Vice-President Agnew. That was candidate Nixon complaining to his aides about the heckling of Vice-President Humphrey, back in September 1968.

It was soon to get worse.

On April 21, 1971, the Mayday Movement—a part of the radical antiwar "People's Coalition"—issued a press release threatening that unless Congress legislated total withdrawal from Vietnam by May 1, protesters would stage a massive civil-disobedience action on May 3 and 4 designed to close down the city of Washington and prevent the government from functioning. Congress did not do as the Mayday Movement ordered, and tens of thousands of demonstrators, as threatened, laid siege to the city. A "tactical manual" put out by the Mayday Tribe described its aims: "Mayday is an action, a time period, a state of mind and a bunch of people. . . . The aim of the Mayday actions is to raise the social cost of the war to a level unacceptable to American rulers. To do this we seek to create the specter of social chaos. . . ."

On the morning of May 3 protesters massed on the major bridges leading into the city and on other major arteries within Washington, in an attempt to block traffic and forcibly prevent people from getting to their jobs. Washington's entire 5100-man police force was mobilized to keep the city open, backed up by 4000 army troops in battle fatigues and 1500 national guardsmen. In the principal battle areas rampaging gangs threatened drivers, accosted pedestrians, smashed windows, slashed tires, overturned trash cans, tore out shrubs, dragged parked cars into the middle of intersections, and hurled anything movable into the street as a potentially lethal traffic hazard, even throwing bedsprings from overpasses into the path of traffic below.

The police responded with mass arrests, rounding up 2000 of the protesters by 8:00 A.M. Those and other thousands arrested later were herded en masse into Robert F. Kennedy Stadium. The next day, May 4, District Superior Court Judge Harold H. Greene ruled that those not charged with a specific offense must be released. On May 5 a federal appeals court upheld the order. Faced with a guerrilla-war situation, Police Chief Jerry Wilson had issued instructions in advance that his men were to dispense with the usual individual arrest forms. Thus there was no paperwork to tie each specific person arrested to a specific offense at a specific place at a specific time. As a result, those caught up in the mass arrests were let out in a mass release. In the years since, a romantic mythology has been built around the Mayday protest, grounded on the fact that the thousands swept up in the police dragnet were released without prosecution. According to the myth, these were wide-eyed innocents victimized by police tyranny, their constitutional rights brutally trampled, and their innocence proved by the judge's action.

As it happened, I spent three hours on the streets that morning, in two of the principal battle areas—Georgetown, where I live, and the George Washington University area near the White House. Whenever there was a major march on Washington, I made it a practice to mingle anonymously with the demonstrators in an effort to pick up some sense of the mood and temper of the crowd. Usually, the vast majority were peaceful. In most cases, in fact, the mood was more of Woodstock than it was of confrontation. But each time there was also a sizable, violence-bent minority who came to terrorize, and did. The chief problem for the police was to contain the violence-prone, while not unduly interfering with the peaceful—no easy task, but one which, by and large, they managed fairly well under the circumstances. Mayday, however, was different. Violence and the threat of violence were the name of the game. Its stated purpose was to paralyze the city by force, intimidation, and terror. I watched as ugly mobs of thugs darted from block to block, with lookouts posted, keeping one scoot ahead of the pursuing police, trashing and vandalizing, destroying property and threatening lives. I saw scores of persons arrested. Without exception, every one of those I saw arrested I had also seen committing a violent act moments before. I saw hundreds commit violent acts without being arrested. No doubt some innocents were picked up along with the guilty; but I doubt that there were many. In any case, as a bystander in what was clearly an emergency situation, I considered it my responsibility to keep out of the way of the police who were trying to cope with it, and not their responsibility to keep out of my way. I arrived at the office that day with my eyes swollen shut and my lungs on fire from tear gas, but I considered that my own fault for having pressed too close to the action.[1]

In the cultural collision that marked the Nixon years, the spiritual heart of the challenge confronting Nixon was located on the college campus. It was there that "the politics of confrontation" was raised to a high art and the new ethic of mass violence was nurtured. It was from the campus—among students and faculty alike —that the assault on old values was mounted. The campus was the home of the new politics, the new morality, the new priorities, the new disdain for "the system" and for all those disciplines associated with it. It was on the campus that the romantic vision achieved its strongest hold. And to me, one of the principal tragedies of that period was that what should be the citadel of reason became the fount of antireason. The institution we chiefly rely on to train the mind in the rigors of left-brain discipline surrendered itself to an orgy of right-brain indulgence.

Perhaps because of my own interest and involvement, the confrontations between campus and White House stand out more vividly in my own mind than they do in the overall history of those years. I had never been as personally uncomfortable with the counterculture as some of my more strait-laced White House colleagues were. I always had friends among their ranks. Back in my

---

1. This was my second encounter with tear gas. The first came on Wisconsin Avenue—Georgetown's main business thoroughfare—one Sunday afternoon during an earlier demonstration. I had run into a neighbor, and we stopped on a streetcorner to chat. Police pursuing a gang of window-smashers loosed tear-gas grenades, and we turned out to be in the path of the invisible gas. The stuff is agonizing; from then on, I could well understand its effectiveness. The neighbor I shared the experience with was CBS White House correspondent Dan Rather.

Herald Tribune days, *The Village Voice,* one of the pioneer journals of the counterculture, once held its annual Christmas party at my New York apartment. Most of what little speaking I did while at the White House was to college groups. I tended to identify with the college campus, and with the needs and feelings of the younger generation—however vehemently I disagreed with much of what they said. I wanted to find ways of reducing the tensions between us and them, for their sake as well as for our own.

One of the things that troubled me most was what I saw it doing to those I considered its principal victims: the students themselves. They were being tempted into a dream world, deceived into believing they could eschew the hard disciplines of learning, separated from reality, stripped of both the intellectual and the psychological armaments they needed if they were to cope successfully with life. They were forever being told that they were the most idealistic generation ever, the brightest, the most mature— and so they believed it.

However, their "idealism" was passionate but superficial, scorning all serious questions of *how* the various millenniums they believed should be achieved could be achieved. They had no patience with process, no comprehension of consequences, no sense of history, no awareness of what the nation had been through to bring it where it was. Each time I talked with a group of students, I was dismayed anew at how abysmally ignorant most of them were—not unintelligent, but uninformed, unaware of even the most elementary facts about whatever issue they were currently inflamed about. They rushed to embrace any rumor, as long as its effect was to discredit the war or the "Establishment." And, sadly, they had no idea of how little they knew, and how much, therefore, they had yet to learn. They were both exploited and pandered to by academic sycophants who cared more about winning their favor than about developing their minds.

They were strangers to linear logic. Yet all the intellectual equipment they so conspicuously lacked was precisely what a college education should have provided—and would have provided, had the nation's universities not bowed to demands that their students should teach before they learned, and had right-brain passion not been allowed, on the campus, to triumph over left-brain analysis.

From their own perspective, of course, it looked different. Their sense of involvement with the world around them, their urgent desire for greater openness, greater frankness, for a greater leaven of humanity against the towering impersonality of institutions in the mass, all had the potential for bringing a more creative balance to the relationship between man and society. I sympathized with many of their wishes. Yet if that potential was going to be realized, if the effect of their new perceptions was, in the final analysis, to be creative rather than destructive, they were going to have to learn some hard lessons about the world and its ways.

By the time Nixon took office, the pattern of campus violence had already been set, starting at Berkeley in 1964 and climaxing at Columbia in 1968. Radical agitators seized on issues with which they could inflame large numbers of students, provoked confrontations, taunted university administrations into countermeasures they could denounce as "repressive," and used these to broaden their base of student support. Their goal was destruction: destruction of "the system," destruction of social institutions, destruction of the university itself. Students were their instrument. Universities, radical leader Tom Hayden declared, "will be caught in the middle. . . . What we are seeking is instability." The protesters, he insisted, "want a new and independent university standing against the mainstream of American society, or they want no university at all. They are, in Fidel Castro's words, 'guerrillas in the field of culture.'" Their tactics were effective.

Coercion, violence, and terror ceased to be aberrational, and became the norm, with arson, bombings, sit-ins, vandalism, intimidation, rifling of files, and destruction of records, all part of the campus scene. Between January 1, 1969, and April 15, 1970, more than 40,000 bombings, attempted bombings, and bomb threats were recorded in the United States. Of those that could be attributed to a specific cause, more than half—8200—were a product of "campus disturbances and campus unrest." In the 1968–69 school year, the FBI reported some 4000 campus protest-related arrests. In the 1969–70 school year, there were 1792 demonstrations, 7561 arrests, 8 people killed and 462 injured (299 of those injured were police). There were 247 cases of campus arson, and 282 attacks on ROTC facilities. When a bomb was set off in August 1970 at the University of Wisconsin, killing one graduate student, wounding four others, and doing $6 million of damage, underground newspapers all across the country gleefully reported that another blow had been struck against the "pig nation."

Though much of the protest action was focused on the war, much was not. Protest itself had become a fashion. It needed only an excuse, not a cause. Many of the "demands" centered on the university itself: grading systems, parietal rules, the right of students to participate in university decision-making. Many centered on race, a carry-over from the civil-rights marches of a few years earlier. If there had been no war, there still would have been an epidemic of violent protest—not least because it was romanticized by the media, and particularly by television.

Actual violence, though serious, was only the tip of the iceberg of campus unrest. More fundamental was the intellectual and emotional climate that nurtured the violence, and in turn was nurtured by it. "Alienation" was the vogue word, and millions of young people did feel alienated from their government, alienated from American society and alienated from its institutions. Even the nonviolent tended, to a dangerous degree, to identify with those who expressed their protest in violent ways. They mouthed the same slogans, supported the same causes, shared the same feeling of fraternal outsiderness. "Dropping out," "turning off," searching for a mystic communion in the unreal world of psychedelics, all were justified by opposition to "the system," however each individual might vaguely define that all-embracing term.

Trying to think through the problem in 1969, it seemed to me that one of the key elements might well be a pervasive fear which they themselves neither articulated nor even explicitly recognized. I developed this in a memo that I distributed among some of the senior White House staff—Kissinger, Garment, and a number of others—many of whom, particularly those who came from the professorial ranks themselves, were spending long hours agonizing over the challenge. In the memo, I suggested that much of the rebelliousness might be rooted in "a fear of failure that saps initiative, and leads the youth to reject a system he's afraid he can't master."

Elaborating on this thought, I wrote:

The most overwhelming characteristic of our society today is its complexity. To those just entering on the mysteries of adulthood, this complexity is not merely a phenomenon to be observed; it is a direct, personal threat to their capacity to manage their own futures, to their achievement of "manhood," to their sense of identity, to their place in a world they yearn to call their own.

From the comfortable vantage point of our own relative self-assurance, we can rhapsodize about "challenges" and maintain that the greater the challenge the greater the adventure, etc. But the key point about a challenge is that the person being challenged must have faith that he has at least a reasonable chance of mastering it. Otherwise the "challenge" becomes a seemingly impassable barrier.

I suggest that a lot of today's young see the complexity of modern life not as a challenge, but as a barrier, precisely because they see no way—viewing it in *personal* terms—by which they can master it; and thus, instead of expending the energy needed to meet the "challenge," they rebel against the system.

If this is the case, what's primarily needed is not exhortation to rise to the "challenge," but rather to convince the young that the challenge is one that *can* be mastered—to chart the ways by which the complexity of life can be overcome, and the freedom and dignity of the individual achieved, *within* the system. . . .

Rebellion can be many things—and one of those things is a crutch for those who fear they can't make it, just as Black Studies is often a crutch for the black student fearful that he can't compete in a white milieu (and for those patronizing white liberals who assume that he can't, and therefore want to provide the crutch). By rebelling against the "system," the youth sets up an excuse for failure; by rejecting its values, he rejects in advance the anticipated negative judgment of the society that embraces those values.

It's no coincidence that so much of the youthful rebellion—the Arlo Guthrie–Woodstock-pot-rock-love contingent—is focused on the search for *simple* answers, *simple* relationships, *simple* truths. Or that in its inarticulateness, this same set—which millions of other youths look to as troubadours of their own discontents—reduces communication to little more than simple grunts and code phrases, rejects precision, and seeks alternatives not only to the values but even to the artifacts of a complex industrial society. It's as though, by instinct, the herd is running from the thunder, seeking shelter: and its shelter is the simple, even the primitive.

Even the turn toward drugs could well be an unconscious response to the same deeply felt but unarticulated fears—a desperate groping for some way of coming to terms with a world that threatens to overwhelm by its complexity and its vastness. The common denominator of today's popular drugs is their hallucinogenic qualities—and the common claim of those who experiment with them is that they bring new perceptions, new patterns, in which the user seems somehow mystically to be in harmony with his surroundings. They give the illusion of replacing discontinuities with continuities, incongruities with congruities—and a common mythology is building up that there is a truth out there beyond the drug wall—a truth of new shapes, new colors, new sounds, a *private* world, from which the "straight"—who create all those dreadful complexities—are excluded, and which contains, somewhere, its own holy grail of mystic communion. . . .

This same set of circumstances might also explain much of the passionate arrogance so characteristic of much of today's youth, and so much more pronounced now than in earlier generations. There are, of course, many other likely explanations, not least of them the combination of permissive child-rearing and the cult of youth, which together have conditioned the young to feel that they are both the center of the universe and the primary custodians of truth. But arrogance can be rooted in fear—and it may well be that the fear of insufficiency in the face of overwhelming and oppressive complexity would produce precisely the sort of arrogance we have witnessed. The youth who fears he can't master the system is forced (unconsciously) to choose: either he is weak or the system is wrong. Unwilling to concede his own weakness, he proceeds *from* the assumption that the system is wrong, *to* a rationale for that assumption. Because his reasoning is not basesd on logic, it's not shaken by logic. In order to reject the system, he must reject also the premises on which it rests. In order to defy the system, he must also defy its authorities—denying not only the rightness of their rules but also their right to rule. The more this whole process leads him into irrationalities, inconsistencies, and absurdities, the more fiercely he has to proclaim his own "truth" in order to preserve it, and the more intolerantly he has to dimiss competing views before they have a chance to upset it—because for him, the stakes are not simply intellectual or political; in a psychological sense, they are survival.

I went on to suggest a number of approaches we might take to demonstrate to the young that the system really was manageable by them, and to engage them in a serious debate over the nation's future. Noting that my basic thesis was that "the ostensible causes of youthful unrest are not the real causes," I argued that "by addressing the real causes, we can defuse a threat to our institutions and at the same time rescue a generation from a despair more deeply felt than its own members would admit."

We passed many such ideas back and forth among ourselves during that period as we groped for answers.

Nixon, too, was searching for ways to deal with the problem. He felt frustrated, constrained by the need to preserve the universities' freedom from government domination, yet keenly aware that the nation expected him to provide at least some form of moral leadership. The question was what form: What *could* he do that would not simply exacerbate an already explosive situation; what *should* he do, believing that the real responsibility had to be taken by university administrators themselves, and that they were caving in to faculty and student pressure and falling down on the job?

As the revolt spilled over from campus to street, it posed what I considered the most profound challenge of this century to the continued stability of the democratic system itself. A militant minority claimed for itself the right to impose its will on society at large, and embraced the tactics of confrontation and terror to enforce that right. And large, articulate, influential segments of the university community gave both material and moral support to that claim. The galvanizing force for the effort to abort the processes of representative democracy was, of course, opposition to the war in Vietnam. The government—led by the President—was determined to follow a carefully balanced course of phased withdrawals, Vietnamization, and diplomacy. The student protesters and their nonstudent allies were equally determined to force the government to do it their way—to get out forthwith, and hang the consequences.

The first major confrontations between these two concepts of how policy should be set came with the "Moratorium Days" announced by antiwar groups for October 15 and November 15, 1969. Hundreds of thousands of people were organized for rallies, marches, speeches, demonstrations in Washington and elsewhere.

As the first of those moratoria neared, there was extensive debate within the White House about what kind of stance to take toward it. Nixon's decision, in effect, was to pick up the gantlet and hurl it squarely back. Asked at a September 26 press conference for his view about the moratorium and other antiwar demonstrations being planned, he replied that "As far as this kind of activity is concerned, we expect it. However, under no circumstances will I be affected whatever by it."

When the protesters marched outside the White House, he further drove the point home by letting it be known that he spent the afternoon watching football on television.

Those twin—and deliberate—presidential cold-shoulders not only inflamed the demonstrators but they also infuriated collegians across the country. They saw it as a spurning of their views and a contempt for public opinion generally, and took it as a personal affront.

But Nixon had a serious purpose. Directly at issue, in his mind, was the question not only of what national policy should be but of how it should be made—by throngs in the streets, or through the constitutional processes of a representative democracy. He was determined that—in that first direct challenge to the constitutional process—there should be no room for doubt, no glimmer of hope that he could be induced to let the challenge succeed. With that point firmly, even brutally made, he was free in the face of later challenges to be somewhat more conciliatory. But, on the theory that the door that invites the pressure is the one slightly ajar, not the one securely bolted, he was convinced that in that first instance it was vital that he give no quarter.

As a device to make this point explicit, we used what was essentially a public-relations gimmick, but one which we hoped would demonstrate that he was not really deaf to the young. The gimmick was to select one letter of protest from among the hundreds he received from college students, to write a reasoned reply, and then to release the exchange of correspondence to the press. The episode provided one of those little ironies that illustrate life's hazards. I sent for the incoming letters, heaped them on my desk, and pored through them looking for the one that would most directly put the challenge he wanted to answer. Once I had selected the best, I made a deliberate point of *not* checking out the writer, so there could be no question, when reporters inevitably went to interview him, of our having selected a patsy. If he were head of the local SDS chapter and used the occasion to blast the President, that would just be the way the ball bounced.

I drafted the President's reply, and he sent it. The letter I selected was from a Georgetown University student named Randy J. Dicks. When the reporters reached him, it turned out that Dicks was not a bomb-throwing radical, but neither was he exactly the representative student we had hoped for. He was, he said, president of the college's Monarchist Club.

In his letter, Dicks branded Nixon's statement that he would not be swayed by the demonstration "ill-considered to say the least," and added: "It has been my impression that it is not unwise for the President of the United States to take note of the will of the people; after all, these people elected you, you are their President, and your office bears certain obligations."

The President replied:

October 13, 1969

Dear Mr. Dicks:

In reply to your comments about my press conference remark that "under no circumstances will I be affected whatever" by the demonstrations planned for October 15, I would suggest that there are several points you should bear in mind.

First, there is a clear distinction between public opinion and public demonstrations. To listen to public opinion is one thing; to be swayed by public demonstration is another. A demonstration—in whatever cause —is an organized expression of one particular set of opinions, which may or may not be shared by the majority of the people. If a President —any President—allowed his course to be set by those who demonstrate, he would betray the trust of all the rest. Whatever the issue, to allow government policy to be made in the streets would destroy the democratic process. It would give the decision, not to the majority, and not to those with the strongest arguments, but to those with the loudest voices. It would allow every group to test its strength not at the ballot box but through confrontation in the streets.

The planned demonstrations will tell us that a great many Americans are deeply concerned about the war; that some of these consider U.S. participation immoral; that many want U.S. troops withdrawn immediately and unconditionally. But all of us in the Administration are already well aware of this sentiment. We are already well aware that it is widespread—indeed, that no matter how many people might participate, there would be many more who share their concern.

Therefore, there is nothing new we can learn from the demonstrations. The question is whether, in the absence of any new evidence or any new arguments, we should be turned aside from a carefully considered course. The policies we are now following reflect our own best judgment, based on exhaustive study of all the available evidence, of how to achieve that goal. To abandon that policy merely because of a public demonstration would therefore be an act of gross irresponsibility on my part.

One further point: I respect the right of each American to express his own opinion. I recognize that many feel a moral obligation to express their opinions in the most conspicuous way possible, and therefore consider such expression to be their responsibility. I respect that. However, my responsibility is different. I must consider the consequences of each proposed course of action—short-term and long-term, domestic and world-wide, direct and indirect. Others can say of Vietnam, "Get out now"; when asked how, they can give the simple, flip answer: "By sea." They can ignore the consequences. But as I consider these consequences, in both human and international terms, I can only conclude that history would rightly condemn a President who took such a course.

One of the first acts of my Administration was to review, exhaustively and comprehensively, every aspect of the nation's policies in Vietnam. We have drastically altered the policies we inherited. We are on the road to peace. That road is not easy. It is not simple. But I am convinced it is the right one. There is no problem to which I have given more of my time and thought. For nine months, we have worked every day for a just end to a conflict which has been building for more than eight years.

On October 15th, I understand, many will simply be saying: "I am for peace." I ardently join with all Americans in working toward that goal.

Sincerely,

Richard Nixon

Between the two moratoria, Nixon delivered what came to be known as his "Silent Majority" speech—or what we in the White House generally referred to simply as the "November 3." It marked a major turning-point in his presidency, and in the Vietnam war. He considers it—I think correctly—the most effective speech of his presidency. He soberly traced through the history of the war, of his own efforts to end it, and of the stakes as he saw them. He made clear that he was going to continue on a measured course, reducing the size of the American force as Vietnamization proceeded, but that he was not going to be stampeded. And he asked "the great silent majority" of the American people to support him in that course. He wrote it himself, working long and laboriously, late into the night day after day, at the White House and Camp David.

The November 3 date was announced before the October 15 moratorium, in order to avoid the impression that he was speaking in response to it. The October demonstration, however, heightened the drama of the backdrop against which he gave it, and almost certainly had the effect of increasing the outpouring of popular support that he got in response, which smothered the critics and established his own command over the process of seeking peace. His Gallup approval rating hit its peak for the year, 68 percent, in a poll taken November 14–17, following the speech. By the time of the November moratorium, some of the steam had gone out of the antiwar protest movement. Because Nixon had managed to galvanize the "silent majority," it was no longer so easy for the vocal minority to convey the impression that they spoke for the nation.

But if he helped drain the venom from the protest with his November 3 speech, six months later he did the opposite with his speech announcing the incursion into Cambodia. Though generally restrained, parts of it were couched in angry, bullying terms— the United States would not be a "pitiful, helpless giant." The speech sent a shock wave across the country, in which the fine distinctions of what he was actually doing were all but lost.

The move into Cambodia was a bold stroke—but strictly limited and surgically swift. The distinction the White House drew between an "incursion" and an "invasion" was scornfully derided, but was both apt and important. It was an action directed not against Cambodia, but solely against the North Vietnamese forces which had invaded, conquered, and occupied portions of Cambodia. It was strictly limited in both space and time: in space, to those North Vietnamese-controlled areas, and in time to a maximum of sixty days—after which U.S. and South Vietnamese troops would withdraw to the Vietnamese side of the border. It was no more an "invasion" of Cambodia, in the usual sense of that term, than, in World War II, a British commando raid on German supply dumps in a Nazi-held area of France would have been an "invasion" of France.

Yet, partly because of the belligerent rhetoric in which it was announced, these distinctions—though spelled out clearly by the President—were lost on much of his audience. All many could imagine was a "new Vietnam," another quagmire, another war. Few of the protesting students I talked with in subsequent weeks were even aware of the limits he had placed on the operation. The reaction was a wave of hysteria, at its most intense in the campus community but not confined to it. There were measured objections as well—W. Averell Harriman, Paul C. Warnke, and Johnson's commerce secretary, John T. Connor, were among those who publicly objected to the move, though Johnson himself called for support for the President—and national polls showed that a majority did support the action. But the intense emotionalism of the campus reaction admitted of no debate, no analysis, no rational discussion. The hysteria was intensified when four students were tragically killed in a clash between rock-throwing demonstrators and armed national guardsmen at Ohio's Kent State University on May 4. Ten days later, at Jackson College in Mississippi, two more students were killed by police during a night of violence outside a women's dormitory.

By the second week of May, 448 colleges and universities were closed or on strike. Nearly 100,000 demonstrators gathered on the Ellipse, to listen while speakers denounced the war and denounced Nixon.

For years radicals had been working to "politicize" the nation's universities. The extent to which they succeeded was evident in the wake of Cambodia and Kent State, when entire universities were, in effect, mobilized against the national administration.

On May 3 the editors of eleven major Eastern college newspapers agreed to run a joint editorial the following day urging "the entire academic community of this country to engage in a nationwide university strike" in protest against the war. The presidents of thirty-seven colleges and universities sent a joint letter to the President protesting "the incalculable dangers of an unprecedented alienation of America's youth" because of the Cambodian action. At Yale, where widely feared violence had barely been averted days earlier as twelve thousand students and others rallied on New Haven Green in support of Black Panthers on trial for murder, President Kingman Brewster led a delegation of more than a thousand students and faculty to Washington to lobby—as a university —against the administration policies (this was an action which particularly outraged me, as a member of the Yale community). Brandeis, Haverford, the University of North Carolina, and other colleges also sent large delegations. All across the country, students, faculty, and college administrators joined in abandoning scholarship for political action.

At Princeton, the faculty voted for a plan—which, as "the Princeton Plan," was widely copied—to provide a two-week recess immediately before the coming November's elections, so that students and faculty could work for the election of antiwar candidates to the Congress. Scores of other colleges hastily rearranged their academic requirements to give students time for political activities, canvassing homes and churches and gathering signatures on antiwar petitions.

Some of the protests were peaceful. Some were not.

University of Maryland students, after ransacking the ROTC offices (cost: $10,000 damage, twenty-five arrests, fifty injuries), showed their continued displeasure by blocking traffic on a major highway, until Governor Marvin Mandel called out the national guard and dispersed the rock-throwing students with tear gas. At Stanford, protesting students set fires that did $100,000 in damage and destroyed the work of ten visiting scholars.

By June a Gallup poll showed that a majority of people in the United States considered campus unrest the nation's number one problem. And millions of young people seemed by then to be genuinely convinced that their government was at war with them, that it was unfeeling, uncaring, not listening, bent only on widening the war in Southeast Asia and "repressing dissent" at home by the bloodiest means available.

New York University philosophy professor Sidney Hook, in that summer of 1970, declared that "American colleges and universities today face the gravest crisis in their history. . . . The problem and threat is not academic unrest but academic disruption and violence which flow from substituting for the academic goals of learning, the political goals of action. . . . The objection is not to controversy, for intellectual controversy is the life of mind. The public objection is to *how* controversy is carried on—to the use of bombs, arson, vandalism, physical assault, and other expressions of violent strife and turmoil."

Lamenting that "on many American campuses today academic freedom has been severely crippled," Hook argued:

At scores of universities speakers are shouted down, sometimes assaulted. While spokesmen for movements hostile to the government have unlimited freedom to incite to violent action in opposing government policies, spokesmen for these policies are often barred from campuses or can appear only under heavy police escort.

By and large, in these institutions faculty and administration either remain silent or issue ineffectual releases mildly deprecating the worst excesses. Even when official guests of the university have been insulted or scandalously mistreated, they seem loath to introduce or enforce disciplinary action. On some campuses fanatical student extremists have disrupted with relative impunity classes of professors of whom they have disapproved.

And most shameful of all, these students have faculty allies who encourage and extenuate attacks on the academic freedom of their colleagues. . . . Although opportunistic administrators with flexible backbones have opened the doors to the academic vandals, in the last analysis it has been the faculties who have been chiefly responsible for the decline in academic freedom. For they have lacked the moral courage to uphold the professional standards of their calling as teachers and seekers of the truth.[2]

Part of the problem was a cast of mind shared, in those tumultuous days, by many academics, and described this way by the University of Chicago sociologist the Reverend Andrew Greeley, S.J.:

"The academic is convinced in his heart of hearts that those on the outside are not virtuous, because of ignorance or malice or both; therefore, he sees no choice but to constrain them to virtue. It is but one logical step, then, to argue that since one cannot get virtuous action by majority rule, one must abandon majority rule; and it is

2. *Los Angeles Times*, 30 August 1970.

but one more logical step to sympathize with, and even applaud, violence as a means for forcing society to be virtuous."

Unlike the politician, Greeley argued, "the academic seems to be subject to the temptation to take his rhetoric not only seriously but literally. . . .

"If he compares the United States frequently enough to Nazi Germany, he begins to believe that there are Nazi stormtroopers in the streets, that Richard Nixon actually is an Adolf Hitler who intends to cancel the 1972 election, that John Mitchell really is a Heinrich Himmler who is setting up concentration camps, that the United States has really embarked on a policy of genocide against the black and brown people in its midst, and that Daniel Berrigan, in a mad exercise of romantic narcissism, has become Dietrich Bonhoeffer reincarnate."[3] (Two years later, commenting in *Change* magazine on the collapse of "The Movement," Greeley specified some of his targets. He was "furious," he wrote, "at many of my colleagues in the academy who pandered to the worst in the romanticism and the irrationality of Movement folk: Kenneth Kenniston, who told them they were morally superior to previous generations. Margaret Mead, who let them believe that they were a whole generation who lived not in the past or the present but in the future. Herbert Marcuse, who let them think that they were three-dimensional men. Charles A. Reich, who agreed that they were a new messianic people. And Theodore Roszac, who equated irrationality with creative vitality.")

One of the bitterest student grievances during that period was their injured sense that they were not being "listened to" by people in authority. Time and again, in my own conversations with them, they complained that because of this the only way they could be heard was to demonstrate. But on probing more deeply, it often became evident that—either consciously or unconsciously—they had become conditioned to equating being "listened to" with having their demands met. I particularly recall the plaintive intensity with which one student at Yale, in the fall of 1969, put the question to me: "But when simply registering our opinions doesn't work, what else can we do but take to the streets?" Many apparently found it difficult to believe that anyone in authority could listen to their arguments and not share their own passionate conviction that theirs was the only truth. Thus, when they saw what to them were self-evident "truths" dismissed by the "power structure," this simply

3. *Los Angeles Times,* 11 October 1970.

proved to them that the "power structure" was corrupt and intractable.

During the post-Cambodia march on Washington, one delegation of eight students and one faculty member from Colgate was received by Secretary of State William Rogers in his eighth-floor inner sanctum at the State Department. The members of the delegation had written Rogers earlier, demanding that he resign both as secretary of state and as a trustee of Colgate. He politely heard out their objections to the Cambodian move, then calmly suggested: "You may be right. But have you considered the possibility that the President of the United States may be right?" It was a new thought, which one member of the delegation admitted had never even occurred to them.

Nixon delivered three major addresses on college campuses dealing specifically with the problem of youthful unrest. The first, on June 3, 1969, was almost completely ignored by the media, and therefore had almost no effect. (A major wire service devoted eleven paragraphs to the story, of which four concerned the fact that of the ten thousand students in the audience two carried obscenely worded anti-Nixon signs.) This was a severe disappointment to me, because I had worked long and hard on the speech and thought its message was one which badly needed to be gotten across—and particularly, one which the nation's college students needed to hear from their President. Nixon also considered it important, and he worked over the speech himself with great care. When we had completed the final draft, he called in Henry Kissinger and, with Kissinger and me seated beside his desk, read long passages aloud, and then asked Kissinger what he thought. Kissinger, deeply troubled by the campus turmoil, was enthusiastic. But we and the ten thousand students who heard it were virtually its only audience. (One reason was that he delivered it on a relatively obscure campus in Madison, South Dakota, General Beadle State College [now South Dakota College], at the dedication of a library to house the papers of his long-time friend Senator Karl Mundt. Although the White House press corps were there in full force, they were too busy deriding the fact that his first campus appearance was at a small Western college rather than a large Eastern one, and trading jokes about its name, to pay much attention to what he said.)

Essentially, the speech was an effort to bridge what he called the "chasm of misunderstanding" that separated old and young, to define those public values that were essential if the "process of freedom" was to be preserved, to recognize that many students had legitimate grievances, but also to defend the rule of reason against the rule of force in the academic world.

Though that first speech never reached its intended wider audience, his second did—spectacularly. This time the setting was the thirteen thousand–seat field house at Kansas State University, the date was September 16, 1970, and the occasion was the college's annual Landon Lecture.[4]

It was a hard-hitting speech. I worked with Nixon on it, and he spent many hours on it himself. In our usual pattern of collaboration, we swapped ideas back and forth and sent drafts back and forth, as he polished and refined precisely what he wanted to say. But in this case, as important to its success as the content was the audience. Twenty or thirty noisy hecklers, strategically located front and center in the huge field house, tried to shout down the President. They in turn were shouted into submission by the thousands of students who gave Nixon repeated standing ovations, punctuating and underlining his message:

There are those who protest that if the verdict of democracy goes against them, democracy is at fault, the system is at fault—who say if they don't get their way the answer is to burn a bus or bomb a building. . . .

Those who bomb universities, who ambush policemen, who hijack airplanes and hold their passengers hostage, all share in common not only a contempt for human life, but also a contempt for those elemental decencies on which a free society rests—and they deserve the contempt of every American who values those decencies. . . .

What corrodes a society even more deeply than violence itself is the acceptance of violence, the condoning of terror, the excusing of inhuman acts in a misguided effort to accommodate the community's standards to those of the violent few.

It is time for the responsible university and college administrators, faculty and student leaders to stand up and be counted. We must remember that only they can save higher education in America. It cannot be saved by government.

When he called on the responsible leaders to "stand up and be counted," the audience rose in a thunderous, prolonged ovation, clearly and conspicuously directed toward the disrupters in their

4. The Landon Lecture series at Kansas State honors Kansas's former governor Alf M. Landon, the losing Republican candidate for the presidency against Franklin D. Roosevelt in 1936. Landon, then eighty-three, introduced Nixon, and later called his speech "a turning point in the continuing struggle to preserve freedom in the United States."

midst—and the television film of that moment made Nixon's point more dramatically than he could ever have made it himself. He was calling on the university community to save itself—and, there in Kansas, the community responded.

Two days later Nixon wrote to the president of Kansas State University, James A. McCain:

Your students demonstrated dramatically that the mindless disrupters are not the voice of America's youth, and not the voice of the academic community. They showed that decency and courtesy are still cherished. By their example, and by their massive response to the few who did attempt to disrupt the meeting, they showed that there is a responsible majority and that it, too, has a voice. . . . Their example will hasten the day when leaders in public life once more can routinely appear on college campuses, to meet with students, to discuss the great issues with them, to listen and be listened to—and when it will cease to be news that they are able to do so. It will hasten the day when respect for the rule of reason rather than the rule of force is once more recognized, in all of our great educational institutions, as the first prerequisite of academic life.

Nixon also received a warm note from an old antagonist:

September 17, 1970

Dear Mr. President:

I heard your excellent address at Kansas State University. I have just finished reading the text of what you have had to say.

I congratulate you on a message that was needed and one that was stated with clarity, understanding and firmness. It is my view that the basic struggle in our country today is not between the liberal and the conservative, but rather between those few who would destroy our system and those of us, liberal and conservative alike, who seek to use it and make it work.

Congratulations on your address.

Respectfully yours,
Hubert H. Humphrey

Having confronted the disrupters at Kansas State and triumphed over them, in his next campus address Nixon was able to go a large step further. Speaking on January 14, 1971, at the University of Nebraska, he called for "an alliance of the generations," telling his young audience: "My generation has invested all that it has, not only its love but also its hope and its faith, in yours. I believe you will redeem that faith and justify that hope. . . . Let us work together to seek out those ways by which the commitment and the compassion of one generation can be linked to the will and the experience of another so that together we can serve America better and America can better serve mankind."

What was, to me, one of the most poignant moments in the whole troubled progress of Nixon's relationship with the campus community came in May 1970, during the post-Cambodia march on Washington. During that protest, the White House aim was unambiguously one of trying to calm the troubled waters—not trimming policy sails with regard to the war itself, but at least trying to make clear to the protesters that we did hear them, we did care, and even if we disagreed with them we respected their disagreement with us. Teams of young White House staff members went out into the streets, inviting groups of demonstrators, at random, to come in and talk with various White House aides (I was one of those they were brought in to meet with). Declaring that "this is a time for communication rather than violence, and above all for mutual understanding," Nixon announced the appointment of Alexander Heard, chancellor of Vanderbilt University, as a special adviser "to help present to this administration the views and sentiments of the campuses around the country." At a televised news conference on Friday evening, May 8, Nixon firmly defended his Vietnam policies, including the Cambodian action, but went out of his way to do so in terms that stressed the way in which those policies were intended to achieve what the protesters also wanted—an end to the killing, an end to the war, an end to the draft. And then, a few hours later, he embarked on one of the most extraordinary—and most extraordinarily misrepresented—acts of his presidency.

As widely reported and generally remembered, he suddenly showed up in the early predawn hours at the Lincoln Memorial, where some thirty or forty students had taken shelter, and—to their annoyance—began talking to them about football and surfing. This impression was largely formed because of the response of one of the students who, when queried by a reporter afterward, complained: "I hope it was because he was tired, but most of what he was saying was absurd. Here we come from a university that's completely up-tight, on strike, and when we told him where we were from, he talked about the football team. And when someone said he was from California, he talked about surfing."

Nixon made his visit to the Lincoln Memorial without telling the press, or even Press Secretary Ziegler—in fact, he gave orders to the Secret Service that no one on his staff should be notified. As usual when there was a demonstration, however, Egil ("Bud") Krogh was working quietly behind the scenes to keep it as peaceful as possible. He was in the Secret Service command post, and happened to hear the radio traffic. He sped to the Lincoln Memorial, with Ziegler following behind. After returning to the White House, Nixon briefed an early arrival, Jack Horner of *The Washington Star*, on what had taken place, and Horner and Ziegler then together filled in the rest of the press corps. But the play given to the reaction of that one disgruntled student (and one or two others in a similar vein) so poisoned the reception of the gesture that, to this day, most who remember the incident remember it as the one in which the President showed himself so detached from the reality of the students' concerns (a "dialogue of the deaf," *The Washington Post* called it) that all he could talk about was football and surfing.

A couple of days later, Nixon dictated his own recollections. Bob Haldeman passed them along to me with a covering memo:

MEMORANDUM FOR: MR. RAY PRICE

Attached is a memorandum of what actually took place at the Lincoln Memorial on Saturday morning.

After you read it I think you will probably have some feelings as to how our coverage of this activity could have been better and perhaps some ideas on steps that might be taken now to follow up on this.

It gives us a unique opportunity to communicate on matters that may in the long run be infinitely more important than the material specifics—that is the qualities of spirit and emotion which the President's visit to the memorial was really about.

The President has since made the point that he realizes that it would have made more news from the standpoint of the students for him to engage with a spirited dialogue with them about why we were in Cambodia—why we haven't ended the war sooner—the morality of the war, etc. This kind of conversation would have been infinitely more easy for him, it would have made more news, but as he evaluated the situation he had the feeling that this was the one time this group of students most of whom appeared to him to be middle class or lower middle class—that this was the only time they would ever talk to a President of the United States. He felt they would see him many times in TV, etc., discussing the heated, angry subjects that they would hear later at the rally and that they hear in their classrooms. He felt that perhaps the major contribution he could make to them was "to try to lift them a bit out of the miserable intellectual wasteland in which they now wander aimlessly around."

He further makes the point that he was trying to get something across in terms of what a President should mean to the people—not in terms of news gimmicks, but in another way. He realizes all of the gimmickry stuff with full television coverage is big stuff and makes big news. He then says, "But on the other hand, I really wonder in the long run if this is all the legacy we want to leave. If it is—then perhaps we should do our job as easily as we can—as expeditiously as we can—and get out and leave the responsibilities of the government to the true materialists—the socialists and the totalitarians, who talk idealism but rule ruthlessly without any regard to the individual considerations—the respect for personality that I tried to emphasize in my dialogue with the students."

As you will note the attached memorandum is a rough draft of the President's recollection of the episodes and is sent only for your background and thought. It should be considered, of course, highly confidential.

H. R. Haldeman

Attachment

These are excerpts (somewhat abridged) from the President's dictated recollections:

I completed returning my calls at approximately 2:15 in the morning.

I then went to bed, slept soundly until shortly after four o'clock. When I woke up I got up and went into the Lincoln Sitting Room and was listening to an Ormandy recording with Entremont playing a Rachmaninoff concerto for piano and orchestra. Manolo apparently heard it and came down to the Lincoln Sitting Room and asked if he could get me some coffee or hot chocolate or something else.

I told him no, but then as I looked out of the window and saw the small knots of students beginning to gather on the grounds of the Washington Monument, I asked him if he had ever been to the Lincoln Memorial at night. He said he had not.

I got dressed and at approximately 4:35 we left the White House and drove to the Lincoln Memorial.

Manolo and I got out of the car at approximately 4:40 and walked up the steps to the Lincoln statue. I showed him the great inscription above the statue and told him that that, along with the inscription over the Tomb of the Unknown Soldier, was, in my opinion, the most moving sight in Washington. Then I showed him the Gettysburg Address on the left and Lincoln's Second Inaugural on the right.

By this time a few small groups of students had begun to congregate in the rotunda of the Memorial. I walked over to a group of them and shook hands. They were not unfriendly. As a matter of fact, they seemed somewhat overawed and, of course, quite surprised.

When I first started to speak to the group there were approximately

8 in it. I asked each of them where they were from and found that over half were from upper New York State. I told them I wanted them, of course, to attend the anti-war demonstration, to listen to all the speakers, but I hoped they had the time to take a tour of the city and see some of the historical monuments.

I told them that my favorite spot in all of Washington was right where we were standing—the Lincoln Memorial at night—that I had not been here at night for ten years, and I had come down here because I had awakened early after my press conference and wanted Manolo to see this wonderful sight.

Two or three of them volunteered that they had not been able to hear the press conference because they had been driving all night in order to get here. I said I was sorry they had missed it because I had tried to explain that my goals in Vietnam were the same as theirs—to stop the killing and end the war and bring peace. Our goal was not to get into Cambodia by what we were doing, but to get out of Vietnam.

They did not respond, so I took it from there by saying that I realized that most of them would not agree with my position, but I hoped that they would not allow their disagreement on this issue to lead them to fail to give us a hearing on some other issues where we might agree. Particularly, I hoped that their hatred of the war, which I could well understand, would not turn into a bitter hatred of our whole system, our country and everything that it stood for.

I said, I know that probably most of you think I'm an SOB, but I want you to know that I understand just how you feel. I recall that when I was just a little older than you, right out of law school and ready to get married, how excited I was when Chamberlain came home from Munich and made his famous statement about peace in our time. I pointed out, too, the fact that I came from a Quaker background. I was as close to being a pacifist as anybody could be in those times. As a result, I thought that Chamberlain was the greatest man alive, and when I read Churchill's all-out criticism of Chamberlain I thought Churchill was a madman.

In retrospect, I now realize I was wrong. I think now that Chamberlain was a good man, but that Churchill was a wiser man and we in the world are better off because Churchill had not only the wisdom but the courage to carry out the policies that he believed were right even though there was a time when both in England and all over the world he was extremely unpopular because of his "anti-peace" stand.

I then tried to move the conversation into areas where I could draw them out. I said I hoped that while they were young they would never miss an opportunity to travel. One said he didn't know whether he could afford it, and I said I didn't think I could afford it either when

I was young, but my wife and I borrowed the money for a trip to Mexico and then one to Central America. You must travel when you are young. If you wait until you can afford it you will be too old to enjoy it.

I urged them to start with the United States. I told them that as they went West, I particularly thought they should go to places like Santa Fe and see the American Indians. I pointed out that I knew that on their campuses the major subject of concern was the Negro problem. I said this was altogther as it should be because of the degradation of slavery that had been imposed upon the Negroes, and it would be impossible for us to do everything we should do to right that wrong, but I pointed out that what we had done with the American Indians was in its way just as bad. We had taken a proud and independent race and virtually destroyed them, and we had to find ways to bring them back into decent lives in this country.

I said that in California the Mexican-Americans were from an economic standpoint even worse off than the Negroes. I said that we needed to open channels of communication to Indians and Mexicans as well as to Negroes, and I hoped that they would do so.

At that time a girl joined the group, and since I had been discussing California I asked if anybody there was from California. She said she was from Los Altos and I said that was one of my favorite towns in northern California and I hoped it was as beautiful as I remembered it. She did not respond.

In trying to draw her out, I told the rest of the group that when they went to California they would see what massive strides we could take to deal with the problem of the environment. I said that right below where I live in California there was the greatest surfing beach in the world, that it was completely denied to the public due to the fact that it was Marine Corps property, and that I had taken steps to release some of this property for a public beach so that the terribly over-crowded beaches further north could be unburdened and people could have a chance to enjoy the natural beauty which was there. I said that one of the thrusts of our whole "quality of life" environmental program was to take Government property and put it to better uses, and not simply to continue to use it for military or other purposes because it had been used that way from time immemorial.

Most seemed to nod in agreement when I made this point.

I then spoke of how I hoped they would have the opportunity to know not only the United States but the whole world. I said Europe was fine, but it's really an older version of America. It is worth seeing, but the place I felt they would particularly enjoy visiting would be Asia.

I told them my great hope that during my administration, and certainly during their lifetime, the great mainland of China would be opened up so that we could know the 700 million people who live in China, who are one of the most remarkable peoples on earth.

I then went on to say, however, that they should not overlook the people of India. The people in India are terribly poor, but they have a history, a philosophical background and a mystique which they should try to understand. I also touched lightly on places like Malaysia.

I then moved on to the Soviet Union. One of them asked me what Moscow was like, and I said "gray." If you really want to know Russia, its exciting variety and history, you must go to Leningrad. I said the people were really more outgoing there since they were not so much under control and domination of the central government.

I said they would find Prague and Warsaw of much more architectural beauty than Moscow. I made this point because I was speaking directly to one of the students who said he was a student of architecture. But the most important point I made about Russia was that they should go to places like Novosibirsk, a raw, new city in the heart of Siberia, and Samarkand in Asian Russia where the people were Asians rather than Russians.

One of them asked whether it would be possible to get a visa to such cities, and I said I was sure they could and if any of them took a trip to Russia and wanted to contact my office I would help out. This seemed to get a little chuckle from them.

I then moved back to my thrust that what really mattered in the world was people, rather than cities and air and water and all the other things that were material. I said, for example, of all the countries I have visited in Latin America Haiti is probably the poorest but that the Haitians, while they were poor, had a dignity and a grace which was very moving.

By this time the group around me had begun to get considerably larger. I would say that the original group of approximately 8 to 10 had now become perhaps 30 and some of those who seemed to be more leader types and older began to take part in the conversation.

One spoke up and said, "I hope you realize that we are willing to die for what we believe in."

I said, I certainly realize that. Do you realize that many of us when we were your age were also willing to die for what we believed in and are willing to do so today? The point is that we are trying to build a world in which you will not have to die for what you believe in, in which you are able to live for it.

I put in one brief comment with regard to the point I had made in the press conference, that while we had great differences with the Russians we had to find a way to limit nuclear arms and I hoped we could make some progress in that direction. They seemed to have very little interest in that subject.

Then another spoke up and said, "We are not interested in what Prague looks like. We are interested in what kind of life we build in the United States."

I said the purpose of my discussing Prague and other places was not to discuss the city, but the people. For the next 25 years the world is going to get much smaller. It is vitally important that you know and appreciate and understand people every place, wherever they are, and particularly understand the people in your own country.

I said, I know the great emphasis currently being put on the environment—we have a very bold program going further than any has ever gone before. But I want to leave just one thought with you. Cleaning up the air and the water and the streets is not going to solve the deepest problems that concern us all. Those are material problems. They must be solved. They are terribly important. But you must remember that something completely clean can also be completely sterile and without spirit.

What we all must think about is why we are here. What are those elements of the spirit which really matter? And, here again, I returned to my theme of thinking about people rather than about places and things. I said candidly that I didn't have the answer, but I knew that young people today were searching, as I was searching 40 years ago, for an answer. I just wanted to be sure that all of them realized that ending the war, and cleaning up the streets and the air and the water, was not going to solve spiritual hunger—which all of us have and which, of course, has been the great mystery of life from the beginning of time.

I realized that the Secret Service were becoming more and more concerned. By this time the dawn was upon us. The first rays of the sun began to climb over the Washington Monument. I said I had to go, and shook hands with those nearest to me, and walked down the steps.

A bearded fellow was taking a picture as I began to get in the car. I asked him if he wouldn't like to get in the picture. He stepped over with me, and I said, look, I'll have the President's doctor take the picture. Tkach took the picture. He seemed quite delighted—it was, in fact, the broadest smile I saw on the entire visit.

As I left him I said I knew he had come a long way for this event, and I knew, too, that he and his colleagues were terribly frustrated and angry about our policy and opposed to it. I said, I just hope your opposition doesn't turn into a blind hatred of the country. Remember this is a great country, with all of its faults.

He smiled and took it all in good humor. We shook hands, and I got in the car and drove away.

THE FOURTH ESTATE

Of all the running wars Nixon was engaged in throughout his presidency, the one I found personally most painful was that with the media. Most of my working life had been spent as one of "them." I felt a bit like a member of one of those families torn by the Civil War, with one son fighting under the Union flag, and another in the uniform of the Confederacy. Many of our bitterest "enemies" in the press were people I liked personally, and some were people with whom, in the past, I had worked professionally. I understood the pressures under which they operated. I knew that most of them really did believe they were engaged in a search for the "truth." Their blindness to their own biases was a genuine blindness; truth, to them, was what they *believed* to be true, and because most of them shared the same biases, they reinforced one another in the belief that theirs was the real "truth." We did often lie, mislead, deceive, try to use them, and to con them, and I could appreciate their resentment. Further, most of them did take a fierce professional pride in their work, identifying their own interests with the national interest.

Having been on both sides of the fence that separates journalism from government, I could readily see how very differently things appear from one side than they do from the other. This was hardly a unique perception. Everyone I know who has been on both sides has shared it. Back in my days as a *Herald Tribune* editorial writer, I occasionally traveled to Washington for a few days at a time to pick up a feel for what was going on—meeting, on a background basis, with people in Congress and the administration, talking with Washington-based newsmen, trying to get the Washington perspective, and at the same time to learn something of how things looked from the inside. I became convinced that on those trips I learned more during evenings spent at the National Press Club bar than anywhere else. It was there that correspondents from the various bureaus expanded on the stories-behind-the stories, gave me their assessments and interpretations, and told me about the strengths and weaknesses of various public figures and about the unseen interplay of forces that shaped the news. It was fascinating. After a few months in Washington as a member of the administration, I still felt that in those earlier visits the Press Club bar was where I had learned the most—but that 90 percent of it had probably been untrue.

Complaints by public officials that what gets reported as "news" is largely untrue are virtually universal. A. H. Raskin, a veteran reporter, editorial writer, and editor of *The New York Times,* once noted: "No week passes without someone prominent in politics, industry, labor, or civic affairs complaining to me, always in virtually identical terms: 'Whenever I read a story about something in which I really know what is going on, I'm astonished at how little of what is important gets into the papers—and how often even that little is wrong.' The most upsetting thing about these complaints is the frequency with which they come from scientists, economists, and other academicians temporarily involved in government policy but without any proprietary concern about who runs the White House or City Hall." But in the past—until Vice-President Agnew went public with his attacks on the media in November 1969— political leaders did their fuming in private.

The media were sacred cows, immune from censure by public officials, for one simple reason: they always had the last word, and they retaliated ruthlessly against any official rash enough to call them to account. The retaliation was not a calculated policy. Rather, it was an instinctive, defensive reaction, made more intense by the fact that they were so unaccustomed to being on the receiving end of criticism. (A good example is the obsessive reiteration by the press of Nixon's comment, after his 1962 defeat, that "you won't have Nixon to kick around anymore." That one, rather mild, comment was made 16 years ago, and the press had, after all, kicked him around rather brutally. Yet it was so unthinkable for a politician to address such a comment to the press that it has reverberated in the press ever since, becoming probably the most-quoted line he ever spoke.)

Of the lines most often cited by editors writing hymns to the press, one of the all-time favorites is Jefferson's assertion, before he became President: "If I had to choose between a government without newspapers and newspapers without a government, I would pick the latter." However, they seldom cite Jefferson's later private comments—for example, in a letter to James Monroe: "From forty years' experience of the wretched guesswork of the newspapers of what is not done in open daylight, and of their falsehoods even as to that, I rarely think them worth reading, and almost never worth notice." Or his complaint that the way the press dealt with public issues was "an evil for which there is no remedy," or that "nothing can now be believed which is seen in a newspaper." Perhaps, like so many of his successors, Jefferson simply recognized that public flattery of the press was the surest way to win praise from the press, or perhaps experience changed his views.

I used to be a member both of the National Conference of Editorial Writers and of the American Society of Newspaper Editors, the latter of which could fairly be called the most "exclusive" of the major journalistic professional societies (exclusive because each of the nation's daily papers, depending on its circulation, is allowed only one, two, or three memberships and these usually go to the paper's top editors). Editors' conventions are orgies of mutual self-celebration—interesting gatherings, because editors tend to be interesting people, but cloying to the point of embarrassment in their paeans to their own collective virtue. Hardly a word is breathed in the official sessions—or at least this was the case when I used to go—about the news business *as* a business, with its hype and its hard-sell and its competitive effort to con the reader into believing that the patchwork of fact, guesswork, and invention he reads is really true.

Jefferson once facetiously suggested that a newspaper should be divided into four sections: (1) Truths, (2) Probabilities, (3) Possibilities, and (4) Lies. Without going quite that far, newsmen could —and should—go much further than they ordinarily do in identifying the degrees of certainty about what they write. A few, but only a very few, do that. The competitive pressures of the news business all push them in the direction of pretending that what they report is the "real, inside story," even when it may be only rumor, gossip, or speculation.

One of the few who do resist these pressures is John Osborne, White House correspondent for *The New Republic*. Osborne was one of Nixon's severest critics. But he retained exceptionally good sources at the White House because he retained the respect of his sources. Osborne is a man of rigorous intellectual integrity and great personal decency. More to the point, he is, to me, a "professional's professional" as a newsman. In effect taking a leaf from Jefferson, he meticulously separates what he knows from what he surmises, and leads the reader through the degrees of probability in what he reports. While presenting both fact and opinion, he distinguishes between the two. He tries scrupulously to be fair. When he discovers later that something he reported in a previous column was wrong, he makes a point of reporting that discovery. In short, he makes it possible to disagree entirely with his conclusions, while still entirely respecting both the process by which he reaches those conclusions and the manner in which he presents them. His work is not error-free—no reporting could be—but he never tries to con the reader; he never pretends to a greater authority than he has; he announces his biases and attempts to discount for them; and he corrects his mistakes. Moreover, he was one of the relatively few reporters with whom I felt free to discuss a complex problem, confident that some one phrase would not be lifted out of context to smear or distort.

The troublesome thing about Osborne's reporting is that it is so remarkable because it is so rare.

It was Nixon's misfortune to be in office when both "advocacy journalism" and the notion that the media should be "adversary" to the government enjoyed their greatest modern-day vogue. Under these twin doctrines, the primary purpose of journalism is not to explain, but to "challenge," on the theory that in such a clash truth will survive and untruth be demolished. The weakness of this theory, of course, is that truth is no more immune than falsehood to the ravages of a sustained assault by those who command the lines of communication.

Even those old-fashioned journalists who still believe that the function of news is to present the facts have to depend on their own subjective judgments.

Henry Fairlie recently wrote:

The flattest and most flatulent lie that is told every night in the world today is when Walter Cronkite says: "That's the way it is. . . ." It is *not* the way it is. How can Walter Cronkite ever know that "That's the way it is . . ." in the world? All he knows is what he is told; and all we know is what he and the staff of CBS News choose to tell us. . . .

News is not what has happened—it is not "the way it is"—it is an account of what a few people, journalists like myself, *think* has happened. Out of what we think has happened, we select and elaborate; and we provide each day what is called the news.

This is our job: *to make the news up*. That may sound a shocking confession; it is, in fact, the only honorable description of journalism. We are engaged in "making up" stories about the little we know of what has gone on in the world in the near past.[1]

A rather arbitrary "dirty dozen" of my own concerns about the media, as those concerns have developed over more than two decades on both sides of the fence, would include:

1. They have acquired a power out of proportion to their accountability, and out of proportion to the ability—or inclination—they have yet shown to use that power responsibly. When I was a newsman, I viewed that power as a good thing. Having seen it now from the opposite perspective—and having felt its force in the White House—in brooding moments I wonder how long the country can survive it in today's world.

2. They pretend to far greater accuracy than they deliver, to far greater authority than their reports really have, and to a high-minded pursuit of truth even when they really are maneuvering to keep the facts from getting in the way of a good story. The late Edward R. Murrow once wisely commented that because one's voice could be heard from one end of the country to the other did not mean that it had more content than it did when it could be heard only from one end of the bar to the other. Newsmen routinely pass public judgment on matters they understand only dimly or not at all. To some degree this is unavoidable, given the increasing complexity and sophistication of those matters that enter into the news. What is avoidable, however, is the false mask of authority they assume when doing it, and the cavalier, even snide, manner in which they often dismiss the views of those who do understand.

3. They display too much bias, and bias too unbalanced on one side. Every newsman worth his salt knows perfectly well that his colleagues, as a group, stand substantially to the left of the general public. Lowell Thomas, the dean of radio correspondents, somewhat overstated it when he declared a few years ago that "I have spent my life in the communications world and I have discovered that perhaps ninety-five percent of all those involved, reporters, editors and so on, are definitely to the left." But the imbalance is serious enough that the media should acknowledge it, and face up to its implications.

1. *The Washington Post*, 10 October 1976.

One reason for this imbalance, I think, is that the kinds of people who are drawn to journalism tend to be the kinds who flock to liberal causes: activists, reformers, those who identify emotionally with the underdog, those who are skeptical or cynical about established institutions, and see journalism as a vehicle for "exposing" the sins of those institutions. They like to think of themselves as being on the cutting edge of social change. Also, for whatever reasons, the world of literature is basically a "liberal" enclave, as are the arts, the academy—and writers and reporters tend to identify more with artists and intellectuals than they do with businessmen and engineers.

Through its structure of rewards and incentives, the industry also perpetuates its own bias. Pulitzer prizes are awarded for exposing the sins of a Richard Nixon, not those of a Ralph Nader. In journalism as in life—just as with love among the hippopotami—beauty is in the eye of the beholder. To one hippopotamus, the most beautiful creature in the world is another hippopotamus. To a liberal editor or network chief, the most impressive work is that of his like-minded colleagues. The next time you encounter someone from the world of network news, ask him to name one political conservative who was hired or promoted by his news department in the last twelve months.

4. They are too self-righteous. The media regularly exempt themselves from the moral standards they impose on everyone else, piously condemning the sins of others while practicing the same sins themselves. (Examples: Columnist Jack Anderson first leapt to public attention nearly two decades ago when, as an assistant to the late Drew Pearson, he was caught eavesdropping electronically on a Washington hotel room. *The Washington Post's* Woodward and Bernstein, in their pursuit of Watergate scoops, tried to get grand jurors to violate their oaths. CBS's Watergate scourge Daniel Schorr, when he first was fingered as the person who gave a copy of the secret House Intelligence Committee report to New York's *Village Voice*, issued a frantic flurry of denials—until his effort to cover up fell apart.) They exempt their own operations from the scrutiny to which they subject everyone else's. They shade, embroider, and distort the truth for their own purposes, while demanding truth from everyone else.

The news business, like government, is populated by fallible human beings, on balance not much better or worse than the rest of us. As do politicians, newsmen have to sell themselves to their audience and so they pretend to be what they are not. Unlike politicians, they have no probing press to expose their failings. So they get away with it better. Too often, getting away with it goes to their heads, and they begin to believe their own notices.

5. Competitive pressure to get the story first translates into a pattern of scrambling to report the news before it happens, and as a result reporting it wrong, often grossly distorting it. Newspapers and networks rush to get out ahead of one another with what *will* happen, rather than what *has* happened. Because they seldom know what will happen, they guess, they grasp at clues, they let themselves be manipulated by "sources" with an ax to grind—and then present their reports with a wholly false air of authority because that, too, is part of the competition: to appear more certain of your material than the other fellow is of his. (This was how a lot of the Watergate myths were created. Day after day, the media breathlessly reported new scandals which, according to "sources," were about to break. Most of the time the facts failed to bear out the predictions. But the damage was already done. The false report had already been drummed into the public consciousness. And the cumulative impact of those false reports probably made up at least three-fourths of the public perception of Watergate.)

6. The "mirror" they hold up to society is a distorting mirror, and therefore they should stop pretending that what it shows "reflects reality." It reflects those portions of reality that are sufficiently *atyp*-ical, sufficiently *un*usual, to be news, or that have an *un*common enough element of human interest or drama to be exciting. Because crime and violence, doom and disaster, conflict and confrontation, all titillate, these loom disproportionately large in the "news." These are legitimate items of news as entertainment, but trying to pass off the result as an accurate picture of the United States is deceitful. Surveys have repeatedly shown that people in all parts of the country are more up-beat in assessing their own lives and their own communities than they are about the nation. One reason is obvious: the one they see with their own eyes, while they judge the other on the basis of "news" reports. A half-hour news program that truly represented "reality" would include fifteen minutes of silence, representing all those things that hummed smoothly along, not causing upsets and therefore not making news.

7. A sort of cultural and professional insularity creates a sameness among the constituent elements of the "media monolith" which almost totally dominates national news coverage, and which originates entirely from New York City and Washington, D.C. The three television networks, *Time* and *Newsweek, The New York Times* and *The Washington Post* are as incestuous as they are competitive. Intellectually, they are built with interchangeable parts. Replace the

staff of any one of the seven with the staff of any other of the seven, make a few technical adjustments and hand out a set of style-books, and the product would be virtually unchanged.[2] Those who see a "conspiracy" among the national media miss the point. There is no "conspiracy," no sinister plot, but they do all view the world through essentially the same set of lenses. Further, they constantly reinforce one another. The editors of *The New York Times* watch CBS News and read *Time* and *The Washington Post*. The news directors at ABC read *The New York Times* and *The Washington Post* and *Time* and *Newsweek*. The editors of *Newsweek* read *The Washington Post* and *The New York Times* and watch NBC and CBS. Together, they blanket the country. The nightly news programs of the three networks, broadcast from New York, are carried by more than 600 local stations, and reach a nightly audience of more than 50 million viewers; further, practically all the filmed reports of national and world news that appear on local newscasts originate with one of the three networks. *Time* and *Newsweek* reach a combined weekly audience of more than 7 million. The *New York Times* news service and the combined *Washington Post–Los Angeles Times* news service have a subscriber list of more than 750 newspapers, and those two papers are not only the daily reading of practically everyone who puts out the network television news and the weekly news magazines, but also of the editors of the two national wire services, Associated Press and United Press International.

Those who wrote the First Amendment never envisioned a situation in which so much power would be concentrated in so few media hands, with so little means of effective challenge to that power. The purpose of the First Amendment was to insure diversity. Its result, increasingly, is conformity. This is not to suggest limitation of the First Amendment. But it is to suggest that those whom the First Amendment protects should pay more attention to its spirit, providing within their organizations more of that diversity it was meant to insure. Just as the Supreme Court keeps the Constitution as a whole alive by reinterpreting its provisions in the light of changing circumstances, the national media should reinterpret their own First Amendment responsibilities in the light of their increasing monopoly power.

8. The media display an excessively defensive, even paranoiac reaction to criticism. An institution that prides itself on its ability to

2. If Roone Arledge, the new president of ABC News, follows through on the things he was saying as he took charge in mid-1977, ABC may become an exception—though even his comments did seem to address style more than substance.

dish out criticism ought to learn to take it, too, without hiding behind the skirts of the First Amendment whenever someone complains of unfairness or untruth.

9. A misperception of the role of the media has badly distorted a lot of recent coverage. The currently fashionable doctrine that the role of the media is to "challenge" government is as wrongheaded as would be its opposite, that the role of the media is to support government. The role of the media is to inform the public, as fully and fairly and truthfully as possible, letting the chips fall where they may. If that hurts the government, fine. If it helps the government, fine. If it hurts or helps Cesar Chavez or Jerry Rubin or Ralph Nader or any of the other media favorites that too is fine. The role of the media is neither to promote the government nor to promote the government's adversaries. Those who tout the "adversary" role of the press tend generally to identify with those adversaries, so that the role becomes, in effect, flackery for their own side. (Some in the media see their role as "challenging" not just the government but the "power structure." If it were this, they should start by challenging themselves.)

10. They show a fascination with fashion, to the point where the faddish becomes a fetish. This is harmless enough when it involves hemlines. But it becomes exceedingly harmful when it involves serious national issues, or when, as in the late 1960s, the fad is protest that spreads by contagion through the media, frequently involving demonstrations staged specifically for the cameras. (The youthful antiwar, antiestablishment protesters were almost always portrayed in a heroic, or at least sympathetic, light, even when violent; they were in fashion. But when angry construction workers attacked antiwar demonstrators in New York and beat up some of them, the workers were portrayed as ignorant thugs. When the workers themselves—a hundred thousand strong—staged their own peaceful rally two weeks later in support of Nixon's Vietnam policies, the media treated the event as an affront. The word "hardhat" became a favorite media epithet. The staged demonstration was almost as much the rule as the exception. In a typical example, I remember watching during one of the marches on Washington as a band of demonstrators lounged on their signs by the entrance to the Justice Department, waiting for the invited camera crews to arrive at the appointed hour. The crews arrived, the demonstrators thrust their signs in the air and marched in a circle, brandishing their fists and chanting their slogans in a fearsome voice. As soon as the crews had their footage the cameras were turned off, and the demonstrators melted away peacefully into the crowd.)

11. Like surgeons, newsmen bury their mistakes. Partly because credibility is one of their most vital assets, and partly because they see little "news" value in a correction, both editors and reporters fiercely resist setting the record straight except when absolutely necessary. Even then they usually do so as inconspicuously as possible. They also get extremely defensive about their mistakes, and often go to extraordinary lengths to find ways of justifying them. (When someone turns out to have been falsely maligned in a news story, a common response by the reporter is to try to dig up some other dirt, so as to protect his own reputation at the expense of his subject's.)

In 1974 NBC's Carl Stern broadcast a report that Richard A. Moore, special counsel to the President, had been named an additional unindicted co-conspirator in the Watergate cover-up case. The report was devastating to Moore, a lawyer with an unblemished reputation for integrity. It was also totally false, and the special prosecutor's office promptly issued a statement saying it was false. Moore called Stern, asking if NBC would at least make some mention of the correction. Stern replied: "I'd like to, but as a television man you know that's not the nature of the beast." (Before joining the administration, Moore was president of a television station in Los Angeles.) The item went uncorrected.

One example I found particularly aggravating involved what was probably the most serious single charge leveled at us in the entire Watergate affair: the *Washington Post*'s accusation (in a September 21, 1975, story written by Bob Woodward) that unnamed White House officials had conspired to murder syndicated columnist Jack Anderson. The *Post* bannered its charge across eight columns at the top of page 1. As a result of the story, the Senate Intelligence Committee launched an investigation. In June 1976 the committee issued a report, stating that there was no evidence to support the charge. The wire services and the *Times* carried the story—but not the *Post*. Infuriated, I wrote to the *Post*'s ombudsman, Charles Seib,[3] protesting that since the original charge was "emblazoned across the top of page one in an eight-column headline, and written in such a way as to smear everyone who had been a White House official at the time with the tar brush of conspiracy to commit murder," the Senate report finding it groundless "deserves, if not

---

3. The *Post*'s establishment of an ombudsman to look into complaints about the paper's treatment of the news represents, I think, an important forward step. Judging from the columns he occasionally writes about the controversies that crop up, Seib seems to be handling an inherently difficult job with both courage and responsibility. More papers should follow suit.

equal treatment, at least one of those 14-point 'correction' heads on a paragraph somewhere east of Ann Landers and west of the used tire ads." A month later, on an inside page, the *Post* did carry a rather grudging story: "No Evidence Found of Plot to Kill Anderson." Seib sent it to me, with a covering note saying it was the result of my letter. Had I not protested, even that gross libel would have been allowed, by the *Post*, to stand as uncontroverted truth.

12. Since encountering the right-brain left-brain phenomenon, I have often puzzled over the ways in which it helps shape the strange and often contradictory folkways of the journalistic tribe. They seem pulled in two directions. Verbal skills are left-brain skills, and many journalists take particular pride in their analytic reasoning, their capacity to marshal facts, and process information in a classically linear manner. Many also emphasize what they see as their special talent for intuitive perceptions, for gut reactions, for cutting through the facts of a story to extract the human interest— speaking directly to the emotions of the reader or viewer. These two thrusts are in constant conflict with one another, producing a sort of professional schizophrenia. Much more than most journalists would admit, the presentation of the news tends to be governed by right-brain perceptions, by emotional triggers, by a "romantic" cast of mind. Journalism has become one of the "glamour" professions, "creative," reformist, with a self-perception of knight-errantry and derring-do, of dragon-slaying and maiden-saving.

The romance of journalism attracts the romantic into it, and the "romantic" values in journalism sell newspapers and attract viewers. There may, as a practical matter, be little that can be done about this, except to recognize it and try to take it into account. The important thing is not to confuse romantic truth with empirical truth, and not to fall into the trap of making empirical judgments on the basis of romantic perceptions.

Once, comparing the liberal columnists Shana Alexander and Meg Greenfield, I commented that the difference between them is that Greenfield thinks before she writes, while Alexander writes before she thinks. I was, of course, using "think" in its linear-logical sense; both of course think, but Greenfield reasons *toward* a conclusion, while Alexander starts *from* an intuitive perception or an emotionally charged value judgment.

Television has vastly changed the nature of the news business, and the nature and significance of that change are still only dimly understood. People turn to the news, whether print or broadcast, for both information and entertainment. Whereas print journalism has tended more toward the presentation of information that entertains, the structure of television news is such that it is designed to be an entertainment that informs. And this in turn has increased the competitive pressure on the print media to be more entertaining. As people grow acclimated to the dramatic nature of television reporting, they develop, subliminally, an expectation of drama, an appetite for it, when they pick up a newspaper or a magazine. They want their pill sugar-coated.

Misinforming the audience is still regarded as a journalistic fault, but as a lesser fault than boring the audience. The reason is strictly a business one. Misinforming merely abuses the audience; boring loses the audience.

Reuven Frank, former president of NBC News, once laid down this rule for television: "Every news story should, without sacrifice of probity or responsibility, display the attributes of fiction, of drama. It should have structure and conflict, problem and denouement, rising action and falling action, a beginning, a middle and an end." The problem, of course, is that this cannot be done "without sacrifice of probity or responsibility." The news does not happen that way. Real events seldom come in such neat, dramatic packages. They have to be molded, squeezed, formed—to fit the formula, news has to be *created*, just like fiction itself.

CBS commentator Eric Sevareid has complained that "show-business aspects of news broadcasting will always be there, but the pressures for these aspects to dominate are becoming too strong." Irving Kristol goes further, calling television "the greatest disaster that journalism has ever experienced." Television news, Kristol points out, "is the slave of that most superficial and unenlightening of perceptual instruments: the camera. Without the tyranny of the camera, television is a boring lecture or recital; surrendering to its tyranny, television news is an exciting, dramatic, and grossly oversimplified presentation of events. . . . The camera cannot unravel complex intellectual issues, it cannot distinguish important from trivial detail, it cannot follow an argument to a reasoned conclusion. . . . What television *can* do, however—and do with extraordinary power—is to mobilize the audience's emotions around a vivid, simplified, essentially melodramatic vision of the political world, in which praise and blame are the magnetic poles. What television can do, in other words, is what demagogic rhetoric used to do less efficatiously."[4]

The seldom-acknowledged secret of journalism is that what sells is not truth, but drama. The illusion of truth enhances the drama,

4. "Press, Politics and Popular Government" (Washington, D.C., 1972).

but the drama is what sells. Journalism is less concerned with pursuit of the truth than it is with pursuit of a good story. It of course is preferable if, as Henry Kissinger once remarked in another context, the story "has the added virtue of being true." The undramatic truth sparks little journalistic interest. If a dubious story is sufficiently dramatic, the media race to present it before the facts have a chance to catch up.

The plain fact is that the journalist, the politician, and the soap-peddler all are in the same business: selling. And all three know that the way to hook the audience is to picture things larger than life. In the soap commercial, getting out that stubborn grease or grime is a matter of life or death. The housewife's whole world is going to crumble until—hosannah!—she finds her washday miracle. In real life, one soap is about the same as another, and a stubborn stain is simply a stubborn stain. But in the commercial, all is hypoed.

In the news, too, all is hypoed. Reporters are made or broken, publications live or die, ratings are gained or lost by the ability to command attention. One of the fiercest—and least reported—contests in the nation is the contest among network reporters to get their own stories, and therefore themselves, on the evening news. The way to get on is to make the story *seem* dramatic. For a journalist, it becomes very easy to persuade himself that a story achieves nothing unless it grabs the reader or the viewer, and therefore that hypoing the lead is a service to essential truth even if not to literal truth. It also becomes very easy to fall into the trap of believing that what sells papers or boosts ratings is news, and thereby to imbue sensationalism with an overlay of moral virtue.

Watergate, of course, had all the elements of the most dramatic story of all: high stakes, fast action, famous stars, mystery, suspense, confrontation, good guys, and bad guys. Further, it was the best kind of story, from a newsman's standpoint: not a one-day story, but a building story, the sort that engages the audience's interest and holds its attention, promising a continuing series of dramatic denouements. It is on such stories that journalistic legends are built, for such stories that journalistic prizes are awarded, and from such stories that reporters and editors reap fame and fortune.

All this, and Nixon too.

"The notion that Mr. Nixon is a sort of monster," the late columnist Stewart Alsop once wrote, "has been almost an article of faith among liberal politicians and journalists." By the fall of 1970, *Christian Science Monitor* correspondent Courtney Sheldon noted that "the ancient jousting between the press and government officials" had "reached a new level of acerbity," while syndicated columnist Harriet Van Horne helped drive his point home by shrilling that Washington was "a city under enemy occupation." In early 1971, exhorting a mostly student crowd of two thousand at an antiwar teach-in at Harvard to "engage in civil disobedience of all kinds," *New York Times* columnist Tom Wicker declared: "We got one President out and perhaps we can do that again."

The media hostility that dogged Nixon through most of his political life probably passed its point of no return on November 13, 1969. Speaking at a Midwest Regional Republican Committee meeting in Des Moines, Iowa, Vice-President Agnew—at Nixon's instigation, and with Pat Buchanan writing the speech—launched a blistering attack on the three television networks' news coverage. Stressing that he was "not asking for government censorship or any other kind of censorship," he asked "whether a form of censorship already exists" by the networks themselves, with "a small and un-elected elite" who lived and worked entirely in the "geographical and intellectual confines of Washington, D.C., or New York City" determining for the nation what its people would see and hear. He protested the "instant analysis and querulous criticism" of the President's speech to the nation on Vietnam ten days earlier, when "the audience of seventy million Americans—gathered to hear the President of the United States—was inherited by a small band of network commentators and self-appointed analysts, the majority of whom expressed, in one way or another, hostility to what he had to say." He declared that the networks' "endless pursuit of controversy" had produced "a narrow and distorted picture of America." He called on members of the media to "turn their critical powers on themselves," and to "direct their energy, talent and conviction toward improving the quality and objectivity of news presentation." And he called on the public to "let the networks know that they want their news straight and objective. . . . This is one case where the people must defend themselves . . . where the citizen—not the government—must be the reformer."

A week later, before the Montgomery, Alabama, Chamber of Commerce, Agnew returned to the attack—this time broadening his list of targets to include *The New York Times* and *The Washington Post,* and declaring: "The day when the network commentators and even the gentlemen of *The New York Times* enjoyed a form of diplomatic immunity from comment and criticism of what they said is over. . . . I do not seek to intimidate the press, the networks, or anyone else from speaking out. But the time for blind acceptance of their opinions is past. And the time for naïve belief in their neutrality is gone."

The reaction from the media was swift, explosive—and predictable. CBS president Frank Stanton called it "an unprecedented attempt by the Vice-President of the United States to intimidate a news medium," and raised the specter of a press "subservient to the executive power of government." NBC president Julian Goodman lashed out that it was "an appeal to prejudice," and added, echoing Stanton: "Evidently he would prefer a different kind of television reporting—one that would be subservient to whatever political group was in authority at the time." Others in the industry responded that it was "sinister, ignorant, and base," that it was an "implied threat to freedom of speech in this country," that it was "one of the most sinister speeches that I have ever heard made by a public official." (The purple-prose prize, however, probably goes not to a network official but rather to New York mayor John Lindsay's cultural commissioner, Thomas Hoving, who declared that it "officially leads us as a nation into an ugly era of the most fearsome suppression and intimidation—the beginning of the end for us as a nation . . . the most shocking use ever of political power.")

Though in some respects Agnew overstated his case, I thought that basically what he said needed saying. I tried—unsuccessfully —to get his second speech toned down somewhat, and objected to the idea of his going to Montgomery to attack the *Post* and the *Times*. (I did see a draft of the second speech before it was given, but did not see the first.) But the issues he raised were serious issues, which deserved a serious debate—and in particular, as he urged, a serious and searching debate by journalists themselves.

Of course, the networks quite correctly perceived that he was not only calling for debate but also challenging their own credibility. There was nothing subtle about this, and most of us at the White House hardly felt any apologies were in order. The question, in our minds, was not whether news organizations should be "subservient" to the administration—a silly straw man—but whether we had a right to warn the public not to be misled by reporting that we considered heavily biased, sometimes propagandistic and often untrue. We thought we had that right. (Whether tactically it was a wise course is another question.)

But the networks took it as a declaration of war, trying to escalate every criticism into an attack on the First Amendment. At various times Walter Cronkite accused the administration of "a grand conspiracy to destroy the credibility of the press," "a clear effort at intimidation," a "very serious assault" on the press, and of trying "to suggest in every possible way that the press has no privileges in this society." In a *New York Times* round-table discussion in 1973 Cronkite declared that the Nixon administration had "created two Americas—one that believes in freedom of speech and press and one that doesn't." At the same round-table, ABC's Howard K. Smith more levelheadedly argued: "I think that if we give them hell they're entitled to give us hell, as long as they don't suggest restrictions on freedom. . . . May I observe that we've planted seeds of doubt in the public's mind about the credibility of people in government. And I don't think it's bad if they criticize us. I don't think we're above criticism, as long as there are no specific restrictions of freedom of the press, which I think was basically the position of Agnew."

(The peculiar ferocity of the networks in responding to every criticism as if it were an assault on the First Amendment was not limited to those leveled by the administration. In 1971 quite a contretemps arose over a CBS documentary called "The Selling of the Pentagon." The network was caught in some very shady editorial practices, including splicing together speeches and transposing questions and answers from an interview, all done so as to make military spokesmen appear in a bad light. *The Washington Post* criticized CBS editorially, noting that such practices do "in fact result in a material distortion of the record." CBS News president Richard Salant angrily accused the *Post* of suggesting that "sound journalistic ethics and the First Amendment are somehow divisible" between print and broadcast media. NBC News president Reuven Frank branded the *Post*'s criticism "arrogant . . . frightening. . . . I had thought we were at least a decade past those days when newsmen considered freedom to gather and transmit information freely according to the tradition of their craft was somehow a chemical component of ink. But when *The Washington Post* can Agnewize in this fashion I hear a bell tolling.")

Shortly after the 1976 election, Richard Reeves, the lively and literate political correspondent (since resigned) for *New York* magazine, delivered a commentary on the campaign refreshing for its candor and remarkable for its rarity. He recounted watching on television as Jimmy Carter said a tearful "thank you" to his neighbors in Plains, and then as Gerald Ford appeared before cameras in the East Room to concede the election. "I was moved, deeply," he wrote, "by the grace of the man in transferring power without public bitterness or self-pity. Inside, Ford must have been dying—to come *so close.* I wondered whether I could do what he was doing and was proud to be part of a country where governments are changed that way."

This was a gracious concession by Reeves, who had been biting in his characterizations of both men during the campaign. In itself it was hardly unprecedented; in the emotional aftermath of an electoral decision, reporters often warm toward their former targets. But then he went on to add the uncommon comment:

"These were the two clowns I have been hearing about and reading about, and watching and writing about. There was something very wrong with this campaign, and in the final analysis, it was not them and it was not the American people; it was us, the Press. John Chancellor, Eric Sevareid, Roger Mudd, and a lot of the best people I have ever known—and me. We were pompous and petty, overbearing and adolescent." He pointed out that it was not the candidates who had waged a trivia campaign, but rather the media who focused on trivia to the exclusion of all else, and then added: "I don't think there is anything wrong with making fun of politicians and presidents—actually, I make a living doing it. They *are* laughable a good deal of the time. But there is more to them than that, and if we don't start showing what it is, we are going to be the ones laughed at—or stoned, by someone more credible than Spiro Agnew. Perhaps the first stones will be thrown by the teams of social and political scientists currently preparing learned treatises on the 'interaction' between press and politics in the 1976 campaign. I hope so; it's time."[5]

Spiro Agnew could hardly have said it better, if he were still around. Or Richard Nixon, if he were still around.

At its best, American journalism is penetrating, insightful, public-spirited, responsible, courageous, thoughtful—and it goes without saying that it is utterly necessary. In letting its anger boil over, the Nixon administration often overreacted to reporting that was frequenly less unfair than it seemed. By the same token, the media overreacted to administration displeasure with their performance. As the relationship soured, both sides lost. The administration lost much of the support that it might otherwise have found. The media lost some of the professionalism that they might otherwise have shown. Anger, grievance, resentment, fear, all have a way of warping judgments and blighting performance. I wish those years could be replayed with less ingrained hostility on both sides. They might have ended very differently.

5. *New York* magazine, 15 November 1976.

XII

"A FREE AND OPEN SOCIETY"

Two days before the 1972 election, Nixon gave an interview to Garnett Horner of *The Washington Star* about his plans for the second term, for publication on the Sunday following the election. As written up by Horner and published by the *Star*, it provided a wide-ranging preview of what Nixon had in mind: He intended to "shuck off" and "trim down" those 1960s social programs that he believed had turned out to be expensive failures, to appoint additional conservative judges, to stand firm against tax increases, to reduce the size of the federal bureaucracy, to "find a way to reform our government institutions so that this new spirit of independence, self-reliance, pride that I sense in the American people can be nurtured." If he could get the needed support in the Congress, he declared, his administration would accomplish "more significant reform" than any since Franklin Roosevelt's—but reform "in a different direction," one which would "diffuse power throughout the country." The 1972 election, he predicted, would demonstrate that "the American people will thrive upon a new feeling of responsibility, a new feeling of self-discipline, rather than go back to the thoughts of the 1960s that it was government's job every time there was a problem, to make people more and more dependent upon it, to give way to their whims."

In driving home his point, he used a familiar figure of speech: "The average American is just like the child in the family. You give him some responsibility and he is going to amount to something. He is going to do something. If, on the other hand, you make him completely dependent and pamper him and cater to him too much, you are going to make him soft, spoiled and eventually a very weak individual."

It seemed to me that his meaning was "perfectly clear," to borrow a phrase Nixon purged from his vocabulary early in his presidency. In context, the remark was thoroughly consistent with the basic themes he had been hammering at throughout his four years in office: that the federal government should be less patronizing, less intrusive, that power and responsibility should be dispersed so that people could make more of their decisions themselves—that they should be treated as responsible, independent adults, not as incompetent wards of the state. Yet the ink was barely dry before a chorus of media commentators seized on his "child in the family" analogy to portray it as exactly the opposite: he had, they trumpeted, callously shown his contempt for the American people by saying they "should be treated like children."

In the Horner interview, Nixon was basically repeating the theme of a nationwide radio address he had given just a few days earlier, in which he also used the "family" analogy: "In a family, when a father tells the rest of the family what to do, that's called paternalism. In a business, when an employer tells workers he knows what is best for their future, that is called paternalism. And in government, when a central authority in Washington tells people across the country how they should conduct their lives, that, too, is paternalism. . . . It is time that good, decent people stopped letting themselves be bulldozed by anybody who presumes to be the self-righteous moral judge of our society. . . . We have achieved a high degree of leadership throughout our history because we have put aside the notion of a 'leadership class'. . . . This is the land where an alien paternalism has no place at all—because we deeply believe in a system that derives its power from the consent of the governed."

Two months later Nixon again returned to this same thought as the central theme of his second inaugural: "Abroad and at home, the time has come to turn away from the condescending policies of paternalism—of 'Washington knows best.' A person can be expected to act responsibly only if he has responsibility. This is human nature. So let us encourage individuals at home and nations abroad to do more for themselves, to decide more for themselves. Let us locate responsibility in more places."

But still, because in that one interview he had used the analogy of the family to frame the same argument, the media continued to hammer into the popular mythology: Nixon thought that the American people should be treated like children.

If this illustrates the difficulty we had in communicating ideas accurately through the distorting prisms of the media, it also points up the sometimes curious nature of the struggle.

One of the truly great ironies of the Nixon era is that the President portrayed, in his disgrace, as a power-mad fiend whose removal was necessary to the preservation of America's liberties, spent most of his presidency trying to get rid of power. Though portrayed as the architect of the Imperial Presidency, it was he who tried to reverse four decades of increasing centralization of authority. And, in a double irony, his efforts to disperse power away from Washington, to reduce the role of the federal government, to relocate authority and responsibility outward, helped create the hostility of those who, because of that hostility, portrayed him as power-mad. Many of his struggles with the Congress were over precisely that—pitting congressional determination to expand federal powers against Nixon's determination to reduce federal powers. One of the reasons for his difficulties with the media was that they, by and large, subscribed to the bigger-government-is-better school, and strongly disapproved his efforts to limit government. And one of the reasons (in addition to the war) for his unpopularity among "activist" youth was that they, too, had been conditioned to equate meeting national needs with expanding federal programs.

Within the federal government, there were several overlapping power struggles. There was the one between the Congress and the executive, and the one between the White House and the executive departments, and the one between the "political" members of the executive branch—the President and his appointees—and the permanent bureaucracy. In these, the Congress tended to be a natural ally of the bureaucracy against the political leaders, and of the departments against the White House—because of the cozy arrangements that had grown up over the years between congressional committees and the various bureaus and their staffs within the executive departments. The President is legally, constitutionally, and politically responsible for the performance of the executive branch, and for the formulation and direction of executive-branch policies—but like others before him, Nixon was constantly thwarted by the bureaucracy nominally under his command. In Nixon's case, the contest was heightened by the fact that he was trying to shift policies in a fundamentally new direction, which would have the effect of cutting back the functions of the federal bureaucracy.

Common Cause founder John Gardner, former secretary of health, education and welfare, has noted that "questions of public policy nominally lodged with the secretary are often decided far beyond the secretary's reach by a trinity consisting of (1) representatives of an outside lobby, (2) middle-level bureaucrats, and (3) selected members of Congress, particularly those concerned with appropriations. In a given field, these people have collaborated for years. They have a durable alliance that cranks out legislation and appropriations on behalf of their special interests."

John Whitaker, former Nixon White House aide and later under-secretary of the interior, has argued that "This 'iron triangle'—composed of the vested interest, select members of Congress, and the middle-level bureaucracy—runs the federal government." Because of this "iron triangle," Whitaker argues, "to attempt fundamental reorganization of the government is to take on a political fight almost impossible to win. The lobbyists do not want change. After all, many have spent their adult lives getting to know the players in the other two corners of the triangle. The bureaucrats do not want change. No matter how often they are assured that they will not lose their jobs when they are transferred to some new and strange departments, they are bound to worry. . . . Finally, the members of the congressional committees resist change since the longer they hold their committee assignments, the more influence they can exert on the departments under their jurisdiction."[1] Or, as Nixon himself put it early in 1971, as he exhorted his cabinet and subcabinet members to fight for his proposals to streamline and reorganize the executive branch: "Everybody, whether in government, in business, in labor, and any kind of group, has a vested interest in keeping things the way they are, because he knows all those plays. He doesn't like to change the system, have to learn a lot of new signals and all the rest. If he does, he thinks somebody will knock them over, so he prefers to keep it in those lines. That doesn't mean he's a bad man. It simply means he is being normal because it is very difficult to change."

When he presented those 1971 State of the Union proposals— somewhat grandiloquently dubbed the "New American Revolution" —Nixon knew he was in for a fight. They included a wholesale reorganization of the executive branch, and also a wholesale turning away from the old system of "categorical grants" that had federal bureaucrats second-guessing every sort of local decision from the height of buildings to the location of sewer lines. (He also knew he was inviting criticism with the "New American

1. *Striking a Balance: Environment and Natural Resources: Policy in the Nixon-Ford Years* (Washington, D.C., 1976).

Revolution" label, which did stick in the throats of quite a few commentators, and brought editorial rebukes even from such relatively sympathetic sources as *The Wall Street Journal.* When he first lobbed it at me, as we worked on the speech, he did so with the comment: "We've been searching for a slogan. What I've decided on—it's going to shock the people like yourself, the purists, the intellectuals—it's the New American Revolution. But it really *is* a new American revolution—for the first time since 1790 this really marks a change in government in America."

Nixon was concerned that unless the direction of change was shifted, America would soon go the way of Britain. In that 1971 State of the Union, he noted that at each great turning-point in the nation's history when the question had been between the states and the federal government—and dramatically so in the 1930s—that question had been resolved in favor of a stronger central government. He argued: "During this time the nation grew and the nation prospered. But one thing history tells us is that no great movement goes in the same direction forever. Nations change, they adapt, or they slowly die." He rejected "the idea that a bureaucratic elite in Washington knows best what is best for people everywhere and that you cannot trust local governments," declaring that this "is really a contention that you cannot trust people to govern themselves. . . . Local government is the government closest to the *people,* it is most responsive to the individual *person.* It is people's government in a far more intimate way than the government in Washington can ever be."

Getting to the heart of the political problem, he spoke directly to the members of Congress: "I realize that what I am asking is that not only the executive branch in Washington but that even this Congress will have to change by giving up some of its power. Change is hard. But without change there can be no progress. . . . Giving up power is hard. But I would urge all of you, as leaders of this country, to remember that the truly revered leaders in world history are those who gave power to people, and not those who took it away."

In his proposed reorganization, Nixon urged that the twelve cabinet departments be cut down to eight, with State, Defense, Treasury, and Justice kept substantially intact and the others consolidated into four new departments: Human Resources, Community Development, Natural Resources, and Economic Development. (Later, under intense political pressure, he revised this to retain Agriculture as a separate department, though drastically reduced in size.) The purpose was to make the executive branch manageable—reducing the number of officials reporting directly to the President, and reducing the number of conflicts that had to be resolved at the White House. By organizing according to function, and consolidating those bureaus and agencies with related functions under a single department, more questions could be resolved at the department level. (As examples of the fragmentation Nixon faced, nine federal departments and twenty independent agencies were involved in education matters, seven departments and eight agencies in health. Federal recreation areas were administered by six different agencies scattered in three departments. Seven different agencies provided assistance for local water and sewer systems. One result was to create an administrative nightmare; another result was constantly to require resolution of differences at the White House level, which, as a practical matter, frequently meant by White House staff members operating out of their depth.)

But however much it might have been needed, reorganization faced one hurdle that turned out to be insuperable: the congressional committee structure was geared to the old organization. Reshuffling committees would mean tampering with the seniority positions of committee members. It would also break up the cozy arrangements committee members and committee staffs had with the old departmental bureaucracies. So reorganization got nowhere. (At the start of his second term, Nixon tried to achieve administratively what he had not been able to get approved legislatively. He designated four cabinet officers as counselors—"supersecretaries," they came to be called—for Natural Resources, Human Resources, Community Development, and Economic Affairs,[2] gave them White House offices, and set them up as cabinet-level referees of interdepartmental disputes. But with Watergate pressures mounting, and with John Ehrlichman's departure in April 1973, this never really got off the ground.)

While reorganization was designed to make the federal government manageable, the philosophical heart of the "New American Revolution" was revenue sharing. This, more dramatically than any other single initiative, was aimed at cutting back the functions of the federal government, substituting local judgment for federal judgment, restoring local initiative, and encouraging local responsibility. It reflected a belief, as Pat Moynihan used to express

2. The four were Agriculture Secretary Earl Butz for Natural Resources, HEW Secretary Caspar Weinberger for Human Resources, HUD Secretary James Lynn for Community Development, and Treasury Secretary George Shultz for Economic Affairs.

it, that the federal government is "very good at collecting revenues, but very bad at dispensing services." It also reflected a belief that local elected officials rather than distant federal bureaucrats should decide priorities for their own communities.

The proliferation of federal "categorical grant programs" had been staggering. In just ten years, from 1962 to 1972, they rose from 160 to more than 1000. The common denominators of these programs were red tape, paperwork, federal approvals, federally required reports, federally mandated standards, enforced conformity, long delays, rigidity, bureaucratic second-guessing—and an erosion of local responsibility.

Federal education grants, in 1971, were being made available to local schools through 38 separate authorizations for "instruction," 37 separate authorizations for low-income students, and 22 separate authorizations for reading instruction. School districts had to hire whole special staffs just to process applications, and to keep track of guidelines and reporting requirements; rational budgeting was impossible because of the year-to-year uncertainty over whether applications would be approved. Urban renewal grants were so tangled in red tape that federal participation involved some 300 separate procedural steps, and it took an average of three years for an urban renewal plan to be developed and accepted, ten years for it to be completed.

Nixon proposed to sweep away whole clusters of these programs, and instead to provide the money to states and localities for certain broad purposes—education, law enforcement, manpower development, rural development, transportation, urban community development—with local officials free to make their own decisions about what to spend it on within those categories. (These conversions of categorical grant programs were dubbed "special revenue sharing"; he also pressed for—and got—a program of "general revenue sharing," in which federal funds were passed out to states and localities on a formula basis for whatever uses they chose.) This would have the effect of abolishing whole bureaucracies, and of sharply cutting back the power of the federal government—including individual members of Congress and congressional staffs, through their leverage on the bureaucracy—to interfere in local government, and to promote pet projects at the expense of others. As the Brookings Institution's Richard P. Nathan has pointed out, "Despite the fact that both decentralizing and centralizing proposals were part of the Nixon program, the important direction of change was *decentralization.* Coming at the end of a thirty-year period in which the predominant trend of domestic policy had been to increase the responsibility of the national government, Nixon's program marked an important shift. At its roots, the New Federalism program involved basic social values; it was designed to reinforce *a sense of community* and thereby to increase the capacity of individuals to influence events."[3]

Of the "special revenue sharing" proposals, two were finally enacted—those for manpower training and urban community development. It was only a start, but it was a start. Combined with a significant slowing-down of the creation of new categorical grant programs from that of Johnson's Great Society period, it did mark the beginning of a new approach to the allocation of power and responsibility between the federal government and the nation's other institutions.

Nixon's judicial appointments were also, quite deliberately, a part of his drive to make government less meddlesome and less intrusive.

Nixon's first nomination to the Supreme Court, ironically, marked the end of a judicial era that began with Eisenhower's first Supreme Court nomination. The first vacancy filled by Eisenhower came with the death of Chief Justice Fred M. Vinson. He named California governor Earl Warren, and the Warren Court was born. Nixon's first nominee was for the seat of retiring Chief Justice Warren, and he chose Warren E. Burger, a justice of the U.S. Circuit Court of Appeals in Washington. If some saw a symbolism in the unusual reversal of names—Warren Earl Burger for Earl Warren—Nixon hoped the shift would be more than symbolic. Warren had come to symbolize judicial activism—the wholesale intrusion by the federal courts into areas of policy choice traditionally the province of the legislative and executive branches, and of states and localities. Nixon was a firm believer in the principle of judicial restraint: that it was the Court's role to construe the Constitution and interpret the laws, not to make social policy; that its function was to decide whether a legislative enactment was constitutionally permissible, not whether it was good or bad.

Burger was confirmed with little difficulty. But not so with Nixon's next two nominees, Clement F. Haynsworth, Jr., and G. Harrold Carswell. One evening in 1975, as we sipped after-dinner brandy in the study of his home in San Clemente, I mentioned to Nixon that if I had been a member of the Senate I would have

3. *The Plot That Failed: Nixon and the Administrative Presidency* (New York, 1975), p. 22. Nathan served as assistant director of the Bureau of the Budget at the start of Nixon's first term, and contributed importantly to Nixon's early "new federalism" proposals.

voted for Haynsworth and against Carswell. I thought Haynsworth had been shot down in a shoddy display of political hypocrisy, sectional prejudice, and interest-group pressure, and would have been a highly distinguished addition to the Court. But I thought Carswell was a judicial mediocrity who had no business being on the Court. With the benefit of hindsight, Nixon agreed.

At the time, however, Nixon gave no quarter in either confirmation fight. When the Senate's rejection of Haynsworth[4] was followed by its rejection of Carswell, an angry Nixon strode into the press room, glowered at the television cameras, and declared: "I have reluctantly concluded that it is not possible to get confirmation for a judge on the Supreme Court of any man who believes in the strict construction of the Constitution, as I do, if he happens to come from the South. Judge Carswell, and before him, Judge Haynsworth, have been submitted [sic] to vicious assaults on their intelligence, on their honesty, and on their character. They have been falsely charged with being racists. But when you strip away all the hypocrisy, the real reason for their rejection was their legal philosophy, a philosophy that I share, of strict construction of the Constitution, and also the accident of their birth, the fact that they were born in the South."

Throughout the 1968 campaign Nixon stressed his belief that the courts, and especially the Supreme Court, had gone too far in the direction of free-wheeling judicial activism; that they were usurping the prerogatives of Congress and infringing the prerogatives of the executive; that he would use his power of judicial appointment to sway them back toward the traditional mold of judicial restraint—of "strict construction" of the Constitution. He also had stressed his belief that the South had been discriminated against too long, and that a century after the Civil War it was time to begin treating the South once again as a full-fledged part of the union.

For years, ever since *Brown* v. *Board of Education* in 1954, the federal courts had been imposing draconian decrees on Southern states and communities, as they sought to break up generations-old patterns of racial segregation. Yet when Nixon became President, the Court had only one member from the South: Hugo L. Black of Alabama, who, with William O. Douglas, had long held down the most liberal end of the judicial spectrum. Nixon reasoned—correctly, I think—not only that the overwhelmingly conservative

---

4. Haynsworth was nominated for the seat of Associate Justice Abe Fortas, a Johnson nominee—and crony—who resigned under a conflict-of-interest cloud. When Haynsworth was rejected, Nixon nominated Carswell for the same seat.

South deserved representation by at least one conservative South-erner on the court that was rapidly remaking the South's institutions but also that its decisions would be better received in a South that had such representation. Besides, he was serious both about his belief in strict constructionism as a basic constitutional principle, and about his belief that it was time to bring the South back within the union. So, for his next Court vacancy after the Chief Justice, he sought not only a distinguished jurist with experience on the federal bench but quite specifically a judicially conservative one from the South. The Justice Department served up the name of Clement Haynsworth of Greenville, South Carolina, chief judge of the Fourth Circuit Court of Appeals, legal scholar, grower of prize-winning camellias, pillar of the community and of the bar, a judge highly respected by his colleagues in the bar and on the bench. On August 18, 1969, Nixon submitted his name to the Senate.

Civil-rights groups angrily protested, charging that Haynsworth was a racist because some of his judicial opinions had not gone their way. The AFL-CIO protested, charging that he was antiunion because some of his decisions had not gone their way, and vowed an all-out fight to block his confirmation. Indiana's Senator Birch Bayh, whose campaigns were heavily funded by AFL-CIO unions, led a vicious character-assassination campaign, first in the Judiciary Committee and then on the Senate floor. Bayh charged conflict of interest, claiming that Haynsworth had repeatedly sat in judgment in cases in which he had a "substantial" financial interest in the outcome.

On examination, the Bayh charges utterly and completely evapo-rated. Typical of those cases in which he charged a "substantial interest" for which Haynsworth should have disqualified himself, and from which Bayh insinuated Haynsworth profited, was *Farrow v. Grace Lines, Inc.* Haynsworth (a wealthy man, with a substantial and diversified stock portfolio) owned 300 shares in W. R. Grace & Co., of which Grace Lines was one of 53 subsidiaries, contributing some 7 percent of the parent company's $1.6 billion revenues. What Haynsworth's Fourth Circuit Court of Appeals did in *Farrow* v. *Grace Lines* was unanimously to uphold a lower court's $50 judg-ment against Grace Lines, the subsidiary of the $1.6-billion-a-year company in which Haynsworth held a minuscule 300 shares of stock.

Of such vaporous stuff were the Bayh charges against Hayns-worth made. (Judges are required by statute to disqualify them-selves in cases in which they have a "substantial" interest. However the courts had repeatedly ruled that judges had a positive duty *not* to disqualify themselves in cases where their interest is not substantial. Congress later—in 1974—modified this "duty-to-sit" rule.)

In all the "conflict-of-interest" cases trumpeted by Bayh, the largest amount by which the court's action in any one of them could even theoretically have affected the value of the millionaire Haynsworth's holding was $5. The conflict-of-interest charges against Haynsworth were sham and pretense. Those professional colleagues who knew him best, the other six judges of the Fourth Circuit Court of Appeals, took the rare step of stating publicly their "unshaken confidence" in Haynsworth's ability, honesty, and integrity. Sixteen former presidents of the American Bar Association joined in rejecting the smear campaign against him, and urging his confirmation. But the real case against Haynsworth was that he was a Southern conservative. Though personally untainted by racism, he fell victim to the anti-Southern bigotry that was then still fashionable—and which was cynically used by interest groups whose interest lay in keeping conservatives off the court. After intensive lobbying by the AFL-CIO, by the NAACP, and by the Leadership Conference on Civil Rights, the Senate rejected Haynsworth's nomination on November 21 by a vote of 55 to 45.

Determined not to take the Haynsworth defeat lying down, Nixon sent word to the Justice Department that he wanted another nominee from the South: a sitting federal judge, a judicial conservative, and a Republican. These criteria sharply limited the available pool, but the department came up with one who looked good on paper: G. Harrold Carswell. Carswell had served five years as a U.S. attorney, eleven years as a federal district judge, and only a year earlier had been unanimously confirmed by the Senate as a judge of the U.S. Circuit Court of Appeals—the next highest tribunal to the Supreme Court itself. As Nixon later pointed out in a letter to Senator William B. Saxbe of Ohio, Carswell had had "longer and more complete judicial service than any Supreme Court appointee in recent decades other than Chief Justice Burger." But as the increasingly stormy hearings on his nomination wore on, it became increasingly clear that the most apt defense was the one offered ineptly (or perhaps tongue-in-cheek) by Nebraska's Senator Roman L. Hruska: that, after all, mediocrity too deserved representation on the high court.

What first galvanized opposition to Carswell was a charge of racism—a charge based flimsily on a speech he had made twenty-two years earlier, as a young candidate for office in the still rigidly segregated Deep South, and on the fact that he had once been involved, fourteen years earlier, together with other community leaders, in the incorporation of a racially restricted golf club. But the charge was so flimsy that, had he been qualified, he almost certainly would have been confirmed. To do otherwise would have exposed too glaringly the hypocrisy of the campaign against Haynsworth. But mediocrity does not deserve representation on the Supreme Court, and even his initial supporters in the Senate were left with little enthusiasm for the fight. On April 8, 1970, the Senate rejected Carswell, 51–45.

In his press-room reaction, Nixon may have been genuinely angry, or he may have been posturing for political effect—reminding the South that he had tried, even as he turned north for his next nominee. Within a week he named Minnesota's Harry A. Blackmun, who for eleven years had been a judge of the U.S. Circuit Court of Appeals for the Eighth Circuit. This time, Nixon met personally with Blackmun before announcing his selection. The following year, with two vacancies to fill simultaneously,[5] he abandoned his criterion that the nominee must be a sitting federal judge. To one of the vacancies he named William H. Rehnquist, a brilliant young assistant attorney general. For the other he chose Lewis M. Powell, Jr., a Richmond attorney and former president of the American Bar Association. Both were exceptionally well qualified, both were judicial conservatives—and, in Powell, he at last had his conservative justice from the South.

Probably the most emotionally charged continuing domestic issue of the Nixon years was school desegregation in general, and busing in particular. Nixon was antisegregation, but he was also antibusing, as that term came rather loosely to be used. He bitterly resented court decrees which, he felt, went beyond the legitimate authority of the courts in fashioning wholly new requirements not only that officially sanctioned segregation be abolished, but also that racial balance be enforced. In his view, the courts that did this were not protecting constitutional rights but infringing constitutional rights, in a display of judicial activism verging on judicial tyranny.

The issue was a bloody one within the administration as well as between the administration and its critics, both left and right. I was deeply involved in it. I wrote the "white paper" on school desegregation policies that Nixon issued on March 24, 1970—an eight thousand-word examination of the legal history and social ramifications of the problem, in which Nixon spelled out his own policies while trying to calm some of the passions, raise the level

5. Replacing Associate Justices Hugo L. Black and John Marshall Harlan.

of debate, and, quite deliberately (although not acknowledging that this was one of its purposes), to lead the Supreme Court. This was the most comprehensive treatment of school-desegregation issues that had ever been issued by any president. The following year, I also wrote a similar white paper on housing discrimination, and in 1972 wrote Nixon's message to Congress proposing new legislation to limit busing, to provide a hierarchy of alternative remedies, and to impose a temporary moratorium on new busing orders.

Of all the hundreds of thousands of words that I wrote during the White House years, one of my favorite passages was a section from that 1970 school-desegregation statement. It is among my favorites because I think it successfully defined an important part of what Nixon was trying to achieve domestically:

The goal of this administration is a free and open society. In saying this, I use the words "free" and "open" quite precisely.

Freedom has two essential elements: the right to choose, and the ability to choose. The right to move out of a mid-city slum, for example, means little without the means of doing so. The right to apply for a good job means little without access to the skills that make it attainable. By the same token, those skills are of little use if arbitrary policies exclude the person who has them because of race or other distinction.

Similarly, an "open" society is one of open choices—and one in which the individual has the mobility to take advantage of those choices.

In speaking of "desegregation" or "integration," we often lose sight of what these mean within the context of a free, open, pluralistic society. We cannot be free, and at the same time be required to fit our lives into prescribed places on a racial grid—whether segregated or integrated, and whether by some mathematical formula or by automatic assignment. Neither can we be free, and at the same time be denied—because of race—the right to associate with our fellow citizens on a basis of human equality.

An open society does not have to be homogeneous, or even fully integrated. There is room within it for many communities. Especially in a nation like America, it is natural that people with a common heritage retain special ties; it is natural and right that we have Italian or Irish or Negro or Norwegian neighborhoods; it is natural and right that members of those communities feel a sense of group identity and group pride. In terms of an open society, what matters is mobility: the right and the ability of each person to decide for himself where and how he wants to live, whether as part of the ethnic enclave or as part of the larger society—or, as many do, share the life of both.

We are richer for our cultural diversity; mobility is what allows us to enjoy it.

Economic, educational, social mobility—all these, too, are essential elements of the open society. When we speak of equal opportunity we mean just that: that each person should have an equal chance at the starting line, and an equal chance to go just as high and as far as his talents and energies will take him.

Nixon also particularly liked that passage, and had me quote it in his housing message the following year. (When presidential candidate Jimmy Carter stubbed his political toe in 1976 with a defense of ethnic neighborhoods, I thought he got a bum rap—and that what he really meant was something like this.) Somewhat more succinctly, I returned to the same essential thought in the 1972 busing message: "The essence of a free society is to restrict the range of what must be done, and broaden the range of what may be done."

To me, this cuts to the heart of the basic domestic-policy debate between Nixon and his "liberal" critics. Essentially, it was a debate over how much compulsion is too much compulsion. The 1960s liberals had a passion for laws, guidelines, controls, regulations—for all the paraphernalia of enforcement that they imagined could impose their vision of an ideal society on a nation of frequently resistant people. Nixon strongly believed that government had grown too meddlesome, too intrusive, too arrogant—that people had a right to make more decisions for themselves. Elliot Richardson once mentioned to the cabinet that when he had been HEW secretary, he used to insist to reporters that "there was no major issue involving HEW pending before the Congress in which the common distinctions of liberal-vs.-conservative were even relevant." For example, he argued, "is it really more 'liberal' to have a social worker make decisions for a family, rather than letting the family make those decisions for itself? Is it really more 'liberal' to encase programs in a strait jacket of regulations imposed by Washington than to let choices be made in the community itself?"

When Nixon took office, fifteen years had passed since the Supreme Court ruled, in *Brown* v. *Board of Education,* that separate schools were inherently unequal. Fourteen years had passed since, in *Brown II,* the Court ordered that dismantling of the old dual school system should proceed "with all deliberate speed." Yet when Nixon became President, only 5.2 percent of black children in the eleven Southern states were in schools defined by the courts as "unitary" systems. Within less than two years that was increased to 90 percent—and, by and large, the change was achieved peacefully. Nixon inherited a dual school system declared unconstitutional fifteen years earlier, but still stubbornly persisting. He quietly engineered its dismantling.

One reason he succeeded where his predecessors failed was, of course, that with the passage of time the courts became more insistent, their patience shorter. But another important reason was the way he approached the task: firmly, but with respect for the affected communities, offering a helping hand rather than self-righteous lectures, systematically engaging state and local leaders in the effort, treating desegregation as a national rather than a sectional problem, emphasizing the need for solutions that were educationally sound, reining in integrationist excesses even while refusing to tolerate segregationist evasions.

In January 1970, after lengthy discussions with John Ehrlichman, Len Garment, and Harry Dent (a South Carolinian who dealt mostly with political matters at the White House, but had a keen feel for Southern sensitivities), Nixon decided to create an informal Cabinet Committee on Education. Its chief task would be to devise ways of enlisting Southern cooperation in the process of school desegregation—while, as an essential part of the process, also extending federal cooperation in working out the problems incident to desegregation. By stressing education along with desegregation, and cooperation rather than confrontation, he hoped to ease compliance into more peaceful paths. The cabinet committee in turn formed state advisory committees in most of the affected Southern states. At first glance, this seems trivial and bureaucratic. In fact, it represented an entirely new approach to that most intractable challenge of domestic policy. Because for the first time it enlisted a broad cross-section of local leadership, it proved the key to success.

Vice-President Agnew chaired the cabinet committee, but its prime moving force was its vice-chairman, George Shultz, then secretary of labor.[6] A skilled labor negotiator, Shultz has a special genius for getting people on opposing sides of an issue to work together. This was precisely the skill that was needed if desegregation were to be achieved peacefully and cooperatively in the final bastions of last-ditch resistance.

Part of Nixon's strategy was to make clear, quietly but beyond any doubt, that 1970 was the year in which the old dual systems were going to be ended. Another part of his strategy was to place squarely on local leaders the responsibility for making desegregation

6. Nixon later named Shultz director of the Office of Management and Budget, and then secretary of the treasury.

work, while offering every available federal assistance in those local efforts. The state advisory committees provided the bridge that made this possible.

Shortly after the cabinet committee was formed in February 1970, its members and staff began a series of meetings with Southern governors. They also began taking extensive soundings on whether state advisory committees could feasibly be formed, and if so how they could best be structured. They settled on the toughest state of all, Mississippi, in which to try the first. In early June they began approaching a broad cross-section of prominent Mississippians, explaining the purpose and asking if they would be willing to serve. Some declined, but fifteen—nine white, six black—accepted. The formation of the committee itself marked a milestone in Mississippi's racial history. Deliberately, it included not only blacks and whites but liberals, conservatives, segregationists, integrationists, educators, and industrialists. Shultz invited the fifteen Mississippians to meet with the cabinet committee in Washington on June 24. They were brought to the White House. For more than an hour, in an atmosphere electric with tension, they met in the Roosevelt Room. Shultz was there, together with other members of the cabinet committee: HEW Secretary Robert H. Finch, Attorney General John N. Mitchell, Postmaster General (and Alabamian) Winton M. Blount, OEO Director Donald H. Rumsfeld, presidential counselors Bryce N. Harlow and Pat Moynihan.

It was clear from the outset that the Mississippians were unsure whether they could trust one another, much less the federal government.

Shultz, presiding, opened the meeting by reiterating Nixon's call for a "special partnership" between the federal government and the districts most directly affected by desegregation orders—a call Nixon had made in proposing to Congress an emergency school-aid act to provide additional funds to help with the costs of desegregation. Shultz stressed that the advisory committee would be central to that partnership, but also emphasized that it would not be involved with the development of actual desegregation plans, and would not function in such a way as to interfere with the actions of HEW, the Justice Department, or the courts. The questions raised by the Mississippians were referred by Shultz to one or another of the cabinet members, as he tried quietly to drain away some of the tension. At 12:30, by prearrangement, they all moved across the hall into the Oval Office, where each of the Mississippians was greeted personally by the President. One of the black members, as he shook Nixon's hand, commented: "Day before yesterday, I was in jail for going to the wrong beach. Today, Mr. President, I am meeting you. If that's possible, anything can happen."

From the Oval Office, they were taken to the State Department for a luncheon in the Jefferson Room; Shultz had invited Mississippi's two senators and its five congressmen to the lunch. All had declined. (One of the seven told the cabinet committee's staff director, Robert C. Mardian: "You've been around long enough to know I'm against desegregation, and most of all against eating with niggers.") Throughout the meeting, the cabinet committee members had maneuvered urgently to keep the fledgling advisory committee from breaking apart: the experiment in cooperation was crucial, and it also was delicate. Both the whites and the blacks had been reluctant to serve: the whites because they could be badly hurt by being associated with desegregation, the blacks because they feared the committee might prove a sham. At lunch, the cabinet committee members intensively lobbied the Mississippians, stressing the importance of the task they were being asked to undertake.

One of the white members, Warren Hood, president of the Mississippi Manufacturers Association, had been asked by the cabinet committee to serve as chairman. A black physician, Dr. Gilbert Mason, president of the Biloxi chapter of the NAACP, had been asked to serve as vice-chairman. Neither wanted to do so, each pleading the press of other business. At the luncheon, Shultz and Mardian sat at the same table with Hood and Mason. Shultz urged that, because of the credibility each man had with different factions in the state, their serving together would vastly increase the credibility of the advisory committee itself. Shultz deftly played on their sense of duty; then, just as he seemed to be making headway, he excused himself from the table and motioned for Mardian to follow. Catching up, Mardian asked why they were leaving, protesting that Hood and Mason seemed almost ready to agree.

"I learned long ago," labor negotiator Shultz replied, "that when parties get that close to a decision, there's only one way they can complete it—by themselves."

Back at the table, Mason was telling Hood: "If you and I can't do this, nobody else in Mississippi can. We're probably the only black and white men in the state who can get together on something like this." And with that, the two shook hands.

With that handshake, the Mississippi committee's future was secured. Soon similar committees were formed in South Carolina, North Carolina, Georgia, Arkansas, Louisiana, and Alabama.

The members of all but the Louisiana committee were brought to

Washington, where they met at the White House with the cabinet committee, with its staff, and with the President. When the Louisiana committee was formed, Nixon took the cabinet committee to New Orleans. He also brought in the chairmen and vice-chairmen of the other state committees, and met with them all at the Royal Orleans Hotel—first with the Louisiana committee, and then, for more than two hours, with the representatives of all the committees. Desegregation was going to take place with the opening of schools that fall. When it did, he told them, "You can have good schools, inferior schools, or no schools." It was up to them. But the federal government stood ready to help. When the meeting ended, he went before the television cameras in order to drive his message home: "The highest court of the land has spoken. The unitary school system must replace the dual school system throughout the United States." If the widely predicted difficulties take place, "those who suffer will be primarily the next generation, the students, the children in the school district involved. . . . We believe, all of us, in law and order and justice. We believe in enforcing the law. But I also believe that leadership in an instance like this requires some preventive action. . . . To me, one of the most encouraging experiences that I have had since taking office was to hear each one of these leaders from the Southern states speak honestly about the problems, not glossing over the fact that there were very grave problems, telling us what was needed to be done from the federal standpoint, telling us also what they were doing at the local level. It was encouraging to see this kind of leadership come. Time will tell how successful we have been, but I do know this: As a result of these advisory committees being set up, we are going to find that in many districts the transition will be orderly and peaceful, whereas otherwise it could have been the other way. And the credit will go to these outstanding Southern leaders. . . ."

Essentially, what the committees did was to shift the debate throughout the affected area from *whether* desegregation would finally take place to *how* it would take place—peacefully or violently, with the schools saved or destroyed. Because the committees were broad-based, and because they were local, they were able to enlist a broad base of local support for the goal of making the transition peacefully and constructively. And when the schools opened that fall, it was done that way.

Yes, Nixon did have a "Southern strategy." But it was a strategy not of racism, but of respect: of ending the South's century-long isolation from the rest of the country, and addressing it cooperatively rather than punitively. A lot of myopic Northern commentators either could not or would not see the distinction. But Nixon saw it clearly. In essence, his Southern strategy was really a national strategy, one of inclusion rather than exclusion, of a single standard rather than a double standard. That Southern strategy made peaceful desegregation possible. Also, in a final irony, it made Jimmy Carter possible. Lyndon Johnson introduced a Texas drawl to the White House. But in 1968, it would still have been unthinkable for a governor from the Deep South to be elected president. By the end of Nixon's time in office, in large measure because of his deliberate efforts, for the first time since the Civil War we were one nation again. A former Georgia governor could be elected.

Because school desegregation was an intensely emotional issue, the debate over it was an intensely emotional debate. Angry conservatives pressed Nixon to denounce integration itself as a failure, and, in effect, to defy the courts. Angry liberals denounced as racist any approach that tried to place limits on federal compulsion. Politically, the issue was explosive. Blacks—even many of those who themselves opposed busing—were extremely sensitive to anything that could be interpreted as a retreat from the basic goals of racial integration, and the press were quick to brand as such a retreat any choice of the less extreme of two possible approaches. Compulsory busing was bitterly opposed in the North, South, East, and West. (A Gallup poll in April 1970 found that those questioned were against busing for racial balance by an 8–1 margin. Quite a few surveys found a majority of blacks as well as of whites against it.) Yet many of the lower courts continued to plow forward with new, sometimes radical, busing orders, some of which sent shock waves of fear across the country about what might be coming next. In February 1970, in what was probably the most extreme such decree that had yet been issued, a California state court judge ordered the Los Angeles school board to establish a virtually uniform racial balance throughout its 711–square-mile district, which then had 775,000 children in 561 schools.

It was against this background that in March 1970, in the eight thousand-word "white paper" which I wrote, Nixon set out to define his policies and to lead the courts. In saying "I wrote" this paper, I use the term rather loosely. As with most major presidential pronouncements, a number of hands were involved. With this one in particular, various aides and advisers—myself included—fought fiercely over words and phrases, with Nixon himself working it over repeatedly. I wrote the first draft, as well as putting together the subsequent drafts that incorporated the various changes that had been thrashed out. Ordinarily, the "definitive" presidential statement on a subject of this magnitude and this degree of intense public concern would have been given in the form of a televised address to the nation. He chose a written statement for this, principally for two reasons: technically, because the complexities of legal history and legal analysis that he wanted to discuss did not lend themselves to the television format; and tactically, because one of his aims was to reduce the emotional intensity of the debate, so that the difficult problems it presented could be approached more rationally. This required doing it in a low-key way.

In the paper, Nixon stressed that the desegregation issue was "not partisan" and "not sectional," and he stated explicitly that one of his purposes was "to reaffirm my personal belief that the 1954 decision of the Supreme Court in *Brown* v. *Board of Education* was right in both constitutional and human terms." He made clear that he would enforce the law, and that there would be no turning back. He stressed the importance of local leadership in adapting desegregation plans to local circumstances. His effort to lead the courts had three basic elements: (1) a careful analysis of what had been finally determined by the Supreme Court, and what had not; (2) in those areas not yet determined by the Supreme Court, an analysis of the "prevailing judicial view" as shown in rulings by the various circuit courts of appeals; and (3) an appeal to the nation to "create a climate in which these questions, when they finally are decided by the Court, can be decided in a framework most conducive to reasonable and realistic interpretation." This, he urged, required "good faith" in devising and carrying out plans that *would* meet the full constitutional requirements: "We should not provoke any court to push a constitutional principle beyond its ultimate limit in order to compel compliance with the Court's essential, but more modest, mandate. The best way to avoid this is for the nation to demonstrate that it does intend to carry out the full spirit of the constitutional mandate."

The most critical of the questions unresolved by the Supreme Court was whether so-called "*de facto*" racial separation fell under the same constitutional strictures as "*de jure*" segregation: that is, whether racial imbalance that was not the result of deliberate official action was to be outlawed along with that which did result from deliberate official action.

Some lower courts were moving dangerously into the *de facto* area, stretching legal points to find a constitutional rationale for massive compulsory busing even where officially sanctioned segregation had never existed. The Los Angeles case was an extreme example, but not an isolated example. Further, they were being prodded in this direction by pro-busing litigants; the Los Angeles decision came in a suit brought by the American Civil Liberties Union. In essence, those pressing the courts in this direction sought to require racial balance as a constitutional principle. Nixon feared —and I emphatically agreed—that if this view ever were adopted by the Supreme Court, the results would be catastrophic, not only a devastating disruption of the nation's educational system but also a near-revolution on the part of the people. Not to mention that it was totalitarian in concept, and racist in fact.

In our review of the prevailing trend of judicial opinion, we were able to point out that the higher courts had drawn "a fundamental distinction between so-called *de jure* and *de facto* segregation: *de jure* segregation arises by law or by the deliberate act of school officials and is unconstitutional; *de facto* segregation results from residential housing patterns and does not violate the Constitution." And, in cases of genuine *de facto* segregation, "school authorities are not constitutionally required to take any positive steps to correct the imbalance."

In this and the rest of our rather extended legal analysis we were, both in effect and in intent, writing a brief for the Supreme Court, and trying to create a public climate in which the Court would be more inclined to decide that way. In a separate section, outlining ten principles that Nixon said would guide administration officials in their enforcement policies, the statement included two principles which we devised in the process of preparing the statement, and which we hoped (though again, without acknowledging it) would eventually be adopted by the Court:

—Racial imbalance in a school system may be partly *de jure* in origin, and partly *de facto*. In such a case, it is appropriate to insist on remedy for the *de jure* portion, which is unlawful, without insisting on a remedy for the lawful *de facto* portion.

—*De facto* racial separation, resulting genuinely from housing patterns, exists in the South as well as the North; in neither area should this condition by itself be cause for federal enforcement actions. *De jure* segregation brought about by deliberate school-board gerrymandering exists in the North as well as the South; in both areas this must be remedied. In all respects, the law should be applied equally, North and South, East, and West.

This was an effort to get at the problem with a surgeon's knife rather than a woodsman's ax; to excise the cancer without killing the patient. It was also very consciously a part of the approach to the problem as national rather than sectional, seeking not to punish the South, but to reduce racial frictions and enhance education both South and North.

Dismantling the dual school system was clearly a national imperative. So, too, was rooting out deliberate racial discrimination under cover of a supposedly unitary system. But conscripting schoolchildren to impose an artificial racial balance was not.

In his approach to school desegregation, Nixon's aim was to use the minimum coercion necessary to achieve the essential national goal, to encourage local initiative, to respect diversity, and, to the extent possible, to treat the entire nation equally—blacks equally with whites, the South equally with the North. Like most complex and controversial public issues, it was one in which no solution could be completely satisfactory. It was one on which he was brutally assailed by his critics in the media. But it was one in which important principles were established, and important progress made.

At the end of 1970 Pat Moynihan left the White House. On December 21, at a gathering of the cabinet, the subcabinet, and the White House staff in the East Room of the White House, he rose to deliver an emotional farewell. The two years had been tumultuous for Moynihan. I was sorry to see him go. We were friends. We had shared many of the same hopes, and the same enthusiasms. He had weathered his disappointments gamely, if not gladly. Now, with perhaps a couple of hundred people seated on little gold-colored chairs, his colleagues and co-workers, he stood beneath the crystal chandeliers, every eye fixed on him as he spoke.

He recalled the nation's condition two years earlier, when Nixon was elected:

It seemed the worst of times. It was the habit then to speak of the nation as divided, and to assert that the situation was grave beyond anything since the Civil War itself. This was misleading. The country was not so much divided as fragmented; it was coming apart. . . .

The agony of war was compounded by and interacted with the great travail of race which, once again, not so much divided as fractured the society. . . .

An ominous new racial division made its appearance, and with it also a new sectional division, unattended and underappreciated, but not less threatening. . . .

The President, on taking office, moved swiftly to endorse the profoundly important but fundamentally unfulfilled commitments, especially to the poor and oppressed, which the nation had made in the 1960s. He then moved on to new commitments to groups and to purposes that had been too much ignored during that period, and beyond that to offer a critique of government the like of which has not been heard in Washington since Woodrow Wilson. In one message after another to the Congress, the fundaments of governmental reform were set forth. . . .

Since that time, mass urban violence has all but disappeared. Civil disobedience and protest have receded. Racial rhetoric has calmed. The great symbol of racial subjugation, the dual school system of the South, virtually intact two years ago, has quietly and finally been dismantled.

All in all, a record of some good fortune and much genuine achievement. And yet how little the administration seems to be credited with what it has achieved. . . .

Depressing, even frightening things are being said about the administration. They are not true. This has been a company of honorable and able men led by a President of singular courage and compassion in the face of a sometimes awful knowledge of the problems and the probabilities that confront him. . . .

I am one of those who believe that America is the hope of the world, and that for the time given him the President is the hope of America. Serve him well. Pray for his success. Understand how much depends on you. Try to understand what he has given of himself. This is something those of us who have worked in this building with him know in a way that perhaps only that experience can teach. To have seen him late into the night and through the night and into the morning, struggling with the most awful complexities, the most demanding and irresolvable conflicts, doing so because he cared, trying to comprehend what is right, and trying to make other men see it, above all, caring, working, hoping for this country that he has made greater already and which he will make greater still.

Pat Moynihan—philosopher, scholar, bon vivant, humane idealist and political pragmatist—gave intensely of himself in those years, because he cared intensely. And because Pat cared, because ideas were his life and the translation of those ideas into policy his fulfillment, he could see in the Nixon White House what John Dean could not.

THE GATHERING STORM

Shortly after Nixon's inauguration in 1969, James Humes, a young lawyer who had worked in the Nixon campaign and later become a member of the White House staff, was offered a bet by an old friend. The friend, a North Carolina Democrat and protégé of Senator Sam J. Ervin, Jr., was chief counsel to a key Senate committee. The bet: that Nixon would not complete his four-year term. Explaining his reasoning, the friend pointed out that impeaching a president is a political act, and Congress is a political body. He argued that impeachment is "not such a difficult thing to do," that with its power of subpoena Congress could destroy any president, and that Lyndon Johnson would have been forced out of office if he had not been a Democrat. Further, he said, in Nixon's case the anti-Nixon media would be there in full force to tell the country that all the impeachers were doing was "getting out the facts." Humes thought his friend was being silly, and took the bet, giving 50 to 1 odds. When Nixon completed his first term, Humes collected a dollar. Ruefully recalling it later, he concluded that he had not deserved to collect. (But he kept the dollar.)

On January 3, 1973, the newly elected 93rd Congress assembled. Despite Nixon's sweep of the 1972 presidential vote, the heavy Democratic majorities in the Congress remained virtually unchanged: 57–43 in the Senate, 240–192 in the House (with three vacancies).

During the two months after the election, Nixon had spent much of his time secluded on the Camp David mountaintop, directing the final diplomatic and military moves to end the war in Vietnam and shaping his new administration. As the rumblings from the mountaintop rolled over Washington, they sounded to many like political thunder. It was clear beyond question that Nixon intended to use his electoral mandate. The sounds were less of conciliation than they were of confrontation. Having been stymied by the Congress in his earlier efforts to reorganize the executive branch, he set out to achieve at least some of the aims of reorganization by rearranging the lines of communication within and among the departments, and between the departments and the White House. He was determined to get mastery at last over the bureaucracy, and to make it responsible to presidential policies. He plainly intended to wrestle Congress for control of the government. He also plainly intended to fashion his "new majority" into a powerful political force capable of leaving his stamp on public policies for a generation, just as Franklin Roosevelt's Democratic coalition had done during the middle third of the century.

House Democratic leader (now Speaker) Thomas P. ("Tip") O'Neill, Jr., a wily, street-wise, intensely partisan Boston politician, later boasted to his Boswell, Jimmy Breslin, that by January 1973 he had already decided Nixon would be impeached. From then on, at every step of the way O'Neill maneuvered, sometimes stealthily, sometimes brazenly, always craftily, toward that goal.

On the other side of the Capitol, the Senate Democrats wasted no time in setting their own wheels rolling. On January 11, just eight days after Congress reconvened, the Senate Democratic caucus voted unanimously to stage an investigation of Watergate and other Republican misdeeds in the 1972 presidential election.

Because this was an inaugural year, and he was therefore delivering an inaugural address during what traditionally is State of the Union season, Nixon chose to forego the usual State of the Union address to a joint session of Congress that year. Instead, he sent a series of written "State of the Union" messages, organized by topic —one on economic affairs, one on natural resources, etc. He introduced these with a short "overview" message on February 5. In it, he reminded Congress that American strength was essential for world security, and promised that the series of messages to follow would be "a blueprint for modernizing the concept and functions" of the federal government.

On the same day, February 5, following the mandate of the Democratic caucus, Senator Ervin introduced a resolution to establish the Senate Select Committee on Presidential Campaign Activities—the Watergate committee.

As usual, several members took to the floor that morning to place various newspaper clippings in the *Congressional Record.*

One of these was Minority Leader Hugh Scott of Pennsylvania. Twelve days earlier, the combination of renewed bombing and intense diplomatic pressure had finally brought agreement in Paris on a cease-fire to end the Vietnam war. Scott introduced a selection of commentaries. "The cease-fire finally is a tribute to Mr. Nixon," declared *The Cleveland Plain Dealer.* "His global poker game has paid off in the face of pressures of all kinds at home and abroad. For our 37th President, this has been his finest hour." The *Richmond News Leader* said pointedly: "He did it when many of the persons who should have supported him most enthusiastically had curled up in the corner like a sulky dog. He made up his mind and dug in his defenses and persisted. Now he has prevailed." Publisher William Randolph Hearst, Jr., wrote in his column that Nixon "pulled off one of the greatest pieces of diplomacy in my lifetime. I will have to admit that I was critical of the President a few weeks ago for not informing Congress and the people of his reasons for launching the massive air attacks against Hanoi and Haiphong. But now I understand that he had to remain silent if there was any hope of getting a settlement in Paris. His eye was on the forest while the rest of us had ours on the trees."

Another who had a clipping to place in the *Congressional Record* that morning was Majority Leader Mike Mansfield of Montana. He introduced an article from the previous day's *New York Times,* by James M. Naughton, headed "Ervin Assumes Leadership in Effort to Reassert the Authority of Congress." Ervin, Naughton noted, was going to be tangling with the White House in a whole series of challenges to presidential authority: impoundment of funds, executive privilege, the power to enter into executive agreements with other governments, the power of pocket veto. And he would also chair the Senate's Watergate investigation. "If the Congress does more this year than just talk about reasserting its authority," wrote Naughton, "it will be largely because of Mr. Ervin."

The resolution to establish the Ervin committee sparked a sharp debate on the Senate floor over how partisan the inquiry should be.

The first test came over composition of the committee. Ervin's resolution called for a Democratic majority. Republican senators argued for a committee split evenly between the two parties, following the precedent of other politically sensitive inquiries—including those that had led to the censures of Senator Joseph R. McCarthy and of Senator Thomas J. Dodd. Ervin would have none of it. Knowing he had the votes in his pocket, he wisecracked his way through the debate. The Republican-controlled 80th Congress, he argued, "established a Special Committee to Reconstruct the Senate Roof and Skylights and Remodel the Senate Chamber. The membership of that committee consisted of three Republicans and two Democrats. If we are going to have a majority and a minority party on the Select Committee to Study the Reconstruction of the Senate Roof and Skylights and Remodel the Senate Chamber, where there are present no political overtones of any kind, we certainly should have a division which would enable the committee to be established by Senate Resolution Sixty to function in the event of disagreement between the members of two different parties on the committee."

When Ervin raised the specter of "stalemate" if the committee were evenly divided, Senator Howard Baker, Jr., of Tennessee (later the committee's vice-chairman and ranking Republican) offered to provide in the rules that in case of a tie vote, the side favored by the chairman would prevail. But the wily old "country lawyer," Ervin, would have none of this either, protesting that "the best way to make certain that there will be no stalemate is to have a committee which has a majority on one side or the other." New Hampshire's crusty Senator Norris Cotton finally revealed that it was he, in a conference between the joint leadership of the two parties, who had first put forward the tie-breaking idea as a compromise proposal. "The one thing I noted," he added, "was that the attitude of everyone on the other side of the aisle engaged in that conference was completely adamant. . . . It was, to me, very clear in our conference that the plan is fixed, that the majority are pledged to it, and that this matter of making speeches about these amendments is an exercise in futility."

A more fundamental dispute centered on the scope of the inquiry. The Republicans argued that if it was really aimed at finding out what happened in presidential campaigns and reforming the election system, rather than at politically inspired muckraking of exclusively Republican sins, it should cover the last three presidential campaigns, and not be limited to that of 1972. If the majority really wanted a bipartisan cast, they insisted, this was the way to do it, and quite appropriately so: the losing candidates of 1964 and 1968, a Republican and a Democrat respectively, were themselves members of the Senate. They also pointed out that whereas the Watergate offenses had already been investigated and widely publicized, the allegations of comparable offenses in the two previous campaigns had never been gone into, and that not only fairness but also thor-

oughness therefore argued for examining the uninvestigated as well
as the previously investigated abuses. But the Democrats would
have none of this either. In a party-line vote, the Senate strictly
limited its inquiry to the offenses of 1972—the year there was a
Republican in the White House.

In the course of the debate on the rejected Republican amendments, Minority Leader Hugh Scott deftly nailed what was afoot:
"This resolution is limited to a single occurrence because the majority view here is that they do not wish to know of anything else.
This is 'See no evil, hear no evil, speak no evil, except the evil we
demonstrate, which we will define carefully.' " The majority, he protested, "does not want to know what the majority party or its friends
or supporters did. . . . It is afraid to let us go into the 1964 campaign
and the 1968 campaign; and that is what is bugging them and not
electronic surveillance."

At first, Ervin also stoutly, even sharply, resisted Republican demands that the minority should be allowed to choose one-third of
the staff, as it could by statute for standing committees; he insisted
that selection and allocation of staff should be his sole preserve, and
that the minority should rely on his benevolence. Eventually he did
back down, but not until after Scott bitterly protested that "perhaps
we should leave the whole thing to the majority. Let them hold their
proceedings. Let them be as 'star chamber' as they wish to be about
it. Let them make all the charges they want. Then let the United
States see for itself that what is going on is not a bipartisan inquiry
in support of legislation but a partisan political effort to extract the
last bit of juice from an already considerably squeezed lemon. . . .
It is obvious that in vote after vote, what we are getting is a determination to ride us down, to roll us over, to seek the maximum
political benefit which can be obtained from a single incident, without the slightest scintilla of curiosity about what may have happened at another time and another place in other elections."

Much later a senior Republican Senate aide commented to me
that the battle had been lost in that first skirmish. The Democrats
had the votes, and they wrote the rules, and they wrote them to
insure the mortification—exclusively—of Richard Nixon's political
flesh. Humes's wagering North Carolina friend may have had his
timing wrong, but he knew his Congress.

Past congressional investigations, particularly when members of
one political party sought to expose politically associated misdeeds
of the other party, routinely were treated with at least some measure
of skepticism by the press. As the Watergate committee hearings

became the media event of the year, however, the committee's elaborate professions of impartiality were taken at face value. Sam Ervin became a folk hero, while the reporters covering the hearings functioned as his claque.

For Ervin, it must have been a moment to savor. Only a few years earlier, defending the doctrine of states' rights, filibustering against the march of civil-rights laws, he had been portrayed as a racist and treated as a pariah by much of the national media. Now, with Nixon in the dock, he found himself celebrated by the same media as a stalwart guardian of American liberties and hailed as a constitutional oracle.

For the nation, establishment of the Ervin committee was the start of a wild ride on the Watergate roller coaster. Within the White House, it was the start of a battle that seemed to lurch from disaster to disaster. We were heavily outgunned. With fewer than a dozen lawyers—who also still had to handle the routine business of the presidency—the White House counsel's office faced a hundred or more working for the special prosecutor, the Senate Watergate committee, and the House Judiciary Committee, not to mention the other committees that kept getting into the act. Confused, uncertain, often operating in the dark ourselves, buffeted by a constantly shifting gale of charges, their sources frequently as elusive as the wind itself, we struggled for the President's survival. Like the wind, even those charges that were all air and no substance left destruction in their wake. It is an old but true journalistic cliché that the correction never catches up with the error. In Watergate, the accusations, the innuendos, the predictions of charges to come, all followed one another so rapidly and in such profusion that in the public mind there was soon no line of demarcation between true and false.

At first, the White House response to the Ervin committee's establishment centered on formulating the rules of executive privilege as they might apply to the production of White House documents, or to testimony by present or former White House aides. Congress had never before armed itself with subpoena power to investigate the campaign practices of a president, much less a president of the opposite party. We fully expected a political circus, with White House aides called by the committee to jump through congressional hoops while the television cameras ground away.

Until Watergate, it had been a firmly established custom that officials of the executive departments did testify before congressional committees, but members of the President's personal staff did not. Through the years there had been very few congressional requests for appearances by White House aides, and those that were made were routinely declined. The rationale for this distinction lay in the Constitution. Cabinet departments are established by statute, and therefore cabinet secretaries and their aides are statutory officers, answerable to some extent to the legislative branch. The presidency, by contrast, is a constitutional office, invested exclusively with the executive power and independent of the legislative branch. The President, therefore, cannot be called before Congress. Since his assistants are extensions of the presidency, neither can they. Or so it was until Watergate.

At issue in those early weeks of 1973 was whether Nixon would invoke the traditional standards of executive privilege in the Watergate inquiry, and also in other related congressional hearings. The Senate Judiciary Committee, for one, was asking John Dean to testify in its hearings on the nomination of Acting Director L. Patrick Gray 3rd as director of the FBI. Besides Nixon, those chiefly involved in formulating his position on executive privilege were Dean and John Ehrlichman. All three, as it later became clear, had reasons of their own to want White House aides protected from testifying. But the principle was important, nevertheless, and when Nixon finally issued his statement on executive privilege on March 12—several weeks after he had promised it—I was glad to see that he took a firm stand: his policy would be to provide "all necessary and relevant information through informal contacts," but present and former members of his staff would not testify. The policy lasted thirty-six days.

During those early weeks I was only a spectator, more irritated than alarmed at what seemed to be unfolding. The Senate hearings on Gray's nomination raked through the FBI's handling of the Watergate case, and through the old charges that ITT had contributed to the 1972 Nixon campaign in return for favorable antitrust treatment. (Actually, the "contribution" was never made, and it was not ITT but rather its subsidiary, the Sheraton hotel chain, that offered to put up the money. Traditionally, host cities offer to defray part of the costs of national political conventions. When the 1972 Republican convention was being planned for San Diego—it later was shifted to Miami—Sheraton, which wanted the prestige and publicity of having its newly opened hotel in San Diego used as presidential headquarters, offered to put up between $200,000 and $400,000 as part of San Diego's package bid. Despite determined political and media efforts to tie this to the Justice Department's out-of-court settlement of an antitrust suit against ITT, these efforts failed. The out-of-court settlement imposed on ITT was the largest

divestiture in antitrust history.[1]) Judge John Sirica imposed bail of
$100,000 each on convicted Watergate defendants G. Gordon Liddy
and James McCord, and declared that he was "not satisfied" that
the whole truth had come out. Senator Ervin, on "Face the Nation,"
threatened to seek the arrest and jailing of any White House aide
who obeyed the President's orders and refused to appear before his
committee. But Watergate still seemed a relatively small and very
political cloud on the second term horizon.

But that soon changed, quickly and drastically.

For most of us, the change came suddenly on March 23, when
Judge Sirica read in open court a letter from James McCord charging that perjury had been committed at the Watergate trial, and
that there had been "political pressure" on the Watergate defendants
to plead guilty and remain silent. Later that day, and again the following day, March 24, McCord met with the staff of the Ervin committee. Monday morning, March 26, the Los Angeles Times reported
that McCord had told the committee staff that Dean and Jeb Magruder, deputy director of CREEP, had advance knowledge of the
Watergate burglary.

Two days before Sirica read the McCord letter, John Dean had
his "Cancer on the Presidency" meeting with Nixon and Haldeman.
From then on, Nixon himself became more and more deeply immersed in Watergate.

By early April Dean and Magruder both were talking with the
prosecutors, laying out their stories and trying to strike their bar-
gains.

On March 26 the Watergate grand jury reconvened. On April 5
Gray's nomination was withdrawn. On April 15 Nixon met with
Attorney General Richard G. Kleindienst and Assistant Attorney
General Henry E. Petersen, chief of the Justice Department's crimi-
nal division (a Democrat, and a career Justice Department lawyer).
Because, by now, the case was reaching John Mitchell and other
close Kleindienst associates, Kleindienst recused himself from it,
and left the Justice Department investigation in Petersen's hands.
On April 17 Nixon announced that on March 21 he had begun
"intensive new inquiries" as a result of "serious charges which came

1. The ITT charges were the principal issue in the Senate Judiciary
Committee's protracted hearings on Richard Kleindienst's confirmation as
attorney general. The committee concluded that the settlement "was reached
on the merits after arm's length negotiations," and that it was "not the
product of political influence." Solicitor General Erwin Griswold told the
committee he "believed that the government would have lost in the Supreme
Court," and that the settlement was "a very substantial victory for the
government."

to my attention, some of which were publicly reported." He dropped his previous objections to testimony by White House aides, saying they "will appear voluntarily when requested" by the Ervin committee and "will testify under oath and they will fully answer all proper questions."

The pressure continued to mount. On April 19 Dean publicly warned that he would not "become a scapegoat," and leaked word to the press through associates that he was prepared to implicate people "above and below" if he were singled out for prosecution. Meanwhile, another grand jury in New York was probing allegations that a $200,000 campaign contribution by financier Robert L. Vesco had been aimed at influencing an SEC investigation in which he was charged with securities fraud. (In the Vesco case, Mitchell and former Commerce Secretary Maurice Stans were indicted; in April 1974 both were acquitted. We were at Camp David when the acquittal was announced. Within minutes, Nixon was on the phone to me. He was elated—and he wanted to hit hard at the way both had been convicted in the press, then acquitted by a jury.) On April 26 reports surfaced in the press that Acting Director of the FBI Gray had destroyed documents taken from Howard Hunt's White House safe and turned over to him by Ehrlichman. Gray resigned the next day, April 27. On that same day, in Los Angeles, Federal District Judge William M. ("Matt") Byrne, presiding in the Pentagon Papers trial of Daniel Ellsberg, released a Justice Department memorandum stating that two of the Watergate defendants had broken into the office of Ellsberg's psychiatrist, Dr. Lewis Fielding. On April 30, on nationwide television, Nixon announced the departures of Haldeman, Ehrlichman, and Dean from the White House staff, and Kleindienst's replacement[2] as attorney general by Elliot Richardson, with authority, if Richardson chose, to name a "special supervising prosecutor" for Watergate-related matters.

By early May Washington was awash with leaks from the various investigations. They alleged widespread campaign sabotage and espionage, wiretapping of reporters, early involvement in the Watergate cover-up by high White House officials, hush-money payments to the Watergate defendants. On May 4 Dean gave Judge Sirica the key to a safe-deposit box where, he said, he had stashed away classi-

---

2. As Nixon was careful to make clear in his speech, Kleindienst had no personal involvement in Watergate. But because of his close association with Mitchell and other potential defendants, he and Nixon agreed that he should leave. Kleindienst was unhappy about having his resignation announced in a package with the White House departures. He thought—correctly—that doing it this way would leave him unfairly stigmatized. But he went along with it.

fied White House documents that "may have a bearing" on the Watergate investigation. On May 14, the new acting director of the FBI, William D. Ruckelshaus, announced at a press conference that missing records of seventeen FBI wiretaps on newsmen and government officials had been found in a safe in Ehrlichman's office. On May 15 Missouri Senator Stuart Symington released a summary of testimony before the Senate Armed Services Committee by CIA Deputy Director Vernon A. Walters, in which Walters said Haldeman and Ehrlichman tried to get the CIA to head off the FBI investigation of Watergate, and Dean tried to get the CIA to put up bail money for the defendants. On May 17, Senator Ervin gaveled open the Senate Watergate committee hearings, declaring that "those who are entrusted with power are susceptible to the disease of tyrants," and that an "atmosphere of the utmost gravity" demanded a probe into charges that "the very system itself has been subverted and its foundations shaken."

Through May, June, and July the televised hearings ground on,[3] finally ending with Henry Petersen's testimony on August 7. Carefully orchestrated for maximum impact, the hearings mesmerized the nation. I watched them most days in my office, as did many others on the White House staff. We felt besieged. Dean, waging his immunity campaign through the press, kept raising his bid by promising more and more lurid revelations. Nixon's accusers were lionized by the media, his defenders pilloried.

At the White House Correspondents Association's annual dinner in the spring of 1973, I ran into my old friend Harry Rosenfeld. Harry had been foreign-news editor of the *Herald Tribune;* now he was metropolitan editor of *The Washington Post*—and, as such, the man responsible for the *Post's* Watergate coverage. We talked at length about that coverage, and for a while I was almost persuaded that the *Post* was honestly pursuing what it considered a thoroughly professional journalistic course. Rosenfeld explained that he was sure similar events had taken place in most past administrations, "but I wasn't here then. I didn't have the story. If I had, I'd have gone after it just as vigorously." It was simply Nixon's bad luck, he suggested, to have been the President whose administration got caught in the *Post's* wringer. He also stressed the meticulousness of what he said was the *Post's* insistence on factual accuracy, claiming

3. From the beginning through principal accuser Dean's testimony during the final week of June, the hearings were covered live by all three networks. When the hearings then resumed on July 10, with Nixon defender John Mitchell as lead-off witness, the networks shifted coverage to a rotating basis, with only one network covering each day's hearings live.

that no "fact" would be printed until it had been "triangulated"—
that is, as I understood him to mean, verified by three separate
sources. (Later, from Woodward and Bernstein's first book, it became clear that the rule was two sources, not three; apparently I
misunderstood.)

I was impressed. I had always had a high regard for Rosenfeld,
and I trusted him personally. Because of this, I was also troubled,
even shaken—might there be more truth to the *Post*'s reporting than
I had given it credit for?

But, though I often reflected back on that conversation in the
months ahead, the momentary thaw it brought in my feelings toward the *Post* did not last long. The hypoed leads, the loading of
stories—selecting from the facts only those that would support the
most sensational interpretation, and studiously ignoring those that
pointed in the opposite direction—continued to belie any professions of objectivity. And however much they might technically bind
themselves to "triangulation," the internal evidence of the stories
repeatedly suggested that they were cheating on their own rules.
One Woodward-Bernstein technique that was both pervasive and
transparent was, as I sometimes complained, to "interview the
cleaning woman and cite her as a 'White House source.'"

That is, an unnamed member of the White House staff would be
quoted in a damaging way, to buttress the writers' thesis about
whatever might be the purported villainy of the day—although to
an insider it was clear from the quote itself that the "source" had
no knowledge of the facts, or no familiarity with the subject. But
this fine distinction would be lost on the general reading public, to
whom the attribution to a "White House source" would, by itself,
convey the appearance of authority.

At that same 1973 correspondents' dinner I met both Woodward
and Bernstein for the first time. We chatted amiably. They seemed
earnest, engaging, and of course both professed to be anxious not
to be unfair to the President. But I remained wary, and continued
to leave their phone calls unanswered. Later there was occasional
speculation that I might be "Deep Throat." I was not, and in fact
have always been skeptical about whether such a character actually
existed.

Meanwhile, on May 18 Elliot Richardson announced his selection of Archibald Cox as special prosecutor, thus clearing the way
for Richardson's own Senate confirmation as attorney general.
Judge Sirica ordered the documents in Dean's safe-deposit box
turned over to the Ervin committee; on May 31 Ervin declared
that these revealed a "Gestapo mentality," and would be "a great

shock to the American people if they were released." The papers included the 1970 memos prepared by White House aide Tom Charles Huston, recommending a variety of domestic intelligence-gathering techniques, some of them illegal, to deal with the mounting domestic violence. The memos were leaked to *The New York Times,* which printed them on June 7. They did shock the American people.

On and on it went. Dean accused Nixon of knowledge of the Watergate cover-up, and produced a White House "enemies list." News stories flashed across the nation declaring that unidentified "investigators" for the Watergate committee had reported that Nixon's San Clemente home was bought with $1 million in unreported 1968 campaign funds. (The story was a total fabrication, appearing first in a local southern California newspaper, but it was picked up and spread nationally by the wire services, and it dogged Nixon's footsteps ever afterward—even after the entire documentation on his purchase of the property was made public.)

Shock followed shock. Nixon was discovered to have taped his office conversations. He refused to give up the tapes. Vice-President Agnew was reported under investigation by federal prosecutors for possible involvement in a bribery scheme while he was Baltimore county executive and governor of Maryland. Agnew protested his innocence, and then struck a plea-bargaining deal: he resigned his office, and pleaded no contest to a single count of tax evasion. Cox took Nixon to court to get the tapes. Nixon offered a compromise. Cox refused it, defying Nixon at a nationally televised news conference, and Nixon ordered Cox fired. Barred by the guarantees he had given the Senate from carrying out the order to fire Cox, Richardson resigned as attorney general. Deputy Attorney General Ruckelshaus left with him. "Saturday-night massacre" was put into the national lexicon. In the "firestorm" that followed, Nixon backed down, and told the court he would give up the subpoenaed tapes. Then two of the tapes turned out not to exist. A third was found to have a suspicious eighteen-and-a-half-minute gap at a crucial point.

Nixon's approval rating as measured by Gallup plummeted from a high of 68 percent in early February to a low of 27 percent in November. As it looked from within the beleaguered White House, 1973 was not a good year.

But what were we to make of it all?

There were complex questions of fact to be sorted out, and even more difficult questions of interpretation. Were we in the White House to believe what we read in the morning newspapers and saw on the evening news, or what we saw with our own eyes and heard with our own ears? Day after day, we were treated to lurid descriptions of an administration hell-bent on savaging America's institutions, contemptuous of its liberties, corrupting its values. Yet this was not the administration we knew. The shoe didn't fit.

Soon after my own first immersion in Watergate—the April 30 speech—I was back in the swim of it again, drafting a white paper that the President issued on May 22. By then, we had a hastily assembled new team. Al Haig, who had left his post as Henry Kissinger's deputy eight months earlier to become army vice-chief of staff, returned to take Bob Haldeman's place as White House chief of staff. Len Garment replaced John Dean as counsel to the President. J. Fred Buzhardt, general counsel of the Defense Department, joined the White House as special counsel handling Watergate matters. Bryce Harlow, who had left his post as counselor to the President two years earlier, was pressed back into White House service. The white paper was the new team's first major joint effort. We set out to make it as definitive an answer as we could prepare to the major questions that had been raised, and that we knew soon would be raised. Among those we knew soon would be raised were those involving the Huston plan.

Tom Huston first came to the White House at the start of the administration as a member of the writing staff. An intense, cadaverous, fiercely conservative former national chairman of Young Americans for Freedom, he had always seemed to me rather overly obsessed with such matters as internal security, and insufficiently sensitive to civil liberties. Somewhere along the way he had gradually disappeared from the writing staff, slipping away into a double-locked office down the hall doing nobody seemed to know just what. Now I knew.

We had learned that it was a copy of the Huston plan that Dean had made off with and squirreled away in his safe-deposit box, ostentatiously giving the key to Sirica. We knew, therefore, that it was likely very soon to be in the public domain. Buzhardt set about trying to learn its background, and what had happened to it.

It turned out to have been born in response to the wave of violent destruction that swept the country at the turn of the decade, and to the collapse of cooperation within the intelligence community. As he grew testier in his final years, J. Edgar Hoover had also grown more jealous, reprimanding subordinates for cooperating with other intelligence agencies and finally, by May 1970, shutting off the FBI's liaison with the CIA altogether. Mob violence and widespread sabotage had, meanwhile, reached crisis proportions. The 1969–70 school year brought 247 cases of arson on college campuses. Bombings became commonplace; in one twenty-four-hour period there were 400 bomb threats in New York City alone. When a town house in New York's Greenwich Village blew up accidentally, in March 1970, it turned out to have been a full-scale bomb factory operated by the militant "Weathermen." Guerrilla-style groups were staging pitched gun battles with police. In the spring of 1970, announcement of the Cambodian operation was followed by a new wave of violent campus demonstrations, climaxing in the shooting tragedies at Kent State and Jackson State; in the wake of those, disruptions became so severe that scores of colleges were forced to close down altogether. There were indications, never confirmed but widely credited, that some of the disruptive activities were getting support from hostile foreign powers. Whether or not there was outside support, the violence was clearly—sometimes openly, sometimes covertly—being planned, provoked, and often directed on a national scale. There was no way of knowing whether it was going to continue to get worse. Lives as well as property were being lost. People were being terrorized. Any government that failed to try to counter the threat would be failing in its first responsibility.

Against that background, on June 5, 1970, Nixon called a meeting of the heads of the government's various intelligence agencies: Hoover of the FBI, Richard Helms of the CIA, General Donald Bennett, director of the Defense Intelligence Agency, and Admiral Noel Gayler, director of the National Security Agency. They discussed the need for better intelligence, and for better coordination within the intelligence community. Nixon named Hoover as head of an interagency committee to draw up recommendations. Huston served as staff coordinator. Working with the committee, Huston put together a list of recommendations for expanded authority— basically, a return to the use of techniques that had been employed since Roosevelt's time, but had been ordered stopped in 1966. These included clearly illegal measures such as breaking and entering, and mail opening. (The Senate Intelligence Committee later disclosed that CIA mail openings had never stopped; neither, it now appears, did the FBI ever completely stop its "black-bag jobs." Through the Huston plan, it now appears the CIA was trying to get presidential authorization for the illegal mail opening that it was already conducting without the President's knowledge.) All members of the committee except Hoover joined in recommending that the expanded procedures be authorized. Hoover—worried less about civil liberties than about what would happen to the FBI's image if it were caught, or if the plan leaked out—dissented. Nixon gave his approval. Hoover took his protest to John Mitchell, who took it up with Nixon. Nixon then reversed himself, and five days after initially giving his approval, withdrew it. That was the end of the Huston plan.

The plan was distasteful, and the shrill rhetoric with which Huston urged that Hoover's objections be overridden verged on the hysterical: "At some point, Hoover has to be told who is President. . . . For eighteen months we have watched people in this government ignore the President's orders, take actions to embarrass him, promote themselves at his expense, and generally make his job more difficult. It makes me fighting mad, and what Hoover is doing here is putting himself above the President. . . . He had absolutely no interest in the views of NSA, CIA, DIA, and the military services, and obviously, he has little interest in our views, or apparently even in the decisions of the President. . . ."

I was glad Nixon had reversed himself, and turned it down. But the significant points, it seemed to me, were that he *had* reversed himself; he *had* turned it down; the authorities being recommended were ones that *had* been used in prior administrations; and, however improper it would have been to reinstitute them, the problem of mass, organized violence he was trying to meet was a real one, which also threatened American liberties. And the inflamed rhetoric was Huston's, not Nixon's.

Others saw it differently, and the Huston plan became one of the prime exhibits in the display of Nixon sins. Writing in *The New York Times* in August 1973, historian Barbara Tuchman declared: "The Domestic Intelligence Program of 1970, authorized by the President, and 'mind-boggling' in its violation of the citizen's rights, would alone be sufficient to disqualify him from office. Indeed this item is the core of the problem for it indicates not only the administration's disregard for, but what almost seems its ignorance of the Bill of Rights." Even apart from her disregard of the fact that the plan was never put into effect, the comment illustrates what we saw ourselves as being up against. The authorities in the Huston plan, which Nixon ultimately rejected, had actually been exercised under the five presidents before Nixon. But it was Nixon, not they, who in Tuchman's rabid eye was rendered unfit to govern. It was the old double standard, with a vengeance: what was acceptable for FDR and his successors to do was unacceptable for Nixon even to think about doing—even if he decided not to.

Of all the specific charges made in the Watergate committee hearings, the one that sparked the greatest outrage seems to have been one John Dean handed the senators on his second day of testimony, while he was being questioned by Connecticut Senator Lowell P. Weicker, Jr.

Weicker had been pressing Dean for examples of political abuse of the nation's security agencies. Dean tried to oblige, but could come up with little. Then, however, Dean volunteered that he did have a memorandum, prepared by himself, on how "to attack the enemies of the White House," and added that "there was also maintained what was called an enemies list, which was rather extensive and constantly being updated."

He produced the memo, and the nation's attention was riveted on its opening paragraph:

"This memorandum addresses the matter of how we can maximize the fact of our incumbency in dealing with persons known to be active in their opposition to our Administration. Stated a bit more bluntly—how we can use the available Federal machinery to screw our political enemies."

He proposed that there should be a "project coordinator," who would determine "what sorts of dealings these individuals have with the Federal Government and how we can best screw them (e.g., grant availability, Federal contracts, litigation prosecution, etc.)," and who should have "access to and full support of" the principal officials of the various federal departments and agencies.

Somewhat plaintively, he added: "I have learned that there have been many efforts in the past to take such actions, but they have ultimately failed—in most cases—because of lack of support at the top."

He also produced several lists of names. One was a "priority" list of twenty persons, which he had attached to his memo. The other lists ran into the hundreds, ranging from the obvious (Bella Abzug) to the absurd (New York Jets quarterback Joe Namath).

Reaction was thunderous.

The *Miami Herald* protested that "Watergate has produced no more disgusting act in the process of undermining democracy than these virtual *lettres de cachet*, a device of the Bourbon kings whose reigns, it appears, have come alive again in the White House."

Columnist Tom Wicker wrote that "The lists confirm what the 1970 internal security plan and the Ellsberg break-in suggested—that the Watergate burglary itself was only the tip of the knife, that American democracy has been retrieved in the nick of time from the police state it so nearly became." In Washington, the lists were called the new Social Register. Columnist Mary McGrory, brandishing her own inclusion, gleefully denied the allegation that she wrote daily hate-Nixon columns, explaining that she wrote only four times a week.

The project was sleazy and sophomoric, and if there had been any serious, sustained follow-through it would have deserved much of the hyperbole it sparked. There is nothing new about presidents trying to make life uncomfortable for their political adversaries, but organizing it in such a fashion marks a qualitative as well as a quantitative difference. Further, it reflects a climate that did exist in some quarters of the White House—especially in the Colson environs—which, in turn, was an extension of the dark side of Nixon. But what actually was it, and what actually happened?

The answer, on both counts, seems to be: not very much. Dean's recommendation of a "project coordinator" languished and died. Lists were churned out by junior staff members and circulated to various White House offices. (Examples of the lists: one was a personnel list of the McGovern campaign staff; another was a list of eleven people "involved with the National Committee for the Impeachment of the President"; another was a list of "Democrat Contributors of $25,000 or More in 1968 Campaigns.") Dean himself, in reply to further questioning, acknowledged that the lists had largely piled up, ignored, in his own filing cabinets.

I never took the "enemies lists" seriously, largely because I assumed that if there really had been a concerted, coordinated White House campaign of harassment and intimidation under way I would have heard about it, somehow, sometime, from someone. What it sounded like to me was a combination of Colson bluster and efforts by junior staffers to win a few "tough-guy" Brownie points for themselves—a self-serving purpose for which a lot of memos were written through the years on many subjects, wasting time and paper and resulting in nothing.

Since most of the people on the various lists were, in fact, ardent anti-Nixon advocates, many bragged about being on "Nixon's enemies list," enjoying the celebrity of having supposedly been personally singled out by the chief executive. Others, equally opposed to Nixon, took strong personal offense. Yet there was no evidence that Nixon even knew about the lists, much less that he knew who was on them. I called them "Dean's enemies lists." After all, it was Dean who proposed the unused plan to "screw our enemies," and Dean who collected the lists in his filing cabinet.

Dean did do one thing with the lists which was serious. He took copies of them to Johnnie Walters, the commissioner of Internal

Revenue, with a request that Walters "undertake examinations or investigations." As a result, virtually everyone whose name appeared on the lists, and who had his tax returns audited, blamed the audit on Nixon and his "enemies list." And the public, quite understandably, was appalled at this abuse of the IRS.

Again, however, when we look at what actually happened when Dean took those lists over to Walters, a somewhat different picture emerges. Because of the charges that were made, the staff of the Democratically controlled congressional Joint Committee on Internal Revenue Taxation conducted an exhaustive investigation, including a detailed examination of how IRS handled the tax returns of every one of the more than seven hundred persons whose names appeared on one or another of the Dean lists.

Walters, according to his sworn deposition, told Dean it would be "disastrous" to do as Dean asked but, in the face of Dean's insistence, he promised to take it up with Treasury Secretary George Shultz. Shultz told him not to do anything with the lists, so Walters simply stuffed them away in his safe. A week later Dean called, pressing Walters on it again. Walters agreed to take it up again with Shultz. Shultz again told him to ignore the Dean demand. That was the end of the matter. Dean was not heard from again, and the lists remained locked in Walters' safe.

Nevertheless, the committee staff went on with their detailed examination of how the returns were handled. They checked how many were audited, and how each one was selected for audit, in each case double-checking for supporting evidence that the listed reason was the real reason. Their conclusion: There was "no evidence that any returns were screened as a result of White House pressure on the IRS." They even examined the revenue agents' reports and the workpapers of each audit, to judge whether the audits were conducted "without undue harassment or undue strictness." Their finding:

Income tax audits necessarily involve some inconvenience for the taxpayer being audited. However, the staff has found no evidence that revenue agents attempted to increase unnecessarily this inconvenience for people on the political opponents lists. In some cases, the agents were relatively strict. However, this was usually motivated by a previous lack of cooperation on the part of the taxpayer. In an equal number of cases, the agents were somewhat lax. The staff has found absolutely no evidence that audits of people on the political opponents lists were on the average conducted more harshly than normal.

The staff has also reviewed the collection activities of the IRS concerning people on the lists. It has found no evidence that the IRS has been more vigorous in its attempts to collect unpaid taxes from political opponents of the White House than normal. Indeed, if anything, the opposite is true. Several individuals on the list appear to pose collection problems for the IRS. The Service has been quite lenient in granting extensions to file in many cases, and has not yet attempted to collect taxes from several political opponents who have failed to file returns or even to ascertain the reasons for the failure to file.

The staff has also found no indication that the IRS was more vigorous than normal in recommending prosecution for tax violations in the cases of political opponents of the White House.

Because the newspapers had been filled with flat assertions—many by persons who themselves had been audited—that specific tax audits had been politically inspired, the staff gave special attention "to the cases of those individuals mentioned in the press as victims of politically motivated audits." Their conclusion: "In none of these cases has the staff found any evidence that the tax-payer was unfairly treated by the Internal Revenue Service because of political views or activities."

Besides trying to peddle his lists to Walters, Dean did try to get one particular person's tax returns audited. That was Robert W. Greene, a reporter for Long Island's *Newsday*, who had written a particularly vicious series on Nixon's friend Bebe Rebozo. In that case, Dean was reduced to having an aide write an anonymous "informant's" letter, just as any private citizen might do. Greene's return was audited, but the staff found that even Greene's had been selected in the normal way, and by New York State rather than the IRS.

If Nixon had had a "wish list," one of the items high on it would have been more political leverage on agencies such as the IRS and the FBI. He envied the leverage that Roosevelt, Kennedy, and Johnson had had—and had exercised—and he was frustrated at not having the same leverage himself. In an ideal world, none would have had it. But Nixon himself had had portions of his own tax returns leaked by the IRS to columnist Drew Pearson in 1952, when he was a candidate for vice-president. He himself had been blatantly harassed by the IRS when Kennedy was President. After he lost the 1962 race for governor of California, his returns were checked three times, and the Los Angeles supervisor sent a report back to Washington that they were in order—and three times orders came back to the supervisor from Washington to investigate anyway. Nixon knew perfectly well, as he later put it, that "use of the IRS for the purpose of investigating the returns of people in political life had been common practice in previous administrations." His point was not that it was right for him to have tried it—but that it was no more wrong for him than it was for FDR, JFK, and LBJ. The difference, of course, was that they could use it, and did, while he only wished that he could. And the reason he could not was that if he could choose a John Dean as counsel, he could also choose a George Shultz as secretary of the treasury. No one who knows Shultz would suppose for a moment that he would tolerate political abuse of the IRS—and it was Shultz, not Dean, to whom Nixon gave the actual authority over the IRS.

On March 13, as Nixon and Dean talked about past abuses by the FBI—Nixon wished the story of those abuses could be gotten out, if it could be done without damaging the Bureau—Dean recalled a recent conversation with William Sullivan, long-time assistant director of the FBI. It had been triggered by a *Time* magazine article breaking the story that White House staff and newsmen had been wiretapped. The transcript reads:

DEAN: .... and after going through his explanation of all that had happened, he started volunteering this other thing. He said, "John, what, this is the only thing I can think of during this administration that has any taint of political use but it doesn't really bother me 'cause it was a national-security purpose. These people worked—there was sensitive material that was getting out to reporters."

PRES: (Unintelligible) what we ordered?

DEAN: That's right.

PRES: Of course, (unintelligible) the stuff was involved in the God-damned Vietnam war.

DEAN: That's right.

PRES: That's what it was. (Portion deleted)

DEAN: But he said, "John, what does bother me is that you all have been portrayed as politically using—"

PRES: And we never did.

DEAN: And we never have! He said the Eisenhower Administration didn't either. The only

PRES: Never.

DEAN: times that he can recall that there has been a real political use has been during Democratic tenure.[4]

4. House Judiciary Committee transcript.

As the testimony unfolded—abuse of power, cover-up, espionage, dirty tricks, hardball politics—so much became a matter of perspective. Once during that summer of 1973, as the Watergate hearings ground on, I was sitting by the beach in San Clemente with Rose Mary Woods when her telephone rang. It was James Roosevelt calling—the son of FDR, six-term Democratic congressman from California, Democratic candidate for governor in 1950, the same year in which Nixon defeated Helen Gahagan Douglas for the Senate. Roosevelt was calling to express his outrage—not his outrage at what Nixon had done, but his outrage at what the press and the Democrats in the Congress were making of it. "Everything they're accusing him of," he protested, "my father did twice as much of!" During that same summer, at a party in Washington, I ran into Thomas Corcoran, who as "Tommy the Cork" was one of the whiz kids of Roosevelt's New Deal. Flashing his Irish grin, his eyes twinkling, he said to me: "The trouble with your people is that they're always writing memos. When we did that sort of thing, we never put it on paper!"

XIV

THE DELUGE

A couple of days after Elliot Richardson's appointment of Archibald Cox as special prosecutor, a half dozen of us were gathered around a conference table late at night working on the Watergate white paper Nixon released on May 22. We relieved the mood with occasional banter, and I concocted a bit of whimsy, suggesting a scene in the Oval Office with the President talking to the attorney general: "Archi—Archi—*Archie* Cox? I thought you said you'd picked *Eddie* Cox!" (Nixon's son-in-law Edward Cox was a recent law-school graduate.)

Though we could joke about it, our concern over the Cox appointment was serious. Harvard Law School professor, Kennedy braintruster in the 1960 presidential campaign, John and Robert Kennedy's solicitor general, high guru of the Cambridge chapter of the Kennedy government-in-waiting, Cox represented the quintessence of the Kennedy establishment. Rubbing salt in the wound, Edward Kennedy and Ethel Kennedy stood conspicuously among the guests at Cox's swearing-in ceremony. The team of eager young prosecutors he assembled was overwhelmingly liberal, Democratic, Harvard, Kennedy-connected, and politically oriented. All but one were Ivy League. Their average age was just under thirty-one. Of the upper echelon, only two were Republicans. Among the politically associated aides Cox chose were: his deputy, Henry Ruth, who served under Robert Kennedy when Kennedy was attorney general; James Vorenberg, a member of George McGovern's staff in the 1972 presidential race; Philip B. Heymann, assistant to the solicitor general in the Kennedy and Johnson administrations; James Neal and Thomas F. McBride, both special assistants to Robert Kennedy; William H. Merrill, chairman of the Michigan Citizens for Robert Kennedy in 1968; George T. Frampton, speechwriter for Kennedy brother-in-law and McGovern running mate R. Sargent Shriver; Robert M. Witten, a Kennedy campaign aide in the 1968 Oregon primary.

In selecting Cox, Richardson chose a man whom he knew and trusted personally, and who was sure to command public confidence. But he was equally sure not to command the confidence of the White House, or to inspire the sort of trust required for a harmonious working relationship in an essentially adversary and intensely political situation. As he assembled his staff, with one after another former Kennedy or McGovern aide named, our initial suspicions mounted exponentially. Even after Cox was replaced as special prosecutor by Leon Jaworski, Jaworski retained the same overwhelmingly Democratic and Kennedy-connected staff. Over the months, as that staff demanded virtually unlimited access to the most sensitive files of the Nixon White House, our visions of the political uses to which those files might be put grew more inflamed by the day.

If the special prosecutor's staffing was insensitive to the need for at least some semblance of balance, the Senate Watergate committee's staffing was insensitive even to more basic requirements. The committee adopted strict rules against leaks to the press, but these quickly became a mockery. The committee was a sieve. Committee members leaked, members' staffs leaked, and the committee staff leaked, and the leaks were not only of information given to the committee in confidence and testimony—often uncorroborated, always incomplete—given in private but of information and testimony leaked with an interpretive spin, almost invariably anti-Nixon. This always is particularly troublesome in an investigation. There is no way to cross-examine a leak, which comes attributed only to an "informed source." Yet it was these leaks which principally commanded the headlines, and the often inflammatory interpretations in which they came wrapped that became embedded in the popular mythology.

One senior member of the majority staff with a particular reputation as a leaker was Scott Armstrong, suspected of being a principal source for the *Washington Post's* team of Woodward and Bernstein. Armstrong was a close personal friend of Woodward—and, incredibly, he was hired by committee counsel Samuel Dash not in spite of his friendship with Woodward, but as a result of it. Dash first approached Woodward, offering him a place on the staff. Woodward declined, preferring to remain at the *Post,* but offered Dash the name of his friend Armstrong instead. Dash hired Armstrong, who became one of the most aggressive and most belligerent questioners of administration witnesses. Thus, through Dash's good offices, the *Post* not only penetrated the supposedly confidential recesses of the committee with its own "friend in court," but on top of that a friend armed with subpoena power, which could be used to badger witnesses from the administration or the re-election committee. With the Senate hearings over and the committee's work completed, Armstrong surfaced as best man at Woodward's wedding and collaborator with Woodward and Bernstein on *The Final Days.*

Another senior committee staff member with a penchant for savaging witnesses friendly to the administration was thirty-three-year-old Terry F. Lenzner. In 1970 Lenzner had been fired from his job as head of the Office of Legal Services in the Office of Economic Opportunity, the antipoverty agency. He left with an angry blast at the President: "The Nixon administration has made it clear that it will trade the right of the poor to justice for potential voters." (The administration was trying to depoliticize the Office of Legal Services, which had become a hotbed of left-liberal political activism at taxpayer expense.) Lenzner had also worked as defense counsel for the Berrigan brothers. Lenzner's most memorable moment in the limelight came on July 12, 1973, during sixty-year-old special counsel to the President Richard Moore's first day of televised testimony. Knowing Moore's testimony would contradict Dean's, Lenzner tried to destroy him with a blizzard of belligerent questions about meetings on specific dates, totally irrelevant to what Moore had been told he was called for questioning on, for which Moore was unprepared and, understandably, could not remember. Lenzner's brutal blind-siding tactic achieved its purpose: it left the grandfatherly Moore looking befuddled. But it had nothing to do with a search for the truth. Lenzner also took special aim at Nixon's friend Bebe Rebozo, directing an extended staff inquisition into the minutest details of Rebozo's personal and business life that soon acquired the dimensions of a vendetta. (The staff not only subpoenaed all of Rebozo's own business records for a six-year period; they also subpoenaed the records of everyone Rebozo had done business with for the same six-year period. They staked out the bank Rebozo headed, checking everyone who entered or left. They got the toll records for eleven telephones Rebozo had had access to during the six years, and grilled him on more than four hundred telephone numbers, demanding to know who he talked to and what they talked about. And, as the committee's minority counsel, Fred Thompson, has since written, "It soon became almost routine, after a batch of Rebozo's records were examined, that newspaper reports would appear quoting sources 'close to the committee' and referring to the Rebozo investigation in ways that were damaging to Rebozo. One day Carmine Bellino examined the records of all of the loans Rebozo had made over a period of several years. The next morning at 9:30 the *Miami Herald* began calling each of the lending banks to verify information the newspaper had about the loans.")[1]

Among the members of the committee, the one who rubbed nerves rawest and raised temperatures highest at the White House was a Republican, Lowell Weicker of Connecticut. Personally, Weicker can be quite engaging. He was two years behind me at Yale, where I knew him slightly (then, he was known chiefly on campus for being rather ostentatiously snobbish about his wealth; the Weicker family fortune, derived largely from the Squibb pharmaceutical company, was large even by Yale standards). A few days after leaving the White House in November 1974 I went to Nassau as a guest of the Downe Communications Corp., to speak at its annual meeting. Weicker was also a guest at the same meeting. We chatted amiably during our three days there, and rode back to Washington together. I resolved to try to be kinder toward him in the future than I had felt in the past. But during the Watergate hearings, few people infuriated me more. I called him "Windmill Weicker," because my principal mental image of him was of his huge arms waving as he bellowed in self-righteous outrage (which I assumed was largely show) at the witnesses who were paraded before him. Playing to the gallery as he did, he seemed to me, in his own way, to be as much the political opportunist as Colson. Weicker also was well known as one of the most egregious leakers of confidential materials, invariably with an anti-Nixon bias. It was a standing joke on Capitol Hill that if Weicker's Xerox machine ever broke down, the Watergate press would have nothing to write that day.

At one point, the committee staff got hold of a set of memos written by William Sullivan, the long-time assistant director of the FBI, detailing political abuses of the Bureau by former presidents—including Johnson's deployment of a whole army of FBI

1. *At That Point in Time*, by Fred D. Thompson (New York, 1975). Thompson's book is must reading for anyone who wants an understanding of the inner workings of the Senate Watergate committee.

agents to gather political intelligence, by wiretaps, hidden microphones, and other means, at the 1964 Democratic National Convention. Howard Baker, the senior Republican on the committee, called a meeting of the three minority members to discuss whether Sullivan should be called as a witness. Weicker was adamantly, implacably opposed. It would look, he protested, like an attempt to justify what had been done in the Nixon administration. Sullivan was never called.

That use of the FBI at the 1964 Democratic convention provided a good example of why the Senate Democrats were determined to limit the investigation to the one campaign—1972—when a Republican was in the White House. Because the Senate Watergate committee and the House Judiciary Committee both refused to measure Nixon's conduct against that of past presidents, the story remained covered up until—with Nixon securely exiled in disgrace —the Senate Intelligence Committee broke it open in 1975, as one small item in its catalogue of abuses going back to Roosevelt's time. By the time of the Intelligence Committee's investigation, enough other prior abuses had been uncovered so that it made few ripples. Had the Watergate committee not kept it hidden in 1973, however, it would have seriously undermined the committee's effort to portray sin as a Nixon invention.

In 1964, as the Democrats met in Atlantic City, Lyndon Johnson bestrode the convention like a colossus. I was there, writing the *Trib*'s convention editorials. Johnson was riding the crest of his popularity, an admiring nation still lauding the skill with which he led it out of the trauma of John F. Kennedy's assassination just nine months earlier. The emotional high point of the week was a thundering convention-hall tribute to Robert Kennedy, who was present, and to his late brother, whose presidency was celebrated in a film that held the delegates in somber silence. But the convention was Johnson's, even as he toyed with its patience in an elaborate charade of indecision that humiliated Hubert Humphrey before Johnson announced the Minnesotan as his choice for running mate.

The convention was Johnson's, that is, except for two things. One was the fervent determination of the Kennedy forces to make their presence felt, implicitly confronting Johnson with their emotional tribute to Robert Kennedy. The other was a potentially explosive credentials fight, centered on the Mississippi delegation. A predominantly black Mississippi Freedom Democratic Party (MFDP) was challenging the all-white regular Mississippi delegation. The contest threatened to erupt in embarrassing demonstrations. It was also bitterly divisive. The MFDP had national support among black and civil-rights groups; yet if the regular delegation were defeated, there was a prospect of a walkout by other white Southern delegations, and of large-scale disaffection among other party regulars. It presented a serious political problem, especially for a Texan president in that highly civil-rights–conscious year.

Johnson turned to the FBI. He wanted wiretaps on Martin Luther King, Jr., and on other black leaders. He wanted a monitoring of the MFDP challenge, and he especially wanted information on Robert Kennedy's contacts with black leaders. The FBI deployed a special squad to Atlantic City—made up of twenty-seven agents, two stenographers, and one radio-maintenance technician, with one direct line to FBI Headquarters and another direct line to the White House, bypassing the White House switchboard.

In a confidential memorandum after the convention's close, Assistant FBI Director Cartha D. ("Deke") DeLoach reported that "we were able to keep the White House fully apprised of all major developments during the convention's course."

This, he said, was achieved by means of "informant coverage, by use of various confidential techniques [a standard FBI euphemism for wiretaps and microphone surveillance], by infiltration of key groups through use of undercover agents, and through utilization of agents using appropriate cover as reporters."

During its convention coverage, the FBI supplied White House political aide Walter Jenkins with forty-four pages of intelligence data. "Additionally," wrote DeLoach, "I kept Jenkins and [Bill] Moyers constantly advised by telephone of minute-by-minute developments." Thanks to the FBI, "Jenkins, et al., were able to advise the President in advance regarding major plans of the MFDP delegates. The White House considered this of prime importance."

Some of the specific intelligence coups of which DeLoach boasted were these:

"On Monday, we furnished Mr. Jenkins details regarding the plans of CORE, the American Nazi Party, the Student Non-Violent Coordinating Committee, and initial plans of the MFDP.

"We alerted White House representatives regarding compromise proposals for seating of the MFDP and furnished them information regarding plans of the Progressive Labor Movement groups, ACT, and other dissident organizations.

"Through a highly confidential source, it was learned that CORE and SNCC had been advised that the President was bringing pressure to bear on the delegates of fifteen states to preclude their support of a move to bring the Mississippi delegates issue to the floor of the Convention.

"We submitted reports reflecting that the militant members of MFDP under the leadership of [name deleted] were revolting against the leadership of Martin Luther King and [name deleted]. We advised Jenkins that the MFDP delegates had flatly rejected the compromise proposal to seat the MFDP delegation.

"We also alerted the White House in advance regarding the telegram prepared by ACT demanding amnesty for Harlem rioters and for federal registrars to police Negro voting in the South."

Two weeks after the convention, DeLoach sent a note to Bill Moyers at the White House:

September 10, 1964

PERSONAL

Honorable William D. Moyers
Special Assistant to the President
The White House
Washington, D.C. 20501

Dear "Bishop":

Thank you for your very thoughtful and generous note concerning our operation in Atlantic City. Please be assured that it was a pleasure and privilege to be able to be of assistance to the President, and all the boys that were with me felt honored in being selected for the assignment.

I think everything worked out well, and I'm certainly glad that we were able to come through with vital tidbits from time to time which were of assistance to you and Walter. You know you have only to call on us when a similar situation arises.

Thank you again for taking time out of your busy day to write to me, and I hope we can get together soon.

Sincerely,
C. D. DeLoach

Immediately before the convention opened, the FBI got another, separate request for information on the MFDP. This one asked for FBI name checks on forty persons in the MFDP leadership and convention delegation members. It came from the head of the Justice Department's Civil Rights Division, a man whose name figured prominently in another drama ten years later: John M. Doar.

The Senate committee's hearings on the Watergate break-in and cover-up phase of its investigation constituted the longest uninterrupted congressional hearings in the history of the Congress. The committee staff numbered 97 at its peak, and a total of 157 persons spent varying periods of time on the staff. These included 20 investigators, 25 lawyers, 22 specialized research assistants, 22 assigned to computer work, 8 consultants, and 6 administrators, as well as 51 secretaries and clerical hands and 3 volunteers. During May, June, and July the story was absent from the front page of *The New York Times* only one day of each month. From March to July, *Time* and *Newsweek* each ran 11 Watergate covers. Watergate saturated the television news.

During this period, the high iron fence that surrounds the White House seemed increasingly to separate two different worlds, two different views of reality. One view was hammered into the nation's living rooms every night on the network news. The other view was the one we lived with, struggling to make sense out of the kaleidoscope of impressions. We saw the actors in the drama not as cardboard caricatures but as flesh-and-blood people we knew and worked with, good people for the most part, reluctantly drawn into a web of intrigue spun by hands only partly seen. And the issues we saw were not a simple morality play or a cops-and-robbers drama but a complex interplay of historical and political forces, of high purpose and low politics, criminality and hypocrisy. As for the cover-up itself, the image that came most frequently to my own mind was that of the man who steps into quicksand: the more he struggles to get loose, the deeper in he sinks. Wrongs had clearly been done, but they were not particularly new or unprecedented. What was new was the sustained intensity of the media coverage, the increasingly open animus, even hate, that suffused it, and the collapse of all bounds of restraint as the psychology of the chase took over, with the pack in full cry in pursuit of a single prey.

On June 12, 1973, with New York's Bella Abzug taking the lead, a group of liberal Democrats spent two hours discussing impeachment on the House floor—though they stopped short of introducing a formal resolution of impeachment. *Christian Science Monitor* correspondent Jack Waugh reported that "the House is circling the subject as if it were a scorpion: fascinating. But nobody wants to pick it up."

On July 31 Representative Robert F. Drinan, an acerbic Jesuit priest from Massachusetts, did pick it up. He introduced the first resolution of impeachment, and thereafter sported an "Impeach Nixon" button on his lapel. Drinan was a member of the Judiciary Committee. Other House and Senate Democrats complained that Drinan's timing was wrong, that he was moving too quickly. Majority Leader Tip O'Neill said that he had told Drinan: "It's too early. We've got to wait to get all the evidence." O'Neill urged, according to the next morning's *Washington Post*, "that Democrats should lie low, and let Republicans cut themselves up, rather than do anything precipitate that could make the President a martyr."

One unidentified House Democratic liberal told the *Post*: "We haven't got enough on him. The Senate committee is building a case of massive mismanagement, but that isn't impeachable." Other members, reported the *Post*, "repeated the oft-made statement that no impeachment effort would stand a chance unless mounted by moderates. Drinan lines up with the liberal left." Comment from Senate Democrats "over every hue," added the *Post*, "was that Drinan's resolution was premature."

Meanwhile, other leading Democrats were weighing in with alternative means of reversing the 1972 election. A favorite forum was the op-ed page of *The New York Times*.

As early as May 11 Wisconsin's Representative Henry S. Reuss, lamenting that the nation could not afford to "operate under a damaged presidency" for the next three and a half years, proposed that Nixon and Agnew both resign in favor of the man next in line of succession, House Speaker Carl Albert. In order to "draw the sting of partisanship," Reuss suggested that the Albert administration could then "conduct a bipartisan coalition of national unity," in which Republicans would be allowed to choose the new Vice-President, would be allotted "roughly half the cabinet posts," and could "participate in policy-making at all stages." A nice, generous touch: just turn over the White House to the Democrats, and then "draw the sting of partisanship" by graciously allowing the party that overwhelmingly won the presidential election six months earlier to pick the Vice-President and to "participate" in policy-making.

On June 4 Democratic elder statesman Clark Clifford offered his own scheme for seizing the spoils. Solemnly declaring that "this is no time for partisanship" (coming from Clifford, a clear signal for Republicans to start counting the silver), he urged that Agnew resign, thus creating a vice-presidential vacancy; that Nixon then ask the Democratic Congress for a list of three candidates to succeed to the vacancy, from which he would nominate one, and that on the new Vice-President's confirmation Nixon himself step down. "Under this plan," Clifford cooed, "we would then have a President and a Congress that could function together." All this at a time when no hint of scandal yet attached to the elected Vice-President.

Soon, however, Nixon's own tapes and the series of confrontations over control of them seized the spotlight.

Just down the corridor from my office, a tiny room housed a

Xerox machine and a set of wire-service tickers. Occasionally I strolled down to see what news was coming over the wires from the Associated Press and United Press International. On Monday, July 16, I was there scanning the news reports when Len Garment burst in, looking for me. He was agitated, upset, worried. How would I react, he asked, to news that all the President's Oval Office conversations had been taped? And what would the public reaction be?

I saw nothing wrong with it in principle. From the standpoint of privacy, the only real question was what was done with the tapes. Certainly nothing said to him was meant to be secret from him. If he wanted an electronic *aide-mémoire*, that seemed to me to be within his prerogative. Problems would arise only if he lost control of the tapes. A great deal, necessarily, was said in the privacy of the Oval Office that should not be spread on the public record. If I had been recorded, I said, I took no offense at it.

Len was less sanguine, concerned that public reaction to the existence of a taping system would be explosive—and he told me that there was a taping system, that former Haldeman aide Alexander Butterfield had told the Senate committee staff about it on Friday, and that Butterfield was going to be called by the committee that afternoon to be questioned about the system on television. Butterfield had telephoned Garment at home Sunday night, telling him about his revelation to the committee staff. That was the first notice the White House had that Butterfield had let the committee in on the secret which now, within hours, was going to be shared with the nation.

I was scheduled for a 12:30 luncheon meeting at the State Department that day. I went, then thought better of it, mumbled a probably unconvincing excuse, and headed back to my office.

Butterfield was called to the stand, and was asked if the President had a taping system. He said yes, and proceeded to describe it. The atmosphere in the hearing room was electric. Denunciations rolled in. House Speaker Albert called the practice "an outrage, almost beyond belief." White House lawyer Fred Buzhardt sent the committee a letter confirming existence of the system, and comparing it with the one Johnson had. Former top Johnson aide Joseph A. Califano, Jr., called the Buzhardt letter "an outrageous smear," and declared flatly that there "was absolutely no secret wiring in the place" under Johnson. There was: Johnson himself showed Nixon and his aides the system during the 1968 transition, recommending that he keep it. One of Nixon's first acts was to have it removed, but two years later, with his eye on history, he reversed himself and had a new system installed. Johnson took his tapes to his presidential library in Austin, where he set aides to the task of expurgating those too-unguarded comments he wanted to take to the grave with him. The first President to install a secret recording device in the Oval Office was Franklin Roosevelt, who had the Army Signal Corps place an experimental microphone in one of his lamps. Truman aide Harry Vaughan also revealed that FDR had wiretaps placed on the phones of some of his closest aides, and Vaughan personally discarded the transcripts of those conversations after Roosevelt's death. Kennedy also had tapes secretly made, and those tapes are now in the Kennedy archives.

As soon as the Nixon tapes' existence became known, both the Senate committee and the special prosecutor demanded to have them. They were clearly relevant, and especially to the questions of whether John Dean's version of his conversations with the President was true. They also tantalized the merely curious, irresistibly. Soon a relentless clamor began for their disclosure. Ironically, many of those who had protested most loudly that making the tapes was an outrageous invasion of privacy became the shrillest in demanding that no consideration of privacy must be allowed to shield them, that they belonged not to the President but to the people, and that whatever the prosecutors, the committee, or its staff wanted, they must have.

Many saw the battle over the tapes as simply an open-and-shut case of whether evidence relevant to a criminal investigation on one hand, and to a congressional inquiry on the other, should be provided. But it also had a major constitutional dimension, which to me far outweighed in importance the interests of either the special prosecutor or the Senate committee.

From a constitutional standpoint, the central question was not whether the tapes should be produced but, rather, who should decide. Until Watergate, the only serious challenge to a president's exclusive right to decide which of his private documents should be made available to a court was made by Chief Justice John Marshall to Thomas Jefferson, when Marshall was sitting as trial judge in a federal district court. A former vice-president of the United States, Aaron Burr, was on trial for his life, charged with treason. Burr claimed that certain correspondence in Jefferson's hands—specifically, a letter to Jefferson from one of Burr's principal accusers—would be exculpatory. Marshall issued a subpoena. Jefferson angrily refused to comply, arguing that "the leading principle of our Constitution is the independence of the Legislature, executive and judiciary of each other," and stating forcefully that he would reserve to himself "the necessary right" of the President to decide, "independently of all other authority," what presidential papers "the public interests permit to be communicated, and to whom." The letter was not produced, and Burr was acquitted of treason. But then he was brought to trial a second time, this time on a misdemeanor charge of having begun a military expedition against Spanish territory. Again he asked for the same letter, plus another. Again Marshall issued a subpoena. This time Jefferson chose partial compliance, but he was careful to insist on the basic constitutional principle that he alone would decide what portions of the correspondence should be provided, and what portions kept confidential. He turned over an abridged copy of one letter. Burr was again acquitted. Again Marshall backed down from the constitutional clash, not attempting to enforce his subpoena for the whole letter. And there the matter stood for 167 years, until the doctrine asserted by Thomas Jefferson was invoked by Richard Nixon.

The basic constitutional issue was well summed up by a unanimous Supreme Court in 1935, which held, in *Humphrey's Executor v. United States:*

"The fundamental necessity of maintaining each of the three general departments of government entirely free from the control or coercive influence, direct or indirect, of either of the others, has often been stressed and is hardly open to serious question. So much is implied in the very fact of the separation of the powers of these departments by the Constitution; and in the rule which recognizes their essential co-equality. The sound application of a principle that makes one master in his own house precludes him from imposing his control in the house of another who is master there."

Not only had every President since Washington successfully insisted on being "master in his own house," the courts and the Congress were equally jealous of their own independence. Each house of Congress always insisted that it alone would decide what should be provided, if anything, in response to a judicial subpoena. This standing doctrine was summed up in a 1962 Senate resolution in connection with subpoenas issued in the trial of Teamster leader James Hoffa, which read: "Resolved, that by the privileges of the Senate of the United States no evidence under the control and in the possession of the Senate of the United States can, by the mandate of process of the ordinary courts of justice, be taken from such control or possession, but by its permission. . . ."

In the Vietnam-atrocity court-martial of Army Lieutenant William L. Calley, Jr., Calley's attorneys asked for the production of testimony that had been taken by a House Armed Services subcommittee in executive session. The subcommittee chairman, Louisiana Representative F. Edward Hebert, refused, declaring that the Congress is "an independent branch of the government, separate from but equal to the executive and judicial branches," and that accordingly only Congress can direct the disclosure of legislative records.

Equally, the courts have always treated the privacy of judicial deliberations as sacrosanct, insisting that neither of the other branches may invade judicial privacy. In refusing to respond to a subpoena from the House Un-American Activities Committee, Supreme Court Justice Tom C. Clark stated in 1953 that "the independence of the three branches of our government is the cardinal principle on which our constitutional system is founded. This complete independence of the judiciary is necessary to the proper administration of justice." In 1971 Chief Justice Burger analogized the confidentiality of the Court to that of the executive, and said: "No statute gives this Court express power to establish and enforce the utmost security measures for the secrecy of our deliberations and records. Yet I have little doubt as to the inherent power of the Court to protect the confidentiality of its internal operations by whatever judicial means may be required."

The general applicability of the basic principle was summed up in 1962 by Mississippi Senator John Stennis, in a ruling upholding President Kennedy's refusal to provide information sought by a Senate subcommittee. Senator Stennis held: "We are now come face to face and are in direct conflict with the established doctrine of separation of powers. . . . I know of no case where the Court has ever made the Senate or the House surrender records from its files, or where the executive has made the legislative branch surrender records from its files—and I do not think either of them could. So the rule works three ways. Each is supreme within its field, and each is responsible within its field."

That was the background against which the battle over the Nixon tapes was joined. In its early phases, the battle ranged the former solicitor general of the United States, Archibald Cox, against one of the nation's leading authorities on constitutional law, Charles Alan Wright, McCormick Professor of Law at the University of Texas. Wright joined the White House Watergate team in June 1973, as a consultant to the President's counsel. He argued the tapes case in Federal District Court and in the Court of Appeals.

Tall, spare, engaging, co-author of the standard text on federal court procedures, Wright is a scholar without scholarly airs. When he was in Washington to prepare his first court brief on behalf of the President, the regular White House lawyers grew increasingly nervous as the deadline approached and Wright had not written a word. I was working closely with our lawyers at the time. Wright joined expansively in our bull sessions about the case, he was amusing over drinks in the evening, he had perceptive advice on the President's public statements—but there was still no brief, not even a first draft, not even a part of a first draft. Then, a couple of days before the brief was due to be delivered in court, he retired to the small office he was using around the corner from Len Garment's, closed the door, lit up the first in a chain-smoked series of cigarettes, and tapped furiously at the keys of his typewriter. In a few hours the draft was done. Stopping by Fred Buzhardt's office that evening, I found Buzhardt, Wright, and Garment going over it, changing a word here and correcting a citation there, and that was it—it went to the printer, brilliantly done, a model of logic and clarity, written with grace, style, even wit.

In terms of its sheer virtuosity, it was a remarkable performance.

Intrigued, I asked him about his writing techniques. He said this was his normal way. He would never start writing until the pieces clicked together in his mind, and when they did, he knew that he had it right. I asked what his speed record was. He said he had once written a law-review article in forty-five minutes. Apparently, he also has one of those rare, genuine photographic memories. I watched him in oral argument before the Court of Appeals. Dueling with Cox, answering Cox's challenges and the judges' questions, he spun off rapid-fire lists of case citations, complete with quotes and page numbers—all without a single note.

Working with Charlie Wright was one of the few pleasures of Watergate. He and Cox used court briefs as dueling swords, oral arguments as rapier thrusts, recognizing that the constitutional ground they were fighting over was vital to the constitutional domain itself, but each approaching it from his own perspective. Wright, who profoundly believed in the rightness of both his cause and his case, saw the key issue as the inviolability of the separation of powers. Cox saw the key issue as the integrity—and the primacy —of the process of criminal justice.

On July 18, two days after Butterfield's testimony, Cox sent a letter to Fred Buzhardt requesting the tapes of eight presidential conversations. On Nixon's behalf, Wright declined the request on July 23. On July 26 Cox formally asked Judge John Sirica for an order to subpoena the tapes. The two sides filed briefs with Sirica's court on August 7, and on August 22, before Sirica, Cox and Wright met in their first courtroom clash over the issue. Wright argued that while "getting to the truth of Watergate is a goal of great worth," there "may well be times when there are other national interests more important than the fullest administration of criminal justice."

Sirica by then had become practically an arm of the prosecution in the Watergate case, and the general feeling among the White House lawyers was that there was little prospect of getting a favorable ruling from him. Hopes were higher, however, that the case could be won on appeal.

On August 29, as expected, Judge Sirica ruled in favor of Cox, but with the stipulation that the tapes, instead of being turned over directly to Cox, should be delivered to Sirica, with specific claims of executive privilege to be reviewed by him, and then whatever portions of the tapes he decided were not covered by valid claims of privilege handed to the special prosecutor. The White House and Cox both appealed, with Cox insisting the tapes should be given directly to him, without judicial review. On September 11 the case was argued by Cox and Wright before the Circuit Court of Appeals, and on Friday, October 12, the Court of Appeals handed down its decision: 5–2 in favor of Cox.[2] Wright was in Texas, teaching his classes and preparing an expected appeal to the Supreme Court.

Meanwhile, in late September Nixon had begun secretly preparing the way for a possible compromise, working toward some means of making the information from the subpoenaed tapes available without accepting the principle that any of the four hundred federal district courts could invade presidential privacy at will, and without carrying the case to the Supreme Court for a final judicial determination that could upset those delicate constitutional balances which often work best when shrouded in some measure of ambiguity—and a compromise which at the same time could stanch the hemorrhaging of presidential confidentiality. Secluding himself at Camp David, together with Rose Mary Woods and White House aide Steve Bull, he began the process of preparing transcripts of the subpoenaed tapes. Bull located the particular conversation on the tape reel. With tape recorder and typewriter, Rose then

2. The U.S. Court of Appeals for the District of Columbia Circuit had a reputation as the nation's most "liberal" circuit court, and thus not a hospitable one for the Nixon case. Two members considered part of the court's conservative wing, Roger Robb and Edward A. Tamm, disqualified themselves. The prevailing guess among White House lawyers was that if the full nine-man court had participated, the vote would have been 5–4.

attempted to identify the voices, sort out the jumble of words, and get the conversations down on paper. (In the months that followed, Rose and Fred Buzhardt often spoke to me of the sheer torture that it was to transcribe the tapes and check the transcripts. The voice-activated recording system was frequently started by the rustling of papers or the rattling of a coffee cup. The placement of the microphones, whether a person spoke with his head up or down, whether he had a higher- or a lower-pitched voice, all served to render words distinct or indistinct. Often two or more people spoke at once, their words tangled together on the tape. Fred Buzhardt commented to me several times that an hour of listening at a time was all he could physically endure. (On the first tape she transcribed, Rose spent more than twenty-five hours trying to get a one-hour conversation on paper.)

In handing down its decision, the Court of Appeals stayed it for five working days, to provide time for appeal to the Supreme Court. That gave the President one week—until Friday, October 19—to comply with the decision, to defy it, to appeal, or to work out a compromise.

Crisis was piling on crisis. Six days earlier, on October 6, a major war had broken out in the Middle East, shattering the cease-fire Israel and Egypt had agreed to in 1970. And just two days earlier, on October 10, the proud Vice-President of the United States, Spiro Agnew, scourge of the lawless, resigned his office in disgrace and, in a federal courtroom in Baltimore, entered a plea of no contest to a charge of income-tax evasion.

The Middle East crisis erupted suddenly, unexpectedly, menacingly; the day before it broke out, the CIA had reported to the President that an Egyptian attack was possible but unlikely, and so he had gone off to Key Biscayne. He turned around and rushed back to Washington. But the Agnew crisis had been building for months. Early in 1973 an investigation by the Maryland U.S. attorney, George Beall, of corruption in Baltimore County began turning its focus toward Agnew, a former Baltimore county executive and, later, governor of Maryland.

The story that Agnew was a target of the investigation broke publicly in *The Wall Street Journal* on Tuesday, August 7. At least since spring, through reports from Agnew himself as well as from the Justice Department, the White House had been aware that there was a potential problem, though its nature and extent were uncertain. That day, the seventh, Nixon and Agnew held their first face-to-face meeting to discuss it. That evening I had dinner with Nixon aboard the *Sequoia,* cruising down the Potomac and back again. The purpose of the dinner was to talk over a speech and statement on Watergate that the President planned to make the following week. But as we sat on deck before dinner, relaxing over drinks while the river breeze cooled the sultry heat of early evening, he talked about the Agnew case. He was clearly troubled, and clearly torn. He had met the day before with Elliot Richardson, who laid out what appeared to be the case against Agnew. It sounded devastating. But Agnew himself steadfastly maintained his innocence. And Nixon was deeply suspicious of the prosecutors handling the case in the U.S. attorney's office in Baltimore, the most aggressive of whom was an antiwar activist who had worked in Muskie's 1972 presidential campaign. Political contributions by contractors were commonplace in a lot of states, not only Maryland. Agnew insisted that this was all that was involved, and that the whole thing was just politics—politics as usual by him, and a political vendetta by his opponents, plus an effort by some of those involved to win immunity for themselves by falsely pointing fingers of suspicion at him. To Nixon, the crucial question was which version was true. He was prepared to move against Agnew if he had to, but not unless and until he was convinced of the facts—and he was not yet convinced. Emotionally, he declared that he was damn well not going to stand for having the Vice-President of the United States pilloried unless the case against him was solid. Beyond his distrust of the local prosecutors, he was concerned that Richardson's own judgment might be warped by his political differences—and potential direct political rivalry—with Agnew. So, he said, he had asked for a searching independent evaluation of the evidence by Henry Petersen, the career Justice Department attorney who headed the department's criminal division. He had confidence in Petersen. He was going to withhold judgment himself until he had Petersen's assessment.

Watergate was trouble enough. This was an extra burden we hardly needed. Nixon was acutely, personally aware of what it meant to be an embattled vice-president, and if Agnew were the victim of a smear, Nixon was determined to stand by him. But the cost could be high. And whatever the outcome, it could only further exacerbate his own difficulties. Having a vice-president faced with criminal charges would be bad enough for any president, in any circumstances. For a Nixon embattled over Watergate, it was devastating. His hopes now rested on Henry Petersen: hopes that Petersen would examine the case, and find it insufficient.

But Petersen found it sufficient.

During August and September, sniping between Agnew and the

Justice Department grew sharp and acerb. Leaks about the investigation filled the newspapers, with each side blaming the other. Nixon, uncomfortably, tried to isolate himself from the fray as much as possible, neither condemning Agnew nor supporting him unequivocally. Publicly, Agnew swore his innocence and vowed to fight on. Privately, his attorneys began negotiating a plea bargain with the Justice Department. At last a deal was struck. Resignation as Vice-President. *Nolo contendere* plea to a single count of income-tax evasion. Entry into the public record by the Justice Department of a complete statement of the evidence, including voluminous testimony of bribes and kickbacks. No prison sentence.

Agnew was bitter, still maintaining that he had been hounded from office and falsely accused. To those of us in the White House, myself included, who liked Agnew personally, and who had admired his courage in fighting for what he believed in, it was a sad, even a tragic moment. Yet it was impossible to read the statement of evidence without feeling betrayed.

Agnew's resignation solved one problem, but posed another: nomination of a successor. And this had to be done with an eye to the problems of confirmation. This would be the first use of the 25th Amendment to name a new vice-president. He had to win confirmation by both houses of Congress. In the Watergate climate, that could be a bloody business. The Democrats could be expected to try to do maximum political damage to any nominee they saw as a prospective presidential candidate in 1976. A Rockefeller or a Reagan, identified as strongly as both were with the factional divisions of the party, would split the Republicans.

My own recommendation—which I made in a memo to the President—was Bill Rogers. I had always thought Rogers was one of the most underrated members of Nixon's cabinet. He was one of the few people I knew whom I considered capable of handling the presidency, if it should come to that. His solid reputation for decency and integrity, and his experience as Eisenhower's attorney general would also, I thought, stand us in good stead in the Watergate battle. I thought Nixon was probably leaning toward John Connally, and, though I admired Connally's abilities, if he were nominated I shuddered at the thought of what Congress would drag him through in the confirmation process. I was afraid that anyone who had become a millionaire in Texas law and politics as a protégé of Lyndon Johnson must have something in his background which, in that Watergate climate, could be used to destroy him, however unfairly—and that Congress would stop at nothing if it saw a chance to destroy Nixon by destroying Connally. I just did not think we could afford the fight. (In 1975 I mentioned to Bill Rogers that I had recommended him. He grinned, and said he was glad Nixon had not taken my advice—otherwise he'd be saddled with being President.)

Nixon would, I think, have named Connally if he could have. But in the circumstances, the certainty of a bruising and possibly losing political donnybrook of a confirmation fight made it unrealistic. He turned instead to a friend of twenty-five years, not brilliant, not colorful, but solid, with the strength to handle the presidency if he had to, and liked and respected by his colleagues on both sides of the aisle in Congress. On the evening of Friday, October 12—the day of the Court of Appeals ruling—in the East Room of the White House, Nixon announced that his nominee for the vice-presidency would be Gerald R. Ford, Jr., Republican leader of the House of Representatives.

Now Nixon had to deal with the court, and also with the war.

On October 10 the Soviets had begun airlifting supplies to the Arab forces. Slashing through red tape and bureaucratic timidities, on the night of October 12, Nixon ordered an American airlift—using "everything that flies"—to resupply the threatened Israeli forces. The war raged, and the ominous prospect of a great-power confrontation in the explosive Middle East loomed suddenly as an imminent possibility. But to the courts, this was irrelevant. They were concerned solely with the orderly functioning of the criminal-justice system, and court timetables made no allowance for matters of war and peace. The special prosecutor had cases to prosecute, and his convenience must take precedence over an outbreak of war that threatened to engage the superpowers and engulf the world.

To me, that in itself was a compelling illustration of the utter asininity of the doctrine that where the interests of the courts conflict with other national interests, the courts alone should set the priorities and decide the conflict—not as equals in a government of separate powers, but as self-proclaimed first among equals.

With one week in which to try to resolve a major constitutional confrontation, while at the same time trying to end the war in the Middle East and avert a superpower collision, Nixon came up with the "Stennis compromise." Under this plan, a "summary" of the subpoenaed tapes would be prepared by the White House. This was to be a verbatim transcript, except that it was to be rendered in the third person, with unrelated matters omitted and, where the language was too coarse, the words were to be cleaned up but the sense retained—in effect, expletives would be deleted. Nixon chose Senator John Stennis as a highly respected outside authority, whom he trusted, to authenticate the transcripts. A Democrat, a former judge, chairman of the Senate Armed Services Committee, Stennis had a reputation among his colleagues as a person of absolute integrity. Under the plan, Stennis would be given the transcripts, together with the complete tapes. He could listen to the tapes as long and as often as he wished, and make any corrections in the transcripts that he felt were necessary. These authenticated transcripts would then be furnished to the court in lieu of the actual tapes.

Under this arrangement, the court, the special prosecutor, and the grand jury would get the substance of the conversations— including the specific language—as they related to Watergate, but the *principle* of presidential control over private presidential conversations would be maintained. The principle would be destroyed if the tapes themselves were submitted to the court, and if the President agreed that the court had authority to compel such submission. Then the way would be open for any of the four hundred federal district judges to assert a similar claim, in any future case in which either prosecution or defense might argue that presidential recordings or presidential documents could be relevant. The principle would be maintained if transcripts were authenticated by an outside person of the President's choice, and then made available at the President's initiative.

However, if this compromise were to moot the constitutional challenge, one other element was obviously essential: The special prosecutor would have to agree that this was the end; that, having been given the authenticated transcripts of those conversations he originally subpoenaed, he would not go to court seeking more; that he would not then press the same constitutional confrontation on the same issue all over again.

Richardson and Wright tried to persuade Cox to accept the compromise. Cox agreed that the idea of an authenticated transcript was, in itself, "not unacceptable," but he insisted on conditions that were clearly unacceptable to the White House. One was that any authenticators be appointed "special masters" of the court, which would have meant abandoning the basic constitutional principle Nixon was determined to maintain—that the President, not the courts, has ultimate authority over private presidential documents. Another was a guarantee that the actual tapes would be produced if needed for later trials. And a third was that Cox insisted on the right to continue pressing, through the courts if he chose, for any additional private presidential tapes or documents he might want.

Richardson has since argued that, given somewhat more time—

if the President had not insisted on meeting the Court of Appeals' October 19 deadline—he might have been able to reach an agreement with Cox, in part by leaving the question of future access to additional tapes for further negotiation when requests were made. Maybe. Yet, given Cox's adamant insistence on the right of access to whatever private presidential tapes and papers he wanted, it is hard to see how anything acceptable to Cox would ultimately have been acceptable to the White House, or vice versa. To the extent that the White House aim was to moot the constitutional issue by stopping court suits for private presidential papers, Cox's position was so absolute as to be irreconcilable. Perhaps Richardson could have postponed the ultimate confrontation, but he could hardly have averted it.

As it became increasingly evident that accommodation with Cox was impossible, the White House strategy shifted. On Friday the nineteenth, Senators Ervin and Baker were hastily summoned to the Oval Office. Two days earlier a federal court had thrown out a suit brought by the Ervin committee for presidential tapes; now, Nixon offered them the Stennis-authenticated transcripts. They accepted enthusiastically. With that to buttress him, and with Cox adamantly refusing to reach agreement, Nixon acted unilaterally. At 8:15 P.M.—less than four hours before the court-imposed deadline—the White House released a statement by the President, in which he announced that he would not appeal the Court of Appeals decision, but rather would "voluntarily" provide both to the Senate committee and to Judge Sirica the record of the conversations, authenticated by Senator Stennis. He also stated that "though I have not wished to intrude upon the independence of the Special Prosecutor, I have felt it necessary to direct him, as an employee of the executive branch, to make no further attempts by judicial process to obtain tapes, notes, or memoranda of presidential conversations. . . . I believe that by these actions I have taken today America will be spared the anguish of further indecision and litigation about tapes."

Cox responded immediately with his own press statement: "In my judgment, the President is refusing to comply with the court decrees. . . . The instructions are in violation of the promise which the Attorney General made to the Senate when his nomination was confirmed." For him to agree, Cox said, "would violate my solemn pledge to the Senate and the country. . . . I shall not violate my promise." At 1:00 the following day, Saturday, Cox held a nationally televised news conference in the National Press Building, at which he repeated his defiance, and suggested that he might ask the court to cite the President for contempt.

Confronted both with the offer of authenticated transcripts and with the order not to pursue further tapes through court process, Cox could have followed any one of four courses. First, he could have accepted the compromise, recognizing that it might bar him from some evidence he would later want, but recognizing also that accommodation of competing principles requires compromise on both sides. Second, he could have accepted the transcripts, examined them, and *then* decided whether he needed more, and, if so, sought them first through negotiation with the White House—postponing an actual confrontation until he could see whether it was really necessary. Or, if he concluded that the terms were unacceptable and his position untenable, he could still have done either of two other things. He could have resigned, leaving his friend Elliot Richardson as attorney general. Or he could force Nixon to fire him, knowing that this would also force Richardson's resignation—because he knew that, technically, his firing would have to be done by the attorney general, and he knew Richardson was barred from doing it by the pledge he had given the Senate.

He chose neither to compromise, nor to wait, nor to resign, but rather to force Richardson out of office with him. This has to have been deliberate. Cox played hardball politics to the end.

After Cox's press conference, there was no way Nixon could have avoided firing Cox, even if he had wanted to. Cox had challenged him, defied him, and gone on national television to do it. The only remaining question was whether he could, at the same time, keep Richardson. He called Richardson to the Oval Office, argued with him, pleaded with him, urged him to think first of the world crisis— "He was concerned," Richardson said later, "that my resignation would jeopardize his efforts in Moscow, jeopardize the cease-fire in the Middle East. He really put it on me. He was really tough."

But Richardson was tough, too. He had given his word to the Senate. He could not fire Cox. Another attorney general would have to do it. The deputy attorney general, William Ruckelshaus, felt equally bound by Richardson's pledge. So he, too, stepped aside. Richardson, Ruckelshaus, and the third-ranking official of the department, Solicitor General Robert Bork, had agreed earlier that Bork should stay at his post and carry out the order. In a brisk two-paragraph letter, Acting Attorney General Bork dismissed Archibald Cox as special prosecutor.

In firing Cox, Nixon also announced that the special prosecutor's office would be abolished and its functions returned to the Justice Department, where the Watergate prosecutions would continue to be pursued "with thoroughness and vigor." (This was a short-lived resolution; under intense public and congressional pressure, Nixon soon agreed to a new special prosecutor.) With reports reaching the White House that members of the Cox staff were making off with the files, FBI agents were called out to guard the offices (as well as those of Richardson and Ruckelshaus), in order to make sure that the files were kept intact. This was a precaution which also had been taken several months earlier with Haldeman's and Ehrlichman's offices when they resigned.

At 8:31 P.M. the news flashed over the wires:

BULLETIN. WASHINGTON (UPI)—PRESIDENT NIXON ACCEPTED AT-TORNEY GENERAL ELLIOT L. RICHARDSON'S RESIGNATION SATURDAY NIGHT AND FIRED WATERGATE PROSECUTOR ARCHIBALD COX.

The television networks broke into their regular programming to deliver the terrible news, the reporters breathless. The networks rushed on the air with "special reports."

On NBC, the network's normally unflappable anchorman John Chancellor intoned ominously: "The country, tonight, is in the midst of what may be the most serious constitutional crisis in its history. . . . That is a stunning development, and nothing even remotely like it has happened in all of our history. . . . You are watching a Special NBC Report of another event this year that we never believed would have happened in the history of this Repub-lic. . . . A constitutional situation that is without precedent in the his-tory of this Republic. . . . In my career as a correspondent, I never thought I would be announcing these things. . . ."

If the firing of Cox and the Cox-forced resignations of Richardson and Ruckelshaus were a "Saturday-Night Massacre," as they were quickly and indelibly dubbed, then those television specials might equally be called "Saturday-Night Specials," the television equivalent of those cheap but lethal handguns that have given Saturday night a bad name.

I was away from Washington that weekend, in the remote eastern reaches of Long Island, without television, with only a transistor radio and the newspapers through which to follow the news. There-fore, it was not until I returned Monday morning that I got the full impact of what the television coverage had been. The one word I heard most from those White House colleagues I talked with was "hysteria."

Pundits and politicians quickly fanned the flames of that hysteria.

The New York Times' Anthony Lewis gasped in his Monday column that "over this extraordinary weekend, Washington had the smell of an attempted coup d'état."

The *Times* itself shrilled editorially: "The desperation of President Nixon's moves . . . makes it plain that neither law nor orderly government process now stand as obstacles to the exercise of his will. . . . This espousal of absolute rule has thrown the country into a governmental crisis of fearful dimensions. . . . Using the Federal Bureau of Investigation in the manner of a totalitarian police force, the President directed its agents to swoop down on the special prosecutor's offices. . . . One Cox associate, confronted by this gross abuse of police power, commented aptly that 'one thinks in a democracy this would not happen.' " (FBI Director Clarence M. Kelley commented shortly afterward that "it didn't occur to me that there might be any objections" when FBI agents moved in to guard the Cox files, because his purpose was to protect "the substance of our own investigation.")

To Harvard Law School professor Raoul Berger, Nixon's actions were "obviously more serious than the Middle East war"; the nation was on "the road to tyranny, dictatorship, and Hitlerism." Ralph Nader declared that the President was acting like a "madman, tyrant or both." Maine Senator Edmund Muskie cried "dictatorship!" West Virginia Senator Robert C. Byrd, the assistant Democratic leader, denounced what he called a "Brown Shirt operation," and "Gestapo tactics." Massachusetts Senator Edward M. Kennedy called it "a reckless act of desperation by a President . . . who has no respect for law and no regard for men of conscience." *The* (London) *Times* correspondent, in a line widely quoted by his admiring colleagues, cried that "the whip of the Gestapo was in the clear October air."

In the course of his brief conversation with William Ruckelshaus on Saturday, after Elliot Richardson's resignation, Haig had asked if Ruckelshaus were willing to carry out the order to fire Cox. Ruckelshaus said no. Then, as Haig recalled it a few days later, he commented: "Well, you know what it means when an order comes down from the Commander-in-Chief and a member of his team can't execute it." To which Ruckelshaus replied that yes, he understood. And, as Haig explained, "I think we both understood at that moment that he was neither fired nor resigned, but somewhere in between, with a happy mutual term that I haven't developed."

As reported in the press, however, Haig—the four-star general —had simply barked at Ruckelshaus: "Your Commander-in-Chief has given you an order!" And, in the October madness, this sent the pundits into another frenzy. *The New York Times'* Anthony Lewis frothed: "There it was, naked: the belief that the President reigns and rules, that loyalty runs to his person rather than to law and institutions. It is precisely the concept of power against which Americans rebelled in 1776, and that they designed the Constitution to bar forever in this country. It is in fact a form of power that no English monarch has exercised since George the Third."

Congress returned on Tuesday the twenty-third. The evening before its return, Monday, the network news programs ran nineteen separate attacks on the President, balanced by two defenses. The air of both houses sizzled with denunciations. In the House, eight resolutions of impeachment, co-sponsored by thirty-one Democrats, were filed the first day. When Tennessee's Representative Dan Kuykendall urged his colleagues to "go slow and don't be part of a legislative lynch mob," he was hissed at from the aisle and the gallery. Mail and telegrams poured in from constituents, over-whelmingly against the President. By October 23 Western Union's Washington office reported the heaviest concentrated volume of telegrams on record.

A short while later Senator William L. Scott of Virginia found himself rather puzzled by the flood of anti-Nixon mail, and had his staff do some quiet checking. He noted that over the space of two weeks he had received a thousand letters and telegrams, running 10–1 against the President, yet Virginia had voted 70 percent for Nixon and, in "open-door" sessions in his Richmond office, he had continued to find substantial Nixon support, even during the "fire-storm." So he had his staff phone the people who had written, thanking them for their views and trying to find out something about them. The results: of those writing, 77 percent had voted for McGovern; 3 percent did not remember or would not answer; only 20 percent had voted for Nixon, and some of these described him as "the lesser of two evils." Beyond this, 36 percent belonged to Common Cause, and 29 percent volunteered that *The Washington Post* was their chief source of information. As Scott put it on the floor of the Senate: "These calls indicate that the people who are asking for impeachment are consistent. They did not vote for the President last year and they do not want him this year. Our col-leagues in the House who filed impeachment resolutions are also consistent. They also supported Senator McGovern last year and now want to impeach the man who defeated him!"

On Tuesday the twenty-third, Elliot Richardson tried to pour oil on troubled waters. A private citizen now, he held a news conference in the Great Hall of the Justice Department, entering to a thunderous round of applause from the Justice Department employees. In his usual calm manner, he outlined the steps of his negotiations with Cox during the previous week, setting forth both his agreements and his disagreements with the positions Nixon had taken, recognizing that different perspectives would lead to different conclusions.

Repeatedly pressed, he repeatedly refused to give the events the kind of characterization the reporters wanted. For example:

Q. Mr. Richardson, you say you see no evidence of a new cover-up. What do you think is going on if it is not a cover-up?

RICHARDSON: I can only say that you have here a situation in which the President, and I know nothing to call this into question, believed that the principle of the confidentiality of communications to the President was fundamentally important. . . . He was weighing the question of whether or not the Court of Appeals decision should be appealed to the Supreme Court of the United States, and then he decided that he would, instead, make available an authentic, verified version of the tapes which I think he believed would fully serve the purposes for which those tapes had been sought in the first place.

I think he felt that a refusal by the Special Prosecutor to accept that proposal was, from his perspective, unreasonable, and that if he couldn't accomplish this, if he couldn't get the whole situation wrapped up by that move, that the Special Prosecutor persisted, as, of course, he did in seeking other tapes and documents and questioned the adequacy of the verified record itself, then he felt that his only course was to discharge him.

Q. Did White House sources say that the President was confident that the Supreme Court would uphold his position? Are you aware of that confidence, and if it is true, why didn't he wait for the Supreme Court to act?

RICHARDSON: His lawyers told him certainly, I think, in the beginning that his chances were good. I understood them to tell him that they were better than even. As of Thursday of this week, Mr. Charles Alan Wright told me that the President had a fifty-fifty chance of winning in the Supreme Court of the United States.

The reason I think why it was decided to pursue in this way, the one I have given, is that he felt that this was a way of providing a record which his lawyers believed would be acceptable in the lower court and, therefore, in effect make unnecessary any further litigation resting on a refusal to provide any version of the tapes whatsoever.

To a reporter who complained that Senator Stennis "has been a partisan of the President in the past," Richardson answered that "the only reason for approaching Senator Stennis for this purpose was that he did have so firmly and does have so firmly established a reputation for integrity. I personally believe, and I think everybody who knows Senator Stennis would agree, that he would rather have his toenails pulled out one by one than swear to anything that he thought was in the slightest degree untruthful, and he was being asked to swear to the adequacy and completeness and truthfulness of the record he was being asked to prepare."

But even as Richardson was meeting with the press, the President, with the firestorm bearing down on him, was preparing to execute another dramatic about-face. At noon, he gave his decision to his astonished counsel, Charles Wright. At 2:00 Wright announced it in Judge Sirica's courtroom. At 2:26 the news clattered over the AP wire:

BULLETIN

WASHINGTON (AP)—President Nixon agreed Tuesday to comply in full with the U.S. Court of Appeals ruling directing him to give the White House tapes to a federal judge.

The announcement came as the House of Representatives began preliminary investigation into whether the President should be impeached.

Nixon's surprise announcement was made to U.S. District Court Judge John J. Sirica by Charles Alan Wright, lawyer for the President.

Wright told Sirica that the President had hoped that the compromise he announced Friday night would end the constitutional crisis.

"Events over the weekend made it very apparent it did not," Wright said.

The announcement shocked spectators in the packed courtroom who had been waiting to hear how Sirica would respond to the President's proposal to summarize the tapes and have his summary verified by a senior member of the Senate.

His back against the wall, Nixon took the step he had determined never to take.

During the next forty-eight hours, the United States and the Soviet Union moved to the brink of confrontation in the Middle East. UN cease-fire resolutions adopted on Monday and Tuesday, October 22 and 23, were accepted by Israel and Egypt, but both sides complained of truce violations. On Wednesday, the twenty-fourth, Cairo asked that both U.S. and Soviet troops be sent to Egypt to check on reported violations. The United States, determined to keep troops of both superpowers out of the area, refused. Leonid Brezhnev sent a message, which Nixon later described as "ominous," indicating that the Soviets were preparing to send troops unilaterally. Intelligence reports indicated that one Soviet ship in the area had nuclear components aboard. In the early-morning hours of Thursday, October 25, U.S. forces were placed on a worldwide alert, as part of a campaign of pressure to prevent the introduction of Soviet forces. On the diplomatic front, Nixon exchanged urgent messages with Brezhnev, pressing the Soviets to agree on creation of a UN peacekeeping force made up exclusively of troops from the smaller nations. Brezhnev assented, and later that day, with the United States and the Soviet Union jointly supporting it, the Security Council passed a resolution creating such a peacekeeping force. The superpowers moved back from the brink.

In Congress, at the same time, the anti-Nixon forces rushed toward the brink. House Majority Leader O'Neill decided conditions at last were ripe; the time had come to move in for the kill. On Tuesday, October 23, he declared on the floor of the House: "No other President in the history of this nation has brought the highest office in the land into such low repute. His conduct must bring shame upon us all. . . . He has left the people no recourse. . . . In their anger and exasperation, the people have turned to the House of Representatives. . . . The case must be referred to the Judiciary Committee for speedy and expeditious consideration. The House must act with determined leadership and strength." The next day, Wednesday, October 24, after conferring with the other nineteen Democratic members of the committee, Judiciary Committee Chairman Peter W. Rodino, Jr., announced that the committee would "proceed full steam ahead" with an inquiry into the possible impeachment of Richard Nixon, 37th President of the United States.

Clare Boothe Luce quoted the owner of a large newspaper chain as gloating: "Nixon will resign in a matter of weeks. No man can stand up to what we are pouring onto him and not crack up." Writing in *Newsweek*, columnist Stewart Alsop noted gloomily that "President-destruction seems to be becoming as popular a pastime in the United States as regicide was in England. . . . There is a fever abroad in Washington, uncomfortably like the ferocious fever that sometimes seizes a fight crowd when the knees of punch-drunk fighters begin to wobble."

"THE GRAND INQUEST"

On April 29, 1974—a Monday—Nixon and I were at Camp David, working on the speech he would give that evening announcing the release to the public of the White House transcripts. With the work on the speech finally done, and with our return to Washington scheduled shortly, the President invited me to join him for a drink on the Aspen terrace. Evening was falling. The spring air was crisp but comfortable. Below, the lawn sloped gently, peacefully, down toward the enveloping forest. We sipped our martinis, and reminisced about the dramatic weekend we had spent at Camp David exactly one year earlier. As he had often done since, the President again wondered aloud whether he had done the right thing in deciding then that Haldeman and Ehrlichman should go. The question still troubled him. We talked about the struggles since then—not just those over Watergate, and now over the impeachment inquiry, but also the Middle East, the economy, the energy crisis, the battles with Congress over war powers and budgets, the search for a durable accommodation with the Soviets. As we reviewed the year, I turned to him and said—with feeling—that I had never admired him so much as I had for the way he had stood up under the pressures of those twelve months. And I meant it. Few could have withstood them. Clare Boothe Luce's friend was right about the strength of the pressures, wrong about the strength of their target. Neither of us fully realized how much those pressures would intensify in the weeks to come.

The House Judiciary Committee's inquiry was styled by committee counsel Albert Jenner as "the Grand Inquest of the Nation," and by Ron Ziegler, in a San Clemente news briefing, as a "kangaroo court." It had aspects of both. But from first to last, it was an intensely political proceeding. Among some members on both sides of the issue, there was serious soul-searching. There were genuine disagreements over what the definition of an "impeachable offense" should be, over what standards should guide the committee's actions, over what level of proof should be required. On both sides there was grandstanding, there were leaks, there was politicking over rules.

Among those committed to impeachment, there was a dogged determination to use any means to achieve that purpose.

Throughout the impeachment battle, our general White House assessment was that we had our best chance of winning in the Senate, our second best on the floor of the House, and our slimmest chance in the Judiciary Committee. Whatever hope we might have had at the outset that articles of impeachment could be defeated in the committee soon dissipated. The question became not whether the committee would recommend impeachment, but what form the articles would take, how sharply partisan the split would be, and how the publicity generated by the committee would affect the climate of public opinion in which the full House would act. The committee showed itself early as a hanging jury.

Committee member William L. Hungate, a Missouri Democrat, helped set the tone. Accompanying himself at the piano, he played and sang for television cameras a little ditty of his own composition: "Come, come, come play with me/ Down at the old Watergate/ Come, come, come love and lie with me/ Down at the old Watergate/ See the little German band/ Ehrlichman und Haldeman/ Don't Martha Mitchell look great!" He also recorded the song, so that it could be played on a telephone call-in service operated by the Democratic National Committee. (Later, as committee counsel John Doar and his staff made their "evidentiary" presentation to the committee, Hungate commented slyly that it was "just like piano lessons—we're learning the keyboard.")

One of the crucial early decisions that shaped the committee's action was on the structure of its staff.

Ordinarily, congressional committees operate with "majority" and "minority" staffs, thus insuring that members of each party will have some members of the staff to whom they can turn, who will be responsive to their views or their wishes. At the outset, however, Rodino determined that the impeachment staff should be "nonpartisan." This was designed partly as a cosmetic measure to give an aura of objectivity to the investigation. But it also had a practical advantage, from the pro-impeachment side's standpoint: what it meant, in effect, was that the *entire* staff would be subject to the chairman and the majority members, and that there would be *no* minority staff.[1]

The Republican members did have a "minority counsel," Albert E. Jenner, but he was a minority counsel in name only. From the outset, he was committed to impeachment. He worked (when he worked at all) as Doar's deputy, not as the agent of the minority members. Barely six days after his appointment, he declared on a television show that the President should be considered impeachable for acts by his aides even if he had no knowledge of those acts.

Jenner was notorious for his absences; when there was work to be done, he was often off somewhere lecturing. At the White House, however, we so thoroughly distrusted him that we preferred his absences to his presence. When the White House transcripts were made public, Nixon offered to let Chairman Rodino and the committee's ranking Republican, Edward Hutchinson, come to the White House and listen to the actual tapes, to check the accuracy and completeness of the transcripts (a point conveniently forgotten by those who insist that the White House transcripts were deliberately "doctored"). The public rationale for limiting the offer to Rodino and Hutchinson, rather than including Doar and Jenner, was one of "principals only"—the President himself had reviewed the tapes for the White House, and made the decisions on what to include and what to exclude, and therefore it should be the chief elected officials of the committee, not staff employees, who did it for the committee. An unstated contributing reason, however, was distrust of Jenner. When Jenner finally was replaced by the committee's Republican members, just a few days before the public debate began, he was not dismissed but was simply given a lateral transfer as "associate counsel"—making official what had been fact throughout, that he was part of the prosecution staff. An assistant to one of the key Republican members of the Judiciary Committee, who worked closely with the committee staff, said later that he believed that the principal reason Jenner took the job in the first

---

1. A third of the staff were chosen on the basis of recommendations from the minority side, but all worked as a single, integrated unit under John Doar's direction—not as separate majority and minority staffs. The committee's senior Republican, Edward Hutchinson of Michigan, challenged the concept of a single, unified staff, but he lost. The minority, he explained later, "simply didn't have the votes."

place was that he wanted the glory of arguing an impeachment prosecution before the Senate.

Committee counsel John Doar was more circumspect, maintaining a pretense of neutrality until July 19. At that point, presenting the committee with five sets of proposed articles of impeachment together with a 306-page summary of "evidence," Doar gave up the pretense and delivered an emotional plea to the committee members that they vote for impeachment.

For months prior to that, in keeping with Chairman Rodino's cosmetic effort to give an appearance of fairness, Doar had insisted that his was an impartial, purely professional role. Members of his staff were warned that they could be fired for publicly expressing a personal opinion on the question of impeachment.

According to author Renata Adler, Doar actually worked primarily with a small group—about seven people—of which she was one, five of whom were old friends not on the regular committee staff. Adler reports that there was never any doubt among this group, including Doar, that unless there were "overwhelming evidence of Nixon's innocence," the object of the exercise was to impeach him. She describes Doar as having been "the second nonradical person I knew, and the first Republican, to advocate impeachment—months before he became special counsel, long before the inquiry began." While Doar and Rodino spoke publicly in almost cloying terms of "fairness" and "impartiality," with this small group Doar spoke in terms of "war" and "the Cause." Doar's purpose, however, obviously required that he conceal his objective from the committee members as well as from the regular staff. As a result, says Adler, "most of the work, almost all the time by almost all the staff, was a charade."[2]

It was a charade designed to bluff the public, to bluff the committee, to bluff the fawning newsmen, who daily told the nation that the committee was proceeding with scrupulous fairness.

One of Doar's tactics was to assemble such a massive volume of material that its sheer bulk would overwhelm. It was the same tactic I used four years earlier, when writing Nixon's first message to the Congress on the environment. Nixon's then-likely 1972 challenger, Senator Edmund Muskie, had taken early leadership on the environmental issue, which was just then emerging as one with great popular appeal. In late 1969 and early 1970 the administration

2. Renata Adler, "Searching for the Real Nixon Scandal," in *The Atlantic Monthly*, December 1976.

began putting together a comprehensive environmental package of its own: legislative proposals, administrative actions, new policy approaches. It really was a far-reaching, well-thought-out package, which deserved respect on its merits. But if we were to seize the leadership from Muskie, it had not only to *be* sweeping but also to *look* sweeping. By then, from long experience, I had evolved a basic rule for capturing headlines and influencing news leads: reporters can't always think, but they can always count. Give them a thoughtful exposition, and it goes in the wastebasket. Turn the same thing into a five-point program, and it gets a headline. Divide each of the five points into two, so that it becomes a ten-point program, and it gets twice as big a headline. So, in writing the environmental message, I organized it as an unprecedented thirty-seven-point program, fourteen measures being taken by administrative action or executive order, and twenty-three legislative proposals. No president had ever presented a thirty-seven-point program for anything before—and so with this Nixon swept Muskie from the headlines, and from then on Nixon was the leader on environmental reform. Few people remembered what the points were, but whatever they were, he had thirty-seven of them.

Doar knew the same trick: he produced an overwhelming thirty-eight-volume "Statement of Information," which staggered the committee members and the public by its mere presence. California Republican Charles E. Wiggins vainly urged his colleagues to consider "the evidence as distinguished from the material" that had been made available: "Thirty-eight books of material. My guess, Mr. Doar, is you can put all the admissible evidence in half of one book. Most of this is just material. It is not evidence and it may never surface in the Senate because it is not admissible evidence." But by then, by the opening of debate, the books had had their effect. No one cared about their content. The important thing was that there were thirty-eight of them.

Whenever Doar was pressed for specifics, whenever he was asked to tell the committee, please, precisely what it was that Nixon was accused of having done, he pointed to that thirty-eight-volume "Statement of Information." But the answers were not there. As Adler herself concedes, the Doar information-assembling machine produced "no investigation and, in the end, no case. It is commonly said that 'the Case' is in those thirty-odd staff volumes. Only by people who have not read them; hardly anyone has read them."

When the Doar staff made its presentation, there was a hallelujah chorus of awed comments about the crushing impact of the sheer weight of the evidence. Yet most of it had nothing to do with

Richard Nixon. It included pound after pound of tedious detail about the lower levels of the Watergate conspiracy, and reams of conflicting testimony assembled from earlier investigations, but most of it was utterly irrelevant to the impeachment of the President of the United States.

That was the way the committee operated: plodding forward, piling inference on innuendo, accumulating a staggering weight of "facts," testimony from prior hearings, creating an *impression* of massively imposing bulk—but seldom stopping to ask the hard questions, such as "Is it relevant?" "What does this have to do with the impeachment of Richard Nixon?" And, particularly, the committee assiduously avoided such hard but crucially relevant questions as "What has, in fact, been the accepted pattern or practice?"

The Doar "Statement of Information" were organized in volumes and subdivided by paragraphs, with each paragraph a terse, summary-form recapitulation of a particular series of supposed events. The paragraph was then backed up by supporting documents, mostly reproductions of selected pages of testimony from the Senate hearings, from the various grand juries, or from other prior proceedings. The simple fact of inclusion created, for the unwary, the impression that everything was somehow relevant, and that every meeting among minions that was catalogued must in some unspecified way be part of a vast conspiracy leading eventually to the Oval Office. The form of its presentation had another subtle but powerful effect: it heightened the impression of conspiracy by eliminating all other context. In some cases, it created the desired effect by encouraging the reader to fill in the blanks with his own assumptions. A good example of this is Book I, paragraph 4, dealing with G. Gordon Liddy's second presentation of his "intelligence" plan to then-Attorney General John Mitchell. (At an earlier meeting, among Liddy, Mitchell, Jeb Magruder, and John Dean, Liddy had proposed a $1 million scheme that included everything from wiretaps to the use of prostitutes to kidnapping. An appalled Mitchell vetoed it, but did so politely. Liddy was now back with a scaled-down, $500,000 model.) The "Statement of Information" reads:

On February 4, 1972, Attorney General Mitchell, John Dean, Jeb Magruder, and Gordon Liddy met in Mitchell's office. Liddy presented a modified version of his proposal with a budget of $500,000. The proposal included plans for electronic surveillance of political opponents. Magruder and Dean have testified that the targets included the office of Lawrence O'Brien, the Chairman of the Democratic National Committee (DNC); the DNC headquarters; and the Democratic Convention

Headquarters at the Fontainebleau Hotel in Miami, Florida. Magruder has also testified that the office of Henry Greenspun, editor of the *Las Vegas Sun*, was mentioned as another target. Mitchell has denied that there was discussion of specific targets. The meeting ended when Dean stated that these subjects should not be discussed in the office of the Attorney General of the United States. Following the meeting, Dean reported on the meeting to Haldeman.

Period. End of "information." Devastating. Since Dean "reported" on the scheme to Haldeman, we are invited to assume that it had Haldeman's blessing. The impression would have been radically different, however, if the staff had not, with a neat, surgical precision, managed to leave out what happened when Dean reported to Haldeman. According to Dean's own testimony:

"After this second meeting in Mitchell's office, I sought a meeting with Mr. Haldeman to tell him what was occurring. . . . I told Haldeman what had been presented by Liddy and told him that I felt it was incredible, unnecessary and unwise. I told him that no one at the White House should have anything to do with this. I said that the reelection committee will need an ability to deal with demonstrations, it did not need bugging, mugging, prostitutes, and kidnappers. Haldeman agreed and told me I should have no further dealings on the matter."

Much of the impeachment effort was devoted to orchestrating atmospherics, creating a climate of hostility toward Nixon in which the public either would be disposed to believe the worst or would grow so disgusted that evidence of specific impeachable offenses would become unnecessary. Charges made and then abandoned, issues raised and left dangling, red herrings pulled across the path, a constant flood of leaks clothed in prejudicial innuendo, all had their cumulative effect.

Among the major committee leaks was a series of thirteen memos, prepared at the request of several Democratic members by one of the committee's regular staff, William P. Dixon. In 1972, at age twenty-eight, Dixon ran the McGovern campaign organization in Wisconsin. For the better part of two years McGovern's Midwest organizer, Gene Pokorny, had lived in the Dixon household, sometimes relying only on Dixon's credit card for campaign financing. Accused of being a "Nixon-hating partisan" when the leaked memos appeared, Dixon merely smiled shyly and commented that, after all, "this is the third full summer I've devoted to getting Nixon out of the White House."

When the committee leaked one of Pat Buchanan's memos to *The Washington Post*, Buchanan seized on the occasion to lash back in his usual feisty style. "Charles Colson was convicted and faces possible disbarment and possible imprisonment for leaking derogatory information about an individual [Ellsberg] under indictment," he told a press conference. "It seems to me there is no ethical difference, and I doubt there is any legal difference, between that felony and what the nameless, faceless character assassins on the House Judiciary Committee are doing today. . . . Who's doing the systematic leaking, why they are doing it, seems to me to be a news story, a major news story, news that the American people have a right to know."

Toward the close of the proceedings, two committee members spoke frankly about the process. Said Wisconsin Republican Harold V. Froelich: "We went fishing. And we played every issue we could for whatever it was worth. Part of it was creating an atmosphere for impeachment." California Democrat Jerome R. Waldie echoed this: "I think all of these things make an ultimate pattern which influences this vote, even though a member cites another single issue. My guess is that it took this entire pattern of conduct to bring many members to a vote for impeachment. Certainly, it provides a symphony in the background."

One of the most damaging contributions to this process was made by Judiciary Committee member Jack Brooks, an abrasively partisan Texas Democrat, who used his chairmanship of a House government operations subcommittee to further the majority's game plan. In March Brooks issued a subcommittee report on expenditures at Key Biscayne and San Clemente designed to foster the impression that $17 million in federal funds had been used for "improvements" on Nixon's "homes." The three Republicans on the subcommittee denounced the report, refusing to sign it. The senior Republican, John H. Buchanan of Alabama, flatly branded the report "absolutely untrue," and declared that what began as a subcommittee investigation of government spending at all presidents' homes "has degenerated into the worst political witch-hunt I've seen in all my time on the Hill. I was outraged. It was one of the grossest political smears I had ever seen." The subsequent treatment of the Brooks report also marked one of the low points of news malpractice. For months afterward, on the strength of Brooks's grossly distorted report, editors who knew better continued to print references to "the $17 million in improvements on Nixon's homes." The figure—and the false characterization—kept popping up in headlines, and kept being cited in those sections of daily stories that recapitulated the background of events—which is how lies become accepted as truths.

In order to reach his $17 million figure, Brooks swept together everything that had been spent over a five-year period at either the Florida White House or the Western White House, even reaching so far as to add in the value of the Army Signal Corps' sophisticated world-wide communications equipment temporarily located out west. He also included the salaries of all army communications personnel, all security and support costs, and all maintenance and equipment costs for the Western White House office complex located at the adjacent coast guard station. These were not even expenditures on Nixon's "homes," much less improvements. They were the routine costs of operating the presidency away from Washington, the same costs incurred when it was operated from Johnson City or Hyannis Port or Gettysburg or Key West. Most resulted from the deliberate—and widely appreciated—decision to establish a base of White House operations in California, closer to the new population centers in the West. But Brooks was the consummate demagogue, and he found an issue which, dressed up in enough distortions, was guaranteed to outrage a large segment of the American people, and he was totally unconstrained in exploiting it.

Most of the work done at the Nixon houses for the Secret Service was done at the same time the Nixons themselves were, at their own considerable expense, refurbishing their newly acquired homes. There does seem to have been a pattern, in a number of instances, of letting the government pay for changes that served both the government's needs and the Nixons'. (For example, the old heating system at San Clemente was unsafe. The Nixons were going to replace it with a new gas system. The Secret Service insisted on a safer, but also considerably more expensive, electric system. The Secret Service won, and the government paid the bill. It seems reasonable that the government should only have paid the difference between what the Nixons wanted and what the Secret Service wanted—although, on the other hand, it meant that the Nixons were stuck forever afterward with the substantially higher operating costs for the electric system.) The Secret Service insisted on removal or relocation of large numbers of trees and shrubs in order to rearrange sight lines; the grounds also had to be extensively torn up to install alarm systems and underground wiring for security installations. In repairing the damage, the government workmen tried to do so in an aesthetically pleasing way, in some cases replacing old fixtures that had been destroyed with new ones that were more expensive. Sometimes the resulting costs were split, sometimes not.

The staff of the Congressional Joint Committee on Internal Revenue Taxation, after a detailed audit, concluded that some $90,000 of the expenditures billed to the government at both homes had sufficiently benefited the Nixons—even though they also served government purposes—so that they should have been treated as taxable personal income. Perhaps. This was the same committee report, however, that claimed Nixon should have reported as personal income the equivalent in first-class air fare for every ride that a member of the Nixon family or an invited guest ever took accompanying him on *Air Force One,* an assertion so brazen and so unprecedented as to be almost breathtaking. One of the largest items the Joint Committee staff held should have been treated as personal was a $12,679 share of the cost of the security fence built at Key Biscayne—on the theory that an ugly chain-link fence would have served as well to keep intruders out, and would have been cheaper. Some of the widely criticized "government" expenditures—for example, a swimming-pool heater in San Clemente—had in fact been paid for by the Nixons.

Even viewed in the most prejudicial light, these $90,000 of costs that perhaps should have been allocated differently are a far cry from the $17 million that Brooks gulled the American people into believing had been spent on "improving" the Nixon homes. And Brooks was one of those pretending to judge Nixon fairly, judiciously, nonpolitically.

The Joint Committee survey was conducted as a result of widespread public charges that Nixon had underpaid his income taxes. The principal item in dispute was whether a 1969 donation of his papers to the government had been made in time to qualify for the $482,000 in tax deductions he claimed, spread over a period of four years. The question arose because a change in the law, enacted in December 1969 but made retroactive to July 26, 1969, made donations of papers no longer eligible for treatment as charitable contributions. The Nixon papers were delivered in March 1969, but the last of the paperwork was not completed until later. His tax attorneys advised him that it was a legal donation for tax purposes.[3] After his tax returns became a public issue, he submitted

3. On the donation of the papers, a deed was later discovered to have been fraudulently backdated. However, there was no evidence that Nixon was aware of this, and his tax lawyers argued that the deed was unneces-

them to the Joint Committee, agreeing to abide by its determination —in effect, waiving the normal taxpayer's right to challenge an adverse interpretation. The committee staff ruled against him on the papers, and on a wide variety of other questions of the sort accountants argue over, and they produced a report similar in nature to the initial bargaining position of an IRS agent in a tax audit. Nixon's own tax lawyers believed strongly that they had a solid case, and wanted to take it to court. Against his lawyers' advice—and because of the political pressure he was under—he accepted the committee report, and volunteered to pay more than $400,000 in additional taxes, plus interest.[4]

Another example of the Joint Committee staff's tendency to decide every disputed issue against taxpayer Nixon: at Key Biscayne, Nixon bought two adjacent houses, one for use as a residence and the other for use as an office, paying the purchase and maintenance costs for both of them himself. On his tax return, Nixon took the customary deduction for costs of using the one house for an office. The committee ruled that this should be disallowed—on the rather remarkable grounds that the government would have paid the full costs of providing an office facility for him if he had asked for it. So he was left in the same situation the committee placed him in with regard to his papers. On the Key Biscayne house, he had to pay extra taxes because he had footed the bill himself for an office the government would otherwise have paid for. On the papers, the transfer was held complete for the purpose of establishing the government's ownership, but incomplete for the purpose of permitting a tax deduction. At Key Biscayne, the government saved the cost and collected the tax; on the donation of papers, it kept the papers and collected the tax.

From the start of the impeachment inquiry, there was intense controversy over what constitutes grounds for impeachment. The Constitution specifies that it shall be for "treason, bribery, or other high crimes and misdemeanors." The central question was whether it required a specifically criminal act. Quite naturally, those pressing for impeachment pressed for a broad interpretation, not limited to criminal acts, while the White House pressed for a narrow interpretation requiring proof of a criminal act. Both sides marshaled

---

sary—that the actual delivery of the papers before the retroactive cut-off date, with the clear intent that it was a donation, was sufficient to establish eligibility under prevailing legal precedents.

4. He paid $317,848.87, covering additional tax, penalties, and interest for the years 1970–72. He deferred payment for 1969, for which he was not legally liable at the time of the settlement.

impressive mounds of historical data to support their respective positions. We found ours more persuasive. They found theirs more persuasive. Every ten years, the Library of Congress issues a new revision of its standard reference work on the Constitution, *The Constitution of the United States of America—Analysis and Interpretation.* This is the definitive annotation of the Constitution by an arm of Congress, and, by coincidence, its latest decennial revision happened to be issued in June 1974, during the committee's deliberations. While recognizing that the question is shrouded in ambiguity, this stated that "practice over the years . . . would appear to limit the grounds of conviction to indictable criminal offenses for all officers with the possible exception of judges."[5] The committee staff, of course, argued the opposite. The issue was never resolved, but in framing its articles of impeachment the committee majority took the broadest possible view. Those minority members who argued for a narrower interpretation found themselves shouting into the wind.

The basic White House legal strategy in the impeachment battle was twofold: first, to focus the debate on Watergate, on the theory that except for Watergate all the collateral issues would never have been seriously put forward as grounds for impeachment; and second, to join the issue squarely on the question of whether Nixon had, as the impeachment chorus claimed, ordered the payment of hush money to Howard Hunt. This payment was the principal overt act charged against Nixon himself. The strategy was devised primarily by James D. St. Clair, the Boston trial attorney brought in to handle the President's Watergate defense. While legally sound, politically it proved woefully inadequate—and, unfortunately, what we were engaged in was a political rather than a legal battle.

The hush-money charge against Nixon grew out of his recorded conversation with Dean and Haldeman on March 21, 1973—the conversation in which Dean warned Nixon that the Watergate cover-up was becoming a "cancer on the Presidency," told him of Hunt's money demands, and relayed Hunt's reported threat to expose the plumbers' activities unless those demands were met by the time of his sentencing two days later. It was on the basis of this meeting that the Watergate grand jury, on the special prosecutor's recommendation, named Nixon as an unindicted co-conspirator in the Watergate cover-up case.

I first saw that transcript in mid-April 1974 while working on the April 29 speech in which Nixon announced that on the following

5. The situation with regard to judges is somewhat clouded by a separate provision of the Constitution giving them tenure during "good behavior."

day he would release the White House transcripts. Ever since
Dean's testimony (and Haldeman's rebuttal) before the Senate
committee the previous summer, this conversation had been regarded by both sides as crucial to the question of whether Nixon
had been personally involved in obstruction of justice. The Hunt
threat was clearly a hot potato. In the conversation, Nixon bounced
back and forth on the question of whether Hunt's immediate demands had to be met, in order to buy at least a little time in which
to consider what to do. The threat concerned not the Watergate
cover-up itself, but the supersecret plumbers—and their exposure
could well begin a process of unraveling that might reach any
number of areas of genuine national security concern as well as
political embarrassment.

I read and reread the transcript, probably a dozen times. It was
a long conversation, lasting an hour and three-quarters. Nixon
was probing for information, reacting, leaning first one way and
then another about what ought to be done. Any number of individual comments could be lifted out of context to "prove" either that he
did authorize the payment or that he did not. Hunt's demand was
only one of dozens of problems Dean presented. Dean traced
through the background of Watergate, telling Nixon about the
Liddy plans, detailing after-the-fact efforts to cover up, saying
Mitchell might have perjured himself and Magruder definitely had,
discussing other possible criminal liabilities on the part of White
House and re-election committee officials. Part of the discussion
dealt with the likelihood of criminal proceedings, and part with
how to minimize the exploitation—on television—of White House
embarrassments by the Ervin committee.

On the payment itself, Nixon's comments ranged from ". . . for
your immediate thing you've got no choice with Hunt but the
hundred and twenty or whatever it is. Right? Would you agree that
that's a buy time thing, you better damn well get that done, but
fast?" to, somewhat later, "But my point is, do you ever have any
choice on Hunt? That's the point. No matter what we do here now,
John, Hunt eventually, if he isn't going to get commuted and so
forth, he's going to blow the whistle."

As I reread the transcript, however, I found that a clear pattern
did emerge. Nixon kept returning to the possibility of impaneling
a new grand jury, and gradually this evolved into an alternative
means of delaying sentencing, and thus of buying the time that the
Hunt payment would have been designed to buy. It would allow
the attorney general to ask Judge Sirica for a delay—maybe one
week, maybe two weeks. From the time this idea surfaced, through

the end of the conversation, there was no more talk of meeting Hunt's demand. From Nixon's standpoint, as the transcript made clear, the grand jury idea had three main attractions: it allowed him to get in a public position of taking leadership in cleaning up the mess, and of moving it into the criminal justice system; by allowing a delay in Hunt's sentencing, it bought the time he needed; and it could place the questioning of witnesses within the grand jury room rather than in front of the Ervin committee's television cameras.

Having found that pattern, I no longer had any problem with the March 21 conversation, in terms of my own assessment of whether Nixon had authorized the payment. Knowing well his habit of darting one way and then another while considering an issue—of saying "do this" and then "don't do it"—I had no difficulty reconciling his early thoughts that the money should be paid with his later turn to another alternative. And this squared with the recollections of all three participants in the meeting. Nixon insisted that he had not authorized the payment. Haldeman insisted he had not authorized it. Even Dean, in Senate testimony that was all but universally ignored in the dispute, declared: "The money matter was left very much hanging at that meeting. Nothing was resolved." (In fact, at no point in his testimony either before the Senate committee or the grand jury did Dean ever allege that Nixon had authorized any payment to Hunt. Yet it was in that meeting with Dean that Nixon was accused of having ordered it.)

Yet a payment was made. That same evening, former Mitchell aide Fred C. LaRue delivered $75,000 to Hunt's attorney, William O. Bittman. What happened?

One answer is clearly suggested by the indictment returned March 1, 1974, in the cover-up case, as drawn up by the special prosecutor. Another, directly contrary, answer is clearly suggested by the testimony the special prosecutor had before him when he drew up that indictment. The indictment specifies a series of "overt acts," numbers 40 through 43, which were obviously designed to establish a basis for naming Nixon as an unindicted co-conspirator:

40. On or about March 21, 1973, from approximately 11:15 A.M. to approximately noon, Harry R. Haldeman and John W. Dean, III, attended a meeting at the White House in the District of Columbia, at which time there was a discussion about the fact that E. Howard Hunt, Jr., had asked for approximately $120,000.

41. On or about March 21, 1973, at approximately 12:30 P.M., Harry R. Haldeman had a telephone conversation with John N. Mitchell.

42. On or about the early afternoon of March 21, 1973, John N. Mitchell had a telephone conversation with Fred C. LaRue during which Mitchell authorized LaRue to make a payment of approximately $75,000 to and for the benefit of E. Howard Hunt, Jr.

43. On or about the evening of March 21, 1973, in the District of Columbia, Fred C. LaRue arranged for the delivery of approximately $75,000 in cash to William O. Bittman.

The intended meaning was obvious: a chain—Nixon to Haldeman to Mitchell to LaRue to Bittman. Yet when he framed his public indictment, the special prosecutor had secret grand jury testimony establishing an entirely separate chain, in which Nixon was not a link. The chain began not in the Nixon-Haldeman-Dean meeting but a separate conversation, apparently earlier that morning, between Dean and LaRue, in which they discussed Hunt's latest demand. Dean said that he was "out of that business," and suggested LaRue contact Mitchell. LaRue called Mitchell. (Both LaRue's and Mitchell's testimony, confirmed by Mitchell's long-distance toll records, confirm that the call was initiated by LaRue.) According to LaRue's testimony,[6] Dean told him that Hunt wanted $75,000 for attorneys' fees and $60,000 for family support. LaRue said that he decided on his own to limit his discussion with Mitchell to the $75,000 for attorneys' fees. Mitchell agreed that he should pay it. LaRue arranged for delivery. Testimony by Dean, LaRue, and Mitchell all confirmed that this was the actual chain, and this was further buttressed by the fact that the amount delivered was the $75,000 LaRue discussed with Mitchell, not the $120,000 discussed among Dean, Haldeman, and Nixon. Both Haldeman and Mitchell testified that the purpose of Haldeman's call to Mitchell was not to discuss Hunt's demands but, rather, to invite Mitchell to a meeting at the White House the following day. There was no testimony, no evidence to support the inferential chain laid out by the special prosecutor.

The indictment was an artful contrivance, belied by the evidence, designed to support the naming of Nixon as an unindicted co-conspirator. But it served the Judiciary Committee's purpose well. At the same court session in which the indictment was returned, in a theatrical gesture, the assistant special prosecutor also handed Sirica a sealed envelope, together with a bulging suitcase. He

6. In a plea-bargained arrangement with the special prosecutor, LaRue entered a guilty plea on June 27, 1973, to one count of conspiracy to obstruct justice in the Watergate cover-up, and agreed to testify as a government witness.

announced that the suitcase contained grand jury materials, which the grand jury wanted transmitted to the House Judiciary Committee. The assembled media instantly made the inescapable connection.

Why was the special prosecutor determined to name the President as an unindicted co-conspirator? Leon Jaworski himself argues that he believed Nixon guilty (though he clings to the traditional fiction that all actions taken in the name of the grand jury were taken at the grand jury's initiative, an assertion that anyone who knows anything about grand juries knows is not so).[7] Quite probably he did. But it also was an important part of Jaworski's strategy. In arguing his right to the Nixon tapes before the Supreme Court, he leaned heavily on the assertion that the fact of Nixon's having been named "constitutes the requisite *prima facie* showing to negate any claim of executive privilege for the subpoenaed conversations relating to Watergate and is binding on the courts. . . ."[8] In other words, he claimed that his having named Nixon an unindicted co-conspirator left the President stripped of his constitutional defenses, and made absolute Jaworski's own right to whatever he wanted from the presidential files for use in the trials of Mitchell, Haldeman, and the rest.

Prior to the Supreme Court arguments, Jaworski attempted another use of Nixon's unindicted co-conspirator status in his efforts to get additional White House tapes. In early May 1974 he met with Alexander Haig and James St. Clair, special counsel to the President, at the White House, and offered a deal. On May 1 St. Clair had made a court motion to quash Jaworski's subpoena for sixty-four tapes. The fact that Nixon had been named had been widely rumored, thanks to the assistant special prosecutor's bit of courtroom theatrics, but had never been confirmed. Jaworski offered to settle for eighteen of the sixty-four, if St. Clair would withdraw the motion. As an inducement, he told them Nixon had been named an unindicted co-conspirator, and that if there were a court contest over the tapes he would be "required" to reveal this. He then pointed out that an out-of-court agreement would avoid that necessity, at least while the Judiciary Committee proceedings were still continuing. Haig and St. Clair responded politely, saying they would explore the offer with the President. Privately, they were infuriated. They regarded it, Haig told me later, as blackmail. Nixon turned down the offer.

---

7. Jaworski's successor, Henry Ruth, acknowledged in 1975 that in naming Nixon, the grand jury had acted on the special prosecutor's recommendation.
8. Brief for the United States, page 99.

The Judiciary Committee majority made much of the differences between its transcripts of White House tapes and the transcripts of some of those same tapes made public earlier by the White House. So did much of the media, asserting automatically (1) that in every difference between the two, the committee's version was correct and the White House version incorrect, and (2) that the "errors" thus shown in the White House transcripts were the result of "editing." (The White House transcripts were almost always—and always in committee documents—referred to as "edited" transcripts, while the adjective was not used for the committee version, though both were in fact edited to eliminate extraneous material. The White House transcripts were also edited to take out expletives, which turned out to be a costly mistake—people imagined much more colorful language than was in fact there.)

The committee had much more sophisticated equipment, and it had the staff resources to devote many more man-hours to making each transcript. As a result, its transcripts are more nearly complete. Less appears as "unintelligible," and thoughts and sentences flow more freely. Having worked now with both sets of transcripts, I tend to regard the committee's as probably being, on balance, more nearly accurate (and in this book, where I have quoted from transcripts, I have used its version). But at the time, we were as suspicious of the committee's versions as it was of ours.

In July, after the committee published its version, White House lawyers checked those transcripts back against the actual tapes. Among their conclusions, as reported privately to Haig:

—Frequently the committee transcripts show someone laughing or coughing in the middle of a conversation. In almost every case where the transcript shows laughter, there is none on the tape; it appears to be an effort at characterization. The "coughs" are usually extraneous noises such as the rattling of coffee cups.

—Names keep popping up in one transcript, unsupported by the tapes. On March 13 it has Nixon telling Dean to "talk to Elliott Gompers" if he needs anything from IRS. No one had ever heard of an Elliott Gompers, and nothing like it appears on the tape. On March 22 it shows Dean saying "Bull has the matter right now"; the tape says "bullheaded right now." On March 22 a reference to "Mansfield" was really "minefield." And so forth.[9]

—A committee version of the September 15, 1972, meeting of

9. On the lighter side, in a separate incident, one of the transcripts had Rose Mary Woods staying behind in San Clemente to visit with her friends "Sam and Ella." Actually she had stayed behind to recuperate from a near-fatal case of salmonella poisoning.

Nixon, Haldeman, and Dean that was leaked to *The Washington Post* and printed on May 17, 1973, was markedly different from the version officially published by the committee in July. In at least eighty places it had undergone "editing" between versions.

They also sharply disagreed with the committee version of one of the most widely quoted passages in all the transcripts, one in which, by most news accounts, Nixon told Mitchell he wanted everyone to "stonewall" it. Again, the committee produced two versions of this: a leaked version, printed by *The New York Times* on June 21, and the official version published by the committee two weeks later.

The leaked version read:

"And, uh, for that reason, I (unintelligible) I don't give a—what happens. I want you to (unintelligible) stonewall it, plead the Fifth Amendment (unintelligible) else, if it'll (unintelligible). That's the big point. . . ."

The later, official version read:

"And, uh, for that reason, I am perfectly willing to—I don't give a shit what happens. I want you all to stonewall it, let them plead the Fifth Amendment, cover-up, or anything else, if it'll save it— save the plan. That's the whole point. . . ."

After their own review of the tape, the White House lawyers insisted (again, privately, within the White House) that they were totally unwilling to accept the committee version, and said that it was more nearly: "And, uh, for that reason, I am perfectly willing to—I don't give a shit what happens (unintelligible) stonewall it, let them plead the Fifth Amendment, cover-up, or anything else, if it'll save it—save it for them." Though not able to make out what was said in the "unintelligible" section, they were certain it was not "I want you all to . . ." (Their guess was that it was "go down and sto—stonewall.")

What angered us most about the handling of this quote, however, was not the apparent "editing" by the committee, but the clearly deliberate editing of it by the news media. That "stonewall" section —whichever version was correct—was only part of a thought, which, lifted out of context, appeared far different if placed back in context. In the committee transcript, Nixon continued the thought, uninterrupted: ". . . that's the whole point. On the other hand, uh, uh, I would prefer, as I said to you, that you do it the other way. And I would particularly prefer to do it that other way if it's going to come out that way anyway. And that my view, that, uh, with the number of jackass people that they've got that they can call, they're going to— The story they get out through leaks, charges, and so forth, and innuendos, will be a hell of a lot worse than the story they're going to get out by just letting it out there."

The Washington Post bannered the first half of the quote across the top of page one, and buried the second half at the bottom of the story, on an inside page. *Newsweek* ran the first half of the quote as its cover, ignoring the second half. I began an outraged letter to the editor-in-chief of *Newsweek,* an old friend, but then threw it in the wastebasket. What was the use?

There was obviously a good deal of guesswork involved in the production of both sets of transcripts, the committee's and the White House's. At the committee, members of the staff prepared the transcripts originally. Committee members who listened to the tapes and disagreed with the staff transcript were then permitted to make modifications, and these were incorporated into the final, official versions—a process probably accounting for many of the differences between the leaked versions and the official versions. Since trying to transcribe the tapes was, much of the time, a matter of trying to deduce from a scramble of indistinct voices what was *probably* said, the bias of the transcriber was bound to affect the product, whether at the White House or at the committee. The only thing that can be said with certainty about the two versions is that neither is completely accurate. The committee went further than the White House did in trying to fill in the "unintelligibles." In my own comparisons, it seems to me that for the most part the basic differences are minor, and that we could probably have survived the committee's versions better than we did our own version— simply because, being more complete, they read more smoothly (whether accurately or not), and therefore they gave less of an impression of stumbling and confusion.

The first action brought under the Constitution's impeachment clause was directed in 1797 against a senator, William Blount of Tennessee. It moved Thomas Jefferson to write to James Madison: "I see nothing in the mode of proceedings by impeachment but the most formidable weapon for the purpose of dominant faction that was ever contrived. It would be the most effectual one of getting rid of any man whom they may consider as dangerous to their views." In 1973, even while calling for Nixon's resignation, columnist Joseph Alsop wrote: "This reporter has known three different White Houses in the range of very well to exceptionally intimately. They belonged, successively, to Franklin Roosevelt, John Kennedy, and Lyndon Johnson. If these other White Houses had gone through what the Nixon White House has been put through, with informers climbing out the windows and floods of secret papers pouring out the doors, there is no room for doubt that impeachment cries would have been heard in the land."

What, then, was to be the standard for singling out one president for impeachment? Was it to be by counting noses, to see which one a "dominant faction" could muster the votes to impeach? Was it to be by spinning the wheel of chance, singling out the one unlucky enough to have all his most private papers exposed to the public view, thus providing the technical opportunity to impeach? Or was it to be the one whose offenses were so disproportionate that they crossed the line of acceptability, even recognizing that presidents throughout history have found it necessary to bend the law?

The power of impeachment is lodged in the Congress, not in the courts, precisely because it *is* a political process. It requires political judgments, in the highest sense. The question is not one of simple guilt or innocence. Guilt is a necessary precondition, but only a precondition. Impeachment is discretionary, not mandatory. The next question is whether the offense is sufficiently grave to warrant this extraordinary remedy. Unless we want presidents to serve only at the pleasure of Congress, impeachment must be an extraordinary remedy, resorted to only in the most extraordinary circumstances. It must be a resort of necessity, not of convenience, not of opportunity, not of faction.

Clearly, any "grand inquest" worthy of its pretensions must focus broadly on the conduct of the presidency. If one president is singled out for impeachment, it must be because he is singularly impeachable, because his conduct so violates the norm as to require this singular remedy.

Committee member Hamilton Fish, Jr.—a New York Republican who voted to impeach—admitted later that "not a person on the committee had any idea how a president is supposed to act, or even what a president's responsibilities are." Yet the only valid way to measure the acts of one president is against those of other presidents. Justice is blindfolded not only against the influence of prejudice but also against the intrusion of consequence. No other person bears the responsibility a president does, not only for the probity of his actions but also for the consequences of those actions. Every president lauded by history as "strong" has been damned by his contemporaries for trampling the law, for being cavalier toward Congress and even, on occasion, contemptuous of individual liberties.

Jefferson understood this. "On great occasions," he wrote in 1807, "every good officer must be ready to risk himself in going beyond the strict line of the law, when the public preservation requires it."

He elaborated the thought in 1810, after leaving the White House: "A strict observance of the written laws is doubtless *one* of the high duties of a good citizen, but it is not *the highest*. The laws of necessity, of self-preservation, of saving our country when in danger, are of a higher obligation. . . . To lose our country by a scrupulous adherence to written law, would be to lose the law itself, with life, liberty, property and all those who are enjoying them with us; thus absurdly sacrificing the end to the means."

Lincoln understood this. Explaining his own sweeping violations of constitutional bounds, he wrote in a letter in 1864:

My oath to preserve the Constitution imposed on me the duty of preserving by every indispensable means that government, that nation, of which the Constitution was the organic law. Was it possible to lose the nation and yet preserve the Constitution? By general law life and limb must be protected, yet often a limb must be amputated to save a life, but a life is never wisely given to save a limb. I felt that measures, otherwise unconstitutional, might become lawful by becoming indispensable to the preservation of the Constitution through the preservation of the nation. Right or wrong, I assumed this ground and now avow it. I could not feel that, to the best of my ability, I had ever tried to preserve the Constitution, if to save slavery or any minor matter, I should permit the wreck of the government, country, and Constitution altogether.

Lincoln's offenses against the Constitution were no trifling matter. He usurped Congress' constitutional power to "make rules for the government and regulation of the land and naval forces," proclaiming his own elaborate code of laws for the military forces. He spent millions of dollars without authorization. In disregard of both the law and the Constitution, he greatly expanded the army and navy by executive order. He extended his own war powers to free the slaves, and then, two days later, he decreed that all persons "discouraging enlistments, resisting military drafts, or . . . guilty of any disloyal practice affording aid and comfort to the rebels" would be subject to military law and to trial by courts-martial, and he arbitrarily suspended the right of habeas corpus for anyone tried by court-martial or confined in any military prison. (Lincoln was a wartime president, of course. But so was Nixon. Imagine the outcry if Nixon had ordered all persons "discouraging enlistments" tried by court-martial and thrown into a military prison without right of habeas corpus. The hullabaloo over Watergate would have been lost in the din.)

If the committee had considered the Nixon presidency in the light of past presidencies, it might have reached the same conclusions. Or it might not. The damning point, which alone would be enough to condemn it as incompetent, is that it never tried. Democratic member Ray Thornton of Arkansas later defended the committee's blinkered focus on the Nixon presidency *in vacuo*, insisting that no "previous standard" should have been considered—"only the Constitution is the proper standard for presidential conduct." By that criterion, he would clearly have had to impeach Lincoln.

He would also have had to impeach Franklin Roosevelt. No violation of constitutionally-protected individual liberties in American history has approached, either in its sweep or in its audacity, Roosevelt's 1942 order imprisoning 110,000 Americans for no offense other than their ancestry. Of those Japanese-Americans interned by Roosevelt's decree, 73 percent were U.S. citizens born in this country. Nearly all the rest—the older ones—were permanent U.S. residents, and still aliens only because U.S. policy denied them citizenship. This was one of the most disgraceful episodes in the American experience, combining hate, fear, blatant racism, greed, political opportunism, suppression of evidence. Historian James J. Martin has called this mass incarceration "a breach of the Bill of Rights on a scale so large as to beggar the sum total of all such violations from the beginnings of the United States down to that time." The fault was not Roosevelt's alone. It was shared, ironically, by the ambitious attorney general of California, a Republican who hoped to win the governorship on the strength of his leadership in the internment drive: Earl Warren. But it was Roosevelt who, on February 19, 1942, issued the notorious Executive Order 9066, followed soon after by notices throughout the western halves of the Pacific coastal states: "ALL PERSONS OF JAPANESE ANCESTRY, BOTH ALIEN AND NON-ALIEN, WILL BE EVACUATED FROM THE ABOVE DESIGNATED AREA BY 12:00 NOON. . . ." The evacuees were registered, transformed into numbers, given a week to ten days to wind up their affairs and dispose of their belongings, and required to report for internment with bedrolls and baggage, no more than they could carry by hand. Whole families were herded into one bare room. Many were dumped into horse stalls. At some centers, hundreds were packed into a single dormitory. Armed guards stood over them with bayonets. Not in Nazi Germany, but in the United States; not 10, or 110, but 110,000, men, women and children.

But it was not Franklin Roosevelt in the dock when the Judiciary Committee staged its "grand inquest" in 1974. It was Richard

Nixon. And, brandishing its moral calipers, the committee was determined to measure only the distance Nixon might have strayed from the strict letter of the law, not whether he had strayed further or less far than his predecessors, or what the provocations might have been. Not even the hard exigencies of war were to be an excuse. Some members argued vehemently that he should be impeached for having ordered secret bombing missions against North Vietnamese forces in Cambodia—no matter that the bombing was done with the concurrence of Cambodia's chief of state, Prince Norodom Sihanouk, and the secrecy was necessary because, for his own diplomatic purposes, Sihanouk would have had to refuse permission if it were announced publicly. The bombing almost certainly shortened the war and saved American lives. Without the secrecy that made the bombing possible, those lives would have been lost. Some argued Nixon should be impeached for having ordered wiretaps—legal at the time—of four newsmen and thirteen administration officials, in an effort to trace the source of potentially disastrous leaks of highly sensitive diplomatic secrets, including the American fall-back position in the strategic arms limitation talks then in progress with the Soviet Union. (Historian James MacGregor Burns relates an incident in which, in the presence of Attorney General Francis Biddle, J. Edgar Hoover confessed to Franklin Roosevelt that an FBI agent had tried to tap left-wing labor leader Harry Bridges' telephone, and had been caught in the act. Roosevelt, Burns reports, "roared with laughter, slapped Hoover on the back, and shouted gleefully, 'By God, Edgar, that's the first time you've been caught with your pants down!' "[10])

Nor did the committee even require proof that the President had transgressed the law or betrayed his trust. Members argued long and inconclusively over what the standard should be—proof "beyond a reasonable doubt," the less rigorous standard of "clear and convincing evidence," or the flexible criterion of "probable cause" established for grand jury indictments. While the question was never resolved, most of the majority members, in their arguments, were clearly satisfied with the least rigorous standard. And counsel John Doar, in the "summary of evidence" with which he offered the draft resolutions, hardly tried to rise even to the level of probable cause. He piled conclusion on inference on assumption, interpreting even the most elementary political and public-relations moves as evidence of conspiracy. (He argued, for example, that a "decision"

10. *Roosevelt: The Soldier of Freedom* (New York, 1970), p. 217.

by the President to engage in a Watergate cover-up "is the only one that could explain a pattern of undisputed incidents that otherwise cannot be explained." Among those incidents that Doar found otherwise inexplicable: Nixon's instructions to Haldeman to try to counter the political damage by launching a "diversionary" public-relations offensive.) As Republican Wiley Mayne of Iowa put it in committee debate, Doar "had to arrive at his conclusion of presidential involvement by a series of inferences piled on other inferences. And I noticed that every time he made an inference, it was an inference unfavorable to the President of the United States."

Throughout the committee proceedings, the argument was repeatedly made in Congress, the press, and elsewhere that the House should vote impeachment so that the issue could be settled in a Senate trial—that it was there, in the Senate, with more rigorous standards of proof, with opposing counsel to challenge arguments, that the true test should come. This argument was used to justify a lower standard of proof for the House—analogizing the House to a grand jury, with its "probable cause" standard and its absence of procedural safeguards, and the Senate to a courtroom, with its "beyond a reasonable doubt" standard and the presence of safeguards. To me, the argument was specious on its face. A Senate trial would be an intense trauma for the nation, half-paralyzing the presidency for months on end, inviting foreign adversaries to seize the moment for challenges that might rise to the most serious sort, further dividing and demoralizing an already overwrought public. Responsibility for deciding whether to put the nation through that trauma and to invite that risk lay squarely on the shoulders of the House as a body, and of each member individually. Unless the House were truly persuaded that removal of the President was necessary, a vote to put the nation through such a wrenching experience would be a gross irresponsibility—not just toward Nixon but toward the country. This, in turn, meant that if the House were to approach its solemn responsibility seriously, not cavalierly, it had an inescapable duty. That duty was to examine the case in the most rigorous possible way, placing the burden of proof not on the accused but on the accuser, and testing it through the adversary process. One reason why this was not done may well have been provided by Peter Rodino back in October 1973, when he told friends in the House that he expected that Nixon, if impeached by the House, would resign rather than face trial in the Senate. In other words, if a resolution of impeachment could be shepherded through the House, there would be no trial in the Senate. The constitutional process could be short-circuited, and the constitutional standards neatly circumvented.[11]

Not only was the committee slipshod about evidentiary standards. Members even held that Nixon should be impeached for what people said about him. Joshua Eilberg of Pennsylvania thus argued: "Our citizens are afraid that if they take a position on a political issue their telephones will be tapped, their mail opened, and their tax returns audited as a means of punishment. This result makes it imperative that Richard Nixon be impeached." Not, that is, that he should be impeached because the charges were true; rather, that he should be impeached because he had become the victim of hysterical, irrational fears, orchestrated by the committee itself and fanned by demagogues. By the same sort of reasoning, the good people of Salem might have voted to put one of their neighbors to death, not because they believed she *was* a witch, but on the grounds that they had *accused* her of being a witch, arguing that if the fears they themselves had thus aroused were to be calmed, it now became necessary to dispose of the accusation by disposing of the accused. (In Salem in 1692, eleven women and eight men were hanged, one man was pressed to death, and a hundred and fifty others were imprisoned on witchcraft charges. After the hysteria subsided, the twelve men of the jury that condemned those "witches" signed one of the most poignant documents in American history: ". . . we justly fear that we were sadly deluded and mistaken, for which we are much disquieted and distressed in our minds; and do therefore humbly beg forgiveness, first of God for Christ's sake for this our error . . . we would none of us do such things again on such grounds for the whole World. . . .")

The committee voted for three Articles of Impeachment. Article I accused the President of complicity in the Watergate cover-up, charging that he "engaged personally and through his subordinates and agents, in a course of conduct or plan" designed to impede the investigation, with that "course of conduct or plan" carried out through "one or more" of nine means. These nine means ranged from withholding evidence to trying to misuse the CIA, and from condoning false testimony to "making false or misleading public

11. In his actions on the nomination of Gerald Ford to be Vice-President, Rodino provided a fascinating insight into his view of his responsibilities as a congressman. That nomination was also dealt with by the Judiciary Committee. In the committee hearings, Rodino personally supported Ford. But in casting his vote, he voted "no"—citing as the reason his need for "responsiveness" to his largely black constituency in Newark. "That seems the classic example," one newspaper commented, "of the politician who talks out of both sides of his mouth."

statements." Nowhere did the Article specify what was charged against the President personally; with the "one or more" formulation, it was so framed that having made a misleading public statement would be sufficient grounds to impeach. Article I was adopted July 27 by a vote of 27–11. Article III, adopted July 30 by 21–17, charged the President with refusing to comply with Judiciary Committee subpoenas. But it was in Article II—adopted July 29 by 28–10—that the committee majority was at its most artful.

Article II—the "Christmas-tree" article—charged abuse of power, and it had something for everyone. By declaring that Nixon should be impeached for "one or more" of five broad and unrelated categories of alleged abuse, its authors neatly contrived a device by which votes on each of the five would be cumulative. Thus, even if as few as four of the committee's thirty-eight members approved each of the five, there could be twenty votes—a majority—for impeachment under Article II, and if as few as 10 percent of the members of the full House approved each of the five, there could be a majority in the House for impeachment, sufficient to send the case to the Senate. As a group of ten Republican members of the committee later charged: "The real reason for collecting those specifications in a single Article was purely pragmatic. It was correctly perceived that each of the five charges, standing alone in a separate Article, might be unable to command a majority vote. The strategy was therefore adopted of grouping the various charges together under a single umbrella, in the hope that enough Members of the Committee, the House, and ultimately the Senate would be persuaded by one or another specification that the aggregate vote for Article II would be sufficient for impeachment and conviction."[12]

Further, Article II was so broadly drawn that it made no distinction between legal and illegal acts. Its sponsor, Missouri's William Hungate, argued that it was not in fact a criminal charge, but that the President should be held to a "higher standard" than the criminal law. One of its proponents insisted that it should apply to doing "something legal for political or improper purposes." As the dissenting minority argued: "It is a far-reaching and dangerous proposition, that conduct *which is in violation of no known law,* but which is considered by a temporary majority of the Congress to be 'improper'

12. Separate minority views of Messrs. David W. Dennis of Indiana, Edward Hutchinson of Massachusetts, Delbert L. Latta of Ohio, Trent Lott of Mississippi, Joseph J. Maraziti of New Jersey, Wiley Mayne of Iowa, Carlos J. Moorhead of California, Charles W. Sandman of New Jersey, Henry P. Smith III of New York, and Charles E. Wiggins of California. Report of the House Judiciary Committee, p. 428.

because undertaken for 'political' purposes, can constitute grounds for impeachment."

But, by the time the committee voted, that was what it had gotten down to. For the 435 politicians who were members of the House of Representatives to vote to impeach Richard Nixon, it was sufficient that he be found to have done something political. Such was the climate that had been created.

One week later, after the articles were voted, Nixon released the transcript of his June 23, 1972, conversation with Bob Haldeman, in which they discussed using the CIA to head off the FBI's investigation of Watergate. This was the "smoking pistol," the final link in the chain connecting Nixon to the Watergate cover-up. No matter that the only actual result of that use of the CIA was a two-week delay in two FBI interviews. No matter that the conversation also established conclusively that Nixon had no advance knowledge of Watergate. It did show that when the crime took place, when agents of the re-election committee were caught in it, and when it looked as though higher-ups were probably involved, his first instinct was to try to protect his people, to protect his campaign and to protect his presidency: to contain the damage, to limit the embarrassment, to minimize the political consequences, to cover up. And it showed that he did try to use the CIA for that purpose. Those minority members of the committee who had protested so vehemently that in the mass of Doar "materials" there was no evidence, now had their evidence. Technically, Nixon had committed an impeachable offense. Politically, the point had been reached at which a technical offense was sufficient. Sadly—in Charles Wiggins' case, even tearfully—even Nixon's most diehard supporters on the committee announced that they now would support Article I, the impeachment article charging complicity in the Watergate cover-up. But, as one of Wiggins' aides commented later, "It doesn't vindicate the process to know that a lynch mob lynched the right guy."

The New York Times' James Reston revealed more of the process than he may have intended when he wrote in 1975: "It took Vietnam to bring the military under some kind of control, and Watergate to get rid of Richard Nixon."

For years, one of Nixon's most caustic critics was *Washington Post* columnist Nicholas von Hoffman, a left-liberal iconoclast outraged by the war in Vietnam. But it was von Hoffman who punctured the pieties of his colleagues in 1976: "If Richard Nixon is not pure Hitlerian evil, the question of why and how he was removed ceases to be an unalloyed struggle between the forces of darkness and light."

Reflecting on the process, von Hoffman asked:

In fifteen or twenty years what will the revisionist historians make of all the moralistic onanism prompted by the Nixon fantasy figure? For sure, the future historians will make short work of the idea of a diabolic Nixon and will, instead, interest themselves in how and why virtually a whole society lost the remnants of balanced judgment and fell on the man like a compacted mob.

From the summer of 1973 onward, Nixon increasingly became the object of the kind of universal media attack that we have heretofore pretty much reserved for foreign enemies or obscure domestic Communists. These past three years Nixon has had a worse press than Stalin in the height of the Cold War.

The only name for it is hysterical contagion. . . . To the very end, Nixon contended that he conducted the office in much the same fashion as his predecessors, and he was right.

XVI

THE WORLD OUT THERE

June 25, 1974: At 8:30 A.M., *The Spirit of '76* lifted off from Andrews Air Force Base, en route first to Brussels, then on to Moscow. I never got in the habit of calling it *The Spirit of '76*, the new name with which it was christened in 1971 (a name which neatly combined the bicentennial spirit with a subtle suggestion that its principal passenger would still be around after the 1972 election). Just as we New Yorkers ignore the signs saying "Avenue of the Americas" and persist in calling the familiar thoroughfare Sixth Avenue, to me the President's plane was still *Air Force One.* A military version of the Boeing 707-C, it provided the President and his staff with a flying office—worktables, electric typewriters, a Xerox machine, plus telephone and Teletype connections through the army's worldwide facilities. The "staff" section in the middle of the plane seated eight at two tables for four people each, and also seated two more in secretarial chairs at the compact typewriter-desks at one end. A dozen more people could be accommodated in comfortable two-by-two seating in a passenger section just behind it. The press pool that always accompanied the President on flights used a separate section aft, which also had a galley that served press, staff, and crew and that doubled as a bar. The President's cabin was forward of the staff compartment, and also had its own separate galley, bedroom, small office, and separate sitting area for family or guests. Forward of that was a section for the Secret Service, and an elaborate communications center.

One of the luxuries of flying on *Air Force One* was not having to listen through the safety-precaution lectures standard on commercial flights; another was not having seat-belt rules enforced. Sometimes, in fact, we would be standing in the aisles on takeoff or landing—though the President's pilot, Colonel Ralph Albertazzi, always set the plane down so smoothly that the hazard was minimal. (Albertazzi also prided himself on his precise arrival times, usually rolling to the plane's stopping-point within seconds of the appointed minute.) Service was provided by Air Force stewards, wearing blazers instead of uniforms.

Our trips were usually working flights, taking advantage of the time in the air to catch up on some of the work that was never quite done. I sometimes traveled in the staff compartment, but more often in the passenger cabin, away from the distracting conversation across the tables—where Haldeman, Ehrlichman, Ziegler, and Kissinger were often seated with aides. If I were writing on the flight, it would usually be in my seat, working in longhand on yellow pads, though sometimes I would commandeer one of the typewriters. There was a firm understanding that members of the press pool were never to venture forward of their separate section of the plane (unless, as happened infrequently, one was called forward for a prearranged interview with the President). Members of the staff, however, frequently wandered back into the press section, sometimes to provide background briefing, sometimes just to chat informally with members of the press, sometimes to stretch their legs or pick up a drink or go to the head. The spirit aboard tended to be informal, and, if the workload was light, relaxed.

On that June morning, Richard Nixon was on his way to his third summit meeting with Leonid Brezhnev. At the first summit, two years earlier, the two leaders triumphantly signed the first agreement of the nuclear age to limit strategic nuclear arms. Nixon still hoped that the second-stage agreement—SALT II—could be reached at this meeting. But negotiations had lagged. Watergate poisoned all. Head-to-head, Nixon and Brezhnev might be able to close the gap between the two sides that the negotiating teams had not closed. Maybe. This was the great question hanging over the summit; this and the President's future.

Washington was a good place to be leaving behind. It was snarling, bitter, spiteful, cynical as the Judiciary Committee pressed relentlessly toward impeachment. Four days earlier, Judge Gerhard A. Gesell sentenced Charles Colson to one to three years in prison and a $5000 fine. In a plea bargain with the special prosecutor, Colson pleaded guilty to a one-count felony indictment of obstructing justice by disseminating derogatory information about Daniel

Ellsberg and one of Ellsberg's lawyers, Leonard Boudin, during Ellsberg's Pentagon Papers trial. The White House director of communications, Ken Clawson, promptly issued a statement charging that Colson was being sentenced for a felony that had been "standard practice of members and staff of the Senate Watergate committee for more than a year and the same felony being committed daily by some partisan members of the House Judiciary Committee."

During the flight to Brussels, the President called me forward to his cabin. He wanted to talk about the speeches he would be giving, particularly his televised address to the Soviet people. As was the case two years earlier, when he also spoke to the Soviet people on television, I had done some preliminary drafting. But most of the work would be done on the trip.

In talking to the Soviet people, he said, he wanted to touch only briefly on the agreements that had been reached and put into effect since the series of summits began, and "on the progress that's been made—for example, since we met then, the war in Vietnam has been ended; we have hopeful developments in terms of working out a permanent peace in the Middle East, a goal we both support." Then he wanted to look forward, and once more to appeal to that community of spirit that the Soviet people do feel with the American people, to remind them that ours are the two strongest nations in the world, but that "our statesmanship will determine whether that strength will follow the dismal pattern of history where it inevitably leads to war, or whether these two nations use their strengths to build a structure of peace."

The basic theme, he said—"I may use it at NATO, or in the first toast to Brezhnev—would be that naturally the fear of war is what holds an alliance together, and what brings about negotiations to avoid confrontation. That, of course, is simply stating a pragmatic reality of international conduct. But our desire is to have more than that—to build bridges of cooperation, and so forth, so that we're drawn together not just by fear but by hope. Our interests will be different, as they are between any nations. But let's join in the kind of competition in which everybody gains. What our two nations have to create for ourselves, and for all other nations, is a stake in peace."

He was tired, and he showed the effects of the phlebitis attack he had suffered at the outset of his Middle East trip two weeks earlier. He had managed to keep that attack secret throughout the entire grueling Middle East tour, keeping his painful and swollen leg wrapped in an elastic bandage while he met with the Middle Eastern leaders and went through the full panoply of ceremonial routines. The secret broke on the eve of his departure for the Moscow summit. He had insisted on going through with the trip to the Middle East, and on concealing his condition so as not to embarrass his hosts or let it interfere with the mission's diplomatic purpose. Some later speculated that he deliberately courted death on that trip—if not by an assassin's bullet from someone among the huge, volatile crowds, then from the potentially fatal phlebitis itself. He dismissed the suggestion as ridiculous, and as totally out of character, and I doubt that he did so consciously and deliberately. But I thought then and still think that in the circumstances, he was at least more willing than he might otherwise have been to tempt fate in a high-stakes gamble. (Four months later complications from the same case of phlebitis did nearly cost him his life. Reflecting on it afterward, he once commented to me that he thought it probably had been brought on at least in part by the stress he was under. This often is true with phlebitis.)

He rode now with his leg elevated, to help control the phlebitis. His report to the American people on his return this time, he insisted, would be brief, something he would deliver before the television cameras at the airport, and he planned to give it off-the-cuff rather than from a prepared text—"I won't read it, but I'll have time to reason it tightly." Returning to his talk to the Soviet people, he suggested working in a reference to a war memorial he was going to visit near Minsk. "We'll be laying two wreaths on this trip," he mused. "But this—what we're building—this is building the memorial."

This, to Richard Nixon, was what the presidency was about, and to me this was what the struggle over Watergate was about: whether on the ashes of man's past folly a structure could be created that would be proof against future folly; whether the tasks of building so brilliantly begun would be completed or aborted.

In Brussels, headquarters of NATO, the NATO heads of government were gathering to mark the treaty organization's twenty-fifth anniversary, the first such NATO summit in seventeen years. From there we went on to Moscow, returning now in a sort of easy familiarity that stood in stark contrast to the apprehensive tension two years earlier. We returned to the same rooms in the Kremlin's Grand Palace, to the same floors of the Rossiya Hotel, to the same ancient Granovit Hall for the arrival dinner hosted by Brezhnev.

On the serious side, the change in atmosphere between the two summits was signaled, this second time, by Brezhnev's coming per-

'sonally to Moscow's Vnukuvo Airport to greet Nixon—the first time Brezhnev had ever accorded that honor to a foreign visitor. The change also had a lighter side.

At the first Moscow summit, in 1972, there was an almost electric tension in the air. If it was a new experience for the Americans, it was a terrifying new experience for those Soviet security and service people who had to deal with the Americans, and for the bureaucrats in charge of arrangements. The cement of the Soviet system is fear, and in blazing these new diplomatic trails they were seized with the fear of the unknown. The bureaucrat dared not tinker with the rules; nothing could be done without clearance from higher authority. Two years later the difference was striking. Not only were we received in 1974 as old friends coming back for another visit, but geniality sometimes spilled over into downright conviviality.

The itinerary in 1974 included a visit to Yalta, the summer resort of the tsars on the shores of the Black Sea, where Brezhnev maintained a magnificent pre-Revolutionary dacha on a tree-shrouded hillside leading dramatically down to the sea, with acres of formal gardens and what seemed like miles of manicured walks. In 1973 Nixon had entertained Brezhnev at San Clemente; the Soviets were determined that they would return the hospitality in kind. But Yalta! While the trip was in its planning stage, we had gruesome visions at the White House of the cartoons, the stories, the editorials, the network commentators' punch lines, if Nixon went to Yalta. To those who cared about such things and were old enough to remember, Yalta was not a charming, storied seaside resort. It was the site of the 1945 Yalta Conference, where Stalin, Churchill, and a dying Roosevelt divided up Europe as World War II neared its end. Its connotation, at least in many conservative minds, was that of sell-out, surrender, capitulation to a domineering Soviet presence. Not only would it offer an irresistible target for political and media fun at the President's expense, but that fun could even seriously undermine the chances for Senate approval of any agreement that might be reached.

In 1972 the problem might have been insuperable. But by 1974 the American planners' Soviet counterparts had learned something of the flexibility that becomes a part of the advance man's art, and the two sides were even able to laugh together about it. The Soviet and American advance teams put their heads together, and came up with the perfect solution. Brezhnev's dacha, and the adjoining guest dacha that Nixon would use, were not in downtown Yalta, but rather in an outlying neighborhood called Oreanda, three or four miles from the center of town. So the advance teams came up with an ingenious answer. The neighborhood was rechristened as a town. Thus the leaders could meet, not in Yalta, but in Oreanda. By the time we arrived, freshly painted road signs had sprouted everywhere, giving the directions from Yalta to Oreanda. The motorcade from the airport even wound on a roundabout route through the outskirts of Yalta, then, circuitously, for miles through the surrounding hills before it reached Oreanda. Soviet honor was saved; Nixon would be a guest at the Brezhnev dacha. Nixon's honor was saved; the summit was not a second "Yalta" Conference. And it was done without even moving the dacha.

On the afternoon of the second day we were in "Oreanda," Brezhnev hosted a long luncheon cruise on the Black Sea for Nixon, Kissinger, and the senior U.S. aides involved in the SALT negotiations. The Soviet leader had a matched pair of 120-foot yachts standing by, and a few of us who were not involved in the official talks were invited to go along on the second boat. Our Soviet hosts included the deputy chief of protocol and the deputy director of the dreaded secret police, the KGB. We had a long Russian lunch; as the pile of empty vodka, wine, and brandy bottles grew higher, the toasts grew warmer, and at the same time the jokes grew more pointed—especially about the KGB. The KGB man took it in stride, gave as well as he got, laughed along with the rest, and, as the level of camaraderie rose, the cloaks of diplomacy fell. The deputy chief of protocol was a rather small, pleasant, mild-mannered man, whose experience as an inmate of a Nazi concentration camp in World War II lent him a sort of haunting presence. At one point, led on by two of the Americans, the brandy glowing in his face, almost visibly pushing aside the block to the words, he raised his glass high and joined loudly in a raucous toast: "And to hell with the KGB!" All of us, including the KGB man, dissolved in laughter, but I was not the only one among us who felt a stab of worry. The next day, at a ceremony in Minsk, the protocol man seemed unusually subdued. Several of us who had been on the cruise noted it, and hoped it was only a brandy and vodka hangover. We had gotten genuinely to like the fellow, and we hoped it was not a KGB hangover.

Al Haig's aide, George Joulwan—an army major—was one of the Americans along, and his promotion to lieutenant colonel was to become effective that day, at 5:00 P.M., Yalta time (midnight, Washington time). Soviets and Americans together kept up a toast-punctuated countdown, then celebrated his new rank with more brandy and vodka—while, in a mock ceremony, inducting the by-then thoroughly sloshed colonel as an honorary member of the KGB. With our White House penchant for "historic firsts," I twitted him

afterward about being the only officer in the U.S. Army to have
become a lieutenant colonel and a member of the KGB on the same
day—or at least the only one to have done both on the same day
on the Black Sea, aboard Brezhnev's yacht.

In Oreanda, most of us stayed at one of the "sanitoria" that dot
the shoreline—vacation hotels made available to favored workers
and officials for seaside respites. At one point I took a break from
work, and went down to the beach for a swim. The way led along
a winding path through the gardens, to a rather antiseptic-looking
concrete structure housing an elevator, which in turn whisked
beachgoers the hundred feet or so down through the cliffs to the
sea. The beach was not sand, but a narrow rim of large black
stones, washed smooth by the seawater. A half-dozen stalls were
set up for changing clothes. A wooden pier led a short way out over
the water. There were perhaps a dozen lounge chairs set up just
back from the beach, and a couple of Americans, and two or three
Russians, were using them, taking in the sun. A few minutes after
I arrived a young Russian struck up a conversation. His English was
limited but adequate. He professed to be an engineering student. He
had traveled widely and frequently around the Soviet Union. From
the evasive way he answered my studiedly casual questions about
his travels, I guessed he was probably a KGB agent. We chatted. We
swam. (A guard first said, in Russian, that swimming was forbidden
that day because the waves were too dangerous, but he quickly got
the guard to relent—again suggesting to me that his credentials
might be more than those of an itinerant student.) Soon he steered
the conversation around to the impeachment drive. How much
trouble was Nixon really in back home? Would he survive in office?

I told him there was no real chance of removal, explaining the
various constitutional steps involved in the impeachment process. I
told him that the Judiciary Committee would almost certainly vote
to impeach, but said that because of the make-up of that committee
and because of the political nature of its inquiry, this was to be expected. I insisted that impeachment had less chance of passage by
the full House, and that even if it were voted by the House there was
virtually no chance that the Senate would vote for the President's
conviction and removal. I argued this point forcefully, because it
was important that the Soviets believe Nixon was going to survive.
But it was a not-so-subtle reminder of the stakes in the impeachment battle: not just the fate of Richard Nixon but the future of
his efforts to cap the nuclear arms race and to establish a basis on
which the United States and the Soviet Union could live together.

The Soviets were prepared to deal with a Nixon securely in power. They were going to be very cautious about dealing with a Nixon who might soon be toppled from power, and they might or might not deal with an untested successor. To the extent that his reports on our conversation might affect Soviet estimates of Nixon's chances of survival, I wanted to be sure that they would serve to bolster belief that he was going to finish his term.

Even in the Soviet Union, it was impossible to escape what was happening back in Washington. The news summary kept us up to date with Watergate developments. And that unstated question hung over the summit itself: was the series of meetings to continue, or was this the Last Hurrah?

I kept thinking back on other trips, and on the painstaking efforts to build other parts of that interlocking "structure of peace" of which a new U.S.-Soviet relationship might be the capstone.

There was the trip that followed that unforgettable moment, on July 20, 1969, when Neil Armstrong took "one small step for a man, but a giant leap for mankind"—and, as the world watched in awe, he and Buzz Aldrin became the first men to set foot on the moon.

Never one to miss an opportunity of historic proportions, Nixon had already determined to make the most of it. Not only did he go to the far Pacific to welcome the *Apollo 11* astronauts back personally aboard the carrier *Hornet;* he also used their return to launch a tour of his own through the capitals of Asia, capitalizing on the boost their adventure gave U.S. prestige to carry his own message to the Asian leaders. At the core of that message was the need for a new kind of partnership between the United States and its trans-Pacific neighbors. He spelled it out first, publicly, in an extraordinary "background" news briefing on Guam for the press corps traveling with the presidential party.

In that briefing, he noted that a number of Asian leaders were wondering what the U.S. role in Asia and the Pacific would be after the Vietnam war. Would we, because of our national frustration over Vietnam and, earlier, over our involvement in the Korean War, withdraw—as the British and French had done—or would we continue to play a significant role? He noted that "one of the weaknesses in American foreign policy is that too often we react rather precipitately to events as they occur. We fail to have the perspective and the long-range view which is essential for a policy that will be viable." Looking ahead toward the end of the century, he sketched out the threats to world peace that arose from Asia, but also the hope for progress centered there—noting particularly that the fastest rate of economic growth in the world was being achieved by the non-Communist nations of Asia. He stressed that it was vital for the United States to continue to play an active role in Asia, but one "appropriate to the conditions that we will find" there in the years ahead. These conditions, he noted, included a growth both in nationalism and in regionalism, and also a strong feeling among Asians "that they do not want to be dictated to from the outside, Asia for the Asians. And that is what we want, and that is the role we should play. We should assist, but we should not dictate." We should assist with their economic development. We should keep our treaty commitments. But "we must avoid that kind of policy that will make countries in Asia so dependent upon us that we are dragged into conflicts such as the one that we have in Vietnam."

Where future problems of internal security and military defense are concerned, "except for the threat of a major power involving nuclear weapons," the United States "is going to encourage and has a right to expect that this problem will be increasingly handled by, and the responsibility for it taken by, the Asian nations themselves." From his preliminary conversations with Asian leaders, he said, he believed that they were going to be willing to accept this responsibility. "But if the United States just continues down the road of responding to requests for assistance, of assuming the primary responsibility for defending these countries when they have internal problems or external problems, they are never going to take care of themselves."

He was careful to strike a balance: on one hand prodding the Asian nations into doing more for themselves, on the other reassuring them that the United States was not walking out on them, explaining that "one of the reasons for this trip is to leave no doubt in the minds of the leaders of non-Communist Asia that the United States is committed to a policy in the Pacific—a policy not of intervention but one which certainly rules out withdrawal—and regardless of what happens in Vietnam that we intend to play a role in Asia to the extent that Asian nations, bilaterally and collectively, desire us to play a role."

As Nixon fielded the reporters' questions, in a crowded, hastily arranged briefing room at Guam's U.S. Naval Air Station, Henry Kissinger sidled nervously around the edge of the room, visibly unhappy with the President's taking the high-risk course of personally broaching these delicate diplomatic matters in the rough-and-tumble setting of a press briefing before the forthcoming talks had taken place. But it was a calculated gamble on Nixon's part, and it paid off. He wanted to be sure that his basic message was understood, both in Asia and in the United States, and the way the traveling press would report it would be vital to that understanding. Further, the obviously authoritative reports from the President's traveling party—even though under the "background" ground rules they could not be attributed directly to Nixon—had their desired effect of preparing the Asian leaders for what to expect.

When it was over, Bob Haldeman grinned at me and asked if it all sounded familiar. It did; much of it clearly echoed the article Nixon and I had worked on together for *Foreign Affairs* two years earlier. I wondered how much of Kissinger's evident distress stemmed from the fact that the President instead of he was giving the briefing.

Later, the policies enunciated in that 1969 briefing became known as the Nixon Doctrine. But for some time they were referred to as the Guam Doctrine—probably the only time a major turn in international affairs has ever been named for the site of a background briefing.

The Nixon Doctrine signaled a new pattern of relationships between the United States and the non-Communist nations of Asia, which was part of a new pattern of relationships between the United States and both its allies and its adversaries world-wide. Just as he was doing domestically, Nixon sought to put an end to U.S. paternalism abroad, and to do so in a way that would strengthen local responsibility and encourage regional initiatives. He had to reassure the nation's Asian allies—and warn its adversaries—that this was actually a way for the United States to stay in Asia, not a retreat from Asia, but at the same time one that required them to do more for themselves.

At two stops on that trip—in Djakarta and Bangkok—I joined Kissinger in informal meetings with selected groups of young intellectual leaders, some of whom had been students of Kissinger's at Harvard. The concerns they reflected represented some of the realities Nixon had to deal with. At Kissinger's request, I sent him a memo summing up my principal impressions from the meetings:

1. Almost universally, they seemed to have gotten the impression that the U.S. was bent on pulling out of Asia. They were uncertain and apprehensive about what this might mean, how far it would go, what it would involve. I *got a distinct sense that they felt they were being abandoned*—and while they were too polite to say this, and while they might not put it in these terms even among themselves, that they were on the verge, or in the process of, being betrayed by us, as if we had laid out a welcome mat and then pulled it out from under them.

2. *They want the U.S. to play a major role in Asia; they are less worried about the prospect of an American presence than they are about the prospect of an American absence.* In Djakarta, there was great apprehension about what they foresaw as a growing Japanese dominance. They felt unable to keep up, to compete (as one of them put it, while the Japanese raise their per capita GNP to $3000, we'll be raising ours to $300); already they find the Japanese influence in their own lives and economy uncomfortably pervasive, and their dependence on Japanese products uncomfortably heavy. *If they have to rely on an outside power, they would rather it be a distant one than a near one.* They worry about Japanese rearmament—not only because of the lingering shadow of Japanese militarism but also because of what they see as an unbalancing effect on Asia of the combination of Japanese military and economic power.

In Thailand, the worry is not that Japan would move into a vacuum left by the U.S., but that the vacuum would cause an implosion. They worry about containing their own insurgency, and that in Laos, they talk earnestly and worriedly about the need for rural development, and for continued, perhaps increased, assistance in that development. *They have the impression that the U.S. has decided to abandon Vietnam; they are afraid "no more Vietnams" means abandoning Thailand too; and they're scared.* They are keenly aware of the public-opinion problem in the U.S., and also of the congressional problem, and they see these as probably determining what the U.S. *will* do, regardless of what the President might want it to do. They're not satisfied merely with official reassurances; they're trying, for their own purposes, to project what a probable U.S. political response to domestic pressures would be.

3. In both countries there was great concern about Vietnam, about the consequences of a Communist victory. I had a rather tenuous sense—which I can't substantiate, and may be mistaken—that there was a subtle difference in the mood of the two gatherings on this point: In Indonesia, more a hope that we could be persuaded to stick it out in Vietnam; in Thailand, more a groping, still inconclusive, for ways to live with what they feared was a decision already taken to pull out.

That 1969 Asian trip took us to Guam, Manila, Djakarta, Bangkok, New Delhi, and Lahore, with Nixon taking a side trip to South Vietnam—which, for security reasons, was unannounced in advance—while we were in Bangkok. Then, from Lahore, we took off across the rugged sweep of Afghanistan, Iran, and Turkey and, 2970 miles and six hours and fifteen minutes later, the wheels of *Air Force One* set smartly down at Bucharest, Rumania.[1]

That arrival in Bucharest was heady, exciting, unforgettable. For the first time since the Iron Curtain clanged across Europe, an American president was visiting a Communist capital. Rumanian President Nicolae Ceausescu, stubbornly struggling to lessen Soviet domination over Rumania, was gambling his own and his country's future. As the Rumanian military band struck up the unfamiliar strains of "The Star Spangled Banner," it was hard to hold back tears. It was no mere idle ceremonial. History was being made. We knew it, and Ceausescu knew it, and the leaders in the Kremlin, who, after the Nixon visit was announced, had canceled a scheduled July visit of their own to Bucharest to sign a twenty-year treaty of "friendship," knew it. As we rode from the hastily completed new airport in to the city, nearly a million people lined the streets. Many had been brought in government buses—but if the authorities could provide the crowds, only the people themselves could provide the looks on their faces: the hope, the rapture, many in tears, waving, straining for a look. Long into the evening they stayed out on the streets. At midnight, as we left the state dinner hosted by Ceausescu, thousands were still milling about, lining the streets, waving, smiling.

Later that evening, one of those little incidents occurred that can chill even a summer night. We were staying in government guest houses, heavily guarded by Rumanian security forces. Wherever we traveled, the Army Signal Corps set up its own telephone switchboard, and installed special White House phones in our rooms. After returning from the state dinner, my White House phone rang. The President was calling. He was in an ebullient mood, still sailing on an emotional "high" from the day's events. In deciding to make the Rumanian visit, he had overridden strong objections from the State Department's diplomatic professionals. They were concerned about the diplomatic risks. He was convinced that these were outweighed by the diplomatic opportunities, and he thought that he could use

1. On that round-the-world trip in 1969, *Air Force One* logged 25,655 miles, and was in the air a total of 53 hours and 40 minutes. It becomes very easy, after a while, to take for granted some of the unusual facilities available to presidents and their staffs. At one point during the trip, Jim Keogh—my predecessor as head of the White House writing shop—needed to check a couple of facts with our advance man in Bucharest. So he telephoned him. He came back a couple of minutes later, grumbling at the flaws of technology—they had a bad connection. He had placed the call to Bucharest from *Air Force One*, which at the moment was flying at 35,000 feet over the mountains of Afghanistan.

it to give him more leverage, rather than less, with the Soviets; in addition, Ceausescu was actively building his own bridges to Peking, and these could be important to Nixon's own plans. Now the visit was actually taking place, and it had begun in unalloyed triumph. The press had flocked to Bucharest from all over a fascinated Europe—some five hundred reporters were there to cover it. Nixon had the initiative, and he was grasping it eagerly to usher in a new era of diplomacy. He talked about the day, about the emotional impact of it, asking me for my own reactions, asking if it was not true that he had been right and his critics wrong—savoring the triumph, basking in it. We must have talked for at least twenty minutes. Then, as I finished my answer to one of his questions, there was no response. The phone line was still open. But, where a moment earlier I had been talking with the President of the United States on the first night a U.S. president had ever spent in a Communist capital, now, suddenly, there was no president on the other end.

Visions of all the gory possibilities flashed through my mind, as I wondered what to do. He had probably dropped off to sleep. But, in the circumstances, "probably" was not enough. Toward the end of the conversation he had gotten slurry and repetitive. I had occasionally seen this happen on the campaign trail, when, at the end of a particularly intensive day, he tried to wind down with a beer and at the same time took a sleeping pill. While not wanting to seem alarmist, I hardly wanted to take any chances—and I was probably the only person who knew that the President had suddenly "vanished" in the Rumanian night. I hung up the phone, then picked it up again and asked the signal corps operator if the President's phone was still off the hook, with the line open. He said it was. I asked him to ring Walter Tkach, the President's doctor. I explained the situation to Tkach and rather apologetically asked him to get up and go check on his patient. Then the signal corps operator came on the line. He had a better idea. He could contact the Secret Service agent posted by the President's door, and have him check. Good idea, I said, wishing I had had the good sense to think of it myself before waking Tkach. A few moments later the operator called back. Yes, the agent had found the President safely sitting in his chair, asleep, with the phone in his hand. It was the best news I had had all day.

Many of Nixon's antagonists felt confident that they could depose the President without sacrifice of American foreign-policy interests, because Henry Kissinger would still be there. I never saw it that way. Nixon needed a Kissinger, but Kissinger also needed a Nixon. The two worked well together because they shared the same world-view. They were both men of exceptionally facile intellect, both deeply concerned for the future of the nation and the world, both convinced that the strength of America's will would be a crucial determinant in the world's future. Neither was paralyzed by an excessive squeamishness about means when ends that they considered vital for the nation were at stake.

Nixon and Kissinger both are conceptualizers, and both are accustomed to thinking in long-range terms. Both can be tough. Kissinger, with his academic air—and his academic credentials—was better able than Nixon to present what they were trying to do in terms that would win the acceptance, if not the acquiescence, of the academic community and of the media. Kissinger, because he was more adept than Nixon at manipulating the media (he leaked more, and flattered them more) often won their praise even while they condemned Nixon for policies the two developed jointly.

Perhaps because I had worked with Nixon for nearly two years before Henry came on board, I saw the principal foreign-policy designs as Nixon's rather than Kissinger's. They flowed organically from the ideas Nixon had expounded—repeatedly and in great detail—before he met Kissinger; they reflected insights developed in Nixon's own quarter-century of involvement in world affairs. Many of America's moves in this period originated with Kissinger, but Kissinger was operating within the Nixon framework.

It took someone of Kissinger's grasp and drive to carry out the Nixon design, and it took the meticulously detailed staff work that Kissinger directed to make it possible. Nothing was left to chance. Options were prodigiously researched, differences dissected, alternatives analyzed, consequences plotted. But in the final analysis, each major turn got down to a presidential decision, and Nixon gave more care to these decisions than to anything else in his presidency. It also, very frequently, got down to raw presidential courage. The gambles were Nixon's, not Kissinger's. And it was Nixon, not Kissinger, who had to take the torrents of abuse for those unpopular acts that made the later triumphs possible.

Kissinger was a master of bureaucratic manipulation, an exceptional negotiator, a prodigious worker. He was deferential toward the President, genial toward his peers, rude and tyrannical toward his aides.

I got along well enough personally with Kissinger, though I never fully trusted him. I had a high respect for his abilities, and thought he performed an essential function exceptionally well. But from the earliest days of the administration onward, one of his traits— which he seemed to carry to compulsive extremes—always particularly irritated me, and contributed to my feeling of distrust: his incessant backbiting of anyone who in any way might be perceived as his rival for power or influence. While cordial enough to their faces, he was ruthless behind their backs. I first saw the pattern during the early months in the White House, when I occasionally met Kissinger and two or three of his aides for breakfast to discuss particular speeches or papers we were working on for the President. The entire meeting would be punctuated with Henry's put-downs of those in State or Defense or one of the other agencies who had anything to do with the project. The constant theme of these animadversions was that unless checked (implicitly, by Henry himself), these others would undermine all that the President was trying to do. I had to assume that as soon as my own back was turned, I was subject to the same treatment.

When Nixon resigned, he strongly urged President Ford to keep Kissinger on, and he strongly urged Kissinger to stay. I too hoped he would stay, though I worried about whether Kissinger could function without a Nixon to take the heat for the unpopular moves while Kissinger took credit for the popular ones. Nixon could do this because he was perceived as a foreign-policy president. Thus, when it became necessary to go into Cambodia, or to mine the harbor at Haiphong or to bomb North Vietnam in December 1972, the waves of public outrage could be directed at Nixon while Kissinger kept a discreet distance. Kissinger's ego, while enormous, was also fragile. It required constant stroking, constant attention, constant reinforcement, constant protection against the buffetings of criticism. Nixon understood this, and he developed the care and feeding of Henry Kissinger to a fine art. He was sometimes jealous of the Kissinger fan club, but he was willing to do what was necessary to keep Henry's remarkable talents employed in the service of the Nixon policies. For all his faults, Kissinger was an immensely valuable property—valuable to Nixon, and valuable to the nation. As long as Kissinger was able to accomplish what Nixon wanted accomplished, this, to Nixon, far outweighed his personal idiosyncrasies, and made his care and feeding well worthwhile.

"The structure of peace," Nixon argued in 1972, "has to be built in such a way that all those who might be tempted to destroy it will instead have a stake in preserving it." This was the essence of the new pattern of relationships he sought to construct. In his televised address to the Soviet people on July 2, 1974, during the second Moscow summit, he analogized the interweaving of international interests to a cloth: "Just as a cloth is stronger than the threads from which it is made, so the network of agreements we have been weaving is greater than the sum of its parts. With these agreements, we have been creating a pattern of interrelationships, of habits of cooperation and arrangements for consultation—all of which interact with one another to strengthen the fabric of the new relationship. Thus each new agreement is important not only for itself but also for the added strength and stability it brings to our relations overall."

But even as Nixon wove his fabric in Moscow, back in Washington others were tugging at the threads.

XVII

THE LAST HISTORIC FIRST

Returning from that final Moscow summit on July 3, 1974—the eve of Independence Day—Nixon bypassed Washington altogether. *The Spirit of '76* set down first at Loring Air Force Base, in Maine, where, speaking into the network television cameras, the President reported to the nation, describing the agreements that had been reached and placing that summit in the pattern of summitry, of the Western Alliance, and of East-West relations. "The process of peace is going steadily forward," he declared. "It is strengthened by the new and expanding patterns of cooperation between the United States and the Soviet Union. It is reinforced by the new vitality of our Western Alliance and bringing such encouraging results as the new turn toward peace in the Middle East."

It was around 2:00 A.M., the day before, that Al Haig's aide, George Joulwan, called to tell me that the President had changed his mind. Instead of ad-libbing, he now wanted a prepared speech. I went back to sleep, figuring that a few hours' rest would be a good investment before beginning—and especially so, because I had had a stiff nightcap before going to bed just shortly before. It was the shortest notice I had ever had for a major presidential speech, live, on all three networks. Fortunately, from our talks during the trip, I already had a fairly complete idea of what he wanted to say. The National Security Council staff gave me updated briefings on the meetings and agreements. On our departure day, July 3, I was still frantically working on the draft in the NSC's Kremlin offices, while around me the last remaining files and equipment were being

carted out for the return trip home. I commandeered the one remaining typewriter for my secretary to use, while I scrawled paragraphs awkwardly in longhand, skipping the farewell reception in
the white-and-gold splendor of the Kremlin's St. George Hall,
finishing it just in time to catch the motorcade to the airport. Nixon
worked over the speech on the plane, and we were able to put the
draft through one revision during the long, nonstop flight from
Moscow to Loring.

With his report concluded, Nixon reboarded his plane and, with
a few of his aides, flew straight to Key Biscayne. The rest of us
transferred to one of the other planes, and wearily returned to
Washington. It was as if Nixon were avoiding the capital, shunning
the White House he had struggled so long to reach. He stayed in
Florida until the seventh, then returned to Washington only until
the twelfth, when he flew to San Clemente. The Judiciary Committee
ground relentlessly on. From July 3 to 11 the committee heard
witnesses. On the eleventh it released an eight-volume, 4133-page
compilation of "evidence" dealing with the Watergate break-in and
its aftermath. On July 12 John Ehrlichman was found guilty by a
federal court jury of conspiring to violate the civil rights of Ellsberg's psychiatrist, and of three counts of making false statements.
On July 14 columnist Joseph Alsop wrote that "Political Washington
has now become a hateful and degraded place. . . . The mingled
venom and hypocrisy that characterize too many of the President's
enemies are almost as distasteful as the crimes and follies the
President stands accused of. So it is hard to feel much sympathy
for anyone, especially when the guts are meanwhile being torn out
of the most sacred and vital institutions of the American political
system." Even the editorial page editor of *The Washington Post*,
Philip L. Geyelin, commented that "there is, in truth, an ugly
atmosphere in Washington and around the nation today—a prose-
cutorial impulse, a tension and an emotional pitch which makes it
difficult to judge the guilt or innocence, the integrity or the motives,
of public officials caught up anywhere near the eye of the Watergate
storm and difficult for these officials, however uninvolved, to
operate."

By mid-July, Democratic National Chairman Robert Strauss
abandoned his stand that it would be "inappropriate" for him to
comment on impeachment. The time at last was ripe. He would,
he said, be "shocked" if the Judiciary Committee failed to vote
impeachment, and "very surprised" if the full House did not follow
suit. The *Washington Star*'s nonagenarian, no-nonsense weekly columnist Gould Lincoln, surveying the scene from his perch of years,

declared sourly that "an anti-Nixon partisan, political vendetta is in full bloom on this hot July Saturday."

I was trying to put Watergate distractions sufficiently out of the way to work on a speech on the economy Nixon was scheduled to deliver from Los Angeles on Thursday, July 25. I worked on it in Washington, and then, a few days after Nixon's departure, flew to San Clemente, not imagining that this was the last time San Clemente would be the Western White House.

In putting together the economic speech, I worked principally with Kenneth Rush, then a counselor to the President coordinating economic matters in the White House; with Roy Ash, director of the Office of Management and Budget; and with Herbert Stein, chairman of the Council of Economic Advisers. I always enjoyed working with Stein, partly because of his thorough knowledge of his subject, partly because he himself is a highly gifted writer whose editorial suggestions were often as incisive as his substantive contributions.

This speech was, in effect, Stein's swan song as chairman of the council. Three times he had postponed plans to return to private life. Now he was really leaving, to take up a professorship at the University of Virginia at the start of the fall semester. His letter of resignation and the President's reply were released in San Clemente as we worked on the speech. Stein wrote:

No CEA Chairman could want a more supportive and understanding President than you have been. You have been responsible for conducting U.S. economic policy during a turbulent period, when the whole world was swept by storms of inflation. Your policy has been firm and decisive. The results have surely not been all we would have liked, but there has been no serious recession, inflation is less violent than in most other developed countries, and the U.S. has a good prospect for reducing its inflation rate. . . . If there is support for persisting on your present anti-inflationary path the record of your terms will stand high in objective histories of the American economy. You will be recognized as a world leader in the fight against the economic disease of democracies—inflation, just as you are a world leader in the fight against the political disease of nations—wars.

Despite the rising crescendo of the Watergate battle, a Gallup poll released as Nixon began his San Clemente stay showed that the economy was still what troubled the American people most: 48 percent ranked inflation as the nation's number one problem, against 15 percent who cited trust in government, and 11 percent Watergate.

Because of this, there was heavy pressure on the President to mend his political fences with economic gimmickry. But after its shocks and spasms, after the harsh medicine of wage and price controls and then the gradual removal of those controls, what the economy most needed now—or so it seemed to Nixon and his economic advisers—was assurance that there would be no short-term gimmicks, but rather steady policies for the long term. People had to be disabused of the illusion that some miracle cure could replace the basic disciplines of the market place; investors had to be reassured that the rules were not going to be changed in mid-game. So, as the Judiciary Committee prepared to vote for impeachment, he had to try to persuade the American people that there was no quick, painless remedy for their number one problem.

The mood during that final San Clemente visit had little of finality about it. By then, most of us were more or less inured to the strains of the Watergate battle. These were part of the pressures we operated under. The strains grew more or less intense with the flow of the news, but the business of government had to go on. It was clear that the Judiciary Committee was moving inexorably toward voting for impeachment. What was not clear, at the start of the visit, was the margin of the vote, how many of the "swing" Republicans and Southern Democrats would line up on the pro-impeachment side, what the impact of the televised debates would be on the public at large, and what the final outcome in the full House would be.

But from the other side of the continent, the proceedings of the Judiciary Committee looked no more judicious to most of us than they did in Washington. When John Doar finally made his emotional case to the committee for impeachment on July 19, Ron Ziegler angrily accused Doar of conducting a "kangaroo court," and told reporters that the committee had made "a total shambles out of what should have been a fair proceeding." Doar, he declared, "is a partisan, and has been a partisan from the beginning," who was advocating impeachment based on "a lot of theories, speculation, innuendo—but not on facts to support the charges." His description of the proceedings as a "kangaroo court" infuriated several of the committee members, and astonished many of the press. I quietly cheered. I thought it was an apt description, and figured we might as well say so. After all, the committee members were saying a lot about us that was far more unrestrained. Inured to the strains or not, tempers were rising—my own included.

Early in the San Clemente visit, Rabbi Baruch Korff arrived for a call on the President. Starting with $1000 that he and his wife had planned to use for a vacation, Korff had organized a National Committee for Fairness to the Presidency—raising funds, organizing rallies, soliciting members, drumming up support for Nixon, and hammering back sharply at the President's critics. Now Korff was arriving to present Nixon with a copy of Korff's new book, *The Personal Nixon: Staying on the Summit.* Included in the book was an interview Nixon gave Korff three months earlier. It was released to the press when Korff presented the book to Nixon. In the interview, Nixon gave vent bluntly to some of his own feelings. Asked by Korff if he thought there had been a "wholesale smear of the President's men in the Watergate affair," Nixon accused "eager-beaver staffers" in the special prosecutor's office and on the investigating committees of harassing tactics which, in the days of Joe McCarthy, would have gotten them "ridden out of town on a rail." He said he thought that "when it's all sorted out in the end, it will be found that there has been harassment on a massive basis of innocent people, that many without guilt have had their reputations badly damaged." Noting that a lot of people were offended by the "tone" of the White House transcripts, he argued that "if they were to tape the conversations of presidents that I have known, they wouldn't like their tone either. I mean, there has to be at times very pragmatic talk in this office. . . ." One reason Watergate has so "caught the imagination" of the press, he suggested, was that "I am not the press's favorite pin-up boy . . . if I were basically a liberal by their standards, if I had bugged out of Vietnam, which they wanted, Watergate would have been a blip."

On Monday, July 21, there was a momentary respite. Budget Director Roy Ash gathered some hundred and fifty guests, mostly old Nixon friends and supporters from southern California, together with a few of the senior White House staff who were in San Clemente, for a dinner at his lavish home in Bel Air. The house itself—formerly W. C. Fields's—was a vision from a Hollywood legend, and the friendly crowd was a welcome tonic. During the dinner, General Brent Scowcroft, then Henry Kissinger's deputy on the National Security Council staff, kept shuttling hastily between the President's table and a telephone in another room. Bitter fighting between Greeks and Turks had erupted on Cyprus the day before. During the dinner a UN-sponsored cease-fire was being worked out, largely by U.S. negotiators, to take effect the next morning. For that brief moment, Nixon was again in his element: making peace half a world away even as he basked in the company of friends in California, almost as if Rodino, Doar, and company were nothing more than characters in a nightmare.

The champagne was poured, and Ash rose, and offered a toast to the President. Responding, Nixon thanked Ash, and then explained what the mysterious comings and goings of Scowcroft had been about. He went on, extemporizing as usual, to talk about America's role in the world, and about what America had done in the past five and a half years, declaring that "all of us, as Americans, regardless of our partisan affiliation, can be proud of the role America, our country, has played in making this world a safer and better place for all people on it, not just for ourselves." America's participation in the Vietnam war—"difficult, long, arduous as that terrible struggle was"—had been ended "on the kind of a just and honorable basis that was essential if we were able to continue to play the role of world leader." He pointed to the new relationships with China and the Soviet Union, to the new welcome for America in the Middle East, and he looked ahead: "We must recognize that for the balance of our lives, for the balance of this century, and perhaps well into the next century—and no one can look further than that, but certainly well into the next century—a strong, responsible United States of America is indispensable if peace is to be kept in the world. There is no one else that can play that role. There is no other nation in the free world that can take up that great responsibility, and so we have that responsibility.

"We believe that over the past five and a half years that we have met it and met it reasonably well. We think more progress has been made in that period for building a peaceful world than has been made in any similar period, certainly in this century, and probably in this period of modern civilization."

And then, in what none of us there realized was the last dinner toast of his presidency, he led up to what preyed so heavily on his mind:

"There is a very real chance that due to the profound changes that have been made—the new relations with the People's Republic of China, the new relationship with the Soviet Union, the beginning of a peaceful era in the Middle East—that as a result of these profound changes the chance for peace to survive on a world basis is better now than it has been at any time in this century.

"And yet, anytime that we say that, when we have an incident like the one that has occurred over the past few days involving America's friends and allies, it shows us how fragile that structure is. It shows us how much it needs constantly to be tended. It shows us how important it is that not only the United States of America but particularly the leadership of the United States of America assume the responsibility of world leadership which is ours, and never back away from it because that might be the easier course.

"It also explains something else that I think is very important that Roy has touched upon tangentially, at least, and that is apart from the man, the office of the presidency must never be weakened because a strong America and a strong American president is something which is absolutely indispensable if we are to build that peaceful world that we all want."

Back in Washington, the Judiciary Committee Republicans that same day finally dismissed impeachment advocate Albert Jenner as minority counsel. Jenner moved over to become Doar's deputy. Samuel Garrison moved up to take Jenner's place as minority counsel. The next day, July 22, Garrison presented a hastily prepared set of legal arguments to the committee. His arguments came after the die was cast, but they cut to the heart of what the impeachment inquiry should have been, but was not: "The House in the first instance and the Senate thereafter exercise Political judgments with a capital P, which I construe to mean simply balancing the public interests in the premises. The question facing the committee, and thereafter the House, is not simply whether the President did whatever it may be. The question is, did the President do it, and if so, what are the implications of that for the nation in light of all competing public interests?" He pointed out that impeachment is discretionary, not mandatory, and analogized the role of the House to that of the prudent prosecutor: "The prudent prosecutor begins his inquiry without bias toward the suspect. He proceeds to gather the evidence from every source, to reach a judgment as to whether he feels that the individual should be prosecuted." The facts have to be sufficiently clear to establish guilt. The offense has to be a valid constitutional charge. And then the member "must be convinced in the exercise of his political judgment that the best interests of the nation warrant removal rather than retention of the officer." And in establishing facts, inferences are not enough: "Mr. Doar's case of circumstances showing presidential involvement from the beginning is a very, very weak one and the reason is because you cannot simply aggregate suspicions. You cannot aggregate inferences upon inferences. You can only aggregate facts."

With his voice of restraint, Garrison by now was whistling into the wind—and the wind had become a hurricane. Not only Doar but also the news media were daily aggregating "inferences upon inferences," while politics with a small "p" whipped impeachment mania to fever pitch. Committee Republican Lawrence J. Hogan, running hard for governor of Maryland, held up his finger to the political wind, and on July 23, the eve of the opening of televised hearings, he called a special press conference to announce that he would vote to impeach. (In Maryland, Democrats outnumbered Republicans 3–1.)

Of the twenty-one Democrats on the committee, eighteen had been solidly pro-impeachment all along. Of the seventeen Republican members, ten or eleven had seemed all along to be fairly solidly in the anti-impeachment camp. To the pro-impeachment Democrats, it was vital to win the support of enough committee Republicans to give impeachment a bipartisan cast. To the White House, it was vital that we hold at least some of the "swing" Republicans, and also that we win at least one and preferably all of the three Southern Democrats—Walter Flowers of Alabama, James R. Mann of South Carolina, and Ray Thornton of Arkansas. Other members of the House were looking to the committee in making up their own minds how to vote. Among the swing Republicans and the Southern Democrats, one vote in committee was likely to mean five or ten on the floor. If the pro-impeachment votes were cast in committee almost entirely by the partisan Democrats, chances were good of beating impeachment in the House. And if impeachment were voted by the House, but with Republicans and Southern Democrats fairly solidly against it, chances of winning in the Senate would be high.

At the start of the San Clemente visit, the tentative head counts being reported to the White House looked generally optimistic—not in committee, where an impeachment vote was virtually certain, but in the full House. But as the opening of the televised committee debate neared, the pro-impeachment pressures on the uncommitted committee members mounted in intensity. Doar dropped his mask of impartiality, with Jenner following suit. The committtee bombarded press and public with its "statements of information"—those massive compilations of "evidence" that no one read, but which produced saturation coverage in the media, excerpts piled on excerpts, played for sensationalism, interpreted into the appearance of a seamless web of unprecedented scandals. Editorials and commentaries hammered at the theme that, even if hard evidence was lacking, the House had a duty to "let the Senate decide"—to vote for impeachment, so that a trial could take place, and so the truth could be brought out there.

On Tuesday, July 23, at the close of the day, I sent the fourth draft of the Thursday economic speech over to the President. He worked on it late into the evening, while also getting reports from Washington on the erosion of his support in the committee.

The San Clemente offices were housed in two rather small, single-story prefabricated buildings. The President's office was in the "A" building, facing the ocean, together with those of Al Haig, Henry Kissinger, Rose Mary Woods, and a few others. Across a narrow patio was the "B" building, with a conference room, a dining room, Ron Ziegler's office and that of the military aide, washrooms, and several small offices variously assigned to whoever might be along on any particular trip. It also had a stockroom, containing two cabinets of office supplies, a Xerox machine, and AP and UPI news tickers.

Wednesday morning, July 24, I was at my desk in the "B" building working on the economic speech when, shortly after 8:30 (11:30 Eastern time) the news tickers clattered out the word: by a vote of 8-0,[1] the Supreme Court had ordered Nixon to surrender the tapes of sixty-four conversations subpoenaed by the special prosecutor for possible use in the Watergate cover-up trial.

For weeks reporters had been badgering Nixon's lawyers to say whether or not he would comply with a Supreme Court ruling to give up the tapes, and the lawyers had steadfastly refused to anticipate either the Court's decision or the President's response. The previous autumn, when the first tapes' case was making its way through the courts, a presidential spokesman had said rather cryptically that the President would obey a "definitive" decision— but the word "definitive" was carefully left undefined.

Now that the decision had come down, the weeks of refusal by the White House to say in advance what the President's response would be sent the press corps into a frenzy of speculation. Personally, I had favored the refusal to make a commitment, as long as we had no idea what form the decision might take if it were adverse. I could all too readily envision a possible decision so sweeping in its claim of judicial sovereignty that it would have to be defied. We were, after all, dealing with a situation in which the judicial branch itself was a party at interest in the case it was deciding: In practical effect, the judicial branch was acting as both plaintiff and judge, and doing so in a political climate in which judicial aggrandizement was being celebrated as the highest of civic virtues. Many were in fact arguing that where the special interest of the courts—the administration of criminal justice—was or even might be involved, the executive should be defenseless before whatever might be the whim of any judge in the land.

If the Constitution said what I believed it did, then the justices should hold that they had no power under the Constitution to issue

1. Justice William H. Rehnquist, who served as an assistant attorney general in the Nixon administration, abstained.

such an order. If they interpreted their own power over the President more broadly, I thought we should at least reserve the right to examine their ruling to see whether the precedent set by accepting it would breach the bounds of acceptability. I was not willing to concede, as a matter of automatic principle, the unlimited right of the Court to decide unilaterally the extent to which, for its own purposes, it could intrude on the privacy of a co-ordinate and co-equal branch. Another reason for waiting to see the ruling before committing to any particular response was the question of how much "air" there might be in it—the extent to which it might be conditional.

From the first sketchy wire-service reports, it was clear that the Court had left no air on the actual order to turn over the tapes. But it was clear that it had at least acknowledged that "executive privilege" did exist as a constitutional principle, and that there were limits to how far and in what circumstances that privilege could be violated. Thus, I assumed that the President would comply. Wondering what turning over the tapes would cost us—what wealth of new titillating tidbits there might be on them—I went back to the economic speech.

Shortly after the news came across, my telephone rang. It was Rita Hauser, a New York lawyer, Republican activist, and long-time Nixon political associate who had served as U.S. representative to the UN Human Rights Commission. I had known her since my first days with Nixon. She was one of the brainiest of those in the old Nixon entourage, and one who consistently had kept the respect not only of Nixon but also of the Rockefeller and Javits factions in New York. We were friends, and occasionally talked with one another about our concerns.

Rita was worried, urging both that the President must comply, and also that he should do so with a statement clearly showing respect for the Court as an institution. How he did it, she suggested, was almost as important as doing it—both for the Court's sake and for his own. I told her I knew nothing about what his plans were, but that I was pretty sure he would comply, and would do it in an appropriate way. I hoped not to get drawn into it, because the speech deadlines were pressing in on me. But then, reflecting on her call, I studied the wire copy again, returned to my typewriter, and quickly batted out a couple of paragraphs. I sent copies to Haig and Ziegler, with a cover note saying I assumed the decision would be to comply, and, if so, this was something the President might appropriately say in announcing it. In Washington, meanwhile, the President's lawyers had rushed back from the Supreme Court to the White House with the text of the decision in hand, studying it, analyzing it, hastily transmitting a copy to San Clemente by telecopier.

Nixon himself woke late that morning. News of the Court decision had already been broadcast to the nation before he learned of it from Al Haig. As details of the decision came in, it was clear to everyone that it left him no course other than to comply. There was no debate over whether to comply.

At 1:45 Nixon asked me to join him in the second-floor study at his house. I walked through the courtyard, past the fountain, and up the single flight of steps that led from the courtyard to the study. He was in his armchair as usual, the economic speech in hand, while, through the windows, the blue Pacific stretched beyond the eucalyptus trees. He talked about the speech in general, and ran through a number of specific changes he wanted in the next draft, mostly tightening and sharpening—where the draft had read, "I do not intend to return to wage and price controls," he hardened it to a more definite "We shall not return to wage and price controls." He spun out thoughts about how some of the points might be better organized, and sections highlighted: "Let me tell you what we are not going to do"; and "Let me tell you what we are going to do." When he had finished, he handed me the blue folder that held his marked-up copy, with the notes scrawled in the margins, and, as I got up to leave, he remarked that there were going to be some rough days ahead, and we had all better be prepared for some setbacks. Things were looking bad in the House.

I told him I thought we should not give up on the House: that we might still turn things around if we could only hammer home the point that if the House voted to impeach, it would be the House, not the President, that bore the responsibility for putting the country through the wrenching trauma of a Senate trial; that therefore a heavy burden of proof lay on the shoulders of every member in casting his vote. The impeachment lobby, in Congress and the media, had managed to create a climate in which it was increasingly assumed that members should vote to impeach unless the President were proved innocent, and this stood the process on its ear. We had failed to make this point, or at least to make it effectively, and I urged that we ought to make it the central thrust of our campaign for votes on the floor of the House.

He agreed that it was worth stressing, but he still seemed uncharacteristically subdued, almost defeatist, telling me with an obvious effort at good cheer that whatever happened I should keep my chin up.

When I got back to my office, Al Haig was looking for me. Jim St. Clair was going to meet soon with the press at the press center at the Surf and Sand Hotel, fifteen miles up the coast in Laguna Beach, to announce the President's intent to comply with the Court ruling. St. Clair had written out a few thoughts for a statement, mostly dealing with the mechanics of compliance. Haig, Ziegler, St. Clair, and I thrashed it out, working from St. Clair's notes and the short draft I had done earlier. It was already late afternoon in the East, so we had to work hastily. Haig had already discussed it with Nixon. We agreed that the mechanics should be dealt with separately by St. Clair, not Nixon. St. Clair and I moved over to Ziegler's office to patch a draft together and get it quickly typed so that it could be cleared by the President. St. Clair then sped to the Surf and Sand, where he announced to the waiting press that he wanted to read a statement by the President. It was basically what I had written as a result of Rita's call:

My challenge in the courts to the subpoena of the Special Prosecutor was based on the belief it was unconstitutionally issued and on my strong desire to protect the principle of Presidential confidentiality in a system of separation of powers.

While I am of course disappointed in the result, I respect and accept the Court's decision, and I have instructed Mr. St. Clair to take whatever measures are necessary to comply with that decision in all respects.

For the future, it will be essential that the special circumstances of this case not be permitted to cloud the rights of Presidents to maintain the basic confidentiality without which this office cannot function. I was gratified, therefore, to note that the Court reaffirmed both the validity and the importance of the principle of executive privilege—the principle I had sought to maintain. By complying fully with the Court's ruling in this case, I hope and trust that I will contribute to strengthening rather than weakening this principle for the future—so that this will prove to be not the precedent that destroyed the principle, but the action that preserved it.

One subtlety in this was, to me, important as a matter of constitutional precedent: while "respecting" and "accepting" the Court's decision in this case, it did not concede that a president must necessarily do so in all cases. The decision to "accept" the Court's ruling was the President's; therefore, by implication, another intrusion by the courts into presidential prerogatives might not be accepted. Through such subtleties, sometimes, are the delicate balances in a system of separate powers maintained.

Returning to the speech, I pulled the President's copy out of its folder. Stuffed in with it were two pages of notes he had written the night before, on the large desk-top memo pad he sometimes used. Most of the notes were about the speech, outlining it, highlighting particular points he wanted to make. But boxed off in the upper right-hand corner were several names. Among them were Hogan, Railsback, and Flowers of the Judiciary Committee, and "Waggonner"—Joe D. Waggonner, Jr., a Louisiana congressman who often served as an intermediary with Southern Democrats in the House. Beneath these he had drawn another box, and in it had written: "12:01 A.M.—Lowest point in Presidency & S.C. to come."

At the time, just what it meant was a mystery to me, though I was sure it must be related to his parting comments to me that afternoon. I had been slow to recognize these for what they obviously were: an effort to prepare me, as he would prepare others, for the prospect of defeat. He had done that in 1968, as we flew back from Los Angeles to New York on election day, the outcome in doubt; calling us a few at a time up to his cabin to try subtly to soften the blow that might fall that night. I told no one about the notes, but slipped the two pages into his folder along with the next draft of the speech, and, in my covering memo, cryptically alerted him that "I'm also enclosing a couple of pages of your notes that were stuck in with the copy of the 4th draft that you gave me."

It was not until months later that I learned what was behind those notes.

Nixon learned that night that he had lost the three Southern Democrats on the committee: Flowers, Thornton, and Mann. At that point, as he explained it to me later, "I had, for the first time, really to face up to the fact that we'd lose in the House. I had to think about what a Senate trial would mean—in terms of the mini-summit, the 1974 elections, the fact that the economy was becoming a serious problem." It was on that night that he first began seriously moving toward a possible resignation. "It was then that I began to prepare people—even including Al Haig." Sometimes, he added in a rather wistful aside, "people are being prepared even without their knowing it." When the Supreme Court ruling came down the next morning, "all that did really was to confirm the conclusion I'd already reached in my own mind—that we simply couldn't make it."

Of the various considerations he had to weigh, the "mini-summit" was among the most serious. When he and Brezhnev failed to agree on a SALT II pact in Moscow, they made a private agreement to meet again at the end of the year for another try. Nixon saw the time in which a SALT II agreement could be reached slipping away, with the danger mounting that in the absence of an agreement a runaway arms race would begin: "I had to balance the arguments for staying against the consideration that if I were facing trial in the Senate, I would not be able to negotiate with Brezhnev."

On the same day—Wednesday, July 24—that the Supreme Court ordered the tapes surrendered, the Judiciary Committee opened its televised debate, with Massachusetts Democrat Harold D. Donohue moving for the adoption of two articles of impeachment, accusing the President of obstruction of justice and abuse of power. The next day, as scheduled, Nixon helicoptered to Los Angeles, and then motorcaded to the Century Plaza Hotel—the same hotel that had been our headquarters in the final, frenzied weekend of the 1968 campaign, and from which we left to fly East on election day. Now, 1700 guests applauded warmly as he stepped to the podium in the hotel's Los Angeles Room. The occasion was a conference on the economy, sponsored jointly by four California businessmen's groups. He omitted the introductory ad-libbing with which he normally began a speech, and plunged quickly, even brusquely, into his text: "Mr. Smith, all of the very distinguished guests on the podium and in this audience, and all of the millions listening on television and radio: I want to discuss today the major problem confronting America—inflation. And I want to discuss where we are in the fight against inflation, how we got here, and what we are going to do about it. . . ." It was the last speech he gave before announcing his resignation, exactly two weeks later.

Flying back to San Clemente, the helicopter skimmed over the bare, summer-brown hilltops, the spreading semicircles of homes, the miles of broad sandy ocean beaches, before settling softly, precisely, down on the helipad beside the office buildings. As we got off, he stopped to chat with me before climbing into his waiting golf cart for the short drive to his house. He talked easily, amiably, thanking me for my help, and then, with a wave to the staff who had come out to greet him, drove off. The Judiciary Committee was holding its second day of televised debate.

I watched the committee's debates intermittently, too disgusted by the demagogic theatrics of the more acidulous majority members to stomach a steady diet of them. We were scheduled to leave for the return trip to Washington Sunday afternoon. On Saturday, with the committee scheduled to vote on the first article of impeachment, I said to hell with it, and went to the beach instead. As I rather glumly told *The New Republic*'s John Osborne over lunch at the San Clemente Inn, I opted for embeachment rather than impeachment. I went to the beach again on Sunday, stayed longer than I should have, and raced to the Marine Air Station at El Toro barely in time to catch the plane. The sun and the waves were difficult to leave for the jungle that waited back in Washington.

On Monday and Tuesday, the committee voted its second and third articles of impeachment: the second charging abuse of power, the third for defying the committee's own subpoenas. The Judiciary Committee's televised proceedings had a devastating impact on public perceptions. A nationwide Harris poll, taken immediately after the committee debate, showed that the percentage of those polled favoring impeachment had risen from 53 to 66, while the percentage opposing impeachment had fallen from 34 to 27. The percentage favoring conviction by the Senate had risen from 47 to 56; the percentage opposing conviction had dropped from 34 to 31.

During those first days back in Washington, besides following the committee's actions, I had a rather urgent staff matter to take care of. My assistant, Tex Lezar, had left the White House staff a few days earlier. He had enrolled in the University of Texas Law School the previous year, intending to enter for the fall term of 1973, but at the last minute agreed to delay it a year in order to see the Watergate battle through. (This was one of the fringe benefits of having Charles Alan Wright, the University of Texas professor, as the President's lawyer. At lunch one day in the summer of 1973 Tex and I told Wright that Tex was willing to stay at the White House another year if the university would be persuaded to delay his admission until the following fall; Wright called a couple of friends that afternoon, and it was arranged.) I had come to trust Tex completely and to rely on him heavily, and wished he did not have to leave at that critical point—but he was already four years out of Yale, and could hardly postpone law school another year. As a replacement, Tex and Dave Gergen both recommended Ben Stein—a young member of Gergen's writing staff, a close friend of Julie Eisenhower, son of Council of Economic Advisers chairman Herb Stein—a quick, facile writer, fiercely loyal to the President, and a lawyer. Because I worked so often with the legal team, we all were agreed that this could be an additional asset of considerable value.

I knew Stein only casually. But I was impressed with his skills, and was willing to gamble that we could develop the trust I had had with Tex. He moved into Tex's old office, separated from mine only by a rather cramped outer office that we shared, and which was occupied by my secretary, Margaret Foote. During the next few days, the arrangement was to cause both Margaret and me some exceedingly awkward moments.

Thursday afternoon, August 1, I was asked to come over to Al Haig's office at 6:30 for a strategy meeting. I arrived a couple of minutes early. Haig was not yet there, but his aide George Joulwan and Jim St. Clair were. As I entered, they were studying a large chart that was laid out on Haig's conference table. They quickly covered it, and placed it on an easel. Soon others drifted in: presidential counselor Dean Burch, chief of congressional relations Bill Timmons, writers Pat Buchanan and Ken Khachigian, Dave Gergen, communications director Ken Clawson, scheduler David Parker, staff secretary Jerry Jones. While waiting for Haig we milled about, chatting. We watched the first part of the NBC Nightly News on Haig's television set, until Dean Burch—a former FCC chairman—suddenly asked, "Does anybody really want to watch any more of this?" No one did. We turned it off.

At about 6:45 Haig bustled in, apologizing for being late. He explained that he had called us together so we could get organized for the big push ahead, and said it was going to require a "total mobilization" of the sort we had not yet had in the Watergate battle. He ran through the schedule: the Judiciary Committee was to make its report to the full House the following week, probably the eighth, and the Rules Committee would probably report out a rule after that. The House debate was slated for August 19 through August 29. The Senate trial would probably begin in late September or early October; it was expected to run to the first of the year, but probably not beyond.

Haig uncovered the charts, explaining a bit apologetically that in setting up the organization some people might feel they had been slotted in the wrong places; if so, we could make adjustments as we went along. There was to be a "strategy group"—Haig, Ziegler, Burch, St. Clair, Buzhardt, Timmons, and Clawson—that would meet every day, at 9:00 A.M. and 6:00 P.M. Then there would be a "working group"—Jones, Parker, Gergen, together with aides to Timmons and Clawson—that would meet each day at 7:30 A.M. and 4:30 P.M. staying constantly on top of day-to-day developments. A "situation group" would become operational two days before the opening of debate, setting up headquarters at the Capitol. Three separate task forces, one for each of the three articles of impeachment, would marshal the substantive arguments (I was to head the task force dealing with Article I, Watergate, and the cover-up).

There was one urgent, immediate matter: the Judiciary Committee minority report. St. Clair said he had talked with Sam Garrison, the new minority counsel, and Garrison had indicated he would be glad to have help with it. But, because of congressional sensitivities, we would have to be very cautious in the way we approached it—perhaps, St. Clair suggested, filtering whatever we provided through Charles Wiggins, who had been Nixon's ablest and most "lawyerly" defender on the committee. Haig warned that the sixty-four additional tapes that were to be turned over were currently being reviewed, and that some materials on these might affect our line of argument. Therefore, he said, we should be cautious about what we sent to Capitol Hill until we knew for sure what was in these. We should be sure not to send anything that might turn out to be inconsistent with these, and which could put our "committee stalwarts" in the position of relying on materials supplied by us which might not hold up. The review, he said, should be completed by the following week.

At about 7:30 the meeting broke up. Several of us lingered outside, talking in small knots in the corridor. I chatted for a while with Dean Burch and Bill Timmons. Timmons was worried about House Republican Leader John J. Rhodes. Rhodes's fellow Arizonan, Senator Paul J. Fannin, was reporting that Rhodes was likely to desert. Burch—another Arizonan, whom Goldwater had made Republican national chairman in 1964—said that probably the only thing that would help now would be for Nixon himself to get on the phone, and tell Rhodes, "I won't ask you to be with me, but I at least hope you won't be against me." As we were talking, Muriel Hartley, Haig's secretary, quietly motioned me aside. Haig wanted to see me.

When I went back into the office, Haig and St. Clair were sitting at the conference table. Both looked unusually sober. "We need a resignation speech," Haig said.

The charts, the organization, the strategy group, the working group—they were a smokescreen. When the Supreme Court ordered the sixty-four tapes turned over, Nixon had asked Fred Buzhardt to listen to the tapes of his conversations with Bob Haldeman on June 23, 1972. Buzhardt, in Washington, got them out, listened, and reported back to Haig in San Clemente that they were a disaster—that they were the "smoking pistol" that tied Nixon directly, and at the very outset, to the cover-up. At first, Haig had discounted Buzhardt's report. Buzhardt had sometimes been overly alarmist in the past. Now Haig and St. Clair had read the transcripts. They were every bit as bad as Buzhardt had said they were. The tapes had to be turned over, and that meant the battle was lost. Nixon planned a speech from the Oval Office Monday night, August 5, announcing his resignation effective at noon on Tuesday.

June 23—I needed no prodding on what those conversations

were. That was the date on which Nixon had had Haldeman and Ehrlichman call in the CIA's Richard Helms and Vernon Walters, and tell them to tell FBI Acting Director Pat Gray that his Watergate investigation might get into sensitive CIA areas. More than a year earlier, Nixon had publicly acknowledged giving that instruction. We dealt with it in the May 22, 1973, Watergate white paper. Within days of the break-in, the white paper explained, Nixon had been "advised that there was a possibility of CIA involvement in some way. It did seem to me possible that, because of the involvement of former CIA personnel, and because of some of their apparent associations, the investigation could lead to the uncovering of covert CIA operations totally unrelated to the Watergate break-in." Also, Howard Hunt's name had surfaced, "and I was alerted to the fact that he had previously been a member of the Special Investigations Unit in the White House." If the FBI's investigation made the plumbers' existence known, this would lead inexorably to the exposure of sensitive national security matters the plumbers had been engaged in. He had to insure that "neither the covert operations of the CIA nor the operations of the Special Investigations Unit should be compromised." Therefore, he told Haldeman and Ehrlichman "to insure that the investigation of the break-in not expose either an unrelated covert operation of the CIA or the activities of the White House investigations unit—and to see that this was personally coordinated between General Walters, the deputy director of the CIA, and Mr. Gray of the FBI."

One evening, while working on that white paper, I got copies of the "Walters memcons"—memoranda of conversations written for the files by Vernon Walters, describing that June 23 meeting and others that followed. These had not then been made public, but they had been provided to a Senate committee. Walters' memo on the first meeting began:

On June 23 at 1300 on request I called with Director Helms on John Ehrlichman and Robert Haldeman in Ehrlichman's office at the White House.

Haldeman said that the "bugging" affair at the Democratic Hqs at the Watergate Apartments had made a lot of noise and the Democrats were trying to maximize it. The FBI had been called in and was investigating the matter. The investigation was leading to a lot of important people and this could get worse. He asked what the connection with the Agency was and the Director repeated that there was none. Haldeman said that the whole affair was getting embarrassing and it was the President's wish that Walters call on Acting FBI Director Patrick

Gray and suggest to him that since the five suspects had been arrested that this should be sufficient and that it was not advantageous to have the enquiry pushed, especially in Mexico, etc.

Other memcons described Walters' subsequent meetings with Dean, in which Dean pressed to have the CIA provide bail and salaries for the Watergate burglers.

When I first saw the memcons that evening, they appeared devastating. They seemed completely to destroy Nixon's position, showing the initial instructions to the CIA as completely politically inspired, and Dean's subsequent crude efforts to enlist CIA help as simply extensions of a cover-up conspiracy growing out of that first approach. Pat Buchanan and I stayed up half the night, brooding over them, analyzing what they probably meant, thinking through alternative courses—unless Haldeman had acted on his own, and gone beyond what the President intended, it seemed as though Nixon must have tried to cover up and would have to acknowledge it.

It was not until the next morning that I began to see that this was not necessarily so. Fred Buzhardt pointed out that the first Walters memcon, on the June 23 meeting, was not written until June 28—after the pressure from Dean, after Walters' contacts with Gray. And, as Fred noted, taken together they did have a strong "CYA"—"cover your ass"—tone to them, portraying Walters and Helms as dauntlessly defending the integrity of their agency against the nasty White House efforts to compromise it. And Walters and Helms had originally cooperated, not grudgingly but willingly, and it was, in fact, not until July 6, 1973, that the CIA finally told Gray categorically that it had no objections to a full FBI investigation. The Agency might have had more to cover up than we knew about. Further, the original suspicions of CIA involvement had originated in the FBI and been relayed by Gray to the White House. Viewed skeptically, as efforts to make a record that might later be used for Walters', Helms's, and the CIA's own self-protection, the memcons began to look more questionable and Nixon's insistence that his own version was correct more plausible.

Now, fourteen months later, all this flooded back as Haig described the June 23 transcript. Haldeman reported to the President that the FBI was going to be able to trace the money found on the Watergate burglars back to the Committee to Re-Elect the President, and that it had gone through a Mexican bank. Mitchell and Dean recommended that the only way to head it off was to use the CIA—to have Walters call Gray and ask the FBI to limit its investigation. Nixon okayed the plan—not to protect the CIA, but to protect the re-election committee. It was all there on the tape, and the tape had to be turned over.

I agreed that if the tape was as Haig described it, the long fight was over. We might have survived it earlier, but not now. It was not so much the actual use of the CIA as it was what I called the "Profumo factor"—a reference to John Profumo, Britain's former war minister, who was caught up in the Christine Keeler sex-and-espionage scandal in 1963, and finally had to resign, not for what he had done but because he lied to the House of Commons about it. Nixon had protested his innocence too long and too unequivocally. Now, with his support in the Congress and the country already crumbling, there was simply no way he could survive a revelation that six days after the break-in he had directed an effort to cover it up. And if the battle was lost, better to resign quickly and gracefully rather than fight it through to its bitter, rending conclusion.

The President's plan to resign was, of course, as tightly held a secret as any in the White House. And this posed a practical problem for me, which, during the next week, made me feel at times like a character in a Mack Sennett movie. The White House was now a rumor factory, with many of the staff spending half their time scurrying around trying to pry out what was really happening, and the other half frantically gossiping about what they imagined might be happening—and many apparently babbling their imaginings to the press. Keeping secrets in that sort of atmosphere requires not only the will to do so but also, frequently, considerable skill and practice. If Tex Lezar were still there, I could have told him what I was doing. By then he had well-developed habits of discretion, and he had learned how not to violate a confidence. But Ben Stein was a wholly unknown quantity, and I dared not risk letting him in on the secret.

Any appearance of unusual activity in my office was bound to generate a new spate of rumors, which in this case could well prove correct. So I had to keep up an elaborate façade of normality, not only in the rest of the White House but even in my own office—pretending to be working on the Article I arguments, generating make-work projects for Ben to keep him off the trail, discreetly concealing my working papers whenever he burst into my office. It was even more difficult for Margaret Foote, my secretary, working in the outer office, having not only to deal with visitors but also to make sure that as Ben brushed by her desk and typewriter nothing showed that shouldn't. (At one point I invented some cover story or other to tell Ben, explaining that it was a project I was working on in secrecy—figuring that if he thought he knew what I was really doing, he would be less likely to guess the truth. Shortly afterward Dave Gergen phoned him to try to find out what I was up to. I happened to be passing by Ben's open door, and heard him tell Gergen: "I'm not permitted to tell you what it is that he's working on." I practically went through the ceiling. Ben was trying, but he had obviously not learned the techniques.)

The need for total secrecy stemmed partly from the need to make preparations in an orderly way, without letting things fall apart in the meantime. It also stemmed partly from the nature of decision-making. No decision was "final" until it was announced— and on this most final, most personal decision of his presidency, Nixon obviously was going to keep reassessing, keep re-examining, possibly reverse himself. He had done this time and again on lesser decisions, and we understood that this was standard operating procedure. (This same pattern was also one of the reasons why comments from the tapes, taken out of context, were often so misleading —and so damaging.) For years reporters had kept trying to pin down the precise moments at which particular decisions were reached. For years I tried to explain to them that this was simply not possible. He might be 70-percent "decided" on a particular move, then rethink it, and be down to 40 percent, then 80, then 60, re-serving his options until the last moment. He was certainly not going to change the pattern now. And if he did decide to fight on, he would certainly not want it known that he had been about to throw in the towel.

Friday, August 2, during the day, I worked on the speech, while also juggling pretenses and appearances and conferring with others involved in preparing the Article I defense. Early Friday evening we reconvened in Haig's office. This time George Joulwan and Fred Buzhardt were there, and our circle was also joined by Pat Buchanan. Haig said the President was going to want Buchanan's assessment of the political impact of the new transcript, and handed him a copy—not of the full conversation, but of the brief portion dealing with Watergate.

When Haig briefed me the night before, I had not seen the actual transcript. My own belief that resignation was necessary was there-fore based on Haig's description. Later I began having doubts: perhaps Haig and St. Clair had not conveyed it accurately; perhaps they were overreacting; perhaps, as had happened so often before, what seemed at first glance conclusive was really not. Perhaps it was not the end of the road, after all. I wanted to read the transcript for myself. We had just one copy. As Buchanan read, I had him pass the pages along to me. While the others went on with their discussion, I read it, a page at a time, shaking my head sadly: no way. It was worse than Haig had described, not because of the specific acts, but because of the state of knowledge and state of mind it revealed. It obviously related back to previous conversations, and it showed the President and Haldeman discussing not whether to cover up, but how, and seizing without serious question on the cover-up opportunity that had been presented. It might have been manageable fifteen months earlier. But now, with the "Profumo factor," even if by some unforeseeable miracle he survived in the Senate, there would be no way he could govern for the next two years. Everyone in the room agreed that resignation was the only course. And, said Haig, so did Chuck Wiggins. The President had had Haig and St. Clair show Wiggins the transcript that afternoon, to get Wiggins' judgment on its impact. Throughout the impeachment debate, Wiggins had argued forcefully and eloquently that the committee was voting to impeach without evidence. But now Wiggins, too, agreed: here was the smoking pistol.

Saturday noon I was called over to Haig's office again. He and St. Clair were there, and Joulwan, and Ziegler for part of the session. The President had changed his mind. He was still going to release the transcript on Monday, but without resigning. (The tape itself had already been delivered to Judge John Sirica, on Friday.) Nixon still wanted a speech for Monday night, but now it was going to be one explaining the transcript, and stressing the importance of seeing the constitutional process through. Suddenly, everyone except me had flopped over. St. Clair, so strongly in favor of resignation the night before, now argued forcefully that the national trauma of a Senate trial would itself be an essential element in setting the constitutional precedent. It would be disastrous if the process were shortcircuited, and a precedent established that a president could be thrown out of office without going through the deliberately difficult constitutional process. Haig stressed that over the past several days he had kept changing his own mind on whether the President should resign, leaning first one way and then the other. It seemed to me that I was watching a familiar process at work. When the client changed his mind, the lawyer smoothly slipped into reverse and argued the opposite case. When the President changed his mind, his chief of staff changed with him. It was not that simple, of course. It was a difficult choice. There were principles in conflict. We were dealing in guesswork and uncertainty. The stakes were enormous. We were all under strain. Some mind-changing was natural. But when I saw minds changing in unison, I was afraid the President was getting echoes of his own shifting moods, not independent advice. I got Al to promise that he would pass on to the President my own strong dissent. There was no way for him to survive, I insisted, and the only way for him to leave with dignity was to leave now, rather than fight it out and be clawed to shreds.

I went back to my office upset, distraught, shifting gears to write the speech that I thought would be a disastrous mistake. Al Haig called a short while later to say that the President wanted me, Jim St. Clair, Ron Ziegler, and himself to come to Camp David the next day, Sunday, to work on the speech. Al asked if there were anyone else I thought should also be brought along. I said I would want my secretary, of course, and then added that I thought it would be helpful to have Pat Buchanan there. Whatever reason I gave Haig, the real reason was that I still hoped the President could be persuaded back onto the resignation track. Based on his reactions the night before, I thought Buchanan's would be another voice urging that.

Haig said I should plan on having a draft of the Monday speech with me when we went to Camp David. We were scheduled to leave the White House at 1:15 Sunday, to go by car to the Pentagon helipad, and arrive by helicopter at Camp David at 2:00. I put together a draft Saturday night, so that Sunday morning before departure I could incorporate whatever revisions Haig and St. Clair thought should be made. I also wrote a draft of another speech—"Option B," I called it—explaining the transcript and announcing his resignation. I planned to take both, still hoping Nixon could be persuaded—and hoping the speech might help persuade him. In "Option B," I included a section that I guessed was somewhere close to the truth of the matter:

Last week, in my review of the tapes to be turned over to the Special Prosecutor, I discovered one that indicated my own knowledge of the Watergate cover-up was greater than I have previously indicated, and that it came sooner—in fact, that I did learn shortly after the break-in that it was a potential source of severe embarrassment to the Administration and to my campaign committee, and that I did, at that time, approve actions which I hoped would have the effect of covering up the connection.

Rather than withhold that tape, I have turned it over to Judge Sirica. I have also made it available tonight to the House Judiciary Committee, so that its records will be complete.

In the light of this, I owe to you, the American people, an explanation of why until now I have continued to maintain that I had no knowledge of the cover-up until I was told about it by John Dean on March 21, 1973.

With hindsight, it is very easy to say that I should have simply opened up everything at once to the prosecutors, and let the chips fall where they might. Certainly the events that have followed have demonstrated that this would have been the wiser as well as the proper course.

At the time, however—whether rightly or wrongly—I was deeply concerned, in human terms, about the possible impact on valued friends and associates, as well as on others who had done wrong in a cause they believed to be right. Because some of the same people were involved, I was concerned that an unlimited investigation might compromise the genuinely sensitive national-security matters that the so-called "plumbers" had been dealing with. In the midst of a political campaign, I knew that the break-in had the potential for massive exploitation as a political issue—and that if a sufficient connection could be established, it conceivably could even be decisive in terms of the outcome, and therefore in terms of all that was at stake both here and abroad, including the foundation I was trying to build for a structure of peace that could last into the next century.

I thought the break-in itself was stupid, as well as wrong. But once it had taken place, I knew that I had inherited the consequences—and that with the presidency at issue, those potential consequences reached out also to the nation and the world.

In retrospect, it would have been better to have explained this fully and frankly when Watergate and the cover-up again became a national issue early last year—at a time when the cover-up had reached dimensions that I still did not fully comprehend. Instead, I felt trapped by events and chose a different way of attempting to defend what I believed to be the interests of the presidency, and to preserve my capacity to function in what I believed to be the interests of the nation.

I say this not in defense, but in explanation.

I also called Buchanan at home Saturday night. Speaking guardedly, because we were using the telephone, I told him about the change of signals, and about my concern, and arranged to meet with him in his office the next morning at 9:00.

Buchanan had been called over Saturday afternoon to talk with the President's family, who had been strongly against resignation. When I met Buchanan on Sunday morning, I found that he had shifted his own ground somewhat. He still thought Nixon was going to have to resign, but now thought it would probably be better to put out the transcripts first, and let the reaction hit. Then there would be no question about whether it was necessary—Nixon would not live the rest of his life thinking that perhaps he could have made it after all, if only he had not been pushed into quitting by alarmist aides. The more I thought about it, the more Buchanan's argument seemed to make sense. It would be better both for Nixon and for the country if any doubts about the necessity of giving up were resolved. And, of course, there was that slim possibility that we were wrong—that this, too, could be survived. But I had seldom been as sure of anything as I was that it could not.

If Nixon were not to resign when he put out the transcripts, however, there were still two things wrong with the present plan. It would be a tactical mistake to summon the nation to its television sets for a prime-time speech Monday evening, simply to announce that he intended to fight on and to try to explain the new evidence. The prime-time speech was the big gun, and realistically we were only going to have one shot with it: if we were to fight on, better that we save it for a reply to the reaction after it hit. Second, it would also be a mistake to lock himself in too rigidly with a pledge to see the fight through the Senate trial.

When Haig gave me the change of signals at noon on Saturday, he said Nixon wanted to make strongly the argument that the constitutional process must be completed, and that he was going to see it through to its conclusion, whatever the outcome. He also intended to pledge that he would appear before the Senate, and answer under oath any and all questions the senators chose to put to him. Saturday evening, on the telephone with Haig, I had urged strenuously that Nixon at least not include the pledge to appear before the Senate: that making it would gain little, and keeping it could destroy him. If it ever got to that point, and if the President of the United States were to stand ducking and squirming in the well of the Senate, weaving, equivocating, under the barrage of accusatory questions that would be fired at him, it would be an ignominious and pitiable way to end his presidency and his career. At least let the decision be made later: don't lock into it now. For the moment, I had gone ahead and written the draft with those pledges in it. But I hoped we could get it changed at Camp David.

Buchanan and I agreed that he should write a memo to Haig, making some of the points we had talked about. He drafted one quickly, addressed to Haig ("Confidential—eyes only"), and my secretary typed it before we left. Buchanan, Ziegler, and I shared a car for the trip to the Pentagon, and as we rode to the helipad I gave Ziegler my copy to read.

In a last-minute change Sunday morning, our departure from the White House was moved up to 12:30, to arrive at Camp David at 1:15. When we got there, the camp commander told us the President wanted to see Haig alone, and wanted the rest of us to go to Birch. Birch is a spacious cabin near the President's lodge, which Ed and Tricia Cox normally used when they were at Camp David. While waiting for Haig, we debated spiritedly whether the President should resign or fight it out, and whether he should make the dramatic pledge to appear before the Senate. St. Clair, though he now favored fighting it out, agreed that the pledge would be a mistake—as a trial lawyer, he argued that it was always better to make the trial decisions closer to the actual time. It was something we should not give away at this stage.

When Haig rejoined us, he had a new set of signals. No speech—I was relieved—but no resignation either. Nixon was going to release the new transcripts Monday with a written statement dealing solely with the new evidence. I asked if he had passed on my strong urgings that the President should resign. Haig said he had—and then indicated that what the President was now following was a sort of "two-track" strategy. He was not foreclosing resignation. He was simply preserving his options. Publicly, he was going to make the disclosure, try to put the best face on it, and act as if he intended to fight on. Privately, he was going to assess the damage. In his own mind, Nixon still believed strongly that he had not done anything that justified his impeachment and removal. If he could fight on, he probably would. If it turned out that the battle really was over, he would probably resign.

I was satisfied. The two-track strategy made sense. My own belief that he should resign was a pragmatic one. If I were wrong about the transcripts' impact—and I hoped that I was—we might yet turn things around. If I were right, another week or so would make no difference.

We talked about what the statement should say. I ducked into a bedroom to scratch a few paragraphs on a yellow pad, got the others to react, and then had the camp commander set up a typewriter for me in another cabin close to Laurel, the large building that included a dining room and conference room. While I worked at my typewriter, the others went to Laurel for lunch. I did a quick draft, eating a sandwich as I wrote. With Rose Mary Woods helping proofread to speed the process, my secretary retyped and Xeroxed it. Then we all gathered around the conference table in Laurel to go over it, line by line.

In preparing the statement, one of the problems was that Nixon's own recollection of the June 23 conversations was sharply different from the way they appeared in the transcripts—and he insisted that even when he listened to the tapes in May, he had not caught their significance. This was understandable enough. We all misremember, and no one saw the situation at the time as having the significance it later took on. Nixon's lawyers had told him all along —and he believed—that whatever problems were raised by his use of the CIA to head off the FBI were taken care of by his orders to FBI Acting Director Gray, two weeks later, to go ahead with a full and complete investigation. When he listened in May, there was no transcript. He could well have been listening for one thing, and missed another, or his mind could have wandered at the wrong moment. The first conversation, in which Haldeman passed on the recommendation that the CIA be used and Nixon approved it, lasted an hour and thirty-five minutes, of which perhaps six minutes were devoted to this. Nixon probably had a dozen things he was dealing with on June 23 that seemed more important—and, by that Sunday in August, it had all taken place more than two years before. Yet we had to deal not only with his recollections but also with the record—and with likely public perceptions. If even an honest recollection seemed to be contradicted by the record, in the climate then existing, it was going to be branded a deliberate lie. And that could bring down on his head even more trouble than the transcripts.

As we went through the draft, Ziegler suddenly focused on a reference to the President's having begun a preliminary review of the subpoenaed tapes in May, and having listened to the June 23 conversation then but not fully appreciated its significance. He began firing out a series of questions—triggered, as he later explained, by his habit of reading with an eye to what questions reporters might ask. In this case, the questions were directed at why the President was listening in May. Haig and St. Clair quickly realized where the questions were leading. It was in early May that Leon Jaworski secretely proposed an out-of-court compromise of his suit to get the sixty-four tapes: if he were given eighteen of them, he would drop the subpoena, and not—at that time, at least— disclose that Nixon had been named an unindicted co-conspirator in the cover-up case. After considering it for a day or two, Nixon turned it down. It suddenly became vital to know what the sequence was. If Jaworski made the proposal, then Nixon listened, and then Nixon turned it down, then whether Nixon's claim that he had missed the significance was true or not became, as a practical matter, irrelevant. True or not, there was no way it would be believed. If Nixon made the claim, Jaworski would reveal the sequence within forty-eight hours, and that would be the ball game.

As we worked, Haig and Ziegler were constantly calling Nixon and being called by him. He was sure he had not listened until late in May. He thought he had not listened to all three conversations. But a series of calls to Washington pinned down the sequence: on May 5, meeting in the Map Room of the White House with Haig and St. Clair, Jaworski made his proposal. The tapes of the June 23 conversations, along with others, were checked out for Nixon to listen to on May 6. On May 7 Nixon rejected the proposal. The June 23 tapes were not checked out again until July 24, when Nixon asked Fred Buzhardt to listen, immediately after the Supreme Court decision. And the logs showing when the President listened had been turned over to the special prosecutor's office.

Haig recalled the outrage at Jaworski's proposal, the resentment of it as seeming "blackmail," which would alone have been cause enough to turn it down. But there was that damning sequence. Whatever the facts, whatever might really have been in the President's mind, he was going to have to *say*, somehow, that he had listened to the tape, and that even though it clearly contradicted his own public statements he had done nothing about it. This was the only thing that would be believed. Whether true or not, if he said—as he insisted was true—that he had missed its significance, it would not be believed. Or so it seemed to us, in the frenzy of that August afternoon.

In fact, I believe now that Nixon really was confused. Haldeman has since told me that when the White House released the June 23 transcripts, he himself was stunned by them—he remembered the national-security considerations as having been genuine, even though the transcripts showed the motive to have been political. When we issued the May 22, 1973, statement—before tapes were known about, and before they had been reviewed—Nixon had asked Haldeman for his recollection, and Haldeman remembered it as having been for the legitimate national-security purpose. Later, when Haig asked Haldeman if there were any problem with June 23, Haldeman assured him there was none. (Once when I was chatting with Haldeman about another matter entirely, long after Nixon's resignation, I happened to mention to him my feeling that the most damaging thing about June 23 had been the "Profumo factor," and Bob quickly, and I think honestly, disputed me on it. "The President didn't have *knowledge*," Bob argued. "He was asking me questions. I gave him answers that had been given me by other people. I was passing on those answers. There were some of them that I didn't believe, and some others that he didn't believe." He went on to muse rather dejectedly about the apparent inability of so many people to understand "the unimportance of it in our minds at the time it happened," pointing out that it was only on that one day, and then only briefly, that he himself had had any involvement with the CIA whatever about Watergate—and that Watergate was "really only one of maybe fifteen things we were honing in on that day.")

We worked through the afternoon, checking, redrafting, tracking down people in Washington by telephone, trying to pin down facts and sequences, arranging for Steve Bull to meet with us in Haig's office with his logs when we returned to Washington that evening, so we could be sure they showed what he said they showed.

The next day, back at the White House, we continued to check and refine the statement, with Nixon going over the drafts, while the lawyers frenziedly checked and rechecked the transcripts themselves. At 3:30 they were to be shown to some of Nixon's supporters in Congress, and at 4:00 released to the press. We were releasing the full transcripts, not just the fragments dealing with Watergate. In the haste to get them ready, no one thought to "edit"—to excise unrelated material that ought not to have been made public. Thus they appeared with a section in which Nixon, speaking of his long-time friend and communications director, Herb Klein, told Haldeman, "And look, you've just not got to let Klein ever set up a meeting again. He just doesn't have his head screwed on. You know what I mean. He just opens it up and sits there with egg on his face. He's just not our guy at all is he?"

Klein knew Nixon well enough to know that he could say that sort of thing and not really mean it. But the reading public did not know this, and so it was acutely embarrassing, both to Klein and to Nixon.

The transcripts hit with shattering impact that afternoon. "President Nixon stunned the country" and caused a "storm" in Washington, declared the NBC Evening News. CBS reported that "the Nixon presidency is virtually being overtaken by events"—adding that the hard-core Nixon supporters on the Judiciary Committee were as "angry and hot as molten steel." The television cameras showed Charles Wiggins in tears as he read a statement urging that Nixon resign, and declaring that if he did not do so the time had come for his "magnificent public career" to be "involuntarily terminated." House Democratic Leader Tip O'Neill forecast a "tidal wave" for impeachment. The next morning's Washington Post declared editorially that "President Nixon has for all practical purposes pleaded guilty. . . . Basically, he has a choice concerning only one matter and that is the manner in which he will depart the office of the presidency and the degree of effort he will make to salvage its dignity and his own."

The *Post* also, that Tuesday morning, featured a news article—attributed to the usual unnamed "sources"—purporting to give a detailed accounting of what had taken place at Camp David Sunday afternoon. Our trip there had been widely (and erroneously) reported as having been suddenly arranged on Sunday morning, and it sent the press into a froth of speculation all day Sunday and Monday. Now the *Post* described what it said was our meeting with the President, complete with extensive direct quotes, gestures, even tones of voice. The article pictured Jim St. Clair as telling the President his position was virtually unsalvageable, and me as urging that he take his case to the people. Nixon himself, it said, suggested using the 25th Amendment—the one allowing a president to step aside temporarily in case of inability to discharge the powers of his office. "The 25th Amendment alternative," it went on, "was raised by the President after St. Clair and Buchanan brought up the option of outright resignation. Mr. Nixon told his aides he is not prepared to resign at this time and questioned Buchanan and St. Clair about the accuracy of their grim impeachment assessment. St. Clair concentrated on the legal difficulties posed by the President's prospective release of the Haldeman tapes. Buchanan delivered a gloomy political assessment, advising the President that Senate conviction was becoming more likely every day. 'I wish you hadn't said that,' the President reportedly replied in a tone the source described as one of sadness, not of anger." Quite an enterprising piece of "color" reporting—except for the fact that the "meeting" with Nixon it described so vividly never even took place. It was this sort of thing that had long since made us not believe what we read in the papers—especially when it came from those mysterious "sources."

Tuesday was a day of waiting, of assessment, watching as the avalanche cascaded down the hillside. House Republican Leader John Rhodes told a news conference that after reading the new transcripts, unless the President resigned he now would vote for Article I of the Impeachment Articles—obstruction of justice. By midday Tuesday, all ten Judiciary Committee Republicans who had voted against impeachment had announced that they would now vote yes on Article I. Rhodes, Speaker Carl Albert, and other House leaders agreed to cut the time set aside for debate on impeachment from two weeks to one. Crowds three- and four-deep gathered on Pennsylvania Avenue outside the White House, pressing against the high iron fence, while more crowds milled across the street in Lafayette Park.

At 11:00 A.M. the President met with his cabinet. He discussed the pressures for resignation, but told them firmly that he intended to fight on, to see the process through, and urged that during the impeachment crisis they should carry on the business of their departments with extra diligence. Then, sweeping that subject aside, he determinedly led them into a discussion of the problems of the economy.

After the ninety-minute session, reporters crowded toward the departing members as they headed for their cars. Some ducked away, but Treasury Secretary William E. Simon stopped briefly, with Labor Secretary Peter J. Brennan and Commerce Secretary Frederick B. Dent standing at his side. "The President sincerely believes he has not committed an impeachable offense," Simon reported, adding that Nixon had "explained the revelations and the disclosures of yesterday" and declaring that Nixon "intends to stay on" and to follow through the constitutional procedures. Asked if Nixon had sought a vote of confidence from his cabinet, Simon replied: "No, he didn't have to ask for our support. Of course he has the support of his cabinet."

Republican members of the Senate held their regular weekly closed-door luncheon meeting that noon. Vice-President Ford, presiding officer of the Senate, attended as usual, but left after a few minutes. After the luncheon, Texas Senator John G. Tower told a packed press gallery that the senators had discussed how they could "collectively take action" to alert the President to his situation in the Senate, adding that "the majority sentiment among Republican senators is that he should retire from office." Tower said "a little cooling-off-period" of two or three days would pass before the GOP senators decided what to do. Washington's afternoon paper, the Star, bannered: "OUST-NIXON CLAMOR RISES; WON'T QUIT, PRESIDENT SAYS." The only non-Watergate-related film report on any of the three network news programs that evening came from Los Angeles, where two people were killed and thirty-five injured in a bomb blast at Los Angeles International Airport. CBS led with a report that "the Republican party gave up today on President Nixon." ABC declared that "President Nixon appears virtually powerless to control events on Capitol Hill." NBC described Nixon's situation in the Senate as "desperate."

At about 4:20 that Tuesday afternoon Haig's secretary called, saying Haig wanted to see me. I walked the short distance across West Executive Avenue to the West Basement, climbed the single flight of stairs to the first floor, and slipped into his cramped outer office. Muriel motioned me to go on in, and said, "I'll close the door." Haig was reading. I sat at the table, while he continued reading for perhaps a minute. Finally he looked up, turned to me, and said, "We'll need a thousand words."

"He's finally decided?" I asked.

"Yes," he replied.

Nixon wanted a short speech, probably for Thursday night, possibly for Wednesday, to announce his resignation. Not a breast-beating *mea culpa*, not a speech proclaiming a guilt that he did not feel—but a healing speech, one that would help rally the country behind his successor: "This has been a difficult time for all of us. The situation has reached a point where it's clear to me that I do not retain the necessary support to conduct the business of this government in a way that I can be assured that the best interests of the nation and the American people are served. . . . I am taking the action I will announce tonight without rancor of any kind. I will be eternally grateful to those Americans who stood with me during this difficult period, and I understand the considerations of those who have not been able to. . . . As I said when I nominated Gerald Ford as Vice-President, I will leave the country in good hands. But he needs, as does any man who holds this office, your support, your confidence, your prayers." But not, said Haig, written to satisfy those "who crucified him, and are now trying to get him to say they were justified."

As we talked, Haig ate a late lunch from a tray—a sandwich, french fries, Pepsi-Cola. George Joulwan came in and, seeing me there, asked if we were back on the other track.

"We were never really off it," Haig said.

We talked for about fifteen minutes, and then I returned to my office. Haig, with a long series of calls stacked up, was reaching for the telephone as I left. I put a draft together that evening, so that it could be on the President's desk first thing the next morning. I sent it to him with a brief covering memo:

August 7, 1974

MEMORANDUM FOR: THE PRESIDENT

FROM: RAY PRICE

SUBJECT: RESIGNATION SPEECH

A first draft is attached. I'll be working on additional thoughts for it.

As I believe you know, I think this has become a sad but necessary decision in the circumstances. But I do hope you'll leave office as proud of your accomplishments here as I am proud to have been associated with you, and to have been and remain a friend. God bless you; and He will.

Attachment

On Wednesday we worked back and forth on the resignation speech, the President working in his EOB office, while I worked in mine a short way down the hall. We met during the afternoon. He showed the strain of defeat, but he was brisk, methodical, going about the business of resigning as if it were the business of governing, being careful to touch all the necessary bases. On the first draft, he scrawled an insert saying: "I have met with leaders of House and Senate, including my strongest supporters in both parties. They have unanimously advised me that because of the Watergate matter I do not and will not have support in the Congress for difficult decisions affecting peace abroad, and our fight against inflation at home so essential to the lives of every family in America." He had not yet met with the leaders, but he knew what their reports would be. He was not only pained by having to resign, but acutely embarrassed at doing it—embarrassed at quitting in the middle of a fight. "I have never been a quitter," he wrote in another margin. "To leave office is abhorrent to every instinct in my body." He also wanted to be certain, as a matter of constitutional precedent, that his resignation was seen as the constitutional equivalent of having seen the process through. "One thing that is very important," he stressed to me that afternoon, "is basically a recognition that this *is* an impeachment."

He had arranged to meet that afternoon at 5:00 with the Republican leaders of the House and Senate, John Rhodes and Hugh Scott, and with Senator Barry Goldwater, so that they could go through the ritual of delivering their grim assessment. A few minutes before meeting with them, he called me, asking that I have the next draft ready by 7:00, and that I leave it on the footstool in front of the overstuffed chair he worked in in his EOB office. He said that after meeting with the leaders "I'm going to have to talk with the family— that's the hard part." We talked a bit about handling the point about his resignation's being the equivalent of impeachment. I mentioned that I had worked out something on it that I thought made the point without "admitting" guilt. "And that's right!" he said. "That six-minute conversation—Haldeman ran that CIA thing by me—it went by so fast I didn't even pay attention. It was a stupid damn thing—but wrong."

That evening, instead of coming back to the EOB, Nixon stayed in the Lincoln Sitting Room in the family quarters of the White

House, talking with Ziegler and Kissinger and working on the speech he hated to give. At 8:30 he called me again. He said he had "made a few scribblings" on the latest draft, and given it to Ziegler to bring back to me. He also said he wanted to work in one of his favorite quotes from Teddy Roosevelt, one which, he said, he had given copies of to a number of staff and friends after his 1962 defeat—something to the effect that it is better to be the "man in the arena" who tries and fails than one of the timid souls who stand on the sidelines and do nothing. He said Ziegler was going to try to find the quote. And he wanted to add to the speech a "pledge": that "as long as I have a breath of life in my body, I shall continue to fight for the great causes to which I have dedicated my life—peace, not just for America but among all nations; prosperity, justice, and opportunity for all Americans."

He asked for a new draft by 8:30 the next morning.

Later that evening Ziegler located the Roosevelt quote, from a speech at the Sorbonne in Paris on April 23, 1910:

It is not the critic who counts; not the man who points out how the strong man stumbles, or where the doer of deeds could have done them better. The credit belongs to the man who is actually in the arena, whose face is marred by dust and sweat and blood; who strives valiantly; who errs, and comes short again and again; because there is not effort without error and shortcoming; but who does actually strive to do the deeds; who knows the great enthusiasms, the great devotions; who spends himself in a worthy cause, who at the best knows in the end the triumphs of high achievement and who at the worst, if he fails, at least fails while daring greatly, so that his place shall never be with those cold and timid souls who know neither victory nor defeat.

The full quote was pure, quintessential Nixon, and I could understand his wanting to use it at this moment as he tried to salvage some dignity from the darkest day of his life. But if he did it would be taken as kicking the critics, and seized on by them as a reason for kicking back. So, in working it into the speech, I lopped off the beginning and end, and kept just the middle—just the man in the arena, not the carping critics and the timid souls. When I told him why, he agreed.

At 10:35 the President called again. Initially we had avoided detailing any of his specific accomplishments. Now it was obvious that he had been thinking about them, brooding about them, reaching back to his triumphs for solace.

"There's just one thing," he said, his voice melancholy and distant. "If you could add in—with regard to peace—the opening to

China—that we started the process of limitation of nuclear arms—
that we started a process of peace in the Middle East, which hasn't
known peace for a thousand years."

He called again three minutes later, suggesting we might do it as
"sort of a quadriad"—ending the war in Vietnam, the opening to
China, moving toward peace in the Middle East, and starting "the
long process of reducing the horrible danger of nuclear war." Another call came at 11:07: he wanted to deal with this "not in a
bragging way," he said, but he wanted to be sure to get it in.

Outside, I could see the crowds still on Pennsylvania Avenue,
swelled now, intense, maintaining a sort of obscene death watch,
with taunts and chants of "Jail to the Chief." Around midnight Jerry
Warren called. For some time now, Warren—the deputy press secretary—had been handling most of the actual press briefings. He explained rather apologetically that he had gotten several inquiries
from reporters who had noticed the lights still burning in my office,
and who had asked if this meant a resignation speech was in the
works. Somewhat gingerly, he said he didn't know what to tell them.
I thought for a brief moment, and then suggested that he could
honestly tell them he didn't know what I was working on. Warren
thanked me. We both understood perfectly well what I was doing
by saying that: protecting him from actual "knowledge," while letting him guess with 99.9-percent certainty. He could be trusted to be
discreet. But he also had a well-deserved reputation for integrity,
and if I had actually confirmed to him, even privately, that I was
working on a resignation, it would have put him on an impossible
spot in dealing with the reporters' queries. This way he was warned
to be cautious about outright denials, but he could guard the secret
without lying.

It was after 1:00 A.M. when I called for a White House car, and
finished up, wearily, for the night. As the gates swung open and
the driver turned out onto Pennsylvania Avenue, I looked glumly
at the faces of the gathered crowd. The victors. But what had they
won, and at what cost? At home, I poured a scotch on the rocks and
pondered the speech some more while winding down, then finally
went to bed around 2:00. At 4:15 the telephone rang, and the
familiar voice of the White House operator told me the President
was calling.

"I didn't want to bother you at night," Nixon said, "but I know
you work at night. Is that all right?" He was joking. I did sometimes
work through the night—when I had to—but not as a regular practice. But that night, I was not going to begrudge him anything. I
just wanted to do whatever I could to help. He had been thinking

more about the foreign-policy part of the speech, and about ways of fleshing it out. In his earlier calls, in what had seemed to me a mood of deep melancholy, he had dwelt on the past, as if pleading to have it weighed in the balance. Now he was looking to the future, not just what had been done but what remained to be done. Some of his old animation was coming back. In terms of the speech, it seemed to me to make good sense—a way to remind the audience of what had been achieved, yet still to do it in an upbeat, forward-looking way. I made a few notes, made sure the alarm was set to wake me early, and went back to bed. At 4:30 the phone rang again. The President. He had been thinking about it more, working on it more. "What I had in mind," he said, "is a little liturgy—like this." And then he spun it out: "We have ended America's longest war, but the goals ahead are ultimately greater and more important. We've started to limit nuclear arms between the U.S. and the U.S.S.R. But our goal must be not just limitation of nuclear arms, but these terrible weapons that could destroy civilization as we know it must be destroyed— What I'm getting at," he explained, "is reduction, not just limitation—so the terrible danger as we know it must not hang over the world." And then he continued. Noting that "millions of people in Asia, Latin America, the Middle East, live in abject poverty," he told me he wanted the speech to say that our goal "should be to turn away from production for war so that all the people of the earth can live in peace, and can have an opportunity to enjoy the benefits of a decent life." In the Middle East, where "a hundred million people in the Arab world who have been our enemies now want to be our friends," we must, he said, not miss the opportunity this opens up for a stable peace, so that "the cradle of civilization will not be its grave."

He finished the rest of his "litany." Then he asked, "All right?"

"Good," I said.

This time I decided to stay up. I was wide awake by now. There was a lot of work to be done, and, with this new section, it was well on the way to being a far better speech—the kind of exit Richard Nixon should make. I turned to my typewriter, and began.

At 4:45 another call. He had another thought he wanted to get in, another "goal," this one here in America. We're "fortunate," he said, that most of our people live good lives and have good jobs—but our goal should be not only good jobs but "prosperity without inflation," and "opportunity, not just for the few, but for all."

"Okay?" he asked.

"Okay," I said.

The last call I got from him on that long night came at 5:07. It was brief: "I just wanted to say—on this one—don't run it by the NSC, or by Haig, or anyone. Just send it to me. You and I can work it out. On this one, I just want to say the things that are in my heart. I want to make this *my* speech."

At 8:30 Thursday morning, back at the office, I was still working on the section we had been talking about in those early-morning phone calls. So I sent him the fourth draft, done the night before, with a brief covering note:

> This is the draft as I finished it up late last night.
> I'm still working over the changes and additions we talked about early this morning, and will very shortly (I'm almost finished) send you substitutes for the last several pages which will incorporate these— but meanwhile wanted you to have this, so that you at least can start work on the early part.
> I think I've worked out a way to reorganize what in this draft are pages 7–11 to incorporate the new material, and at the same time to make the whole thing flow much better than it does in this draft.

Shortly afterward I sent over the substitute section, which lengthened the speech, noting in my cover memo that "this brings the word count up to 1702." He was always acutely conscious of word counts, trying to discipline both himself and his writers to keep his speeches from getting too long.

At 10:48 Appointments Secretary Steve Bull called. Steve asked if I could come to the Oval Office right away. He said that the President had another meeting at 11:00 and wanted to see me first. I put down the phone, and reached quickly for my copy of the speech —and could not find it. Frantically, I searched through the heaps of papers on my desk, and through my briefcase. Finally I located it, stuck between the pages of a bound copy of the 1969 Presidential papers, where I had been checking a quote. Relieved, I grabbed it, flung on my suit coat, and rushed to the Oval Office.

The President was sitting at his desk, working on the draft. He looked haggard, drawn, a gray tone around the deepened lines of his face. Thinking back on those calls during the night, I wondered how much sleep he had had—or if he had gotten any sleep at all. He asked first about my own personal plans, saying that if he could somehow find the funds he hoped I could find a way to work with him in the future. "You do like California, don't you?" he asked. While sidestepping any commitment—as I had for the past year, I still felt urgently the need to get off on my own—I told him that I at least would certainly be glad to help whenever I could, simply as a friend. And, yes, I did like California.

Nixon had marked several changes in the draft. Explaining them to me, he pointed out how one of them eliminated a redundancy, and made it flow better. Other changes refined a thought here or elaborated one there. He liked the way the new material we had developed that morning worked. For the opening, he suggested that it would be a nice touch to say that "this is the _____th time I have addressed you" from the Oval Office, and said I should check on what the number would be. He asked me to work in these, together with any other changes I thought ought to be made. Then he looked at his watch, and said—rather sadly, rather wistfully, I thought—that he had to meet with Ford at 11:00. I asked when he wanted the next draft. He thought a moment, and said at 2:00. Getting up to leave, I said I did not know whether I would see him that afternoon, but in case not, I wanted to wish him the best. "This afternoon? But of course we will," he said. "We'll focus in hard on the ending then." As it worked out, we did all our conferring that afternoon by telephone. That morning was the last time I met with him as President.

Going back to my office in the EOB, I walked, as usual, across West Exec, up the automobile ramp to the EOB, through the swinging doors to the ground-floor corridor, and up the spiral staircase to my first-floor office. As I came in through the swinging doors to the ground-floor corridor, I suddenly found myself brushing by Gerald Ford, the Vice-President, flanked by his Secret Service agents, looking solemn as he quickly strode the same route in reverse, on his way to be told officially by the 37th President that at noon the next day he would become the 38th.

At 12:30 Ron Ziegler announced to the press that the President would address the nation from the Oval Office at 9:00 P.M. He did not say what the address would be about, but there was no need to. When he stood at the lectern in the press room, he had to struggle visibly to keep himself under control, choking over his words as he made the announcement. Several of the women on his staff went about their work with tears streaming down their cheeks.

During the day, Nixon ran through some of the routine business of the presidency, including vetoing an agricultural-appropriations bill so as not to saddle his successor with the veto as one of his first official acts. He continued working on the speech through the afternoon, conferring occasionally with me by phone. Ziegler's staff were checking the records to see what number we should use for that opening—that this was the "_____th" time Nixon had addressed the nation from the Oval Office. During the afternoon, Ron called. "Would you believe this?" he asked. "Here's a real quirk of history. This is his 37th speech from the Oval Office—and he's the 37th President."

At around 6:00, with the speech done, I noticed that one of the calls that had come in for me during the afternoon was from Clifton Daniel, then chief of the *New York Times'* Washington bureau. I called him back. It was the first press call I had returned in three days. In his usual manner, he was gentlemanly, understanding, diplomatic, explaining that he had a "purely professional question," which, as a former newspaper editor myself, he knew I would understand. He said that for months the *Times* had had a large package of material ready to be run if and when Nixon resigned. They already had it set in the forms to run that night, for the next morning's edition, with the entire first fourteen pages of the paper given over to that and other stories related to the resignation. Daniel's question, he said, stemmed from the way Nixon operated, keeping things close to his chest, sometimes—as this time—not releasing advance texts. Putting it delicately, being careful not to overstep, he asked whether—because of the mechanical problems involved—I could tell him privately just one thing about the speech—"is the word 'resign' there?"

I understood. I knew the mechanical difficulties, and the anxieties the editors of the *Times* must be feeling, and it was no longer really that much of a secret anymore. So I said yes, it was. He thanked me, relieved, saying he had gotten indirect confirmation earlier, but that this was his first direct confirmation from an authoritative source; he had been concerned about the possibility of using the 25th Amendment, or some other arrangement short of resignation, in which case the whole paper would have had to be torn apart just at press time. No, I said, it would not have to be. No 25th Amendment. He was going to resign.

At about the same time Len Garment stopped by my office, dropping in to chat as he had done so often through the years. Earlier in the week he had bet me a dinner that Nixon would not resign within the next ten days. We agreed that I would collect on it sometime soon. He also said that he and Bill Safire were going to have dinner together that evening, and would come back to watch the speech in Len's office; did I want to join them? I said no on dinner. I thought I ought to stick around, just in case there were any last-minute problems with the speech. Besides, I was drained, exhausted, and needed some time alone. And Safire, even though he was a friend and former colleague, was now a columnist for *The New*

York Times. He had stopped by my office that afternoon and pressed me with questions—"for history"—about details of the past few days. I had answered most of them with long silences. At that point I simply did not have the energy or the focus to cope with them, even from Bill. We left it, though, that I probably would join them to watch the speech.

After dinner Len popped in again. Fred Buzhardt had joined them for dinner, and now they were all going to watch in Fred's office. I went down there shortly before 9:00. It seemed an appropriate place to watch it, and appropriate company to watch it in. Fred, Len, and I had fought most of the Watergate battle together, and Bill went back to the beginning—back to the better times. Fred turned on the set. Nothing happened. A West Pointer and one-time army electronics expert, he frantically tried to find the trouble, pushing and pulling at all sorts of mysterious gizmos, while I rather anxiously suggested we all speed down to my office instead. As the clock ticked on, Fred kept trying; finally, about sixty seconds before the hour, another set was hastily rolled in from an adjoining office. We got it turned on just in time to watch: the familiar Seal of the President of the United States, the familiar Oval Office, the familiar desk, the familiar blue suit, the familiar half-smile, the familiar strong voice, speaking firmly now, steadily, as he faced the cameras:

"Good evening.

"This is the thirty-seventh time I have spoken to you from this office, where so many decisions have been made that shaped the history of this nation. Each time I have done so to discuss with you some matter that I believed affected the national interest.

"In all the decisions I have made in my public life, I have always tried to do what was best for the nation. . . ."

And finally, as he closed, his farewell wish:

"There is one cause above all to which I have been devoted and to which I shall always be devoted for as long as I live.

"When I first took the oath of office as President five and one-half years ago, I made this sacred commitment: 'To consecrate my office, my energies, and all the wisdom I can summon to the cause of peace among nations.'

"I have done my very best in all the days since to be true to that pledge. As a result of these efforts, I am confident that the world is a safer place today, not only for the people of America but for the people of all nations, and that all of our children have a better chance than before of living in peace rather than dying in war.

"This, more than anything, is what I hoped to achieve when I sought the presidency. This, more than anything, is what I hope will be my legacy to you, to our country, as I leave the presidency.

"To have served in this office is to have felt a very personal sense of kinship with each and every American. In leaving it, I do so with this prayer: May God's grace be with you in all the days ahead."

It was 9:16 P.M. I looked at each of the others, nodded silently to them, got up, and went out the door, walking back down the long corridor to my own office. It was the only way I could keep my composure. I did not dare even try to speak. I wondered at the strength that had enabled him to get through it.

Now it was all over. Almost.

Earlier that evening, at 7:30, the President had gone to his EOB office to meet with the bipartisan leaders of Congress: with House Speaker Carl Albert, who first came to Congress with Nixon in 1947; with House Republican Leader John Rhodes; with the Majority and Minority Leaders of the Senate, Mike Mansfield and Hugh Scott; and with James O. Eastland, president pro tem of the Senate. Then, at 8:00, he crossed back to the Cabinet Room, where thirty-six of his old friends and colleagues from Congress—veterans of the political wars from both parties, who time and again had stood with him at the critical moments when it counted—had gathered for an emotional farewell. And then to the Oval Office, to the cameras, to make his announcement to the nation.

It was six years to the day since he had stood before a cheering Republican National Convention in Miami Beach to accept the party's 1968 presidential nomination.

Now he still had more bases to touch, more calls to make. Shortly after midnight my home telephone rang, and, for the last time, the White House operator told me the President was calling. He thanked me for my help, and said that after he got to San Clemente he was going to need a few days' quiet seclusion to decompress, but he hoped I could come out there in about a week or so to visit, and to talk with him about the future. I said of course I would. And then, as he did to other friends and staff that evening, he said, almost plaintively, "I just hope I haven't let you down." No, I said, he had not; I was still proud to have been associated with him and to have been a part of his administration.

At 11:02, after the speech, and after the reporters had filed their initial stories, Ron Ziegler gave his last briefing to the White House press. He filled in a few details for them of the past day's activities, and told them about the next day's schedule. At 9:30 the President, together with Mrs. Nixon, Tricia and Ed, and Julie and David, would say farewell to the cabinet and staff in the East Room. Then, at about 10:00, the Nixons would leave from the South grounds by helicopter for Andrews Air Force Base, and fly from there to their home in San Clemente. The President's letter of resignation was to be delivered to the secretary of state at noon. Jerry Warren, Ziegler said, would be available to answer their questions on Friday. Then he added that he would like to take a minute himself to say good-by:

"I hope, over the next few weeks, to have a chance to see each of you personally, but this is the last time we will be meeting in these circumstances. We have met, of course, in this setting many times, here and around the world. I have been proud to be President Nixon's press secretary over the past five and a half years. I have tried to be professional, as all of you are professional, and I hope I have never underestimated the difficulty of your jobs or the energy and intelligence you bring to them.

"We have been through many difficult times together, and we have been through many historic times together. I know that I will remember the good ones, and I hope you will, too. I would just like to conclude by saying that whatever our differences have been, I believe that there are no simple answers to the complex questions that this period poses, but above all, I think I take away from this job a deep sense of respect for the diversity and strength of our country's freedom of expression and for our free press. . . . Thank you very much."

At 9:15 Friday morning I went to the East Room, where the President was scheduled to say farewell to the cabinet and staff at 9:30. Looking to my right as I entered, I was surprised to see the banks of television cameras. I had thought this was going to be a private gathering, and that the announcement speech the night before was his last to the nation. The room was already largely filled. I was quickly ushered down to the front row, to a seat alongside Jim St. Clair. At 9:30 the strong voice of Marine Lieutenant Colonel Jack Brennan—one of the President's military aides—boomed out, for the last time, the introduction that had echoed from those walls so often before: "Ladies and gentlemen, the President of the United States and Mrs. Nixon!" The words unleashed a thunder of applause, the guests all rising to their feet as the Nixons, the Coxes, the Eisenhowers moved to their assigned places on the raised platform set up on the room's east side. As the President moved to the lectern, the applause intensified, continuing, a spontaneous, heartfelt outpouring of emotion. Catching my eye, he smiled and nodded a greeting, as he did with a few others that he picked out of the crowd. The applause went on; many wept, and others choked back the tears. Finally he quieted the room, we resumed our seats, and he began his farewell—rambling, informal, struggling visibly to control his own emotions, having at times to pause before he could go on.

He spoke of having met, moments earlier, with the members of the household staff, and he compared the White House with other great houses of the world. The White House, he said, is not the biggest or the finest. "But this is the best house. It is the best house because it has something far more important than numbers of people who serve, far more important than numbers of rooms or how big it is, far more important than numbers of magnificent pieces of art. This house has a great heart, and that heart comes from those who serve."

Looking out at those gathered in front of him, he said he was proud of his cabinet, proud of his subcabinet, proud of his White House staff. And he said he was proud that no one in his administration had ever profited at public expense. "Mistakes, yes. But for personal gain, never. You did what you believed in. Sometimes right, sometimes wrong." He spoke of "the sacrifices that all of you have made to serve in government," but said that "you are getting something in government. . . . It is a cause bigger than yourself. It is the cause of making this the greatest nation in the world, the leader of the world, because without our leadership the world will know nothing but war, possibly starvation, or worse, in the years ahead. With our leadership it will know peace, it will know plenty."

And then, suddenly traveling back through time, he spoke about his father—"my old man. I think that they would have called him sort of a little man, common man. He didn't consider himself that way." And, his voice choking, about his mother: "Nobody will ever write a book probably, about my mother. Well, I guess all of you would say this about your mother—my mother was a saint. And I think of her, two boys dying of tuberculosis, nursing four others in order that she could take care of my older brother for three years in Arizona, and seeing each of them die, and when they died, it was like one of her own. Yes, she will have no books written about her. But she was a saint."

He talked on about defeat, loss, death, and the need not to surrender to them. Putting on his reading glasses for the first time ever in public, he read a passage from a book that Ed Cox handed to him, a paragraph from the diary of the young Theodore Roosevelt, describing his first wife's death—"And when my heart's dearest died, the light went from my life forever." But, he said, Roosevelt "went on. And he not only became President but, as an ex-President, he served his country always in the arena, tempestuous, strong, sometimes wrong, sometimes right, but he was a man. And as I leave, let me say, this is an example I think all of us should remember. . . . We think that when someone dear to us dies, we think that when we lose an election, we think that when we suffer a defeat, that all is ended. We think, as T.R. said, that the light had left his life forever. Not true. It is only a beginning, always. The young must know it; the old must know it. It must always sustain us because the greatness comes not when things go always good for you, but the greatness comes when you are really tested, when you take some knocks, some disappointments, when sadness comes, because only if you have been in the deepest valley can you ever know how magnificent it is to be on the highest mountain."

He added a parting bit of advice, almost as if the light side of Richard Nixon were lecturing the darker side:

"Always give your best, never get discouraged, never be petty; always remember others may hate you, but those who hate you don't win unless you hate them, and then you destroy yourself."

He concluded, finally, and applause once again swelled through the room, the warmth this time mixed with relief that he had made it through to the end. There were times when he seemed on the verge of breaking down. But each time he pulled himself back from the brink, recovering his voice, and pressed on.

At 11:35, as Nixon flew westward in *The Spirit of '76*, his letter of resignation was delivered to Secretary of State Henry Kissinger, in Kissinger's White House office. At noon, in the East Room, Gerald Ford was sworn in as President by Chief Justice Warren Burger. "Our long national nightmare is over," the new President said. But he added: "In the beginning, I asked you to pray for me. Before closing, I ask again your prayers, for Richard Nixon and for his family. May our former President, who brought peace to millions, find it for himself."

I spent the weekend at home, numbed. Back at the White House on Monday, I dropped in to visit with Rose Mary Woods. Rose had stayed behind to sort out some of the unfinished details, and to take care of the former President's papers and memorabilia. She was in his EOB office. We embraced. There was so much to say, and yet so little that needed to be said. The office was the same. The large desk, that he so seldom used. Against the opposite wall, the red-and-white sofa, with photos beside it of Tricia and Julie. At one end, the large hinged racks of souvenir photos. His collection of gavels. The mementos from his vice-presidential days. The oval mahogany table with its four armchairs, at which I had sat so often as we talked and worked. And, in the corner, the golden-yellow lounge chair with its matching ottoman, in which he did most of his work. On the low square table beside it his paraphernalia were still spread out. A desk-top dictating machine with a round ashtray perched on top of it, a single pipe propped in its pipe rack. An open paper package of Amphora pipe tobacco. A yellow package of Dill pipe cleaners. A single pipe cleaner lying loose. A telephone. Two yellow pencils, his reading glasses, his portable dictating machine. Not neatly arranged, but scattered in working disarray, just as he had left them Thursday afternoon. Just as if "our long national nightmare" had been only a bad dream. Just as if, stepping out of the office that Thursday, only his day's work had been interrupted. Just as if all that Richard Nixon had begun in the world could still be completed.

XVIII

REFLECTIONS

March 10, 1977: At three buildings here in Washington today, members of the Hanafi Muslim sect are holding more than a hundred people hostage at gunpoint, as they have been for the past twenty-four hours. The leader of the gunmen, with the largest number of hostages, is barricaded in the national headquarters of B'nai B'rith, about a half block from my office. The streets in the area are sealed off by police. In our building, we have to come and go by way of an alley leading to the back door. (The other two buildings seized are the District Building—Washington's city hall—and the Islamic Center, in the Embassy Row section of Massachusetts Avenue.) So far, one person has been killed and about eleven injured. The terrorists have demanded that distribution of a movie they object to—*Mohammad, Messenger of God*—be halted (which the distributor has agreed to), and that eight members of the rival Black Muslims now in prison for murder—three for killing Malcolm X, five for the murder of seven people four years ago at the Hanafi headquarters—be delivered into the terrorists' hands, presumably for some form of summary execution. ("We are committed to retribution; our law allows that," the leader of the gunmen said in a telephone interview today. "There is no justice without the sword.") They have also demanded that boxer Muhammad Ali and Wallace Muhammad, head of the rival Black Muslim sect, be delivered to them, for purposes unspecified.

The terrorists have threatened to cut off the heads of hostages and toss the heads out the window. NBC has a news team posted on the top floor of our building, with its cameras trained on B'nai B'rith's windows. The view of B'nai B'rith headquarters is excellent from here. It should provide dramatic film footage.

Sitting here trying to sort through the meaning of the Nixon years, the passing drama so close at hand both distracts and concentrates the mind. The temptation is strong to draw parallels and to search for parables. The temptation needs to be resisted. But not completely.

Today's events are a sharp reminder that we live in an imperfect world; that mindless, irrational violence is a fact of life authorities have to deal with; that remedies have sometimes to be improvised; that simple moralisms are not enough to keep the peace; that the penalties for misjudgment often are paid in the coin of human life. Yesterday morning President Carter promised a terrorist in Ohio that if he released his one hostage, he, the President, would talk with the terrorist, as the terrorist had demanded. At a news conference the President acknowledged that this might set a dangerous precedent. Of course it did. There seems to have been no direct connection between that Carter concession and the Washington incidents a few hours later, but the indirect association must be giving Carter and his aides the willies. It should.

The U.S. government has to deal with other governments that frequently show about the same degree of respect for American standards of proper conduct as do those terrorists down the street. We cannot afford, morally, to let ourselves descend to their level. But neither can we afford to be paralyzed by propriety or immobilized by idealism. I want a president who, in the crunch, will bend the rules if necessary. This is one of the things we elect presidents for: to exercise hard judgment in those situations that were not foreseen when the rules were written—or that were foreseen, with the unstated expectation that the rules would be sacrificed before the nation's vital interests were sacrificed. In the late sixties and early seventies, when antiwar fever coincided with the cresting of a decade of simplistic, anti-intellectual romanticism, the fashionable wisdom was capsuled in the flower children's chant: "Make love, not war." The problem with this, when dealing with actual or potential aggressors, is that the man with a bayonet in his hand making war is going to skewer the one with the flower in his hand making love.

If the terrorists with their hostages remind us of the world's dangers, the coverage of the story also reminds us of the way a sort of Gresham's law operates in the news business. At President Carter's press conference, he also put forth new suggestions for a compromise between Israel and the Arab states in the Middle East; for compromises with the Soviet Union on arms control; for phased withdrawal of U.S. troops from South Korea; and for new initiatives here at home, including a $1.5 billion youth-employment program. Some of his comments on these and other matters were highly provocative, controversial, perhaps reckless—but clearly important. Brooding on the play of the news, James Reston writes:

It is hard to remember any time since the last World War when an American President made so much news in a press conference or anywhere else, proposed so many programs on the home front, suggested so many compromises and innovations abroad, some of them almost offhand and maybe premature or unwise, and yet received so little attention in the newspapers or on radio or television.

The violence in the streets by the Hanafi Muslims drowned him out. With all these serious Presidential suggestions, he didn't even get on the front page of *The Washington Post*, except in a footnote. So far as I can discover few newspapers in the United States besides *The New York Times* printed the text of this remarkable news conference. . . .

Neither the President nor the press has figured out this problem of what is news in the modern world of terrorists, propaganda and ambiguous politics. The men with the guns have dominated the news here this week. The media have followed them on the principle that what is new is news, yet what President Carter said, right or wrong, is clearly more important and more enduring; but nobody could hear him for the noise and the headlines about the terrorists.

For a fleeting moment in history, it was Watergate all over again: the one dramatic story which, because of its drama, eclipsed all else.

Even now, two presidents later, truths are difficult to sort out, and meanings more so. Have I been guilty of a sort of willful self-delusion, refusing to see what I preferred not to see—the reverse of the willful self-delusion of the critics, who saw only what they wanted to see? Perhaps. But the mythmakers have been so busy reinforcing their own creations that, beyond the range of our own direct experience, it becomes impossible to distinguish truth from fiction with anything approaching absolute certainty. The effort is made more difficult by the current fashion of blurring the lines between truth and fiction. On television, dramatizations are presented routinely as "documentaries." In literature, books which a few years ago would have been billed as historical novels are offered now as nonfiction. As part of its livelier "new look," *The New York Times Book Review* changes the headlines on its best-seller list from "fiction" and "general" to "fiction" and "nonfiction." It should change them back again.

The publishing phenomenon of the moment, Alex Haley's *Roots*, has had its luster dimmed by a rising controversy over how much of it is history, how much invention; serious scholars rush to insist that the question is immaterial, because whether factual or not it represents a "symbolic" truth. Perhaps the *Times*' headings should be fiction, nonfiction, and symbolic truth. The publishing phenomenon of 1976, Woodward and Bernstein's *The Final Days*, is breathlessly hailed as true by those who want to believe it true. Its authors invent thoughts which they place in people's heads, words which they place in people's mouths; they boast of having interviewed 394 people, and maintain that every word of their book is true because they include nothing unless confirmed by as least two "sources." What this means is that if two people have heard the same rumor, they weave a story around it, wrap it in manufactured detail and sprinkle it with quotation marks, and present the story as fact. "Journafiction," Bill Safire aptly called it. "Crap," *The New Republic*'s John Osborne called it. "Trash," Richard Nixon called it. Who were the 394? The authors don't tell us. Rather, they artfully contrive to convey the impression that their sources were the principals whose actions, words, and thoughts they purport to describe, rather than admitting that it was gossip from second- or third-hand sources, embellished by the authors. David Eisenhower, doing a little sleuthing of his own, finally identified a college friend as the "source" on whose account the authors based long passages that appeared in the book to have come from David himself. Henry Kissinger appears, through the authors' contrivance, to have been the source of extensive parts of the book, including some of the most sensational. Kissinger spent just thirty minutes with the authors, spoke very discreetly, had two of his aides present, and recorded the conversation. And then, ingeniously, they devise the perfect cover for themselves: They preface the book with a note saying that many of the principals will deny having talked to them, or will deny their account, but the reader should dismiss the denials. Parts of the book are true, parts are not; but the artful interweaving of fact and fiction does a disservice not only to the record but also to the concept of truth itself.

As we look back over the past, sensations crowd the mind, making memory indistinct. Montages of headlines, pictures, unsourced stories, speculation, all run together until we forget where we "learned" those "facts" that we "know." As a newspaper editor, I used to make a firm rule of not letting myself read the late Drew

Pearson's column, because I was afraid I might remember something I read there and forget where it was I had read it—and therefore think it was true. It becomes harder now to enforce such disciplines. The old-fashioned respect for literal truth has been subsumed by the new fashion of reaching for "intrinsic" or "symbolic" truth.

Reading through the flood of postresignation accounts, by journalists and polemicists, of what supposedly happened in the Nixon administration, I kept fuming at their methodology: it was a sham; it was dishonest—not only pretending to an authority they did not have, but in many cases self-evidently written from a pile of news clips and assuming the truth of anything that had appeared in print, as long as it fit the author's particular thesis, then presenting these "facts" not as what a third-hand source claimed or imagined had happened, but as the "real story" of what *did* happen.

I brooded over the transparent dishonesty of all this, and gnashed my teeth a bit at the practitioners of it—until one evening I suddenly realized that I had strayed rather far from my old journalistic moorings. I had forgotten: *This is the way it is done.* The author who cites *The New York Times* as his source, to certificate the truth of what he writes, is following an established journalistic tradition. One of my early jobs was at *Life*, where I was quickly indoctrinated into both the passion at Time, Inc., for factual accuracy and the elaborate methods by which this "accuracy" was assured. Every *Time* or *Life* story was gone over by one of a vast team of researchers. The researcher, not the writer, was held responsible for its accuracy, the better to insure the researcher's diligence and the better to keep the writer from straying. The researcher was required to place a dot over every word, signifying that that word, as used in that story, was accurate, that the fact it represented had been checked and found true. There were black dots and red dots, with the red dots used for numbers and other such facts on which an exceptional degree of precision was required; and the list of authorities that could justify a red dot—"red-check sources," we called them—was extremely limited. The *Encyclopaedia Britannica* was a red-check source. *The New York Times* was a red-check source. In other words, if a "fact" had been reported in the *Times,* then, for the purposes of maintaining this highest of all standards of "accuracy," it could be assumed to be true!

Jolted, suddenly, by this recollection, I could see how a journalist immersed in a pile of old newspaper clippings, especially if they were old *Times* clippings, could construct an account of events he had not witnessed, offer it as the "real story," and still have a clear conscience. As a journalist, he is trained to rely on the "morgue"—on the newspaper library, with its thousands of folders of neatly clipped articles by other journalists. As a practitioner of the dramatic art of daily newswriting, he is trained to reach for the detail that will heighten the drama—and to justify his inclusion of that detail by the fact that it has been printed before. If it turns out not to be true, well—the error is the other fellow's; as long as he can produce the clip, he has someone else to blame. That is the way the art is practiced; and that is the way what one journalist, in the heat of passion and under pressure of deadlines, imagines, becomes, through repetition, set into the cement of "history."

Trying to sort out the meaning of the Nixon years, most have searched for patterns of consistency. The truth probably lies more nearly in the welter of inconsistencies. Life is like that. Human nature is like that. We react to the pressures of the moment, turning first one way and then another. We respond now in a right-brain spasm, now with left-brain analysis. We cherish our binding myths, yet we demand the harsh light of reality—and then we bitterly resent it when that same light exposes the myths as only illusion. Our reactions reflect our moods—changeable, quixotic, sometimes frivolous. One man's truth is another's falsehood—though often these represent simply differing truths, because they are the same truth differently perceived. Ask me how I feel about the events of the Nixon years, and you may get a quite different answer Wednesday morning than you will Thursday afternoon. One way the truth gets so distorted in the first place is by trying to force it into simple, clear, consistent molds.

What happened, and why, in Watergate? I don't know. I doubt that anyone really fully knows. I strongly suspect that there is a lot more to the "why" of Watergate itself than has yet come out, or than Nixon and his people even remotely imagined at the time. The conventional wisdom today is that if only, when the break-in occurred, Nixon had brought down his fist and thrown the villains to the wolves, an approving public would have forgiven and the incident would soon have been forgotten. I doubt it. Watergate was the one issue the Democrats had in 1972, and they would have exploited to the hilt any acknowledgment of higher-level responsibility. The media would have let Kennedy get away with that, but not Nixon. Still, in retrospect, the damage could hardly have been more, and would almost certainly have been less.

Yet could Nixon have done so? My own guess is that, in human terms, he simply could not. We know from the fateful June 23 conversation between him and Haldeman that he thought John Mitchell was probably involved:

P: Well what the hell, did Mitchell know about this?

H: I think so. I don't think he knew the details, but I think he knew.

P: He didn't know how it was going to be handled though—with Dahlberg and the Texans and so forth? Well who was the asshole that did? Is it Liddy? Is that the fellow? He must be a little nuts.

H: He is.

P: I mean he just isn't well screwed on is he? Is that the problem?

H: No, but he was under pressure, apparently, to get more information, and as he got more pressure, he pushed the people harder to move harder—

P: Pressure from Mitchell?

H: Apparently.

P: Oh, Mitchell. Mitchell was at the point (unintelligible).

H: Yeah.

P: All right, fine, I understand it all. We won't second-guess Mitchell and the rest. Thank God it wasn't Colson.

So—was he going to blow the whistle, and send John Mitchell, his friend, confidant, law partner, campaign manager, attorney general, to prison at age fifty-nine? For being somehow involved in bugging the Democratic National Committee Headquarters, when Nixon himself was convinced that he had been bugged by Johnson in 1968? When he had felt it necessary to have his own campaign headquarters in 1968 swept for bugs every week? No—or at least, this is my guess—he damn well was not. He was going to do what FDR probably would have done, or Johnson or Kennedy or Harry Truman. He was going to do what he could to make the whole mess go away—to contain it, limit the political damage, to keep it from reaching Mitchell if Mitchell were involved. Haldeman told him there was a way—Dean had studied it, and Dean and Mitchell recommended it—simply have the CIA tell the FBI that the investigation could lead into CIA activities, in Mexico and elsewhere. Cut the connection that tied it into the higher echelons of the re-election committee. Let it be treated as an ordinary, low-level criminal offense. Make it go away. Get on with the election. Keep Mitchell out of jail. After all, no one had been hurt. It was just politics, politics the way it had been played against Nixon ever since he had been in public life. Make it go away.

Send Mitchell to jail? For *that*? When he had a way to head it off? Unthinkable. And so, same conversation, on to the next subject.

Writing a humorous P.S. on a letter to Emil Mosbacher, who was resigning as chief of protocol, and explaining the joke to Haldeman. Trouble with Wilbur Mills. Democratic politicking over the debt-ceiling bill. Britain's floating of the pound. Arrangements to have pictures taken with Republican congressional candidates—and also with friendly Democrats. A forty-five-second statement on busing that he was going to read that afternoon for the television cameras. Whether Mrs. Nixon and the girls should stay in Key Biscayne during the Republican convention or at a hotel in Miami Beach—if they had to travel by helicopter, they complained, their hairdos would be spoiled. What kinds of campaign events the girls should do. Plans for a reception for Secret Service agents. The 1960 campaign—Nixon had been rereading *Six Crises*. A possible meeting with all-time baseball greats. An hour and thirty-five minutes altogether, with perhaps six minutes devoted to Watergate, the CIA, and the FBI. Six minutes, casual, offhand, given about the same degree of attention as the effect of helicopter blades on Mrs. Nixon's hair. Six minutes that changed the world.

The question of "Why Watergate?" remains one of the most intriguing mysteries of all, and it keeps getting more so. In his March 21 "cancer on the Presidency" conversation with Nixon, Dean explained that it had all started "with an instruction to me from Bob Haldeman to see if we couldn't set up a perfectly legitimate campaign intelligence operation over the re-election committee." Dean selected G. Gordon Liddy, a former FBI agent then working in connection with the White House plumbers, to head the operation, and Liddy transferred to the re-election committee, serving also as counsel to the finance committee. Together with his partner E. Howard Hunt, Liddy came up with the series of schemes that he pressed on a reluctant John Mitchell. After being rebuffed twice by Mitchell on more bizarre, larger-scale proposals, Liddy finally came up with a third, scaled-down version, which Jeb Magruder presented to Mitchell in Key Biscayne, together with a large number of other campaign matters. Magruder claims Mitchell approved this third version. Mitchell claims he did not. My own guess all along has been that he probably did, either after a few drinks too many (he was on vacation in Key Biscayne) or else as a sort of trade-off, figuring that if he agreed to this he could better hold back the dirty-tricks boys on other things. Win a few, lose a few.

Bearing in mind that the bugging and burglary were apparently done without high-level White House knowledge (even Dean said that he thought it had been turned off), and that Mitchell, if he approved the operation at all, did so with obvious reluctance, the puzzle of "why" becomes more intriguing as we look at the cast of characters, as we consider who else might have had an interest in Larry O'Brien's office, and as we trace through the pattern of other Liddy-Hunt endeavors.

Since few other explanations seem to make much sense, let us sit back for a moment and suppose—hypothesize—theorize. Let us suppose that Howard Hunt fancied himself a sort of intelligence entrepreneur, a maestro of clandestine activities, a master cloak-and-dagger operative with a keen eye for targets of opportunity, and particularly for those that offered multiple opportunities— missions he could undertake for profit, for pleasure, or from his own peculiar sense of public service, to be rewarded at one and the same time by the gratitude of his former colleagues at the CIA, by pay from the bulging vaults of the Howard Hughes organization, and by honor and attention from the President of the United States himself and his innermost advisers.

Consider: The break-in at the office of Ellsberg's psychiatrist, the aborted proposal for a break-in at the office of *Las Vegas Sun* publisher Hank Greenspun, and the Watergate break-in itself—all were pressed on the White House or the re-election committee by Howard Hunt and Gordon Liddy. In each case, the CIA and/or the Hughes organization had greater reason to be interested than did the White House or the re-election committee. Each one now appears to have been conceived and promoted by Liddy and Hunt while Hunt was working for Mullen & Co., a Washington public-relations firm which served as a CIA front, which was regularly visited by a CIA case officer, and which had the Hughes organization as its principal client.

The Hughes-CIA-Mullen & Co. links to Watergate have been probed extensively, but never completely or conclusively. During the Ervin committee hearings, committee Vice-Chairman Howard Baker got interested in the CIA angle. Under his direction, three members of the minority staff, headed by Minority Counsel Fred D. Thompson, pried open some of the CIA doors and pried loose some of the CIA's Watergate secrets. By the time the doors clanged shut again, their probe had raised more questions than it answered —and some of those it raised were even more tantalizing than those it answered. Some of what it uncovered is spelled out in Baker's separate addendum to the Watergate committee's final report, and also in Thompson's subsequent book.[1] Other possible pieces of the puzzle emerged later from the Senate Intelligence Committee's investigation, and can be found in its reports. For those searching for the truth behind Watergate, all of these are worth study. Whatever the reasons, the CIA did scramble frantically to cover up. Both in the days immediately following the break-in itself and during the later investigation, its officials consistently pretended to know less that subsequent evidence showed that they knew. They concealed pertinent information from the FBI. They purged files and destroyed evidence. Whatever they were hiding, they were hiding something.

In looking for possible answers to the question of "Why Watergate?" one place to begin is with the "Maheu papers." In late 1970 Howard Hughes fired his once-trusted aide Robert Maheu as boss of the Hughes empire in Nevada. The split was both spectacular and bitter, with multimillion-dollar suits and countersuits. When he was fired, Maheu carted off armloads of supersensitive documents from the Hughes files. Hughes's own passion for secrecy verged into paranoia. And the CIA had at least as much reason as Hughes to wonder what was in those papers, and what Maheu might do with them. The Hughes organization was the CIA's largest contractor—the $350 million *Glomar Explorer* project to raise a sunken Soviet nuclear submarine, which became known in 1975, was only one of many. So to both Hughes and the CIA, the Maheu papers must have seemed as potentially troublesome a security hemorrhage as the Pentagon Papers.

Beyond that, there was Maheu himself. One of the most explosive secrets in the Agency's vaults was its partnership with the Mafia in a protracted effort to assassinate Fidel Castro, an effort which may well have backfired and resulted, instead, in Kennedy's assassination in Dallas. The CIA's contact with its mob partners was Robert Maheu, who was then on a CIA retainer and was used frequently by the CIA during that period for especially sensitive clandestine operations—ones in which, as the Agency's support chief later told the Senate Intelligence Committee, Agency officials "didn't want to have an Agency person or a government person get caught." Maheu recruited mobster John Rosselli for the job, and Rosselli in turn brought Mafia chieftains Sam Giancana and Santos Trafficante into the plot. Maheu then spent the next several months in Miami

1. *At That Point in Time: The Inside Story of the Senate Watergate Committee* (New York, 1975).

with the Mafiosi, shepherding the assassination plots at every step of the way. Later, when the Senate Intelligence Committee investigated the assassination plots, Giancana was murdered just before he was scheduled to testify. Rosselli was murdered just after he testified.

This might seem far removed from Watergate—except that until the Hughes-Maheu split, Larry O'Brien doubled as Democratic national chairman and as Hughes's $15,000-a-month Washington "public-relations" representative, with the money funneled to O'Brien through an intermediary. In the world of Hughes and the CIA, "public relations" can be an innocuous cover for a lot of very unpublic activity, including dealings between the Agency and its contractors. But O'Brien had been hired by Maheu and was a Maheu ally, and when the Hughes-Maheu war broke out the Hughes people shifted their business elsewhere: to Robert Bennett, son of Utah's Senator Wallace Bennett, who brought the account to Mullen & Co. and became the company's president. Whoever was concerned about the Maheu papers would also have been likely, in the wake of the Hughes-Maheu split, to have been concerned about O'Brien.

So: That was the background against which Liddy and Hunt, in the Mullen offices, while Hunt was on the Mullen payroll, planned the break-in at O'Brien's office and peddled it to the re-election committee. What were they after, and for whom? An interesting question.

It becomes more interesting in light of the Greenspun caper. When Hughes established himself in Nevada, Greenspun lavished praise on him editorially, sold him a television station, and negotiated a substantial loan from him. But when the falling-out between Hughes and Maheu came, Greenspun sided with Maheu, attacked Hughes editorially, and held large quantities of the Maheu papers for Maheu in his office safe. Liddy and Hunt also tried unsuccessfully to promote White House sanction for a break-in at Greenspun's office. With Bennett serving as a middleman, they discussed the project with Hughes officials and, together with the Hughes people, began drawing up plans for carrying it out. (Hunt claims the idea came from Bennett; Bennett claims the idea came from Hunt.) The project was finally dropped. Later a break-in at Greenspun's office was actually attempted—but this was two months after the Watergate team were caught. Obviously, someone was still interested—someone else.

Throughout the time Liddy and Hunt worked for the White House and the re-election committee, Bennett seemed to have been deeply involved in their activities. Hunt himself arranged while he was still at the CIA to join the Mullen firm. The firm's founder, Robert Mullen, claims that CIA Director Richard Helms was personally involved in Hunt's placement with the firm; Helms denies it. In any case, when he officially retired from the CIA, Hunt moved directly to the Mullen firm, keeping his covert clearance. Hunt continued reporting to the CIA, even from his White House office—recently declassified materials show that while at the White House he was passing materials to Helms through a secret channel, in envelopes marked "For Helms's Eyes Only." As for Bennett, he coordinated with Hunt the hiring of a young political spy, who worked with Liddy to set up dummy committees as a conduit for Hughes campaign contributions. He coordinated the release of a statement, from Denver, by ITT lobbyist Dita Beard, after contacting Beard's lawyers at the suggestion of a Hughes official. (It was on a trip to meet with Beard that Hunt used his famous red wig, obtained from the CIA.) At one point, when Hughes officials were considering a possible bugging operation directed at author Clifford Irving, author of a spurious Hughes "autobiography," they approached Bennett, who in turn made inquiries of Howard Hunt, who got an estimate from James McCord. According to Hunt—who provided this account to Senate investigators—Bennett relayed the estimate back to the Hughes people, who decided against it on grounds that it was too costly. This seems an unlikely reason for them to have turned it down, but the Hughes-to-Bennett-to-Hunt-to-McCord sequence is, in the wake of Watergate, interesting, to say the least.

Even the wiretap supposedly placed by mistake on the wrong telephone in the Hunt team's first Watergate entry, a month before the one in which they were caught, ties curiously back to Hunt himself and the Mullen firm. The "wrong" phone that was tapped was that of R. Spencer Oliver, Jr.—an odd mistake in the first place, since his desk was at the opposite end of the office suite from O'Brien's. But Oliver's father, R. Spencer Oliver, Sr., was a close friend of the Mullen firm's founder, Robert Mullen, and was used by the Mullen company as Washington lobbyist for the Hughes organization. One of the transcripts of intercepted calls typed by Liddy's secretary, Sally Harmony, was of a conversation between the Olivers—Sr. and Jr. Moreover, Hunt knew Oliver Jr. and loathed him, and bitterly resented what he considered efforts to foist young Oliver off on him as a partner when Hunt had earlier tried to buy the Mullen firm. Young Oliver, who arranged Soviet-American exchange programs, had extensive Soviet contacts, and one reason Hunt loathed him was that Hunt considered him too liberal and distrusted his contacts with the Soviets. One theory held by some investigators is that Hunt hoped to gather information on Oliver for counterintelligence purposes. Whatever the reason—whether that, or spite, or the Hughes connection—it hardly seems to have been accidental. One of the reasons Liddy and Hunt gave the re-election committee for needing a second entry on that fateful June 17 was that one of the original taps had been placed on the wrong phone—Oliver's. Yet when they went in on the seventeenth, they did not remove the tap on Oliver's phone. Interesting.

Shortly after the Watergate break-in Bennett was extensively debriefed by his CIA case officer. The case officer reported on the debriefing in a memo. Because of its sensitivity, the memo was hand-delivered to Helms. Bennett reported detailed knowledge of the Watergate events, and told of his plans for covering up the CIA-Mullen & Co. connection. He said that he had established a "back-door entry" to Edward Bennett Williams, attorney for the Democratic National Committee, in order to "kill off" revelations of the CIA-Mullen & Co. relationship in the course of the DNC's civil suit against the re-election committee. Senate investigators learned that he did in fact supply information to Williams—and that he told Williams more than he had previously told the grand jury. Bennett also served as liaison between Hunt and Liddy after the break-in. Later, as the Ervin committee began investigating, Bennett reported to the CIA that he felt he could handle the committee if the Agency could handle Hunt, and claimed that he was feeding stories to the press aimed at implicating Colson in Hunt's activities and protecting the Agency. In particular, he said he was feeding stories to a "suitably grateful" Bob Woodward of *The Washington Post*, and that Woodward in turn was protecting Bennett and Mullen & Co.

At the time of Watergate, and at the time of the unraveling of the cover-up, I assumed that it was what it appeared to be: a re-election committee venture, undertaken for no clear reason and botched in an amateurish way. Because of a welter of suspicious circumstances surrounding the burglars' capture, many of us quickly came to suspect that a double agent was involved, and that in the execution of the venture we were being deliberately set up, somehow, for political embarrassment. (Not least of the suspicious circumstances was that the alarm went out when a security guard found the door taped, removed the tape, and then found it taped again. The tape was supposed to have been removed—the doors opened from the inside, so there was no need for it once they were in the offices. Instead of being removed, it was left on and then, when the guard removed it, McCord replaced it—not vertically, so is would be hidden, but horizontally; it stood out like a flag.) But as for the motive for the break-in itself, that remained a puzzle. We figured someone at the re-election committee must have had his reasons, even though it was hard to imagine what reasons would have been sufficient to send in what appeared to be a whole squad of Keystone Kops.

Now, however, it seems more likely to me that Hunt was, as I hypothesized above, a sort of packager and promoter of clandestine operations—operating out of the Mullen offices, reuniting his team from the glory days of the Bay of Pigs, seeking sponsorship by the White House and the committee to give his ventures legitimacy, glamor, funding, and cover.

Though a career CIA operative, Hunt also pursued a parallel career as a novelist, turning out a rapid-fire succession of spy stories under a series of pseudonyms. In one of these, the protagonist was a "master spy" who served several clients at once, without letting any of them know that he was also serving the others. I suspect that something of the sort was operating in this case —and that what Hunt hoped to find was something that would make him a hero again in the corridors of the CIA, as he had been once, so long ago, while at the same time making him the new golden boy of the billionaire recluse who had so much potential use for his special skills, and so much money to lavish on them. And, by playing the game right, he could also emerge as the sort of bold soldier whom he imagined that the tough, conniving, driven man in the Oval Office—after all, Colson was his friend, Colson was his contact, Colson was the one through whose eyes he saw the President—would want at his side in a crisis, would rely on when the chips were down.

Just a theory, a speculation.

The break-in at Dr. Lewis Fielding's office, I had assumed, as the President did, was what it appeared to be. But if my theory is correct, that also may have been a package production. That, too, seems now to have originated with Liddy and Hunt. Nixon was in a ferocious mood over the Pentagon Papers leak. It was serious— deadly serious. It was vital to know more about Daniel Ellsberg, what his associations were (there were rumors that he had delivered a copy to the Soviet embassy before giving them to *The New York Times*)—and, with Ellsberg becoming an instant folk hero, there were dangers, in this Xerox age, that others with dreams of glory would follow his example and seek the same route to celebrity.

To Bud Krogh, chief of the leak-plugging White House plumbers, Nixon stressed vehemently the vital importance of the Ellsberg case. The terms in which he did so apparently led Krogh to believe he had authority to do whatever was necessary to find out whatever he could about Ellsberg. Krogh and his partner, David Young, went to Liddy and Hunt. They came up, first, with the idea of having the CIA prepare a psychological profile on Ellsberg—which was done—and later with the idea of breaking into Ellsberg's psychiatrist's office to copy his records on Ellsberg.

Perhaps there was no more to it than that. Or perhaps there was. For the CIA also had its own, very special reasons for being intensely interested in what Ellsberg might have told his psychiatrist, even beyond its automatic concern with a security breach of Pentagon Papers proportion. Ellsberg, it turns out, had a close personal friendship with a woman who might have had access to some of the most sensitive of the Agency's secrets, including even those involved in its assassination attempts against Castro. This was precisely the sort of thing that would have sent senior officials of the Agency into spasms of anxiety when Ellsberg surfaced as the source of the Pentagon Papers. What might she have told him, and what might he do with it? This was unknown to plumbers chiefs Bud Krogh and David Young, whom Liddy and Hunt pressed for approval of the Fielding break-in. But it could well have become known to Liddy and Hunt, who were in a position to learn about it. It was the sort of thing a patient might discuss with his psychiatrist. And any information obtainable indicating what Ellsberg might have told his psychiatrist about this would be something senior officials at the Agency would be extremely grateful to get. If Hunt delivered such a prize, he would indeed be a hero.

What better way to earn the gratitude of his old comrades-in-arms than to deliver into their hands the answers to what must be their frantic questions? So: persuade the White House, also beside itself with anxiety over Ellsberg, that the psychiatrist's records might be vital to its own purposes. Get White House authorization for an entry; and then see what there is to find.

My own guess is that Hunt was not put up to these operations by the CIA—at least not institutionally, and probably not even by any of the particular officials to whom they were of special interest. More likely, if this theory is correct, he was operating as an individual entrepreneur, who knew his market—much as the art dealer does who spies a treasure at auction, and buys it, confident that a customer will want it. He knew or suspected where the bodies were buried. He knew how the CIA worked, what sort of things it would want. Through Bennett, he knew what the Hughes organization wanted. When fate gave him an opportunity to pick up something of special interest to the Agency, he helped the opportunity along—badgering Colson to badger Magruder to get Watergate approved, urging Krogh that a Fielding break-in would help find out about Ellsberg and the Soviets.

So far as I know, I have never met Howard Hunt (or Gordon Liddy either, for that matter). The fact that Bill Buckley is a Hunt friend and admirer speaks well of Hunt to me, at least in terms of his motivations. And he could well have constructed these plots-within-plots in the firm belief that he was serving his country. If people in the CIA were concerned about the Maheu papers, concerned about Ellsberg, they had reason to be; and, loyal as he was to the CIA, Hunt could well have seen these operations as the highest form of loyalty. There is no inconsistency in trying to earn money from Hughes while serving the interests of the Agency and the nation; after all, the interests of the Hughes organization and the CIA are so intertwined as to be almost symbiotic. And, purely as a challenge, as an adventure in cloak-and-dagger gamesmanship, what could be more intriguing—in both senses of the word—than operating such a three-way parlay out of the White House itself, and using the cover of the President to do for the Agency what the Agency was barred by law from doing for itself, while leading the President's men to believe that Hunt was daring all for them?

None of this, even if true, excuses the White House or the Committee to Re-Elect the President. The break-ins and the bugging did take place, and, at one level or another, they were approved by our people for what were perceived to be our own reasons. But it does heighten the irony if, as I now suspect, we were being used as cover for a sort of Special Operations, Incorporated, E. Howard Hunt, Proprietor.

And it makes more understandable the bungling and confusion that followed in the wake of Watergate, with each player assuming that one of the others had been the prime mover—and so covering up, but covering up the wrong people for the wrong reasons, and all the time wondering why.

If the mysteries of Watergate are ever to be resolved—and, like so many other puzzles of history, they may never be—it can only be done in a more dispassionate emotional climate than existed in 1973 and 1974. So, too, will any final judgments on Watergate in particular, or on the Nixon presidency in general, have to wait for a more dispassionate time.

One thing that distinguishes presidents from editorialists is that presidents are responsible for the consequences of their choices. They do not have the luxury of reaching conclusions in a vacuum. They have to make decisions, knowing that the costs of error are going to be paid by hundreds, thousands, or even millions of other people. We live in a messy world, which often fails to respect the high-minded abstractions so beloved by the moralists. The messiness of that world is often what determines the consequences of presidential decisions—and therefore those decisions have to take into account that messiness. A decision on Watergate, for example, which might have the effect of interrupting or even reversing progress toward peace in the Middle East could not responsibly be made without at least taking into account that possible cost.

Watergate is probably unique among major political scandals—no one got hurt except the perpetrators. True, it was an offense against our system of law. But a system of law is flawed if it throws out too many babies with the bathwater. This happened in Watergate. In order to pursue the scandals to their furthest reaches, the country was put through a trauma that came close to wrecking its economy and destroying the most hopeful initiatives toward world peace of the past quarter-century. And those doleful consequences stemmed not from the original offense, but from the process by which that offense was pursued through the avenues of law, journalism, and politics. It was not the cover-up that brought them on, but the relentless, obsessive way in which the cover-up was uncovered.

The currently fashionable wisdom, of course, is to insist that purification was the first necessity, and all else had to be secondary. This is not a hierarchy of values that has much support in history. Absolute moral purity has certainly been far more the exception than the rule among governments, and particularly among governments with great responsibilities.

Was the 37th President, Richard Nixon, statesman extraordinaire, who reshaped the world in the pattern of his own architecture of peace? Or was he Tricky Dick, the shifty political con-man? He was both—and it took a Tricky Dick to bring the dreams of the statesman to reality. It took a consummate politician to put together the electoral majorities that gave the statesman his opportunity. It took a devious manipulator to engineer public consent for national policies that often went against the grain of the voters' private interests, and to line up other nations of the world behind policies that their leaders had vowed never to accept. It took a politician with a keen sense of the possible, with a cynical sense of political reality, with the drive and the ambition and the cunning to pull it off.

A presidential candidate has to win, and a president has to govern, in the face of enormously powerful tides that run against what he tries to do. These are not only tides of public resistance to paying the costs of progress but also tides of political and media antagonism for antagonism's sake, of posturing and demagoguery and manipulation. The cynical Nixon of the transcripts sounded like hundreds of other cynical politicians and commentators and reporters, who present a public face to the world and a private face to their closest associates.

Nixon was destroyed because he was caught. And he was caught, finally, in a web spun of intrigues fully as devious as those of which he himself was accused.

The larger questions concern not the fate of Richard Nixon, but respect for those restraints that reason must exercise on passion. They are not questions of whether we are going to have duplicity in government. We always have had, and we always will have. Rather, they concern the survival of the fragile instruments on which democracy depends, against the concerted onslaught of those with a monopoly of the means by which words and ideas and perceptions of truth reach the public. In today's nation, the people have only their votes. The media have the voice. The votes of the people are registered every two years. The voices of the media are heard every day.

As nearly as I can discern it, a brilliant, complex, dedicated, often devious, sometimes duplicitous president was driven from office not for what he did, but for what, in the protected privacy of his own resentment and rage, he said. What he did was well within the bounds of those trespasses against the letter of the law which in past administrations were routinely blinked at, recognizing that history must judge by the total record, not its isolated fragments. What he said was probably not beyond the range of what other presidents, in their angry or despairing moments, have voiced—but the private outbursts of other presidents were not recorded on tape, or, when they were, the tapes were not wrested from their control and placed on public display. And this withdrawal of the electoral mandate was engineered by an alliance of his enemies in the Congress and in the national media, who exploited as never before the concentrated power which, thanks to the miracles of modern technology, now has a range and impact which would have been undreamed of a generation ago.

After Nixon's resignation, the pressures on those of us who had remained loyal became more rather than less intense: pressure to renounce him, to join the chorus of denunciation, or at least to put some visible distance between ourselves and our former President. Sometimes subtly, sometimes not so subtly, we got the message: turning on Nixon is the price of your readmission into polite society.

In my case, these pressures—which I resented, even when they took the form of advice from well-intentioned friends—simply hardened my determination to stand firm on my own beliefs. But it was easy to see them working on others. Cabinet members who had been staunch Nixon loyalists as long as he held power suddenly began "remembering" their disagreements, their disenchantments, their suspicions—on all of which they had been remarkably silent before. Members of Congress who had clutched at the Nixon coattails or begged for an audience that could be recorded on film, competed with one another in their dark reminiscences of the terrible days of the Nixon presidency. Former staff members, trying to hang on to government jobs or to escape the stigma as they re-entered private life, began focusing on the dark side as assiduously as, in better times, they had focused on the brighter side. The system was working: the system of enforced conformity, of coerced acceptance, of rewards and punishments bestowed by the lords of opinion. And as that system worked, history was being systematically rewritten. No longer was truth a constraint. No longer need writers fear that they might be called to account for lies or distortions. There was no one left to call them to account. Any who might try were automatically discredited by the attempt itself. Any defense of a Nixon action was tagged an "apologia." Any attack, however vicious, was hailed as an enlightened contribution to public understanding.

As Nixon himself hovered for days on the brink of death in Long Beach Memorial Hospital, the hospital's switchboard lit up with calls from protesting citizens. "Let him die!" they declared, their own exquisite moral sensibilities presumably having been offended by the tone of his transcripts.

Nixon's resignation put an end to his presidency but not to the issues over which he had been embattled. But now there was a difference. Like the first green shoots of spring after a long, cold winter, familiar ideas began sprouting in unfamiliar quarters.

California's new governor, Edmund G. ("Jerry") Brown, Jr., was greeted on the national scene as the fresh new voice of the coming generation—yet what he was saying sounded remarkably like what Nixon had been saying eight years earlier. In fact, it sounded a good deal more like Nixon than it did like Brown's own father, Edmund G. ("Pat") Brown, Sr., who defeated Nixon for the California governorship in 1962.

Jerry Brown—and other "new breed" Democrats like him, such as Massachusetts' Governor Michael S. Dukakis—warned of limits to what government can do, of the danger of spending too much, of the spiritual erosion that comes from too much governmental interference. His words struck a welcome chorus among millions of Americans, young people particularly, who suddenly found themselves spiritually suffocated by government. And what he said had such a familiar ring:

"The liberalism of the sixties is dead. The fact that there's a problem doesn't mean that more government will make it better. It might make it worse. . . . Inaction may be the highest form of action.

"Government shouldn't be looked at as an elixir, the all-emcompassing final solution to the human condition. That's a very dangerous predilection on the part of a growing number of people. We can do a lot, and there are a lot of things we have to do, such as full employment and cleaning up the environment. All these things are important, but they have to be approached on an incremental basis.

"You know, there's a tendency in government for mayors to look to governors to look to Congress and the President, as though that were a separate sugar daddy that can provide funding that isn't available at home. I've tried to reject that philosophy."

On the other side of the continent, meanwhile, in the only state carried by McGovern, Massachusetts' Dukakis—once celebrated for his orthodox liberalism by Americans for Democratic Action—was stressing the "work ethic," impounding funds and clamping down on state spending. Addressing the Southern Governors' Conference, the new chairman of the House Ways and Means Committee, Oregon's Al Ullman, accused his fellow Democrats of continuing "to raise the New Deal slogans of the 1930s for lack of real solutions for the 1970s." He complained that his party "must begin to aim programs at specific areas we can win with the resources available rather than continuing to wage war on all social ills—bringing victory to none." Wisconsin's liberal Democratic governor Patrick J. Lucey, just as if it were a new idea, declared that "we are beginning to recognize that there are limits to what government can and should do." Maine's Senator Edmund S. Muskie demanded: "Why can't liberals start raising hell about a government so big, so complex, so expensive and so unresponsive that it's dragging down every good program we have worked for?" No less an expert on the old liberalism than Senator Gary Hart of Colorado, manager of George McGovern's 1972 campaign, was complaining by 1975 that "the leadership of the Democratic party still has its head stuck in the New Deal. The party still feels that if there is a problem, the federal government has a responsibility to solve it with a program and money." California's Senator Alan Cranston was another who spied the new idea: "A great many liberals now see the limits of government's ability to resolve problems," he noted. "They are very concerned about the concentration of power in government, which tends to go down to the executive branch. And they are concerned about government spending in ways that threaten the economy and limit the spending choices of individual citizens."

This "new liberalism" was not yet as sophisticated in its approach as the old Nixonism, with its stress on self-regulating systems, on dispersal of authority, on a careful meshing of national goals and local responsibilities. But at least it was a step in that direction.

In terms of foreign policy, the costs of Watergate are—in the most precise sense of the word—incalculable. There is no way of knowing what would have happened if Nixon had had the freedom of maneuver in his second term that he had in his first. Could he have averted the Arab oil embargo, with its devastating and continuing impact on the world's economy? Would he have managed to persuade, cajole, or pressure the Congress into living up to the terms of the Vietnam settlement, and thereby enabled South Vietnam to defend itself? Could he have brought about that peace in the Middle East which, for the first time, seemed so tantalizingly within reach? In the Watergate frenzy, such questions as these were dismissed as irrelevant. They were not irrelevant to the rest of the world. They are not irrelevant to history.

With a curious circular logic, some critics argue that Nixon's initiatives toward the Soviet Union and China have not, since his resignation, brought the results that had been hoped for from them; and that therefore little was actually lost by his downfall. Of course they have not. They were interrupted in mid-passage. The United States was shaken to its roots by the Watergate trauma, and this was not lost on the leaders of Moscow and Peking. Nixon was no longer there to follow through. Congress, feeling its oats, seized the opportunity presented by political weakness in the executive branch to encroach on executive prerogatives in foreign policy, and did so in a heavy-handed way that conveyed a sense of national irresolution. Instead of strength and purpose, the United States confronted its adversaries in a posture of weakness and uncertainty. And they, quite naturally, stood ready to exploit whatever advantages the situation presented. It was precisely because such an evolution was totally predictable that many of us saw the stakes in Watergate as being so high. Watergate threatened not only Richard Nixon but the entire structure of peace that he and Kissinger had been so painstakingly building.

That structure depended absolutely on American strength—not only military and economic strength but also strength of will and strength of purpose. The Nixon détente was not a substitute for containment. It was a means of containment—a means created for the new strategic environment, in which the United States could no longer rely on the massive nuclear superiority it enjoyed a decade earlier. In this new environment, policies had necessarily to be more subtle and more complex. Unable to dictate to our adversaries, the United States had to weave a fabric of interdependencies that would supplement traditional deterrence with positive incentives to keep the peace rather than to break the peace.

The first rule of regicide is that he who shoots at the king had better be sure he kills. If those who took aim at Nixon believed even a fraction of their own rhetoric about his ruthlessness—and, in their advanced state of paranoia, many seem to have believed more than a fraction—then the fierceness of their determination to insure that his destruction was total is understandable, if not necessarily admirable. But that battle is over. Richard Nixon had hoped and expected to be the bicentennial President, presiding over the nation's celebration of its two centuries of independence. Instead, he watched that celebration as an exile in his own land. Those two centuries have come and gone. His presidency has come and gone. The passions that surrounded its end have not died, but they are subsiding. And the rest of us are left to sort through the wreckage, to search for the lessons. As the passions recede, as we exercise our right brains less and our left brains more, we may find our way to a fuller understanding of that extraordinary period. Just as we search for deeper truths in a synthesis of our differing patterns of perception, we may find a greater insight in the synthesis of differing perspectives. One thing I do know: The battle looked far different from inside the barricades than it did from outside.

APPENDIX

APPENDIX

THE FIRST INAUGURAL ADDRESS

January 20, 1969

Senator Dirksen, Mr. Chief Justice, Mr. Vice President, President Johnson, Vice President Humphrey, my fellow Americans—and my fellow citizens of the world community:

I ask you to share with me today the majesty of this moment. In the orderly transfer of power, we celebrate the unity that keeps us free.

Each moment in history is a fleeting time, precious and unique. But some stand out as moments of beginning, in which courses are set that shape decades or centuries.

This can be such a moment.

Forces now are converging that make possible, for the first time, the hope that many of man's deepest aspirations can at last be realized. The spiraling pace of change allows us to contemplate, within our own lifetime, advances that once would have taken centuries.

In throwing wide the horizons of space, we have discovered new horizons on earth.

For the first time, because the people of the world want peace, and the leaders of the world are afraid of war, the times are on the side of peace.

Eight years from now America will celebrate its 200th anniversary as a nation. Within the lifetime of most people now living, mankind will celebrate that great new year which comes only once in a thousand years—the beginning of the third millennium.

What kind of a nation we will be, what kind of a world we will live in, whether we shape the future in the image of our hopes, is ours to determine by our actions and our choices.

The greatest honor history can bestow is the title of peacemaker. This honor now beckons America—the chance to help lead the world at last out of the valley of turmoil and onto that high ground of peace that man has dreamed of since the dawn of civilization.

If we succeed, generations to come will say of us now living that we mastered our moment, that we helped make the world safe for mankind.

This is our summons to greatness.

I believe the American people are ready to answer this call.

The second third of this century has been a time of proud achievement. We have made enormous strides in science and industry and agriculture. We have shared our wealth more broadly than ever. We have learned at last to manage a modern economy to assure its continued growth.

We have given freedom new reach. We have begun to make its promise real for black as well as for white.

We see the hope of tomorrow in the youth of today. I know America's youth. I believe in them. We can be proud that they are better educated, more committed, more passionately driven by conscience than any generation in our history.

No people has ever been so close to the achievement of a just and abundant society, or so possessed of the will to achieve it. And because our strengths are so great, we can afford to appraise our weaknesses with candor and to approach them with hope.

Standing in this same place a third of a century ago, Franklin Delano Roosevelt addressed a nation ravaged by depression and gripped in fear. He could say in surveying the Nation's troubles: "They concern, thank God, only material things."

Our crisis today is in reverse.

We find ourselves rich in goods, but ragged in spirit; reaching with magnificent precision for the moon, but falling into raucous discord on earth.

We are caught in war, wanting peace. We are torn by division, wanting unity. We see around us empty lives, wanting fulfillment. We see tasks that need doing, waiting for hands to do them.

To a crisis of the spirit, we need an answer of the spirit.

And to find that answer, we need only look within ourselves.

When we listen to "the better angels of our nature," we find that they celebrate the simple things, the basic things—such as goodness, decency, love, kindness.

Greatness comes in simple trappings.

The simple things are the ones most needed today if we are to surmount what divides us, and cement what unites us.

To lower our voices would be a simple thing.

In these difficult years, America has suffered from a fever of words; from inflated rhetoric that promises more than it can deliver; from angry rhetoric that fans discontents into hatreds; from bombastic rhetoric that postures instead of persuading.

We cannot learn from one another until we stop shouting at one another—until we speak quietly enough so that our words can be heard as well as our voices.

For its part, government will listen. We will strive to listen in new ways—to the voices of quiet anguish, the voices that speak without words, the voices of the heart—to the injured voices, the anxious voices, the voices that have despaired of being heard.

Those who have been left out, we will try to bring in.

Those left behind, we will help to catch up.

For all of our people, we will set as our goal the decent order that makes progress possible and our lives secure.

As we reach toward our hopes, our task is to build on what has gone before—not turning away from the old, but turning toward the new.

In this past third of a century, government has passed more laws, spent more money, initiated more programs than in all our previous history.

In pursuing our goals of full employment, better housing, excellence in education; in rebuilding our cities and improving our rural areas; in protecting our environment and enhancing the quality of life—in all these and more, we will and must press urgently forward.

We shall plan now for the day when our wealth can be transferred from the destruction of war abroad to the urgent needs of our people at home.

The American dream does not come to those who fall asleep.

But we are approaching the limits of what government alone can do.

Our greatest need now is to reach beyond government, to enlist the legions of the concerned and the committed.

What has to be done, has to be done by government and people together or it will not be done at all. The lesson of past agony is that without the people we can do nothing—with the people we can do everything.

To match the magnitude of our tasks, we need the energies of our people—enlisted not only in grand enterprises, but more importantly in those small, splendid efforts that make headlines in the neighborhood newspaper instead of the national journal.

With these, we can build a great cathedral of the spirit—each of us raising it one stone at a time, as he reaches out to his neighbor, helping, caring, doing.

I do not offer a life of uninspiring ease. I do not call for a life of grim sacrifice. I ask you to join in a high adventure—one as rich as humanity itself, and exciting as the times we live in.

The essence of freedom is that each of us shares in the shaping of his own destiny.

Until he has been part of a cause larger than himself, no man is truly whole.

The way to fulfillment is in the use of our talents. We achieve nobility in the spirit that inspires that use.

As we measure what can be done, we shall promise only what we know we can produce; but as we chart our goals, we shall be lifted by our dreams.

No man can be fully free while his neighbor is not. To go forward at all is to go forward together.

This means black and white together, as one nation, not two. The laws have caught up with our conscience. What remains is to give life to what is in the law: to insure at last that as all are born equal in dignity before God, all are born equal in dignity before man.

As we learn to go forward together at home, let us also seek to go forward together with all mankind.

Let us take as our goal: Where peace is unknown, make it welcome; where peace is fragile, make it strong; where peace is temporary, make it permanent.

After a period of confrontation, we are entering an era of negotiation.

Let all nations know that during this administration our lines of communication will be open.

We seek an open world—open to ideas, open to the exchange of goods and people—a world in which no people, great or small, will live in angry isolation.

We cannot expect to make everyone our friend, but we can try to make no one our enemy.

Those who would be our adversaries, we invite to a peaceful competition—not in conquering territory or extending dominion, but in enriching the life of man.

As we explore the reaches of space, let us go to the new worlds together—not as new worlds to be conquered, but as a new adventure to be shared.

With those who are willing to join, let us cooperate to reduce the burden of arms, to strengthen the structure of peace, to lift up the poor and the hungry.

But to all those who would be tempted by weakness, let us leave no doubt that we will be as strong as we need to be for as long as we need to be.

Over the past 20 years, since I first came to this Capital as a freshman Congressman, I have visited most of the nations of the world. I have come to know the leaders of the world and the great forces, the hatreds, the fears that divide the world.

I know that peace does not come through wishing for it—that there is no substitute for days and even years of patient and prolonged diplomacy.

I also know the people of the world.

I have seen the hunger of a homeless child, the pain of a man wounded in battle, the grief of a mother who has lost her son. I know these have no ideology, no race.

I know America. I know the heart of America is good.

I speak from my own heart, and the heart of my country, the deep concern we have for those who suffer and those who sorrow.

I have taken an oath today in the presence of God and my countrymen to uphold and defend the Constitution of the United States. To that oath I now add this sacred commitment: I shall consecrate my Office, my energies, and all the wisdom I can summon to the cause of peace among nations.

Let this message be heard by strong and weak alike:

The peace we seek—the peace we seek to win—is not victory over any other people, but the peace that comes "with healing in its wings"; with compassion for those who have suffered; with understanding for those who have opposed us; with the opportunity for all the peoples of this earth to choose their own destiny.

Only a few short weeks ago we shared the glory of man's first sight of the world as God sees it, as a single sphere reflecting light in the darkness.

As the Apollo astronauts flew over the moon's gray surface on Christmas Eve, they spoke to us of the beauty of earth—and in that voice so clear across the lunar distance, we heard them invoke God's blessing on its goodness.

In that moment, their view from the moon moved poet Archibald MacLeish to write: "To see the earth as it truly is, small and blue and beautiful in that eternal silence where it floats, is to see ourselves as riders on the earth together, brothers on that bright loveliness in the eternal cold—brothers who know now they are truly brothers."

In that moment of surpassing technological triumph, men turned their thoughts toward home and humanity—seeing in that far perspective that man's destiny on earth is not divisible; telling us that however far we reach into the cosmos, our destiny lies not in the stars but on earth itself, in our own hands, in our own hearts.

We have endured a long night of the American spirit. But as our eyes catch the dimness of the first rays of dawn, let us not curse the remaining dark. Let us gather the light.

Our destiny offers not the cup of despair, but the chalice of opportunity. So let us seize it not in fear, but in gladness—and "riders on the earth together," let us go forward, firm in our faith, steadfast in our purpose, cautious of the dangers, but sustained by our confidence in the will of God and the promise of man.

ADDRESS ANNOUNCING THE DECISION TO RESIGN

August 8, 1974

Good evening:

This is the 37th time I have spoken to you from this office, where so many decisions have been made that shaped the history of this Nation. Each time I have done so to discuss with you some matter that I believe affected the national interest.

In all the decisions I have made in my public life, I have always tried to do what was best for the Nation. Throughout the long and difficult period of Watergate, I have felt it was my duty to persevere, to make every possible effort to complete the term of office to which you elected me.

In the past few days, however, it has become evident to me that I no longer have a strong enough political base in the Congress to justify continuing that effort. As long as there was such a base, I felt strongly that it was necessary to see the constitutional process through to its conclusion, that to do otherwise would be unfaithful to the spirit of that deliberately difficult process and a dangerously destabilizing precedent for the future.

But with the disappearance of that base, I now believe that the constitutional purpose has been served, and there is no longer a need for the process to be prolonged.

I would have preferred to carry through to the finish, whatever the personal agony it would have involved, and my family unanimously urged me to do so. But the interests of the Nation must always come before any personal considerations.

From the discussions I have had with Congressional and other leaders, I have concluded that because of the Watergate matter, I might not have the support of the Congress that I would consider necessary to back the very difficult decisions and carry out the duties of this office in the way the interests of the Nation will require.

I have never been a quitter. To leave office before my term is completed is abhorrent to every instinct in my body. But as President, I must put the interests of America first. America needs a full-time President and a full-time Congress, particularly at this time with problems we face at home and abroad.

To continue to fight through the months ahead for my personal vindication would almost totally absorb the time and attention of both the President and the Congress in a period when our entire focus should be on the great issues of peace abroad and prosperity without inflation at home.

Therefore, I shall resign the Presidency effective at noon tomorrow. Vice President Ford will be sworn in as President at that hour in this office.

As I recall the high hopes for America with which we began this second term, I feel a great sadness that I will not be here in this office working on your behalf to achieve those hopes in the next 2½ years. But in turning over direction of the Government to Vice President Ford, I know, as I told the Nation when I nominated him for that office 10 months ago, that the leadership of America will be in good hands.

In passing this office to the Vice President, I also do so with the profound sense of the weight of responsibility that will fall on his shoulders tomorrow and, therefore, of the understanding, the patience, the cooperation he will need from all Americans.

As he assumes that responsibility, he will deserve the help and the support of all of us. As we look to the future, the first essential is to begin healing the wounds of this Nation, to put the bitterness and divisions of the recent past behind us and to rediscover those shared ideals that lie at the heart of our strength and unity as a great and as a free people.

By taking this action, I hope that I will have hastened the start of that process of healing which is so desperately needed in America.

I regret deeply any injuries that may have been done in the course of the events that led to this decision. I would say only that if some of my judgments were wrong—and some were wrong—they were made in what I believed at the time to be the best interest of the Nation.

To those who have stood with me during these past difficult months— to my family, my friends, to many others who joined in supporting my cause because they believed it was right—I will be eternally grateful for your support.

And to those who have not felt able to give me your support, let me say I leave with no bitterness toward those who have opposed me, because all of us, in the final analysis, have been concerned with the good of the country, however our judgments might differ.

So, let us all now join together in affirming that common commitment and in helping our new President succeed for the benefit of all Americans.

I shall leave this office with regret at not completing my term, but with gratitude for the privilege of serving as your President for the past 5½ years. These years have been a momentous time in the history of our Nation and the world. They have been a time of achievement in which we can all be proud, achievements that represent the shared efforts of the Administration, the Congress, and the people.

But the challenges ahead are equally great, and they, too, will require the support and the efforts of the Congress and the people working in cooperation with the new Administration.

We have ended America's longest war, but in the work of securing a lasting peace in the world, the goals ahead are even more far-reaching and more difficult. We must complete a structure of peace so that it will be said of this generation, our generation of Americans, by the people of all nations, not only that we ended one war but that we prevented future wars.

We have unlocked the doors that for a quarter of a century stood between the United States and the People's Republic of China.

We must now ensure that the one quarter of the world's people who live in the People's Republic of China will be and remain not our enemies, but our friends.

In the Middle East, 100 million people in the Arab countries, many of whom have considered us their enemy for nearly 20 years, now look on us as their friends. We must continue to build on that friendship so that peace can settle at last over the Middle East and so that the cradle of civilization will not become its grave.

Together with the Soviet Union, we have made the crucial breakthroughs that have begun the process of limiting nuclear arms. But we must set as our goal not just limiting but reducing and, finally, destroying these terrible weapons so that they cannot destroy civilization and so that the threat of nuclear war will no longer hang over the world and the people.

We have opened the new relation with the Soviet Union. We must continue to develop and expand that new relationship so that the two strongest nations of the world will live together in cooperation, rather than confrontation.

Around the world—in Asia, in Africa, in Latin America, in the Middle East—there are millions of people who live in terrible poverty, even starvation. We must keep as our goal turning away from production for war and expanding production for peace so that people everywhere on this Earth can at last look forward in their children's time, if not in our own time, to having the necessities for a decent life.

Here in America, we are fortunate that most of our people have not only the blessings of liberty but also the means to live full and good and, by the world's standards, even abundant lives. We must press on, however, toward a goal, not only of more and better jobs but of full opportunity for every American and of what we are striving so hard right now to achieve, prosperity without inflation.

For more than a quarter of a century in public life, I have shared in the turbulent history of this era. I have fought for what I believed in. I have tried, to the best of my ability, to discharge those duties and meet those responsibilities that were entrusted to me.

Sometimes I have succeeded and sometimes I have failed, but always I have taken heart from what Theodore Roosevelt once said about the man in the arena, "whose face is marred by dust and sweat and blood, who strives valiantly, who errs and comes short again and again because there is not effort without error and shortcoming, but who does actually strive to do the deed, who knows the great enthusiasms, the great devotions, who spends himself in a worthy cause, who at the best knows in the end the triumphs of high achievements and who at the worst, if he fails, at least fails while daring greatly."

I pledge to you tonight that as long as I have a breath of life in my body, I shall continue in that spirit. I shall continue to work for the great causes to which I have been dedicated throughout my years as a Congressman, a Senator, Vice President, and President, the cause of peace, not just for America but among all nations—prosperity, justice, and opportunity for all of our people.

There is one cause above all to which I have been devoted and to which I shall always be devoted for as long as I live.

When I first took the oath of office as President 5½ years ago, I made this sacred commitment: to "consecrate my office, my energies, and all the wisdom I can summon to the cause of peace among nations."

I have done my very best in all the days since to be true to that pledge. As a result of these efforts, I am confident that the world is a safer place today, not only for the people of America but for the people of all nations, and that all of our children have a better chance than before of living in peace rather than dying in war.

This, more than anything, is what I hoped to achieve when I sought the Presidency. This, more than anything, is what I hope will be my legacy to you, to our country, as I leave the Presidency.

To have served in this office is to have felt a very personal sense of kinship with each and every American. In leaving it, I do so with this prayer: May God's grace be with you in all the days ahead.

INDEX